Airline Terrorism

ALSO BY MARC E. VARGO
AND FROM MCFARLAND

The French Terror Wave, 2015–2016: Al-Qaeda and ISIS Attacks from Charlie Hebdo *to the Bataclan Theatre* (2021)

The Weaponizing of Biology: Bioterrorism, Biocrime and Biohacking (2017)

The Mossad: Six Landmark Missions of the Israeli Intelligence Agency, 1960–1990 (2015)

Women of the Resistance: Eight Who Defied the Third Reich (2012)

Airline Terrorism
A History with Case Studies

MARC E. VARGO

McFarland & Company, Inc., Publishers
Jefferson, North Carolina

LIBRARY OF CONGRESS CATALOGING-IN-PUBLICATION DATA

Names: Vargo, Marc E., 1954– author.
Title: Airline terrorism : a history with case studies / Marc E. Vargo.
Description: Jefferson, North Carolina : McFarland & Company, Inc., Publishers, 2024 | Includes bibliographical references and index.
Identifiers: LCCN 2024012957 | ISBN 9781476690841 (paperback : acid free paper) ∞
    ISBN 9781476652283 (ebook)
Subjects: LCSH: Hijacking of aircraft—Case studies. | Aircraft accidents—Case studies. | Terrorism—Case studies. | Airlines—Security measures—Case studies.
Classification: LCC HE9779 .V36 2024 | DDC 364.1—dc23/eng/20240321
LC record available at https://lccn.loc.gov/2024012957

BRITISH LIBRARY CATALOGUING DATA ARE AVAILABLE

ISBN (print) 978-1-4766-9084-1
ISBN (ebook) 978-1-4766-5228-3

© 2024 Marc E. Vargo. All rights reserved

No part of this book may be reproduced or transmitted in any form or by any means, electronic or mechanical, including photocopying or recording, or by any information storage and retrieval system, without permission in writing from the publisher.

Front cover photograph by Hayley Irvine (Shutterstock)

Printed in the United States of America

McFarland & Company, Inc., Publishers
  Box 611, Jefferson, North Carolina 28640
    www.mcfarlandpub.com

For Gloria and Beverly

Table of Contents

Introduction   1

Part I. Aerial Terrorism: History, Motives and Methods

One—Air Piracy: Hijackings   7

Two—Improvised Explosive Devices and Surface-to-Air Missiles   48

Three—Conventional Assaults and Cyberattacks on Airports and Airliners   81

Part II. Case Studies

Four—Up in the Air: The Controversy of TWA Flight 800   111

Five—Over the Skies of Russia: The 2004 Black Widow Attacks   164

Six—Libya and Terrorism I: The Downing of Pan Am Flight 103   182

Seven—Libya and Terrorism II: The Downing of UTA Flight 772   224

Eight—Aircraft as Guided Missiles: Kamikazes, al-Qaeda, and the 9/11 Attacks   243

Index   275

Introduction

It was the world's first terrorist hijacking, or "skyjacking," and an air traffic controller's worst nightmare. After a midnight departure from Rome, El Al Flight 426 was passing over the Isle of Capri when an unfamiliar voice began transmitting messages to the control tower. The speaker's tone was angry, his messages frantic and garbled, and the controller at Leonardo da Vinci International Airport was unable to make out what was being conveyed. Just then, the captain of a nearby Ethiopian Airlines flight overheard the exchange and radioed the specialist on the ground. "Rome," he shouted, "El Al 426 has been hijacked!"[1]

It was an extraordinary act of air piracy, and it occurred on board a Boeing 707 traveling to Tel Aviv on July 23, 1968. The plane carried ten crew members and thirty-eight passengers, the latter including American and Canadian sightseers, Israeli citizens returning home, and a group of Italians on a pilgrimage. Shortly after the aircraft reached a cruising altitude of 33,000 feet, the flight engineer ordered coffee for the cockpit crew, and the captain, Oded Abarbanell, switched off the seat belt sign. Shrewdly, the hijackers chose this moment to make their move. As the flight attendant opened the door to serve the beverages, two armed men appeared behind her, shoved their way inside, and set about pistol-whipping the first officer, or co-pilot. At the same moment, a third operative, clutching a pistol in one hand and an unpinned grenade in the other, planted himself in the aisle of the passenger cabin. "We are Palestinians," he bellowed, "and we have liberated this plane and renamed it the Liberation of Palestine 707."[2]

The hijackers were members of the PFLP—the Popular Front for the Liberation of Palestine—a Marxist-Leninist organization whose broad aim was to force the State of Israel to return the Palestinian land it had confiscated during the Six-Day War. The group further sought the establishment of a sovereign Palestinian state. Uncompromising in its methods, the PFLP was among five factions within the Palestine Liberation Organization (PLO), and it was arguably the most lethal. In the present operation, the group was specifically demanding that Israel hand over a large number of Palestinian inmates in exchange for the El Al aircraft and its passengers and crew. Mistakenly believing that Major General Ariel Sharon of Israel was on the flight, the hijackers were gambling on his status as a hostage to force President Zalman Shazar's administration to bow to their demands.

In this high-stakes mission, the PFLP had secured a partner in crime, Algeria, with the gunmen now ordering Captain Abarbanell to re-route the airliner to the Dar El-Beida Airport in Algiers, 650 miles southwest of Capri. Here, Algerian authorities impounded the plane and, hours later, freed the non–Israeli passengers and crew. A few days later, officials released the Israeli women and children as well, but retained a dozen Israeli men as hostages.

It was, to be sure, a cinematic political event, and television networks around the globe raced to cover the skyjacking. In the process, they introduced much of the world to the Palestinian cause. Although the situation in the Occupied Palestinian Territories was certainly newsworthy, Western media had steered away from covering the Palestinian experience. By securing such extensive media coverage, then, the PFLP's aerial crime brought international attention to the troubled region. And although the publicity was the result of an illicit deed—skyjacking would become a capital offense—the terrorists and their exponents welcomed it all the same. "At least the world is talking about us now," said Zehdi Lahib Terzi, a politician who would become the PLO's principal observer to the United Nations.[3] Echoing this view was George Habash, founder of the PFLP. "The hijacking of a large plane," Habash declared, "has a greater impact in terms of propaganda and the media than killing one hundred Israelis in battle."[4]

Under threat of boycott by the International Airline Pilots Association (IAPA), the Algerian leadership agreed to a deal that would entail it relinquishing the El Al airliner and the remaining captives, while the Israeli leadership would release sixteen Palestinian prisoners. Although Israel sought to portray its concession as a humanitarian gesture, the arrangement was clearly a partial submission to Algeria's demands. "The blackmail precedent had been set," reported *TIME Magazine*.[5]

The fact is, airliners had been commandeered prior to 1968, but the taking of Flight 426 came to be regarded as the birth of international terrorism. In his book *Inside Terrorism*, Bruce Hoffman identifies a number of factors that contributed to the incident's significance, starting with the fact that the PFLP chose for its crime an El Al aircraft.[6] As Israel's national carrier, El Al Israel Airlines was a symbol of the state, such that the militants, by taking possession of one of the company's Boeing 707s, humbled the nation in front of the world. The hijackers also engineered a situation in which they could, at will, harm or kill Israeli citizens. In so doing, they created an untenable state of affairs, one that forced Israel's government to override its policy of non-negotiation. Then too, the hijacking marked the first time that both an airliner and its occupants had been used as political pawns.

In the months that followed, the PFLP seized more commercial airliners and attacked airports in Munich, Athens, Zurich, and Frankfort. Concurrently, El Al introduced an array of tough security measures on its fleet of planes. The upshot: the hijackers had little recourse but to turn their attention to Western airliners as potential targets.

As could be expected in light of the PFLP's gains, other extremist groups soon adopted this ostentatious form of attack, commandeering airliners and using the aircraft, their passengers, and their crews as bargaining chips. By 1971, the practice had skyrocketed globally. "[S]ome 8,000 passengers from 88 countries have, quite unwillingly, experienced the thrill of an aerial hijack," reported the *New York Times*, wryly, in January of that year.[7]

Even as politically-motivated skyjackings increased sharply in the wake of the Flight 426 episode, however, terrorists continued to carry out other forms of air-related aggression. They sabotaged airliners in flight, for instance, typically through the use of explosive devices. They also used surface-to-air missiles to bring down commercial carriers, and repurposed airliners to serve as weapons, most notably in the 2001 attacks on the World Trade Center and the Pentagon.

Today, run-of-the-mill criminals, among them extortionists, have added cyberattacks to their bag of tricks, thus far having targeted specific airline companies and international airports, usually accompanied by financial demands. But a growing concern among experts in the field of aviation security centers on the prospect of terrorist entities exploiting the cybersphere in an effort to conduct cyberattacks on airliners in flight—a chilling scenario, to be sure.

In Part I, numerous terrorist strategies are explored in their historical contexts, including hijackings, bombings, missile strikes, and cyberattacks on both airports and airliners. For each method, a review of the preventive measures instituted by the security community is included.

Part II revisits five air disasters that center on commercial aircraft in flight, each of which illustrates certain elements of the material covered in Part I. Among the cases is that of TWA Flight 800, arguably the most controversial airline disaster in aviation history. An enigma, it continues to be debated by those who insist that the catastrophe was caused by a terrorist missile strike and those who contend that it was the result of an undetermined mechanical malfunction. Also reconstructed are the simultaneous midair bombings conducted by a pair of female Chechen terrorists, so-called "black widows," over Russia. As well, the text revisits two in-flight bombings that transpired over Scotland and the Sahara Desert, both of which were purportedly the work of Libya during its days as a rogue state. The questionable assertion put forth by the United States government, namely, that no other nations or terrorist entities contributed to these sophisticated terror operations, is also evaluated. And lastly, the September 11 attacks are examined, with emphasis on the perpetrators' unprecedented use of commercial aircraft as guided missiles. Collectively, the five cases offer an intriguing sample of terrorist organizations' motives for, and methods of, committing heinous acts of mass murder in the skies.

Notes

1. Oded Abarbanell, "Hijacked to Algiers—Part 1," *Oded Abarbanell*, March 8, 2013, https://odedabarbanell.wordpress.com/2013/03/08/hijacked-to-algiers-part-1/.
2. Terence Smith, "A Hijacked Plane Stirs New Tensions," *New York Times*, July 28, 1968, https://www.nytimes.com/1968/07/28/archives/middle-east-a-hijacked-plane-stirs-new-tensions.html.
3. Jan Laskowski, "Terroryzm Lotniczy—Charakterystyka Zjawiska," *Journal of Humanities and Social Sciences* 7 (January 2013): 146, https://www.researchgate.net/publication/344155565_Terroryzm_lotniczy-charakterystyka_zjawiska.
4. Alex P. Schmidt and Janny de Graff, *Violence as Communication: Insurgent Terrorism and the Western News Media* (London: Sage, 1982), 32.
5. "Drama of the Desert: The Week of Hostages," *TIME Magazine*, September 21, 1970, https://content.time.com/time/subscriber/article/0,33009,942267,00.html.
6. Bruce Hoffman, *Inside Terrorism* (New York: Columbia University Press, 2006).
7. Milton Viorst, "El Al—The World's Toughest Airline," *New York Times*, January 3, 1971, https://www.nytimes.com/1971/01/03/archives/el-al-the-worlds-toughest-airline-el-al-the-catering-is-kosher-and.html.

Bibliography

Abarbanell, Oded. "Hijacked to Algiers—Part 1." *Oded Abarbanell*, March 8, 2013. https://odedabarbanell.wordpress.com/2013/03/08/hijacked-to-algiers-part-1/.
"Drama of the Desert: The Week of Hostages." *TIME Magazine*, September 21, 1970. https://content.time.com/time/subscriber/article/0,33009,942267,00.html.
Hoffman, Bruce. *Inside Terrorism*. New York: Columbia University Press, 2006.
Laskowski, Jan. "Terroryzm Lotniczy—Charakterystyka Zjawiska." *Journal of Humanities and Social Sciences* 7 (January 2013): 133–163. https://www.researchgate.net/publication/344155565_Terroryzm_lotniczy-charakterystyka_zjawiska.
Schmidt, Alex P., and Janny de Graff. *Violence as Communication: Insurgent Terrorism and the Western News Media*. London: Sage, 1982.
Smith, Terence. "A Hijacked Plane Stirs New Tensions." *New York Times*, July 28, 1968. https://www.nytimes.com/1968/07/28/archives/middle-east-a-hijacked-plane-stirs-new-tensions.html.
Viorst, Milton. "El Al—The World's Toughest Airline." New York Times, January 3, 1971. https://www.nytimes.com/1971/01/03/archives/el-al-the-worlds-toughest-airline-el-al-the-catering-is-kosher-and.html.

Part I

Aerial Terrorism

History, Motives and Methods

ONE

Air Piracy
Hijackings

It was only eight years after the Wright brothers took to the skies in the world's first powered aircraft, or "aeroplane," that someone in St. Louis stole one. Crime was now in the air, literally. And while the incident did not inspire a rash of thefts, airplane enthusiasts did continue to "borrow" private aircraft on occasion, most often in search of a joyride.[1]

On February 5, 1919, the world's first commercial airline company was established in Germany, followed three days later by the launch of a French one.[2] Not surprising, perhaps, it was only a few months later that the first hijacking of an airplane in flight took place, and it was executed by Baron Franz Nopsca von Felsö-Szilvás. A Hungarian aristocrat who lived in the region of Transylvania and suffered from bipolar disorder, Nopsca was a renowned scientist who today is hailed as a founder of the field of paleobiology. The reason for his aerial offense, which occurred in a political context, entailed his own survival. It seems that Nopsca lost his wealth, along with his Transylvanian castle, when the Treaty of Versailles was signed, the pact that ceded Transylvania to Romania. A stunning reversal of fortune, it caused both Nopsca and his longtime male lover, an Albanian shepherd by the name of Bajazid Doda, to fall into despair. Even worse for the baron, he found himself in the crosshairs of Hungary's disenfranchised proletariat.

"During the short-lived Hungarian Soviet Republic of 1919, Nopsca was trapped," writes historian Tom Holland, "and in a spectacular turn of events, he became the first person to ever hijack an aeroplane as his means of escape."[3] Boarding a small commercial carrier in Budapest, the baron, once it was aloft, held the pilot at gunpoint and forced him to fly 150 miles to Vienna. Fortunately, no one was injured in the episode, and Nopsca, whom the public continued to hold in high esteem owing to his scientific breakthroughs and noble lineage, does not appear to have been prosecuted for the hijacking.

The year that Nopsca commandeered the plane, 1919, also proved to be a banner year for commercial aviation. At that time, prescient entrepreneurs in Western Europe established the first airline companies and created air routes within and between Germany, France, and England. Since such countries were in close proximity, comparatively short flights were feasible, the upshot being that the continental air industry soon became profitable.

In North America, in contrast, domestic flights surged whereas international ones lagged. Expansive nations like the United States and Canada, with their oceanic borders, found it challenging to reach far beyond the continent. Indeed, it would be another twenty years before transatlantic air routes would be established linking North America to Europe. In the meantime, acts of air piracy would persist, albeit infrequently and without documentation.

The first political hijacking for which an official record does exist transpired in Peru on February 21, 1931. The aircraft was a two-person Ford Trimotor transport plane—it was part of a fleet operated by Pan American-Grace Airways—and the American pilot, Byron Rickards, was delivering U.S. mail to towns across the southern Andes. Although he was familiar with Peru's airstrips, Rickards was unfamiliar with the county's current political situation. More to the point, he did not know it was in the throes of a revolution and was therefore unprepared for the sight of armed rebels racing toward his aircraft as he touched down in the mountain town of Arequipa. "The soldiers had been hiding behind the hangar," he said. "They surrounded the plane and told me to cut the engines."[4] In short order, the revolutionaries seized the aircraft and ordered Rickards to use it to drop political tracts onto the surrounding towns and villages. The pilot refused, however, resulting in a standoff that lasted until the insurgency came to an end, victoriously, as it happened, ten days later.

The seizure of the Pan Am transport plane turned out to be much ado about nothing. And although the rebels did hold Rickards captive throughout the ordeal, he was uninjured and later remarked that his abductors had treated him politely despite his having defied their orders. They were also quick to release him after the insurrection—on one condition.[5] "They let him go," writes Oliver Burkeman, "in return for giving one of them a lift to Lima."[6]

While the Andean incident alarmed officials at Pan Am, the company did not feel it necessary to institute tighter security measures. Rather, they dismissed the seizure of the transport plane as a one-off. And they were right; only a few commercial aircraft would be commandeered during the next seventeen years. But this state of affairs would change off the back of World War II, when the Soviet Union set about subjugating its Eastern

European neighbors, a development that culminated in a spate of airline hijackings in the late 1940s and 1950s.

Iron Curtain Hijackings

Risking their lives to obtain asylum in the West, those who commandeered aircraft in the USSR and the Eastern Bloc nations came from an array of backgrounds and political allegiances. Most often, they were ordinary, non-state actors who were simply trying to return to a less oppressive way of life. "[H]ijacking seemed to offer marginal individuals the opportunity to mount a challenge to Cold War borders and forge global connections," writes Erik R. Scott.[7] As could be expected given the political milieu, the Western press portrayed those who defected in this manner as courageous men and women who thumbed their noses at the communist system and prevailed in their quest for freedom.

Regarding the first such skyjacking, it occurred on April 6, 1948, and involved a Douglas DC-3 owned by Czechoslovak National Airlines (Československé Státní Aerolinie). The pilot and co-pilot, both of whom had served in the Royal Air Force (RAF), planned and executed the takeover, possibly with the advance knowledge and perhaps even the collaboration of some of the passengers.

The hijacking began when the plane's two aviators, who were scheduled to fly from Prague to Bratislava, Czechoslovakia, deviated from the flight plan once they were airborne and re-routed the aircraft to Munich. As a destination, the German city made sense: it was situated in the American Occupied Zone and boasted a key U.S. Air Force installation nearby, the Neubiberg Air Base. "The pilot said he knowingly brought the plane to the American zone and landed," stated a press release from the U.S. military.[8]

Air Force officers escorted the pilot, the co-pilot, and a third crew member to an undisclosed location, together with seventeen passengers who were likewise seeking sanctuary. All would receive it. Not pursuing asylum, in contrast, was the aircraft's navigator, who had been unaware of the intrepid plot and who flew back to Czechoslovakia with five passengers also wishing to return. Today, the incident stands as the first mass skyjacking in aviation history owing to the sizable number of crew and passengers who took part in it.

After the 1948 spectacle, both the management of Czechoslovak National Airlines and the nation's secret police became suspicious of pilots who had served in the Royal Air Force. For this reason, the airline confiscated their passports and relegated them to domestic flights exclusively. It also set about recruiting and training its own aircrews, with each new hire replacing a veteran of the RAF. Of course, this rendered the latter jobless and trapped in a communist country. Worsening matters, some of the pilots' names were rumored to be on an arrest list being compiled by the secret police. By 1950, then, it was obvious that any ex-RAF aviators hoping to escape had better do so while they still had access to a cockpit.

So it was that eight RAF-trained pilots employed by Czechoslovak National Airlines decided they would make their move on March 24, 1950. They would seize three airliners. Those pilots who were not scheduled to fly on that day would simply travel as passengers.

Months in the planning, the triple skyjacking was a complex endeavor. The pilots, like those in the 1948 operation, organized all aspects of it, even selecting the same U.S. air base as their journeys' terminus. If their strategy worked, it would mark the first hijacking in history to involve multiple aircraft and it would be one of the most audacious escapes from an Eastern Bloc nation.

The risks were grave, of course. During this taut Cold War era, Czechoslovakian regulations forbade any passenger from traveling on an airliner if the pilot was a member of their own family. Furthermore, the Czechoslovakian secret police had, by now, come to regard ex-RAF aircrews as actual adversaries, not just suspicious people, and the authorities were merciless to the friends and loved ones of those who defected. Consequently, the pilots, co-pilots, flight engineers, and flight attendants in the present operation would need to be inventive in slipping their families out of the country.[9] And they were indeed creative, their solutions ranging from placing their loved ones on other pilots' flights to instructing female family members to travel under their maiden names. Most challenging, though, the pilots and their crews had to ensure that the three flights were scheduled for the same day, for roughly the same time, and from specific points of departure: the Czechoslovakian cities of Bratislava, Brno, and Ostrava.

Three early morning flights were selected, since the planners, familiar with them, knew that sufficient seating would be available for all of the defectors. The pilots were further gambling on the airports' security officers being less attentive at such an early hour. In all, eighty-five people boarded the airliners, nearly a third of whom were secretly seeking asylum. Besides the aircrew and their loved ones, the latter group included such passengers as the mother of Alena Vrzáňová, a world figure skating champion who had already defected. Also on board, but not defecting, were several Communist Party officials, along with Leopold Thurner, the president of the airline itself. Thurner was known to travel with a pistol.

For two of the planes, all went according to plan and their departures were without incident, but the third encountered an obstacle. "Thirty minutes delayed, the aircraft was ready to depart but, at the last minute, they were instructed to return to the terminal," writes Philip Baum in his book *Violence in the Skies*. "The radio operator pretended not to have heard and the aircraft departed."[10] A little over an hour later, as the hijacked flights entered the American Occupied Zone in Germany, the U.S. Air Force, alerted to the operation, dispatched fighter planes to escort the airliners to the base.

Of the eighty-five people who were aboard the three planes, twenty-seven sought and received asylum. They included the former RAF pilots and their families, two flight attendants, and fourteen passengers. All but one of the latter were aware of the plot in advance. In terms of those who decided to return, the fate of their loved ones who were still living in Czechoslovakia was a principal concern.

In the course of the political firestorm that ensued, the Czechoslovakian government, which controlled the nation's media, initially reported that no airliners had been hijacked. It insisted that all such reports were rumors.[11] Czech officials soon reversed their position, however, falsely accusing the U.S. military of using Gestapo tactics against those passengers who wished to return to Czechoslovakia. They further claimed that the pilots were members of "a subversive terrorist group."[12]

Coconut Curtain Hijackings

As the 1950s progressed, the number of hijackings originating in the Soviet Union and Eastern Bloc nations declined, the last notable incident taking place in 1956 when seven Hungarian college students, using plastic wrenches, overtook a small passenger plane. Yet while air piracy from behind the Iron Curtain abated, it surged unexpectedly in the West and forever changed commercial air travel. Among other developments, it led to a handful of security measures that are still in place today. It was in the Caribbean, in 1958, that this new wave of skyjackings emerged.

The Cuban dictator Fulgencio Batista, at this juncture, was clinging to power in the face of the Cuban Revolution. In the course of the insurrection, Fidel Castro, his brother Raúl Castro, Ché Guevara, and their compatriots created new methods of guerrilla warfare, among them tactics involving commercial aircraft. In particular, it was Raúl—"the father of the modern crime of aircraft hijacking"—who foresaw the benefits that air piracy could bring to a revolution.[13] "Raúl Castro recognised that attacks on aviation were a formidable tool with which he could focus the world's attention on the rebels' plan of an international revolution—not to mention as a powerful political bargaining chip," write Nicoletta Mazzoleni and Massimo Catusi.[14]

To this end, the younger Castro brother and a band of insurgents commandeered a domestic flight on October 22, 1958. The plane, a DC-3, was the property of Compañia Cubana de Aviación, the Cuban national airline, and the purpose was both to unnerve the government and draw public attention to the insurgency. "This was the first instance of [an] aircraft hijacking being used as a guerilla tactic," writes Jin-Tai Choi.[15] It was also the first time that hijackers injured a member of a captured aircrew, the rebels shooting, but not killing, the pilot. As the guerrillas had hoped, the takeover received considerable notice.

Ten days later, the first deaths stemming from a terrorism-related skyjacking occurred on Cubana de Aviación Flight 495, which was traveling from Miami to Havana. Shortly after takeoff, four pro–Castro rebels stormed the cockpit of the four-engine turboprop, strong-armed the pilot, and demanded he divert to a remote location in northeastern Cuba. It was the Preston Sugar Mill, which had a small airstrip.[16] On arrival, the pilot was unable to land because the airstrip was too short and had no runway lights, and, worsening matters, the airliner was low on fuel. Flight 495 crashed into Nipe Bay, killing nearly everyone on board.

Undeterred, Raul Castro's guerrilla forces persisted, overtaking 25 percent of the Cubana de Aviación fleet within days. After yet another incident on November 6, 1958, Cubana de Aviación cancelled nearly all of its domestic flights, a decision that disrupted business transactions and postal communications across the island. A small victory for the insurgents, it foreshadowed the far greater triumph that was about to come.

On New Year's Day, 1959, Batista fled the country, and six weeks later, Fidel Castro was sworn in as prime minister. The revolutionaries had won. Despite the change in national leadership, however, regional airliners continued being commandeered, although now it was for a new set of reasons.

When Castro assumed power, the United States government acknowledged him, but subsequently distanced itself when he nationalized the lucrative U.S. businesses on the island and instituted agrarian reforms. Declaring Cuba to be a Marxist state, Castro had long railed against the United States' exploitation of the island's natural resources, and now he was ensuring it would come to an end. In addition, Castro, partly as a means of protecting Cuba from possible aggression by the United States, formed a political alliance with the Soviet Union, a turn of events that further strained relations between the two North American countries.

In terms of the U.S. reaction to Castro's initiatives, the Eisenhower administration imposed a crushing trade embargo on the Caribbean nation in 1960, the United States suspended all flight service to Cuba in 1961, and the Kennedy administration imposed a naval blockade in 1962. The United States also guided a campaign to expel Cuba from the Organization of

American States, thereby further isolating the struggling nation. As a result of these hard-hitting measures, as well as adverse developments within Cuba itself, the island soon suffered from internal strife and shortages of goods.

So it was that numerous Cubans, both individuals and groups, wished to emigrate, some fearing the Castro administration would punish them because of their Batista-era loyalties, and others simply not wanting to remain on the nascent socialist island despite the leadership's assurances of a more egalitarian way of life. And indeed, they were permitted to leave, although this freedom would soon be rescinded as Castro dropped the "coconut curtain" and prohibited such departures. Even so, those who were truly determined to flee would not be dissuaded. They believed the solution to their dilemma lay ninety miles to the north, the United States being, in their view, a hospitable democracy. Fueling this perception was the American media, which set about celebrating those Cubans who escaped by boat or aircraft, their daring getaways bolstering the narrative that the tiny nation, with its close ties to the USSR, had become an unviable, despotic hellhole. For that matter, the CIA, as a means of further undermining the Castro regime, covertly encouraged hijackings from Cuba by promising the perpetrators automatic asylum.[17] Such refugees were propaganda gold.

As to the commandeered Cuban planes that touched down on American soil, the United States confiscated them pending legal proceedings. By July 1961, it was holding twenty-six such aircraft, prompting Castro to take decisive action. The impounded planes were costly and irreplaceable, and the struggling Caribbean nation could ill afford to lose any more of them.

With this in mind, the Cuban government enacted strict air security measures, one of the earliest administrations in the Western world to do so. First, it ordered the military to become a constant presence at the José Marti Airport in Havana; the rationale was that an armed passenger, faced with a squad of soldiers on patrol, would not attempt to board a commercial plane. Second, the government ordered the nation's airliners to post armed guards on all flights, a backup measure in case the first line of defense failed. Additional security measures were implemented as well. "[T]here is no doubt that the airport security checkpoints that we see around the globe today," writes Philip Baum about the Cuban situation, "were a response to the phenomenon of individuals armed with guns, knives and grenades."[18] Once these initiatives were in place, hijackings from Havana to the United States declined substantially.

U.S. Security Measures. In a curious reversal, hijackings originating in the United States and diverting to Cuba increased during this same period. On May 1, 1961, the first American-owned airliner was commandeered to Cuba, a National Airlines flight departing from Miami. Armed with a pistol and a steak knife, the hijacker insisted he needed to warn Fidel Castro about an assassination plot. The following month, another aircraft was re-routed to Cuba, an Eastern Air Lines jetliner departing from Miami. And still another seizure was attempted ten days later, a Continental Airlines flight departing from Los Angeles. A disturbing pattern, it prompted the Kennedy administration to intervene.

Thus far, the U.S. government had enacted one major piece of legislation focusing on commercial air travel, the Federal Aviation Act of 1958, which created the Federal Aviation Administration (FAA). Broadly speaking, the Act was intended to ensure the safety and security of airborne passengers and crews, as well as persons and properties on the ground, most notably airports, that were involved in, or affected by, air travel. In terms of the administrative organization that the Act established, the FAA, it was charged with overseeing the operation of the airline industry, together with regulating flight activity in the nation's airspace, with the exception of designated military areas. A comprehensive piece of legislation, one that thoroughly addressed the country's aviation needs in 1958, it proved to be deficient three years later with the advent of U.S.-based air piracy. For this reason, President Kennedy enhanced the Act.

On September 5, 1961, Kennedy signed into law a bill that made skyjacking a federal offense. Titled "Public Law 87–197," the text was unequivocal. "Any person who *obtains or attempts to obtain control* of an aircraft by unlawful force or threat of force will be subject to a fine of not more than $10,000 or imprisoned for not more than 20 years, or both," the bill states. "If the act was committed with the use of a dangerous weapon, imprisonment may be for life but not less than 20 years, *or by death if the jury so directs*" (italics in original).[19]

It was also in 1961, and again at President Kennedy's behest, that the FAA set about creating an air security service that would make use of specially-trained border patrol agents. Originally referred to "FAA Peace Officers"—the agents would come to be known as "sky marshals" or "air marshals" by the end of the decade—their training consisted of "FAA policy, unarmed self-defense, legal, search and seizure, airline operations (of which they were already intimately familiar), firearms safety and marksmanship, physical fitness training, and terrorist/criminal mindset," writes former U.S. air marshal Clay Biles.[20] The principal task of these eighteen armed agents was to furnish protection on specific flights at the request of the FBI or an airline company.

Once the FAA Peace Officer program was up and running, episodes of air piracy from the United States to Cuba plummeted, and they remained low in number for the next five years. In the latter part of the Sixties, however, hijackings resumed rather abruptly and soared to hitherto unforeseen levels over the next four years. In 1968, for instance, nineteen airliners were forced to fly to Cuba, with this reflecting the expanding motives for such crimes.

Some were "homesick hijackings," and, as the nickname suggests, they were carried out by people longing to return to their native country. Contributing to their decision was often a concern for the loved ones they had left behind on the island, family and friends who were struggling with life under the Castro regime. Others were draft-age opponents of the controversial Vietnam War. And then there were those whose motives grew out of the political and social idealism that permeated certain segments of American society in that era. Drawn to Marxist ideologies, they romanticized the Caribbean nation as an idyllic destination. And like the homesick hijackers and Vietnam War opponents, they did not resort to physical force when seizing aircraft.

In that such skyjackings were nearly always nonviolent offenses, the decision was made to maintain, rather than upgrade, the existing safety and security measures. It was partly a matter of dollars. It cost an airline less to retrieve a hijacked plane—approximately $20,000—than to purchase and staff expensive security equipment and risk-reduction procedures at U.S. airports, writes Brendan I. Koerner in his edifying text, *The Skies Belong to Us: Love and Terror in the Golden Age of Hijacking*.[21] Simply complying with the perpetrators was more cost-effective. To this end, commercial carriers furnished their pilots with aeronautical charts of the Caribbean and instructed flight crews to cooperate with the hijackers' demands, safe in the knowledge that, based on prior incidents, no one would be injured or killed. "They weren't there to hurt anyone, they just wanted to get to Cuba," says Gloria Willoughby, a former flight attendant for Miami-based National Airlines.[22]

Unfortunately, as it became common knowledge that Cuba-bound hijackings from the United States were occurring frequently and without resistance, a more troubling breed of hijacker materialized. "Seeking political asylum, a haven from racism, contact with Third World revolutionary movements, escape from criminal charges, and adventure," writes historian Teishan A. Latner, "the majority of the hijackers framed their actions in explicitly political terms by invoking left-wing tropes of social justice and political protest."[23]

Among their number were militants such as Raymond Johnson of the Black Panther Party. A twenty-one-year-old student at Southern University in New Orleans, Johnson commandeered a National Airlines flight on November 4, 1968. En route to Havana, he told the passengers what he believed would come next: "[B]lack nationalists are going to hijack a plane every day for the next 100 days to show the white people they can't keep us down."[24] For the next eighteen years, Johnson, who would come to regret his actions, remained in Cuba, where he spent most of his time trying to leave it. In 1988, he was finally permitted to return to the United States. "Maybe it's not wrong to be a fool one time," he said, "but it's wrong to keep being a fool."[25]

In another episode shortly after the Johnson hijacking, an armed couple seized an Eastern Airlines flight departing from New York. Besides training a gun on the pilot, they also took a hostage—a two-year-old boy.[26] Clearly, air piracy was spiraling out of control and the risk of bodily harm to passengers was mounting.

Although the FAA was alarmed by this new threat of violence in U.S.-based air travel, the organization was pessimistic about the measures that might reduce it. An impotent stance, it would be on display during an emergency hearing called by the U.S. Senate in the summer of 1968. A key issue was how to ensure that passengers would be weaponless when entering a commercial carrier. In an era when a paper ticket was all that was needed for boarding, this was considered a tough question. "It's an impossible problem short of searching every passenger," FAA representative Irving Ripp informed the Senate panel.[27] So it was that Senator George Smathers proposed a solution: he suggested that magnetometers, or metal detectors, be used to screen passengers, pointing out that the devices were already in place and functioning effectively in certain military sites and prisons across the United States. "I see no reason why similar devices couldn't be installed at airport check-in gates to determine whether passengers are carrying guns or other weapons just prior to enplaning," he said.[28] But the answer was still no. Neither the airline industry nor the federal government considered it feasible to inspect passengers or their carry-on luggage. The airlines worried that their well-heeled customers would be insulted by such measures and would return to traveling by train, while the government was concerned that metal detectors might alarm passengers unnecessarily or infringe their rights to privacy.[29] Inspection procedures were therefore shelved in the face of increasingly violent hijackings.

As could be expected, not everyone was impressed with such dithering. The Air Line Pilots Association, which was composed of pilots and flight attendants at the time, threatened to go on strike, with its dissatisfaction persisting for the next four years. "If it was in my power alone," said the president of the organization, Captain J.J. O'Donnell, "I would shut down America's air industry until such time as the proper guarantees for safety to passengers and crew were made by the Federal Government."[30]

Individual pilots also spoke out publicly about the escalating danger. Among them was Captain James G. Brown of National Airlines, who had been held at gunpoint and forced to fly to Havana. In that incident, the hijackers had also placed four sticks of dynamite beside the captain to underscore their seriousness. Addressing a congressional committee, Brown emphasized the urgent need for stronger prevention measures. "If anyone has a solution to the problem of hijacking, please do something about it expeditiously," he told lawmakers, "because it is a tragedy waiting for a place to happen."[31]

One solution the FAA did ponder involved constructing, in southern Florida, the façade of the Havana airport. Aircraft that were commandeered in Miami would instead fly to this imitation airport, where police would arrest the perpetrators when they deplaned. One reason this far-fetched solution was not pursued concerned the excessive cost.

Other ideas, some of which were submitted to the FAA by inventors, were even more fanciful. One consisted of a passenger seat that would contain a "hypodermic injection apparatus, arranged for driving the needle of a hypodermic syringe through the seat cushion and into the passenger, to instantly sedate or kill the [hijacker]," says Koerner.[32] A related notion centered on a passenger seat with a built-in ejection mechanism; in effect, a trap door through which the hijacker would plunge into a plexiglass container that would serve as a holding cell. And then there was the short-lived idea of releasing a gas into the passenger cabin so as to anaesthetize everyone in it, the hijacker included. Related to this was the idea of arming flight attendants with tranquilizer darts, or, alternatively, broadcasting the Cuban national anthem over the public address system in order to identify those passengers who knew the lyrics.[33] In the meantime, the FAA continued exploring more realistic measures for putting a stop to air piracy.

In regard to the Cuba-United States hijacking problem, it would be addressed, and rather successfully, on February 13, 1973, when representatives of the two governments signed the "Memorandum of Understanding on Hijacking of Aircraft and Vessels and Other Offenses."[34] The agreement stipulated that the authorities would return a hijacker for prosecution to the nation in which the airline was registered, or, alternatively, the hijacker would be prosecuted by the country in which the aircraft landed. In either case, the perpetrator would face legal penalties. Given that conditions in Castro's prisons were known to approach the barbaric, Americans decided that diverting airliners to the Caribbean nation was not a clever plan. Likewise, Cubans, knowing that convictions and prison sentences awaited them, were disinclined to flee to the United States.

Middle Eastern Hijackings

Unfortunately, skyjacking mania spread to other parts of the world during this period, a foreseeable turn of events in that air piracy in North

America was receiving substantial press coverage. "Newspapers, television, and other mass media constantly carried stories about aircraft hijackings," writes Robert T. Holden, "and it was often suggested that the motivation to hijack planes spread from individual to individual as a result of the media coverage."[35] Holden's research on the subject, which made use of a mathematical model, would bear out such contagion.[36] The ease with which commercial aircraft could be overtaken without resistance illustrated to the global community that hijackings could be a convenient tool for numerous ends.

It was on July 23, 1968, that the episode which was presented in the Introduction, the one in which Palestinian extremists commandeered El Al Flight 426 over the Isle of Capri, transpired. Considering that U.S. airliners were being re-routed to Cuba on a monthly basis during that same summer, it is plausible that the extremists who seized the El Al aircraft were inspired by the North American hijackers.

Lending support to this notion was an episode the following year, one that appeared to have been galvanized by the spate of Cuban-U.S. hijackings and the Cuban Revolution itself. The date was August 29, 1969, and the target was TWA Flight 840 from Rome to Athens, the ultimate terminus being Tel Aviv. (This incident should not be confused with the 1986 terrorist bombing of another TWA Flight 840 over Greece.) The perpetrators were two PFLP members, Salim Essawi and Leila Khaled. Like his comrades who seized El Al Flight 426 eleven months earlier, Essawi made his move at mealtime when an unsuspecting flight attendant opened the door to the cockpit. The terrorist burst in and held the crew at gunpoint in what marked the first case of a U.S. airliner being commandeered outside the Western hemisphere.

In the passenger cabin at this same moment, Khaled, the first woman to hijack an airliner, announced that she and her accomplice were members of the PFLP's "Che Guevara Commando Unit," the moniker constituting a show of solidarity with the guerrilla leader. Essawi and Khaled mistakenly believed that Israeli ambassador Yitzhak Rabin was on board the plane; their aim was to capture him as an act of protest against Israel's unlawful annexation of Palestinian territory. Upon learning that Rabin was not on the flight, the two decided to proceed all the same. To maintain order, moreover, they attempted to frighten the passengers into submission. "Put your hands on your heads, don't move," commanded Khaled on the public-address system, "there are Israeli assassins aboard; we're going to a friendly country."[37] Following a failed landing attempt in Tel Aviv, the Boeing 707, after two more hours of searching for an accommodating airport, touched down in Syria. "We made Damascus on a wing and a prayer as we were almost out of fuel," recalled Del Marinello, a passenger.[38]

Within minutes, the airliner's occupants deplaned using the emergency chutes, one woman fracturing her leg in the process. Concurrently, Syrian forces arrived in trucks and herded the frightened passengers and crew, at gunpoint, to a secluded building. After Essawi and Khaled determined that no one remained on the airliner, they detonated an explosive device, obliterating the TWA's nose section.

Notwithstanding its cooperation after the fact, Syria had played no role in the hijacking and the government was not pleased with serving as the operation's endpoint. The scenario placed Syria in an awkward position, politically. In any event, the authorities promptly arrested the two terrorists and held them for over a month, while quickly releasing the passengers and crew, except for two Israelis. It seems the Syrians, for whatever reason, claimed to find the pair suspicious and contemplated torturing them.[39] The Syrian government also detected a self-serving angle in the madness at the Damascus airport, leading it to propose that Israel release seventy-one Syrian and Egyptian soldiers who were incarcerated in Israeli prisons in exchange for the two "suspicious" passengers. Three months later, Israel did set free thirteen prisoners, thereby bringing to an end the TWA 840 ordeal.

In this pivotal episode, a hijacking that brought international publicity to the Palestinian cause was subsequently capitalized upon by an unrelated third party so as to compel an exchange of passengers and prisoners. For the terrorists, the PFLP, and Syria itself, there was no downside. Naturally, the fact that this single act of air piracy paid such dividends did not go unnoticed by other extremist organizations.

The Flight 840 incident was notable for another reason as well, namely its pugnaciousness, the first hijacking to be so aggressive. "This new type of hijacking was much more violent in nature, and exhibited a shift in hijackings and hijacker tactics," writes Biles. "[It] involved a team of hijacker *terrorists*, as opposed to a lone hijacker *criminal*."[40] Unfortunately, this more belligerent version would proliferate, and swiftly.

Seven days after the TWA 840 episode in the Middle East, student militants in South America orchestrated the first dual skyjacking in the Western hemisphere. In this violent operation, twelve men and one woman, some armed with submachine guns, overtook two airliners operated by Ecuador's official airline, TAME (Transportes Aéreo Militares Ecuatorianos). From the capital city of Quito, they diverted the aircraft to Colombia and Cuba, in the course of which one crew member was killed, another one wounded, and an airliner damaged. The militants explained that the synchronized hijackings were a reprisal for recent law enforcement action at the University of Guayaquil, action in which the police killed several students during a political protest.[41]

More hijackings would transpire in the autumn of 1969, and would involve airliners departing from Argentina, Brazil, Colombia, Ethiopia, France, Honduras, Nicaragua, Poland, South Korea, Spain, and Turkey. It was also during the autumn months—November 10, 1969, to be precise—that the youngest person to attempt to commandeer a commercial carrier appeared on the scene. The would-be hijacker was fourteen years old, angry at his father, and desperate to leave home. To this end, he traveled to the Cincinnati Airport, where he took hostage an eighteen-year-old ballet dancer and boarded Delta Airlines Flight 670. "I was really scared after he put that knife to my side and said 'You're going with me—we're going to Sweden,'" said the young woman.[42] After learning that the McDonnell Douglas DC-9 was not designed for intercontinental travel, the boy released the hostage and surrendered. It later came to light that he had decided to act after viewing television coverage of a similar incident two weeks earlier, one in which a nineteen-year-old U.S. Marine, who was AWOL, seized a TWA jetliner in California and forced the pilot to fly to Rome. Once again, a perpetrator had picked up the idea from a prior episode of air piracy.

Faced with growing concerns over the rise in airline seizures, the FAA now encouraged U.S. airlines to implement a procedure recently developed by John T. Dailey, an educational psychologist and the chief of the FAA's Biomedical and Behavioral Sciences Division. Dailey had assembled a "behavioral profile" of a hypothetical skyjacker. In a preliminary study conducted with the cooperation of Eastern Airlines, the profile, which consisted of six behaviors, appeared to effectively identify potential perpetrators.

In November 1969, a handful of U.S. commercial carriers voluntarily implemented the new procedure, which required ticket agents to gauge each customer's degree of eye contact, nervousness, and other behaviors. If one met the criteria, a security agent would escort the person to a private room for further evaluation, including a scan with a metal detector.

As to the reason that ticket agents were assigned to carry out this important task, it was because ticket counters were the only spot that soon-to-be passengers were required to come to a halt before boarding an aircraft. They had to stop and purchase their tickets. And, as it turned out, this was also a weakness in the profiling procedure. Ticket agents were busy people who served thousands of customers each day and attended to ancillary tasks. They were simply unable to evaluate the behavior of every passenger they encountered. Whereas the concept of behavioral profiling may have been sound, then, its initial application was less than ideal. All the same, it would continue to be used, since it was an effective method of identifying potential hijackers when applied consistently. In fact, its use would increase. "The [behavioral] screening system," writes Dailey, "became compulsory for all airlines in February 1972."[43] In light of the continuing escalation in acts of air piracy, additional forms of prevention were needed as well.

Skyjack Sunday. The inadequacy of the existing security methods would come into sharp focus during a crisis on September 6, 1970, a day known as "Skyjack Sunday." It would be a humiliating moment, and a galvanizing one, for the FAA and the U.S. airline industry, a moment in which they would witness the futility of their prevention measures and, at long last, pledge to transform them.

On this historic Sunday, terrorist teams from the PFLP set out to commandeer four airliners traveling on international routes; the organization's demand was the release of six Palestinian guerrillas incarcerated in Switzerland and West Germany. The perpetrators possessed guns, hand grenades, and aeronautical charts. Because of their anticipant preparations, they would be able to calculate fuel usage rather than trusting the pilots' claims. The flights consisted of the following:

- El Al Flight 219 (Boeing 707), 148 occupants; Amsterdam to New York
- Pan Am Flight 93 (Boeing 747), 169 occupants; Amsterdam to New York
- Swissair Flight 100 (Douglas DC-8), 157 occupants; Zurich to New York
- TWA Flight 741 (Boeing 707), 158 occupants; Frankfurt to New York

For the four sets of hijackers, the scheme was identical: seize the airliners at gunpoint and command the pilots to fly to an isolated airstrip in the Sahara Desert. The location was Zarqa, twenty miles northeast of Amman, Jordan. Zarqa was selected because it was once the home of a Royal Air Force base known as Dawson Field, and it had an abandoned airstrip. Then too, the PLO was based in Jordan, which had a sizeable population of Palestinian refugees, leading the PFLP to assume it could use the airstrip without undue opposition from the country's leader, King Hussein. The hijackers re-christened Dawson Field "Revolution Airport."[44]

The terrorists' takeover of the Swissair and TWA planes proceeded according to plan, with the two aircraft touching down at the desert airstrip in the early evening hours. The Pan Am hijacking was another matter, however. Being one of the company's new Boeing 747s, the wide-body jet was too big to put down on the old military runway, so the pilot proceeded to Cairo. Upon arriving, PFLP guerrillas hustled the passengers and crew off the aircraft, then fire-bombed the 21-million-dollar jumbo jet.

Like the Pan Am 93 skyjacking, El Al Flight 219 also diverged from the plan. In Amsterdam, two PFLP guerrillas boarded the airliner, a

Nicaraguan-American by the name of Patrick Arguello and the aforementioned Leila Khaled, who had grown in popularity in Arab circles since her involvement in the TWA 840 episode the previous year. The twenty-four-year-old Palestinian teacher, touted as the "glamour girl of international terrorism" due to her stylishness and panache, was indispensable to the Palestinian liberation movement not only because of her audacious actions and facility in articulating the Palestinians' grievances, but also because of her persona.[45] It enticed young, would-be guerrillas into the movement.

Prior to boarding the plane, airport personnel in Amsterdam inspected Khaled's luggage and found nothing of concern. Had they more diligently searched Khaled herself, they would have detected two hand grenades concealed beneath her clothing. It is plausible that the security officers did not check her more thoroughly because they did not recognize her. An international fugitive by this point, Khaled had undergone plastic surgery after hijacking TWA 840, thereby making it more difficult to identify her.

Twenty minutes after El Al Flight 219 took to the skies, Khaled stood up, unpinned a grenade with her teeth, then rushed to the cockpit door and demanded that Captain Uri Bar-Lev open it. "I will count," Khaled shouted, "and if you don't open [it] I will blow up the plane."[46] At the same moment, her accomplice grabbed the chief purser, pressed a gun to the man's head, and ordered him to tell the captain to open the cockpit door. "One crew member had passed out upon hearing there was a hijacking," recalled Amit Hasak, a passenger, "and the other advised Uri to let the hijacker in so as not to risk the passengers' safety."[47] But Bar-Lev had no intention of bowing to the terrorists. Instead, he turned to an air marshal standing in the cockpit—the captain had wisely requested extra protection on his flights—and relayed his plan of action. "I told him that I was going to put the plane into negative-G mode," said Bar-Lev. "When you put the plane into negative, it's like being in a falling elevator."[48] And sure enough, those who were upright lurched and dropped to the floor, the two hijackers among them. In the commotion, a second air marshal shot and killed Arguello, while the purser led a handful of passengers in dogpiling Khaled. She was arrested soon thereafter, the airliner making an emergency landing in London.

Of the four New York-bound aircraft that the PFLP targeted, the fact that it was the aircrew of the El Al plane that repelled the would-be hijackers is not surprising. After the seizure of El Al Flight 426 two years earlier, the Israeli airline had invested considerable time and money to ensure that its fleet would be immune to future skyjackings. Among other features, El Al flight crews had now been trained in more advanced safety and security methods; airport staff was more proactive in frisking passengers and hand-searching carry-on bags; and El Al specialists applied stringent behavioral profiling techniques, most notably face-to-face interviews in some cases. In addition, the fleet's cockpit doors were newly fortified, with an updated policy requiring that they be locked shortly after takeoff. Plainclothes sky marshals, armed and seated among the passengers, were also posted on all flights, and "alert" buttons were added so that flight attendants could notify the cockpit of a hijacking in progress. (El Al would also mount double doors leading to the cockpit, one of which had to be locked before the other could be opened. As well, the company would reinforce the floors of passenger cabins to better protect travelers from a bomb blast in the cargo hold, and, for freight, the airline would introduce decompression chambers through which cargo would be passed prior to be loaded onto an aircraft.[49] If a piece of cargo concealed an explosive device that was contingent on altitude for detonation, the decompression chamber would trigger it.)

Three days after the PFLP's multiple hijackings, a fifth team of Palestinian militants commandeered yet another commercial carrier: BOAC Flight 775 (British Overseas Airways Corporation) en route from Bahrain to London. A Vickers VC10, it carried 114 passengers, thirty-four of whom were British nationals. Arriving at Dawson Field in the dead of night, the aircraft made a rough landing on the runway lit by headlights and barrels of fire. As to the rationale for this impromptu act of air piracy, it stemmed from Leila Khaled's arrest in London, the hijackers gambling that, if necessary, they could ransom the BOAC's British passengers for her release.

Whereas the PFLP initially called for six Palestinian guerrillas to be released, this number, with the addition of Khaled, climbed to seven. In terms of the 310 passengers who had been transported to Dawson Field, the hijackers released 254 of them at this juncture, retaining fifty-six as hostages, mostly men. As well, the organization issued a fresh three-day deadline, which, it turned out, was a ploy.

Before the deadline had passed, the hijackers transported the remaining hostages to an undisclosed location, then blew up the TWA, Swissair, and BOAC airliners at Dawson Field. The PFLP was convinced that a Western military operation was in the works, one intended to recover the airliners and those being held for ransom. "It was clear there was a plan to foil our seizure of the planes by imperialistic agents," said a PFLP spokesperson, "therefore we blew them up."[50]

As noted earlier, the PFLP had assumed that Jordan's leader, King Hussein, would tolerate the group's Dawson Field operation, but this did not turn out to be the case. Instead, the criminal spectacle in the Sahara Desert was the last straw for the monarch, who was already exasperated by the PLO's violent deeds within Jordan itself during the preceding three months. So it was that a bloody civil war broke out, one in which Jordanian troops confronted the PLO and its offshoots, which, in turn, attempted to overthrow King Hussein and seize control of the nation. But this was not to be. By the end of the month, the military had trounced the extremist organization and expelled its remaining members. "The PLO leadership was decimated," writes Pierre Tristam, "and between 50,000 and 100,000 people were left homeless."[51] Because the month proved to be a bleak one for Palestinians, many came to refer to it as "Black September."[52] A notoriously lethal offshoot of the organization would soon adopt this term as its name.

On September 27, 1970, Egyptian president Nasser hosted a summit in Cairo during which he negotiated a truce between King Hussein and the PLO's Yassar Arafat. Shortly thereafter, the hijackers at Dawson Field freed the remaining hostages—only six captives remained, the others having been released—in exchange for Leila Khaled and the six imprisoned Palestinian commandos incarcerated in Switzerland and West Germany.[53]

Despite the fact that the multi-plane hijacking sparked unrest in the Middle East and culminated in the PLO and its spinoffs being banished from Jordan, the Dawson Field operation had been a success for the PFLP in certain respects. Once again, Palestine was making headlines around the world, and the terrorist group had compelled three European nations to free seven of its commandos. As well, the Dawson Field drama helped fuel a torrent of extremist missions far and wide, the lion's share stemming from the Arab-Israeli conflict.

"[T]errorist attacks increased drastically all over the world, especially those involving Western targets," writes intelligence expert Avila Guttmann. "In the early 1970s, more diplomats were kidnapped, more airplanes were hijacked, and more politicians were murdered by transnational terrorist groups."[54] Then again, the PFLP's multiple-hijacking scheme and its aftereffects also served as a wake-up call for the West, a call that was long overdue.

"It was not until Dawson Field," writes Nicola Clark, "that the international aviation community began to take coordinated action to prevent hijackings."[55] Bearing out this observation, President Nixon delivered a speech on September 11, 1970, in which he presented the methods the United States would henceforth use to avert hijackings. For starters, the FAA would mandate the behavioral profiling of all passengers traveling on U.S. airlines. Additionally, Nixon announced that a sizable portion of the federal government would be joining the campaign for improved air safety. "I have directed the Department of Transportation, Treasury and Defense, the Central Intelligence Agency, the Federal Bureau of Investigation, the Office of Science and Technology, and other agencies to accelerate their present efforts to develop security measures, including new methods for detecting weapons and explosive devices," he stated. And the president revealed a more daunting mechanism that he intended to put into use right away. "[W]e will place specially trained, armed United States Government personnel on flights of U.S. commercial airliners," he said.[56]

While Nixon was hoping to portray the White House as a decisive force in the fight against air piracy, some of his top advisors questioned his approach. Believing that hijackings would continue to occur at home and abroad, they were concerned that the American public would perceive Nixon as having failed in his mission. Melvin Laird, the Secretary of Defense, was vehemently opposed to the president's decision to place federal agents on commercial flights. "The most preferable course by far is to provide training assistance to the airlines to establish their own guard service," Laird argued.[57] Nixon proceeded with the plan, nevertheless. "Within 24 hours of the president's statement," writes historian David D. McKinney, "federal agents were traveling on commercial flights to prevent on-flight air piracy and working at airports as a deterrent to would-be hijackers."[58]

During his speech, Nixon also introduced a measure that had long been contemplated. "[T]he Departments of Defense and Transportation will work with all U.S. airlines in determining whether certain metal detectors and x-ray devices now available to the military could provide immediate improvement in airport surveillance efforts."[59] Like many of those who were worried about the escalation in violent hijackings, Nixon believed magnetometers held considerable promise.

As it happened, one forward-looking American airport had already initiated a magnetometer trial, the first facility in the United States to do so. It was a project of the New Orleans airport, known at the time as Moisant Field and today as Louis Armstrong International Airport. Commencing on July 17, 1970, and utilizing a walk-through metal detector, security staff required those passengers whose behaviors appeared to match the profile of a hijacker to pass through the apparatus.[60] "For anyone flagged by the system, airline personnel formed the initial gauntlet, and U.S. Marshals Service staffers were called in to investigate unresolved questions," writes George C. Larson.[61] As the New Orleans magnetometer program progressed, it was monitored for accuracy, reliability, and usability, and it was judged to be both precise and practicable.

Sixteen months later, an extraordinary in-flight occurrence once again attracted immense attention and highlighted the need for better security in the sphere of domestic aviation. The episode did not involve a terrorist and was unrelated to political conflicts in the Middle East, but the incident was significant nonetheless and ultimately influential.

It was on November 24, 1971, that a man, Dan Cooper, whose alias the media mistakenly understood to be "D.B." Cooper, purportedly carried a briefcase bomb onto Northwest Orient Airlines Flight 305 in Portland,

Oregon. Once the plane was airborne, he dispatched a note to the captain commandeering the plane and demanding $200,000 in ransom ($1.5 million in 2024). Upon landing in Seattle, receiving the money, and freeing the passengers, Cooper ordered the pilot of the Boeing 727 to return to the air, after which the lawbreaker, spoils in tow, parachuted somewhere over the state of Nevada or Washington.[62] He would never be seen again. As could be expected, the midair stunt packed a wallop, and numerous written and televised accounts of the extravagant plot would be produced in the ensuing years. "It was the saga of Cooper that captured the imagination of the American public," writes historian Janet Bednarek, "and helped transform the perception of the overall threat hijackings posed to U.S. air travel and national security."[63]

Further directing the nation's attention to this topic was an in-flight episode that transpired on November 10, 1972, one that amplified the sense of urgency in the nation's capital. It entailed a hijacked domestic airliner, Southern Airways Flight 49, whose perpetrators threatened to crash the plane if they were not accorded ten million dollars. The heart-stopper: they planned to crash it into a nuclear research reactor at the Oak Ridge National Laboratory in eastern Tennessee. Naturally, the prospect of nuclear terrorism on American soil horrified lawmakers.

Taken together, the Dan Cooper hijacking, the Oak Ridge nuclear panic, the New Orleans airport's success with its magnetometer trial, and President Nixon's favorable attitude toward the use of metal detectors were sufficient to mandate the widespread application of such devices. Clearly, there was a problem and magnetometers appeared to assure at least a partial solution. So it was that the FAA, on January 5, 1973, announced that all passengers at U.S. airports would be required to undergo scanning by metal detectors before boarding a commercial aircraft. In addition, security staff would X-ray carry-on bags. Because the new screening protocol was universal in that it applied to all passengers and their hand luggage, behavioral profiling, which was in place to identify suspicious travelers, would no longer be the cardinal approach.[64] In a sense, all passengers would now be regarded as though they were prospective hijackers.

In terms of the costs of the magnetometer and X-ray operations, they would be borne by the airlines. On this subject, there was no flexibility, with the FAA's mandate becoming a federal law the following year. Known as the Air Transportation Security Act of 1974, it extended the Federal Aviation Act of 1958 to encompass weapons screening, penalties for weapons violations, and the responsibilities of airports in "providing a law enforcement presence and capability."[65]

International Treaties. Due to the steep rise in air piracy in the late 1960s and early 1970s, the United States also revisited the "Tokyo

Convention," officially titled the "Convention on Offences and Certain Other Acts Committed on Board Aircraft."[66] This eight-year-old international treaty centered on "acts which ... may or do jeopardize the safety of the aircraft or of persons or property therein or which jeopardize good order and discipline on board."[67] For an offense perpetrated on an airliner, the agreement laid out responsibilities of the country in which the aircraft was registered. The treaty further designated the captain as the authority while an aircraft was in flight, outlined the conditions for restraining a passenger, and indemnified those who helped maintain safety and order when an aircraft was confronted with a crisis affecting its safety. Among those protected from prosecution were the aircraft's owner, the captain, crew members, and passengers who provided help.[68] Although the United States signed the United Nations treaty on September 14, 1963, and put certain aspects of it into effect on December 4, 1969, the U.S. would henceforth fully adhere to its elements. In addition, the United States, on September 14, 1971, became a signatory to the "Convention for the Suppression of Unlawful Seizure of Aircraft."[69] Prepared at The Hague on December 16, 1970, the treaty focused exclusively on skyjackings.

While many observers, including airline pilots and flight attendants, had long criticized the U.S. airline industry and the FAA for dawdling in the face of the increasingly violent skyjackings of the 1960s and early 1970s, the same two bodies received praise at this juncture for their belated, but nevertheless effective, toolkit of anti-hijacking measures. The protocols they had formulated would furnish passengers with a safer in-flight experience, and with the smallest amount of intrusiveness and disruption possible. Interestingly, the industry's longstanding worry that passengers—paying customers—would be frustrated or insulted if required to undergo security screenings proved to be unwarranted. The preponderance of passengers appeared to understand the need for the new security protocols and accepted them. Many travelers, in fact, seemed reassured by them.

Certainly, there was reason to feel assured, with air travel becoming verifiably safer in the ensuing years. Whereas 277 hijackings occurred worldwide between 1968 and 1972, only seventy-eight transpired between 1973 and 1976. A significant change, this figure represents a nearly 30 percent drop in acts of air piracy after the United States and other nations put into place more stringent preventive measures.

Partners in Crime

Although hijackings were in decline, particularly in North America, they persisted in Western Europe and the Middle East, albeit to a lesser extent. In addition, a twist in terrorist operations was observed during the remaining years of the Seventies, with extremist organizations from culturally disparate nations collaborating on, and even contributing to, one another's schemes.

One advocate of such networks was the infamous Venezuelan terrorist Carlos the Jackal (Ilich Ramirez Sánchez), who believed that extremist groups, by working together, could orchestrate more effective attacks, and with a greater reach, than individual groups acting alone. And he was not alone in this belief; effective alliances among militant political organizations were actively being forged at this time. The PLO, for instance, backed the Provisional Irish Republican Army (IRA), a paramilitary organization that, at one point, trained in Libya alongside Palestinian guerrillas. Similarly, the PLO and the IRA declared their solidarity with the Revolutionary Cells, a West German far-left outfit that overlapped ideologically with the pugnacious Red Army Faction (RAF) and the Baader-Meinhof Gang. Then, too, the IRA supported Basque separatists in Spain, while the PLO extended a welcome to extremists in the Japanese Red Army, Italy's Red Brigades, and Uruguay's Tupamaros.[70] As for skyjackings, the PFLP and West Germany's Revolutionary Cells joined forces in at least two such missions.

The first was set into motion on June 27, 1976, when a quartet of terrorists traveling on Singapore Airlines landed in Athens, then transferred to Air France Flight 139 to Paris. Despite the history of air piracy in the region, the Athens airport remained one of the world's most lax facilities, the diligence of its security staff being particularly anemic. It was therefore a smart choice by the terrorists, who were not patted down or otherwise scrutinized before boarding the Airbus A300 bound for the French capital. Concealed beneath their clothing were handguns and grenades.

The aircraft was in the capable hands of Captain Michel Bacos, who recalled hearing a commotion outside the cockpit door once the plane was aloft. "Seven minutes after departing from Athens we heard screams on board," Bacos said. "We thought there was a fire in the cabin."[71] Instead, the tumult stemmed from two sets of terrorists. One pair was from West Germany's Revolutionary Cells and consisted of a man named Wilfried Böse and his lover Brigitte Kuhlmann. The other was comprised of two high-level male operatives of the Popular Front for the Liberation of Palestine–External Operations (PFLP–EO), Jayel al-Arja and Fayez Abdul-Rahim al Jaber. Using the cabin's public address system, the hijackers announced that they represented the Che Guevara Group and the PFLP's Gaza Unit.[72]

It was now that Böse ordered the pilot to divert the aircraft to Benghazi. After refueling at the Libyan airport, the hijacker next directed Captain Bacos to proceed to Entebbe, Uganda, the East African nation of which Idi Amin was the president. A military officer famous for his brutality, Amin, who was aware of the skyjacking scheme before it was put into motion, personally welcomed the perpetrators and their hostages. At this juncture, five additional terrorists, at least three of whom were Palestinian extremists, joined the original four German and Palestinian hijackers, as did a squad of Ugandan troops.

After transporting the jetliner's 246 passengers and twelve crew members to an abandoned, dilapidated building a mile from the main terminal, the perpetrators laid out their demands: fifty-three militants imprisoned in Israel, Switzerland, West Germany, Kenya, and France were to be set free if the Air France passengers and crew were to be released. The hijackers further insisted that France fork over five million dollars for the return of the plane, an ultimatum that was swiftly rebuffed.

As the days passed and Israel and other nations did not comply with the demands, the terrorists set about separating the Israeli passengers from the non–Israelis, following which the latter were released. According to Ilan Hartuv, a retired member of the Israeli Foreign Ministry who was among the hostages at Entebbe, the hijackers did not target Jewish captives in this process. "There was no selection applied to Jews," Hartuv said. "Entebbe was not Auschwitz."[73] Instead, the groupings centered on nationality, although it should be noted that four Jewish people who were not Israeli citizens were purportedly kept behind with the Israeli captives.[74]

Throughout the ordeal, Captain Bacos, whom the hijackers offered to release, chose instead to remain with the hostages. The Air France crew did the same. The conscientious pilot was steadfast in his conviction that the passengers were his responsibility, and he went all out to help them. "Bacos attended the sick, dispensed medicine, made beds, and even swept the floor," writes author Ira Peck.[75]

Meanwhile, as tensions ramped up in Entebbe, several officers from the Israeli Defense Forces (IDF) mulled over the prospects of a rescue effort. "[W]e looked into range, navigation, fuel requirements, payloads we could carry, how we could fly beneath the radar between Saudi Arabia and Egypt, and weather patterns for the time of year—very general preparations, just in case someone would approach us," said Lieutenant Colonel Joshua Shani.[76] And indeed, someone—Golda Meir—did approach the military.

An astonishing rescue mission, Operation Entebbe, as it was dubbed, was launched at 3:30 p.m. on July 3, 1976. Six planes carrying 100 to 200 Israeli troops took to the air from the Red Sea resort town of Sharm El Sheikh, Egypt, which was under Israel's control at the time. Their destination, Entebbe, was nearly 2,000 miles to the south.

The aircraft that were selected for the mission consisted of four

Hercules C-130 heavy transport planes and a Boeing 727, which served as an airborne command and control center. As to the sixth plane, it was a Boeing 727 as well, and it housed a medical unit equipped with surgical suites. Dispatched to Uganda's neighbor, Kenya, this plane would treat the injured. During the eight-hour flights to the two African nations, all of the aircraft traveled at low altitudes to avoid detection by radar, flying as low as 100 feet over water.[77]

Within ninety minutes of landing in Entebbe, the Israeli planes were airborne once again, the soldiers having fought off the terrorists and Ugandan military while, at the same time, rescuing nearly all of the hostages. Killed in the mission, unfortunately, was a soldier named Yonatan ("Yoni") Netanyahu. The brother of future prime minister Benjamin Netanyahu, Yoni would forever be remembered for his courage. Also lauded would be the Air France captain, who did survive the ordeal. The French government would award Michel Bacos the Legion d'Honneur for having voluntarily remained with, and attended to, the captives of Air France Flight 139. "[I]t would be impossible for me to leave my passengers," Bacos told the BBC, "unimaginable."[78]

As to the second joint operation to be engineered by combination of Palestinian and West German terrorists, it transpired on October 13, 1977. The PFLP and a cell of the Red Army Faction—the cell was known as the Kommando Siegfried Hausner—organized a hijacking that aimed to force the release of eleven RAF and Palestinian terrorists imprisoned in West Germany and Turkey. While much of the planning was performed by the West German cell, the actual act of air piracy was to be executed by four Lebanese and Palestinian members of the PFLP. The team leader was twenty-three-year-old Zohair Youssif Akache, who called himself Captain Mahmoud.[79] In addition to the release of the prisoners, the cell demanded $15 million U.S.

In this incident, the targeted aircraft was a Boeing 737. Designated Lufthansa Flight 181, it departed from the island of Majorca, Spain, with Frankfurt as its destination. As it was flying over Marseilles thirty minutes into the journey, the terrorists commandeered the airliner, stated their demands, and notified the eighty-three passengers and cabin crew that the plane had been hijacked.

What ensued was a five-day odyssey during which Lufthansa Flight 181, after refueling in Rome, bounded across the Arabian Peninsula seeking safe haven as well as refueling in Cyprus, Bahrain, Dubai, and Yemen. The 6,000-mile journey finally came to an end in Mogadishu, Somalia, where the hostages were forced to endure temperatures in the 120s inside the cabin. Extreme heat was not the only issue for them, however, since the hijackers periodically, and intentionally, raised the stress levels. At one point, for instance, a female hijacker by the name of Suhaila al-Sayeh threatened the life of the pilot, Jürgen Schumann, insisting she would douse him with gasoline and set him on fire. The terrorists also affixed what they claimed were explosives to the cabin walls to further taunt the hostages.

In Bonn, meanwhile, the West German government adopted a position of non-negotiation while secretly green-lighting a rescue plan. Code-named Operation Feuerzauber, meaning "Fire Magic" in German, the mission would be the responsibility of an elite tactical division of the German Federal Police known as the GSG-9 (also known as *Grenzschutzgruppe 9* and *GSG 9 der Bundespolizei*). In it, sixty commandos would be flown to Mogadishu and positioned on the runway behind the Lufthansa plane. Two operatives from Britain's Special Air Service (SAS) would be present as well, the pair having been loaned to West Germany for the covert mission.

And so it was that a team of commandos climbed onto a wing of the Lufthansa airliner and, taking the hijackers by surprise, killed three of them in a firefight. Seven minutes later, the GSG-9 mission was over. All of the passengers were now free, along with four crew members. Sadly, the perpetrators had already murdered the pilot during a stopover in Yemen, shooting Captain Schumann in the face because, in their opinion, he had taken too long to inspect the landing gear. The co-pilot, Jürgen Vietor, had assumed control of the plane.

While the GSG-9 received a hero's welcome upon its return, pilots and flight attendants around the world, especially in West Germany, voiced their anger and frustration yet again. Despite the recent enhancements in airline and airport security, they believed additional measures were still needed and they shared this opinion with the media. "The International Federation of Air Line Pilots Associations denounced governments in general for failing to act decisively against hijackers," reported the *New York Times*, "and West German pilots called for a worldwide pilots' strike on behalf of tougher aviation security measures."[80]

The valid concerns voiced by the West German pilots notwithstanding, aviation security had become much more effective in preventing skyjackings now that international airports had begun using metal detectors and X-ray equipment as well as conducting hands-on searches of passengers and carry-on bags. Case in point: after the FAA's updated security requirements in 1973, only one successful hijacking occurred in the United States during the next four years. This is not to say that there was no room for improvement; security vulnerabilities still existed, most notably at airports. "Passengers were allowed to arrive just 30 minutes before boarding, family and friends were allowed at gates and security was often outsourced to underpaid contractors," writes Ashlee Kieler.[81] Unfortunately for the traveling public, these and other security gaps would not be rectified during the remainder of the 1970s. For that matter, they would persist throughout most of the 1980s, a decade when the number of hijackings once again began to rise. Among the terrorist groups orchestrating such attacks was the Abu Nidal Organization (ANO), a Palestinian nationalist group.

Abu Nidal Organization. It was an ANO cell calling itself the "Egypt Revolution" that was behind the seizure of EgyptAir Flight 648 on November 23, 1985.[82] Departing at night, the aircraft was scheduled to travel from Athens to Cairo, but twenty minutes into the flight a hijacker made his way into the cockpit and held the pilot, Captain Hani Galal, at gunpoint. The perpetrator's weapon, like the guns and grenades of his two accomplices, evidently had been sneaked onto the Boeing 737 at the Athens airport, although not by the terrorists themselves. "There have been instances where a man disguised as a member of the ground crew managed to reach the ramp of a plane undetected," says Rodney Wallis of the International Air Transport Association.[83] Wallis noted that the security presence around the aircraft at the Athens airport was inadequate on the night of the hijacking, suggesting this may have been the method used to transfer the weapons.

After commandeering the airliner, the terrorists confiscated the passports of the ninety-two passengers and set about sorting them by nationality. Not surprisingly given it was an Abu Nidal mission, the targets would be citizens of Israel and the United States. Unlike previous skyjackings by Middle Eastern groups, however, no demands would be forthcoming; a disturbing change in aviation terrorism in that the objective appeared solely to horrify.

Moments later, a passenger, an Egyptian secret service agent, got up from his seat and shot a hijacker, killing him. The remaining hijackers returned fire, striking the agent and two flight attendants, with the bullets piercing the fuselage. Cabin decompression became yet another threat to the lives of all on board.

Due to the damage, the plane made an emergency landing at Luqa Airport in Malta, albeit on an unlit runway because Maltese officials refused to turn on the beacons. When the hijackers, once the plane was on the ground, insisted that the Maltese provide fuel and a doctor, the officials again refused to comply. It was at this juncture that the ANO team sequestered the Israeli and American passengers and commenced shooting them at ten-minute intervals. After each shooting, the cell's leader laughed and made jokes, Captain Galal recalled.[84]

The ugly episode finally came to an end one day after it began, when a contingent of twenty-five Egyptian commandos raided the plane, setting off smoke bombs and firing at those they assumed to be hijackers.

The slapdash rescue attempt was roundly criticized; it was suggested that many of the fifty-eight people who died had been killed by the actions of the commandos. Most of the deceased were victims of smoke inhalation, apparently caused by the rescuers' smoke bombs, while a smaller number suffered gunshot wounds.

In the end, the objective of the EgyptAir incident was largely fulfilled. Its intention had been to bring about a shocking event that would terrify passengers and garner international publicity as well as discomfit the governments of Israel and the United States. In light of this accomplishment, it is not surprising that the Abu Nidal Organization conducted another skyjacking a year later.

In this second incident, four members of the ANO carried out a terrorist attack that would quickly devolve into a blood-stained fiasco, and it would happen on board an American-owned Boeing 747, a jumbo jet. "It was exceptionally rare for a Boeing 747 to be hijacked," writes Baum, "as generally terrorists targeted smaller aircraft, which were easier to control."[85] Certainly, this was the case in this latest ANO mission; the perpetrators were so unacquainted with the Boeing 747 that they could not find the cockpit, which, on the jumbo jet, is located on an upper level.

Designated Pan Am Flight 73, the jetliner was on the tarmac at Jinnah International Airport in Karachi, having just arrived from Mumbai (Bombay). After taking on additional passengers in the Pakistani city, it was scheduled to continue on to Frankfurt. It would not, however, leave Karachi.

As passengers were filing onto the plane, four armed men dressed in airport security uniforms sped onto the tarmac in a van and fought their way onto the aircraft. Besides handguns, they were armed with AK-47s and grenades. Despite the shock of the moment—the hijackers were firing into the air and shouting—a fast-thinking flight attendant transmitted the hijack code to the flight deck, thereby allowing the pilot, co-pilot, flight engineer, and navigator to escape through a hatch in the roof. Once atop the aircraft, they climbed down using a rope ladder. "Many have criticized the pilots for leaving the rest of the crew behind," says Sunshine Vesuwala, one of the plane's fourteen flight attendants, "but I was relieved when I saw the pilots were gone, as we were all safer on the ground than we would be in the air." Vesuwala was not alone in her opinion; other crew members likewise championed the flight crew's actions. Exiting the cockpit was Pan Am protocol in such a circumstance.

Now threatening to blow up the airliner, the hijackers demanded to be flown to Cyprus and then to Israel; their aim was to compel the release of their imprisoned comrades in the two countries. To demonstrate their seriousness, one of the terrorists executed a twenty-nine-year-old American passenger, Rajesh Kumar, and kicked his lifeless body off the plane. Realizing, at this point, that the passengers' nationalities might become a matter of life and death, the flight attendants collected all of the travelers' passports except for those of the Americans. It was an attempt to ensure that no other U.S. citizens would be singled out for murder. As for the few American passports that the crew unintentionally gathered, the flight attendants hid them under the seats.

At this juncture, the Pakistani police and a Pan Am official began speaking to the hijackers by radio, conversations that led to Pakistani authorities agreeing to find a replacement pilot to fly the Boeing 747. In reality, the officials were stalling, while the jet's 378 passengers and crew bided their time on the aircraft.

The horrific moment came sixteen hours after the incident began, at 9:00 p.m., when the lights inside the aircraft began to dim. The reason: the plane's power supply was nearly depleted. Yet the terrorists suspected it meant that a special forces team was about to launch a raid on the grounded aircraft. "Shortly thereafter," writes Erica Pearson, "the plane went completely dark as the emergency power ran out, and the hijackers, thinking that the plane was being assaulted by security forces, fired on the hostages with machine guns and grenades."[86] The terrorists exhausted the entirety of their ammunition in the bloodbath. Twenty-two passengers and crew were killed and another 120 were wounded.

After the firing stopped, but before the police apprehended the terrorists, the pilot and other members of the flight crew re-boarded Flight 73, where they joined the cabin crew in helping the injured and disoriented passengers exit the plane. These evacuations were carried out using the emergency chutes or assisting victims in leaping off the rear of the wings. As far as the aircrew could determine, the terrorists were still on board, somewhere in the darkness. For these and other reasons, the selflessness and courage of the Pan Am team in attending to their passengers' needs brought international praise as well as a feature film recounting the actions of one crew member in particular, purser Neerja Bhanot. Shot in the hip, Bhanot, who perished, was honored by the Indian government.

While acknowledging the rise in airline hijackings and the escalating mortality rates resulting from them, aviation officials yet again failed to assess and adjust the existing security measures in any meaningful, systematic fashion. It would not be until the Lockerbie tragedy in 1988, the terrorist attack in which Pan Am Flight 103 exploded at 31,000 feet, that such longstanding lapses would be confronted and the inconsistent implementation of existent procedures corrected. Since the disaster over Scotland did not originate with a hijacking, it will not be revisited at this point. Suffice it to say, the terrorist bombing of Flight 103, which was intended solely to cause the mass murder of passengers and Pan Am crew at Christmastime, culminated in sweeping changes in safety and security practices at airlines and airports around the world. As well, it led the U.S. government to craft new policies targeting those nations that sponsor terrorism, including aviation terrorism.

Owing to such enhancements in skyjacking prevention measures, acts of air piracy committed on commercial airliners dropped from 492 incidents in the 1980s to 200 incidents in the 1990s.[87] This roughly 60 percent decline is impressive, but it means that an unacceptable number of incidents still occurred. In part, this was because certain airports failed to consistently adhere to the mandated preventive procedures. For instance, the Frankfurt International Airport, long regarded as unreliable in its security compliance, would be the departure point for a hijacking on February 11, 1993, one carried out by an amateur with a gun.

The airliner's designation was Lufthansa Flight 592, and it had departed from Frankfurt and was en route to Cairo. As it was crossing the Alps into Austrian airspace, a young Ethiopian man entered a restroom situated between the business-class and first-class sections and emerged moments later sporting a black ski mask and brandishing a pistol. Shoving a flight attendant into the cockpit, the twenty-year-old hijacker demanded that the jetliner be re-routed to the "North Atlantic" and that he be granted political asylum upon landing.[88] Complying with the intruder, the pilot explained to the passengers and crew via the public-address system that a gun was being held to his head and he was being ordered to alter the course of the plane.

Evidently, the hijacker was not entirely rational. "About four hours into the flight," recalled a passenger, "a stewardess said to me that this guy is really nuts, he doesn't have any political agenda."[89] It was this observation, the passenger added, that was most alarming.[90]

Eleven hours later, the aircraft, which had refueled in Hanover, Germany, touched down at JFK Airport in New York, the pilot having convinced the unstable gunman that the plane was running out of fuel. The man surrendered peacefully. It was later discovered that his revolver was actually a "starting pistol" loaded with blanks. All the same, the episode raised questions about how an unsound man had managed, in 1993, to sneak a pistol onto an Airbus A310 at the Frankfurt airport. Obviously, security vulnerabilities persisted.

Although there would be a spike in skyjackings in the year 2000, it was not until September 11, 2001, that the mind-boggling damage that hijacked planes are capable of inflicting would reach catastrophic proportions. As is well known, it was on this day that nineteen terrorists from the al-Qaeda organization, most of them citizens of Saudi Arabia, seized four

U.S.-owned airliners at three East Coast airports and flew them into the World Trade Center in Manhattan and the Pentagon in Arlington, Virginia, near Washington, D.C. Another crashed in a Pennsylvania meadow.

Because the 9/11 hijackings are the subject of Chapter Eight, they will not be revisited in detail at this point. However, the associated security issues will be examined.

In this regard, the airports al-Qaeda selected for its lethal operation consisted of Logan International (Boston), Dulles International near Washington, D.C., and Newark International in Newark, New Jersey. Arriving shortly before their flights were scheduled to depart, the terrorists left little time for security officers to screen them thoroughly on this busy weekday morning. And even when the officers did detect troubling attributes—"red flags"—in some of the men and pulled them aside for questioning, the officers ultimately permitted them to board the planes. We now know that two of the hijackers also triggered the metal detectors, but after the officers hand-searched them, the perpetrators were permitted to proceed. Quite likely, it was their knives and box cutters that set off the metal detectors, but, at the time, these items were allowed on commercial airliners. The fact is, security was applied perfunctorily on September 11, a slackness at domestic airports that was not uncommon. In large part, this was because airline companies outsourced their security services to private firms, which, in turn, delivered protection, often patchily, through unarmed and sometimes inexperienced agents. Contributing to the situation, the FAA did not demand a higher standard of service provision. "The airlines pretended to deliver security," says Mary Schiavo, "and the government pretended to find it okay."[91]

Schiavo's statement is consistent with the conclusion reached by the National Commission on Terrorist Attacks Upon the United States, commonly known as "the 9/11 Commission," following its twenty-month investigation into the terrorist attacks. "Each layer relevant to hijacking—Intelligence, Passenger Screening, Checkpoint Screening, and Onboard Security—was seriously flawed prior to 9/11," states the final report. "Taken together, they did not stop any of the 9/11 hijackers from getting on board four different aircraft at three different airports."[92]

In all, nearly 3,000 people perished in the attacks, roughly 6,000 more were injured, and still another 3,000 are estimated to have died in subsequent years due to long-term diseases, most notably cancer and respiratory conditions, associated with the terrorist strikes. "The rate of some cancers among first responders is up to 30 percent higher than in the general population," says Michael Crane, M.D., of Mount Sinai Hospital in New York.[93]

Seventeen minutes after one of the hijacked airliners slammed into the Pentagon, the FAA Command Center in Herndon, Virginia, ordered a halt to civilian air travel over the United States.[94] "The groundstop," CNN reported at the time of the FAA's announcement, "affects 36,000 to 40,000 flights that take off in the United States daily, as well as general aviation flights."[95] Amtrack and Greyhound, the railway and bus services, likewise suspended operations, specifically in the Northeast. When air travel slowly began to resume two days later, domestic airports and airlines, unlike in the recent past, diligently applied the existent security protocols as well as complied with additional layers of protection that the federal government was now mandating. Passengers, for instance, were forbidden from taking knives, razors, scissors, box cutters, and other sharp objects onto airliners; security officers painstakingly searched all passengers and their carry-on bags; and armed National Guard soldiers patrolled selected airports. Although only a small number of people were choosing to fly at this worrisome and uncertain moment, the enhanced security protocols, in particular the hand searches of travelers and their belongings, generated long lines and lengthy delays at airports from coast to coast.

More substantive action would come on November 19, 2001, when Congress passed, and President George W. Bush signed into law, the Aviation and Transportation Security Act, or ATSA. A direct response to the coordinated strikes on September 11, the legislation created the Transportation Security Administration (TSA), which would federalize aviation security as well as that of rail and inter-city bus travel across the United States. Upon its creation, the TSA functioned as a subagency of the Department of Transportation (DOT), but it was transferred in 2003 to the newly-established Department of Homeland Security (DHS).

As for air travel, the ATSA required federal agents to X-ray all checked baggage at domestic airports, and it also expanded the Federal Air Marshal Service, culminating in a much larger contingent of armed agents on commercial flights. In addition, it required that cockpit doors be reinforced. Until this point, El Al was the only airline in the world that had done so with its entire fleet. "If we had just had good cockpit doors before 9/11," says Captain Tom Bunn, "that would have stopped 9/11 from happening."[96]

The reason that the FAA and airline industry had resisted mandating stronger cockpit doors had to do with the need for a means of escape during life-threatening emergencies. They wanted to ensure that crew members or first responders could kick down the doors in the event of a fire or crash. On top of that, the industry was concerned that retrofitting the aluminum cockpit doors on all U.S.-based airlines would be a costly endeavor. Of course, the pilots whose lives were at stake during skyjackings had concerns of their own, and they did not involve expenditures. Beginning with the string of aircraft seizures that occurred in the late 1960s and early 1970s, they and their organizations had persistently pushed for buttressed doors.

It was to their annoyance, then, that after Congress passed the ATSA and the recommendations for fortified doors became official, it was another nineteen months before all of the airline companies complied. And during this delay, hijackings, like those carried out on September 11, could have happened again. Indeed, there was at least one attempt. "An unruly passenger on a flight from Miami to Buenos Aires," reported CBS News, "managed to kick in a small breakaway panel across the bottom of the door and put his head into the cockpit before a co-pilot clubbed him with an ax."[97]

When U.S. airline companies finally did reinforce the cockpit doors, some were coated in titanium and others in stainless steel. Sheets of Kevlar, which is a bulletproof, synthetic fabric, were installed on a number of them as well. Now, the augmented doors provided the aircrew with greater protection from would-be skyjackers and thus greater peace of mind. (Increasingly, airlines today are also installing a "Flight Deck Secondary Barrier" outside the cockpit door as a backup measure. A low-cost addition, it consists of a wire-grid panel, parallel to the cockpit door, that must be in place when the latter is open.)

And more advancements were forthcoming. In December 2001, the federal government expanded its "No-Fly List," which prohibited individuals deemed suspicious from traveling on an airliner. Although such a list, a small one containing only sixteen names, had been maintained unofficially prior to the attacks on the World Trade Center and the Pentagon, it was formalized and expanded after 9/11, with its existence initially being kept secret from the public. After a few years, tens of thousands of names made the list, which was overseen by the FBI and TSA.

Particularly important, even historic, was a piece of legislation that President Bush signed on November 25, 2002, one that spoke further to airline pilots' safety concerns. Titled "Arming Pilots Against Terrorism Act," or APATA, it authorized airline captains to undergo training in the use of firearms for the purpose of protecting their aircraft against acts of criminal violence or air piracy.[98] Enhancing the APATA, the TSA, in 2003, launched the Federal Flight Deck Officer Program (FFDO), which permitted the agency to deputize as law enforcement officers those pilots and crew members on passenger and cargo aircraft who volunteered for, and successfully completed, specialized instruction. "Participants in the program, known as Federal Flight Deck Officers (FFDOs), are trained and authorized to transport and carry a firearm and to use force, including deadly force," reads the program's description.[99] As with reinforced cockpit doors, many pilots and their principal union had long sought approval to keep firearms on the flight deck.

It was also in the wake of September 11 attacks that the government announced that airlines must confirm that each piece of checked luggage, meaning that which is stored in the plane's cargo hold, is matched to a person who is physically present on the aircraft (i.e., "baggage reconciliation"). Alternatively, the airline could screen the checked baggage by hand searches, bomb-sniffing dogs, or electronic detection devices. Nearly all facilities chose the latter method.

In terms of the public's response to these measures, it was ambivalent. The amount of time required to pass through security, including the fact that travelers were required to arrive at an airport hours before their departure times, was exasperating to many customers despite the fact that, according to their own reports, their sense of security was heightened. And this mixed reaction had an impact on business, most notably in 2002, the first year after many of the methods' implementation.

"Airlines say this has cost billions this year in lost ticket revenue, as some business travelers simply choose not to go," writes Joe Sharkey.[100] In the years that followed, however, the public would, largely out of necessity, come to terms with the time-consuming and often invasive security measures and would gradually return to air travel.

In response to customer complaints about the burdensome inspection procedures, coupled with the cost of screening over two million passengers per day in the United States, the Department of Homeland Security devised "trusted traveler programs."[101] Perhaps the best known is TSA PreCheck.[102] Launched in December 2013, the latter is designed for flyers who pay a fee, sit for an interview, and submit to a background check. In return, those who are approved are permitted to take liquids aboard airliners, undergo less intrusive physical inspections, and are processed by security agents by means of dedicated counters at American airports. The PreCheck procedure significantly shortens passengers' wait-times and accelerates boarding, while also reducing the burden on TSA agents.

All in all, the trusted traveler programs, in concert with the much larger arsenal of innovative security measures introduced after September 11, caused hijackings on U.S. commercial aircraft to plunge. Between 2010 and 2020, for instance, only one or two acts of air piracy occurred each year, with some years having no hijackings at all.

In terms of the other preventive measures that today's travelers routinely encounter, such as full-body scanners, three-dimensional (3D) imaging of carry-on and checked baggage, and related technologies, they will be examined in Chapter Two, which centers on improvised explosive devices (IEDs) or makeshift bombs. Along with air piracy, bombs and bomb threats have long been favored tools of terrorists who target airliners.

Notes

1. Philip Baum, *Violence in the Skies: A History of Aircraft Hijacking and Bombing* (West Sussex, England: Summersdale, 2016).
2. Charles H. Gibbs-Smith, *The Aeroplane: An Historical Survey* (London: Her Majesty's Stationery Office, 1960).
3. Tom Holland, "15 Minutes of Fame | Tom Holland Chooses Franz Nopcsa von Felsö-Szilvás," *History Extra* (BBC), August 31, 2022, https://www.historyextra.com/period/20th-century/franz-nopcsa-von-felso-szilvas-who-life/.
4. Edward R. Mickolus, *Transnational Terrorism: A Chronology of Events, 1968-1979* (Westport, CT: Greenwood, 1980), 8.
5. Marc E. Vargo, *The Mossad: Six Landmark Missions of the Israeli Intelligence Agency, 1960-1990* (Jefferson, NC: McFarland, 2015).
6. Oliver Burkeman, "Can We Ever Stop This?" *The Guardian*, September 28, 2001, https://www.theguardian.com/world/2001/sep/28/september11.usa4.
7. Erik R. Scott, "The Hijacking of Aeroflot Flight 244: States and Statelessness in the Late Cold War," *Past & Present* 243, issue 1 (May 2019): 213, https://doi.org/10.1093/pastj/gty044.
8. Associated Press, "20 Czechs Seize Plane in Midair and Force It to Land in U.S. Zone," *New York Times*, April 9, 1948, https://timesmachine.nytimes.com/timesmachine/1948/04/09/94644837.pdf.
9. Philip Baum, *Violence in the Skies*.
10. Philip Baum, *Violence in the Skies*, 38.
11. FCAFA, "They Flew to Exile 1950," Free Czechoslovak Air Force (FCAFA), March 12, 2011, https://fcafa.com/2011/03/12/they-flew-to-exile-1950/.
12. Dana Adams Schmidt, "Czechs Insist U.S. Send Back Airmen," *New York Times*, March 25, 1950, https://timesmachine.nytimes.com/timesmachine/1950/03/31/94251809.html?pageNumber=16.
13. Jin-Tai Choi, *Aviation Terrorism: Historical Survey, Perspectives and Responses* (New York: St. Martin's Press, 1994), 12.
14. Nicoletta Mazzoleni and Massimo Catusi, "The Cuban Hijackings: Their Significance and Impact Sixty Years On," *Transport Security International*, October 19, 2018, https://www.tsi-mag.com/the-cuban-hijackings-their-significance-and-impact-sixty-years-on/.
15. Jin-Tai Choi, *Aviation Terrorism*, 13.
16. "Compania Cubana de Aviscion Viscount Hi-jacked," *Vickers Viscount Network*, accessed October 2, 2022, http://www.vickersviscount.net/Pages_History/Cubana%20Hijack.aspx.
17. Don Bohning, *The Castro Obsession: U.S. Covert Operations Against Cuba, 1959-1965* (Dulles, Virginia: Potomac Books, 2005).
18. Philip Baum, *Violence in the Skies*, 43.
19. "Legislative Summary—Aviation," John F. Kennedy Presidential Library and Museum, accessed September 22, 2022, https://www.jfklibrary.org/archives/other-resources/legislative-summary/aviation#:~:text=This%20amendment%20to%20the%20Federal,in%20flight%20in%20air%20commerce.
20. Clay W. Biles, *The United States Federal Air Marshal Service: A Historical Perspective, 1962-2012* (Coppell, TX: Wendy de la Cruz, 2013), 39.
21. Brendan I. Koerner, *The Skies Belong to Us: Love and Terror in the Golden Age of Hijacking* (New York: Crown, 2013).
22. Gloria Willoughby, personal communication, September 17, 2022.
23. Teishan A. Latner, "Take Me to Havana! Airline Hijacking, U.S.-Cuba Relations, and Political Protest in Late Sixties' America," *Diplomatic History* 39, no. 1 (January 2015): 16, https://www.jstor.org/stable/26376639.
24. "Will Hijack More Planes, Gunman Says," United Press International, November 4, 1968, https://skyjackeroftheday.tumblr.com/post/49258112380/50-raymond-johnson.
25. Associated Press, "Hijacker Surrenders 18 Years Later," *The Ottawa Citizen*, September 13, 1986, https://news.google.com/newspapers?id=5L4yAAAAIBAJ&sjid=be8FAAAAIBAJ&pg=4605,1535917&hl=en.

ONE. Air Piracy

26. David Bauder, "Woman Arrested in 1969 Hijacking to Cuba," Associated Press, July 26, 1988, https://apnews.com/article/0cf464d520028b772e0bf0b67dfa87a8.
27. Brendan I. Koerner, "How Hijackers Commandeered Over 130 American Planes," *Wired*, June 18, 2013, https://www.wired.com/2013/06/love-and-terror-in-the-golden-age-of-hijacking/.
28. Andrew Hay, "A Brief History of Airline Security, Hijackings and Metal Detectors," IBM, April 24, 2019, https://www.ibm.com/blogs/systems/a-brief-history-of-airline-security-hijackings-and-metal-detectors/.
29. Andrew Hay, "A Brief History of Airline Security, Hijackings and Metal Detectors."
30. Richard Within, "Threat of Strike Raised by Pilots," *New York Times*, November 16, 1972, https://www.nytimes.com/1972/11/16/archives/threat-of-strike-raised-by-pilots-union-presses-demands-for-more.html.
31. Robert Lindsey, "U.S. Is Moving on Two Fronts in Effort to Halt Sharp Increase in Plane Hijacks," *New York Times*, September 5, 1969, https://www.nytimes.com/1969/09/05/archives/us-is-moving-on-two-fronts-in-effort-to-halt-sharp-increase-in.html.
32. Roman Mars (host) and Brendan Koerner (interviewee), "Skyjacking (transcript)," *99% Invisible* (podcast, episode #120), June 23, 2014, https://99percentinvisible.org/episode/skyjacking/transcript/.
33. Melissa Sartore, "In the 1970s, Airport Security Didn't Exist—and the 'Golden Age of Airplane Hijackings' was Born," *Ranker*, March 20, 2020, https://www.ranker.com/list/golden-age-of-plane-hijacking/melissa-sartore.
34. "Memorandum of Understanding on Hijacking of Aircraft and Vessels and Other Offenses," Department of State, February 13, 1973, https://2001-2009.state.gov/documents/organization/52191.pdf.
35. Robert T. Holden, "The Contagiousness of Aircraft Hijacking," *American Journal of Sociology* 91, no. 4 (January 1986), 874, https://www.jstor.org/stable/2779961.
36. Robert T. Holden, "The Contagiousness of Aircraft Hijacking."
37. "The PFLP Hijacking of TWA Flight 840," *Association for Diplomatic Studies and Training*, August 10, 2015, https://adst.org/2015/08/the-pflp-hijacking-of-twa-840/.
38. Ellen Sussman, "GV Woman Recalls Historic 1969 Hijacking," *Green Valley News*, April 30, 2013, https://www.gvnews.com/news/local/gv-woman-recalls-historic-1969-hijacking/article_16fd4f84-a980-11e2-b14e-001a4bcf887a.html.
39. Clay W. Biles, *The United States Federal Air Marshal Service*.
40. Clay W. Biles, *The United States Federal Air Marshal Service*, 57.
41. Philip Baum, *Violence in the Skies*.
42. Seth Hettena, "The Man Behind the Right Wing's Favorite Conspiracy Theories," *New Republic*, December 9, 2019, https://newrepublic.com/article/155896/man-behind-right-wings-favorite-conspiracy-theories.
43. John T. Dailey, "Development of a Behavioral Profile for Air Pirates," *Villanova Law Review* 18, no. 6 (1973), 1011.
44. Associated Press, "RR7038 Guerrilla Hijackings Deadline at Dawson Field," *AP Archive*, airdate September 23, 1970, https://www.youtube.com/watch?v=GDi4wxp5Pz8&t=406s.
45. Philip Baum, *Violence in the Skies*, 55.
46. Philip Baum, *Violence in the Skies*, 82.
47. Amit Hasak, "Uri Bar Lev Thwarted Leila Khaled's Hijacking; I Was a Passenger on That Plane," *Forward*, December 18, 2020, https://forward.com/community/460579/uri-bar-lev-leila-khaled-hijacking-passenger-plane-terrorism-israel/.
48. David Pearce and Ilan Ziv (writers/directors), *American Experience: Hijacked*, produced by WGBH (PBS), season 18, episode 8, aired February 25, 2006, https://www.pbs.org/wgbh/americanexperience/features/hijacked-american-hijacker/.
49. Jonathan Karp, "El Al's Tight Security Methods Are Now Envy of Other Airlines," *Wall Street Journal*, September 26, 2001, https://www.wsj.com/articles/SB1001458258397595640.
50. "12 September 1970—Hijacked Jets Destroyed by Guerrillas," *The Malta Independent*, September 12, 2012, https://www.independent.com.mt/articles/2012-09-12/local-news/12-September-1970---Hijacked-Jets-destroyed-by-guerrillas-315884.
51. Pierre Tristam, "1970: King Hussein Crushes the PLO and Expels It from Jordan,"

ThoughtCo, July 3, 2019, https://www.thoughtco.com/black-september-jordanian-plo-civil-war-2353168.

52. Marc E. Vargo, *The Mossad: Six Landmark Missions of the Israeli Intelligence Agency, 1960–1990*.

53. "Britain Releases Woman Hijacker," *New York Times*, October 1, 1970, https://www.nytimes.com/1970/10/01/archives/britain-releases-woman-hijacker-6-arab-prisoners-in-europe-included.html.

54. Aviva Guttmann, *The Origins of International Counterterrorism: Switzerland at the Forefront of Crisis Negotiations, Multilateral Diplomacy, and Intelligence Cooperation (1969–1977)* (Leiden, Netherlands: Brill, 2017), 99.

55. Nicola Clark, "Why Airline Hijackings Became Relatively Rare," *New York Times*, March 29, 2016, https://www.nytimes.com/2016/03/30/world/middleeast/airline-hijacking-history.html.

56. Richard M. Nixon, "Statement Announcing a Program to Deal with Airplane Hijacking," The American Presidency Project, September 11, 1970, https://www.presidency.ucsb.edu/documents/statement-announcing-program-deal-with-airplane-hijacking.

57. Timothy Naftali, *Blind Spot* (New York: Basic, 2005), 45.

58. David D. McKinney, "Riding the Planes: Sky Marshals Redefined Airline Security in the 1970s," *Frontline* 5, issue 4 (2013) 40, https://www.cbp.gov/sites/default/files/documents/ridingtheplanes.pdf.

59. Richard M. Nixon, "Statement Announcing a Program to Deal with Airplane Hijacking," September 11, 1970, The American Presidency Project, https://www.presidency.ucsb.edu/documents/statement-announcing-program-deal-with-airplane-hijacking.

60. Andrew Hay, "A Brief History of Airline Security, Hijackings and Metal Detectors."

61. George C. Larson, "Moments and Milestones: Perfecting the People Filter," *Smithsonian Magazine*, September 2010, https://www.smithsonianmag.com/air-space-magazine/moments-and-milestones-perfecting-the-people-filter-1490080/.

62. Editors of *Encyclopædia Britannica*, "D.B. Cooper," accessed November 18, 2022, https://www.britannica.com/biography/D-B-Cooper#ref1238764.

63. Janet Bednarek, "D.B. Cooper, the Changing Nature of Hijackings and the Foundation for Today's Airport Security," *The Conversation*, July 11, 2022, https://theconversation.com/d-b-cooper-the-changing-nature-of-hijackings-and-the-foundation-for-todays-airport-security-185562?xid=PS_smithsonian.

64. John T. Dailey, "Development of a Behavioral Profile for Air Pirates."

65. "S.39—An Act to Amend the Federal Aviation Act of 1958 to Implement the Convention for the Suppression of Unlawful Seizure of Aircraft; To Provide a More Effective Program to Prevent Aircraft Piracy; and for Other Purposes (Public Law No: 83-366)," 93rd Congress, Senate Commerce Committee and House Interstate and Foreign Commerce Committee (1973–1974), August 5, 1974, https://www.congress.gov/bill/93rd-congress/senate-bill/39/text.

66. "Convention on Offences and Certain Other Acts Committed on Board Aircraft," *United Nations Treaty Series*, September 14, 1963, https://www.un-ilibrary.org/content/books/9789210548854s003-c001/read.

67. "Convention on Offences and Certain Other Acts Committed on Board Aircraft."

68. "Convention on Offences and Certain Other Acts Committed on Board Aircraft."

69. "Convention for the Suppression of Unlawful Seizure of Aircraft," *United Nations Treaty Series*, December 16, 1970, https://treaties.un.org/doc/db/Terrorism/Conv2-english.pdf.

70. John Follain, *Jackal: The Complete Story of the Legendary Terrorist, Carlos the Jackal* (New York: Arcade, 1998).

71. Simon Dunstan, *Israel's Lightning Strike: The Raid on Entebbe 1976* (Oxford: Osprey, 2009), 11.

72. Marc E. Vargo, *The Mossad: Six Landmark Missions of the Israeli Intelligence Agency, 1960–1990*.

73. Yossi Melman, "Setting the Record Straight: Entebbe Was Not Auschwitz," *Haaretz*, July 8, 2011, https://www.haaretz.com/2011-07-08/ty-article/setting-the-record-straight-entebbe-was-not-auschwitz/0000017f-da7f-dea8-a77f-de7fcaeb0000.

74. "Entebbe Pilot Michel Bacos Who Stayed with Hostages Dies," BBC, March 27, 2019, https://www.bbc.com/news/world-europe-47719367.
75. Ira Peck, *Raid at Entebbe* (New York: Scholastic Books, 1977), 76.
76. Gary Rashba, "Rescue at Entebbe," *HistoryNet*, September 10, 2022, https://www.historynet.com/rescue-at-entebbe/?f.
77. Gary Rashba, "Rescue at Entebbe."
78. Jerusalem Post Staff, "On This Day: The Hijacking That Would Lead to Operation Entebbe," *Jerusalem Post*, June 27, 2021, https://www.jpost.com/israel-news/on-this-day-the-hijacking-that-would-lead-to-operation-entebbe-672145.
79. Eric Sof, "Hijacking of Lufthansa Flight 181 and Brillian GSC 9 Rescue Operation," *Special Ops Magazine*, March 31, 2022, https://special-ops.org/hijacking-of-lufthansa-flight-181/.
80. Henry Tanner, "German Troops Free Hostages on Hijacked Plane in Somalia; Four Terrorists Killed in Raid," *New York Times*, October 18, 1977, https://www.nytimes.com/1977/10/18/archives/german-troops-free-hostages-on-hijacked-plane-in-somalia-four.html.
81. Ashlee Kieler, "The Evolution of Airport Security: From Carry-On Dynamite to No Liquids Allowed," *The Consumerist*, January 24, 2014, https://web.archive.org/web/20181214151230/https://consumerist.com/2014/01/24/the-evolution-of-airport-security-from-carry-on-dynamite-to-no-liquids-allowed/.
82. Jillian Mallia, "35 Years Ago: The EgyptAir Hijacking-Turned-Massacre That Stunned Malta & the World," *GuideMalta*, accessed November 30, 2022, https://www.guidememalta.com/en/35-years-ago-the-egyptair-hijacking-turned-massacre-that-stunned-malta-the-world.
83. Don Podesta, "Terror for Terror's Sake," *Washington Post*, December 1, 1985, https://www.washingtonpost.com/archive/politics/1985/12/01/terror-for-terrors-sake/09a94f88-578d-42f9-a2b6-71543965ce45/.
84. Don Podesta, "Terror for Terror's Sake."
85. Philip Baum, *Violence in the Skies*, 185.
86. Erica Pearson, "Pan Am Flight 73 Hijacking," *Encyclopædia Britannica*, March 16, 2023, https://www.britannica.com/event/Pan-Am-flight-73-hijacking.
87. "Aviation Safety Network: Statistics," Aviation Safety Network—Flight Safety Foundation, accessed December 7, 2002, https://aviation-safety.net/statistics/period/stats.php.
88. Malcolm Gladwell, "11-Hour Hijacking Ends in Surrender at New York Airport," *Washington Post*, February 2, 1993, https://www.washingtonpost.com/archive/politics/1993/02/12/11-hour-hijacking-ends-in-surrender-at-new-york-airport/ab517dab-6f76-4371-89ef-5497e2ca312f/.
89. Malcolm Gladwell, "11-Hour Hijacking Ends in Surrender at New York Airport."
90. Malcolm Gladwell, "11-Hour Hijacking Ends in Surrender at New York Airport."
91. Terry Moran (host) and Brian Ross (reporter), "U.S. Security Flaws Post-9/11," ABC News, airdate August 31, 2011, https://www.youtube.com/watch?v=BZaqhqEhvCg.
92. National Commission on Terrorist Attacks upon the United States, *The 9/11 Commission Report, Executive Summary* (Washington, D.C., 2004), 83, https://www.9-11commission.gov/report/911Report.pdf.
93. Nancy Cutler, "Deaths from 9/11 Diseases Will Soon Outnumber Those Lost on That Fateful Day," *USA Today*, September 10, 2018, https://www.usatoday.com/videos/news/2018/09/10/deaths-911-diseases-soon-outnumber-those-lost-day/37772323/.
94. "National Commission on Terrorist Attacks upon the United States," *The 9/11 Commission Report, Executive Summary*.
95. "All Flights Stopped Nationwide," CNN, September 11, 2001, https://www.cnn.com/2001/TRAVEL/NEWS/09/11/faa.airports/.
96. "Air Travel Before and After 9/11: How the Terror Attacks Changed How We Fly," NBCLX News, September 7, 2021, https://www.youtube.com/watch?v=rJxtpQ6Ce2I.
97. "Bulletproof Cockpit Doors a Reality," CBS News, April 4, 2003, https://www.cbsnews.com/news/bulletproof-cockpit-doors-a-reality/.
98. "H.R. 4635: Arming Pilots against Terrorism Act," 107th Congress (2001–2002), House of Representatives—Transportation and Infrastructure Committee; Judiciary Committee,

accessed December 2, 2022, https://www.congress.gov/bill/107th-congress/house-bill/4635/text.

99. "Privacy Impact Assessment for the Federal Flight Deck Officer Program," U.S. Department of Homeland Security, January 10, 2008, https://www.dhs.gov/sites/default/files/publications/privacy_pia_tsa_ffdo.pdf.

100. Joe Sharkey, "The Lull Before the Storm for the Nation's Airports," *New York Times*, November 19, 2002, https://www.nytimes.com/2002/11/19/business/business-travel-on-the-road-the-lull-before-the-storm-for-the-nation-s-airports.html.

101. "Trusted Travelers Programs," Department of Homeland Security, accessed December 21, 2022, https://ttp.dhs.gov/.

102. "TSA PreCheck," Transportation Security Administration, accessed December 21, 2022, https://www.tsa.gov/precheck.

Bibliography

"Air Travel Before and After 9/11: How the Terror Attacks Changed How We Fly." NBCLX News, airdate September 7, 2021. https://www.youtube.com/watch?v=rJxtpQ6Ce2I.

"All Flights Stopped Nationwide." CNN, airdate September 11, 2001. https://www.cnn.com/2001/TRAVEL/NEWS/09/11/faa.airports/.

Associated Press. "Hijacker Surrenders 18 Years Later." *The Ottawa Citizen*, September 13, 1986. https://news.google.com/newspapers?id=5L4yAAAAIBAJ&sjid=be8FAAAAIBAJ&pg=4605,1535917&hl=en.

Associated Press. "RR7038 Guerrilla Hijackings Deadline at Dawson Field." *AP Archive*, airdate September 23, 1970. https://www.youtube.com/watch?v=GDi4wxp5Pz8&t=406s.

Associated Press. "20 Czechs Seize Plane in Midair and Force It to Land in U.S. Zone." *New York Times*, April 9, 1948. ttps://timesmachine.nytimes.com/timesmachine/1948/04/09/94644837.pdf.

"Aviation Safety Network: Statistics." Aviation Safety Network, Flight Safety Foundation. Accessed December 7, 2002. https://aviation-safety.net/statistics/period/stats.php.

Bauder, David. "Woman Arrested in 1969 Hijacking to Cuba." Associated Press, July 26, 1988. https://apnews.com/article/0cf464d520028b772e0bf0b67dfa87a8.

Baum, Philip. *Violence in the Skies: A History of Aircraft Hijacking and Bombing*. West Sussex, England: Summersdale, 2016.

Bednarek, Janet. "D.B. Cooper, the Changing Nature of Hijackings and the Foundation for Today's Airport Security." *The Conversation*, July 11, 2022. https://theconversation.com/d-b-cooper-the-changing-nature-of-hijackings-and-the-foundation-for-todays-airport-security-185562?xid=PS_smithsonian.

Biles, Clay W. *The United States Federal Air Marshal Service: A Historical Perspective, 1962–2012*. Coppell, TX: Wendy de la Cruz, 2013.

Bohning, Don. *The Castro Obsession: U.S. Covert Operations Against Cuba, 1959–1965*. Dulles, Virginia: Potomac Books, 2005.

"Britain Releases Woman Hijacker." *New York Times*, October 1, 1970. https://www.nytimes.com/1970/10/01/archives/britain-releases-woman-hijacker-6-arab-prisoners-in-europe-included.html.

"Bulletproof Cockpit Doors a Reality." CBS News, April 4, 2003. https://www.cbsnews.com/news/bulletproof-cockpit-doors-a-reality/.

Burkeman, Oliver. "Can We Ever Stop This?" *The Guardian*, September 28, 2001. https://www.theguardian.com/world/2001/sep/28/september11.usa4.

Choi, Jin-Tai. *Aviation Terrorism: Historical Survey, Perspectives and Responses*. New York: St. Martin's Press, 1994.

Clark, Nicola. "Why Airline Hijackings Became Relatively Rare." *New York Times*, March 29, 2016. https://www.nytimes.com/2016/03/30/world/middleeast/airline-hijacking-history.html.

"Compañía Cubana de Aviación Viscount Hi-Jacked." *Vickers Viscount Network*. Accessed October 2, 2022. http://www.vickersviscount.net/Pages_History/Cubana%20Hijack.aspx.

"Convention for the Suppression of Unlawful Seizure of Aircraft." *United Nations Treaty*

Series, December 16, 1970. https://treaties.un.org/doc/db/Terrorism/Conv2-english.pdf.
"Convention on Offences and Certain Other Acts Committed on Board Aircraft." *United Nations Treaty Series*, September 14, 1963. https://www.un-ilibrary.org/content/books/9789210548854s003-c001/read.
Cutler, Nancy. "Deaths from 9/11 Diseases Will Soon Outnumber Those Lost on That Fateful Day." *USA Today*, September 10, 2018. https://www.usatoday.com/videos/news/2018/09/10/deaths-911-diseases-soon-outnumber-those-lost-day/37772323/.
Dailey, John T. "Development of a Behavioral Profile for Air Pirates." *Villanova Law Review* 18, no. 6 (1973): 985–1011.
Dunstan, Simon. *Israel's Lightning Strike: The Raid on Entebbe 1976*. Oxford: Osprey, 2009.
Editors of *Encyclopædia Britannica*. "D.B. Cooper." *Britannica*. Accessed November 18, 2022. https://www.britannica.com/biography/D-B-Cooper#ref1238764.
"Entebbe Pilot Michel Bacos Who Stayed with Hostages Dies." BBC, March 27, 2019. https://www.bbc.com/news/world-europe-47719367.
FCAFA. "They Flew to Exile 1950." Free Czechoslovak Air Force (FCAFA), March 12, 2011. https://fcafa.com/2011/03/12/they-flew-to-exile-1950/.
Follain, John. *Jackal: The Complete Story of the Legendary Terrorist, Carlos the Jackal*. New York: Arcade, 1998.
Gibbs-Smith, Charles H. *The Aeroplane: An Historical Survey*. London: Her Majesty's Stationery Office, 1960.
Gladwell, Malcolm. "11-Hour Hijacking Ends in Surrender at New York Airport." *Washington Post*, February 2, 1993. https://www.washingtonpost.com/archive/politics/1993/02/12/11-hour-hijacking-ends-in-surrender-at-new-york-airport/ab517dab-6f76-4371-89ef-5497e2ca312f/.
Guttmann, Aviva. *The Origins of International Counterterrorism: Switzerland at the Forefront of Crisis Negotiations, Multilateral Diplomacy, and Intelligence Cooperation (1969–1977)*. Leiden, Netherlands: Brill, 2017.
Hasak, Amit. "Uri Bar Lev Thwarted Leila Khaled's Hijacking; I Was a Passenger on That Plane." *Forward*, December 18, 2020. https://forward.com/community/460579/uri-bar-lev-leila-khaled-hijacking-passenger-plane-terrorism-israel/.
Hay, Andrew. "A Brief History of Airline Security, Hijackings and Metal Detectors." IBM, April 24, 2019. https://www.ibm.com/blogs/systems/a-brief-history-of-airline-security-hijackings-and-metal-detectors/.
Hettena, Seth. "The Man Behind the Right Wing's Favorite Conspiracy Theories." *New Republic*, December 9, 2019. https://newrepublic.com/article/155896/man-behind-right-wings-favorite-conspiracy-theories.
Holden, Robert T. "The Contagiousness of Aircraft Hijacking." *American Journal of Sociology* 91, no. 4 (1986): 874–904. http://www.jstor.org/stable/2779961.
Holland, Tom. "15 Minutes of Fame | Tom Holland Chooses Franz Nopcsa von Felsö-Szilvás." *History Extra* (BBC), August 31, 2022. https://www.historyextra.com/period/20th-century/franz-nopcsa-von-felso-szilvas-who-life/.
"H.R. 4635: Arming Pilots against Terrorism Act." 107th Congress (2001–2002), House of Representatives—Transportation and Infrastructure Committee; Judiciary Committee. Accessed December 2, 2022. https://www.congress.gov/bill/107th-congress/house-bill/4635/text.
Jerusalem Post Staff. "On This Day: The Hijacking That Would Lead to Operation Entebbe." *Jerusalem Post*, June 27, 2021. https://www.jpost.com/israel-news/on-this-day-the-hijacking-that-would-lead-to-operation-entebbe-672145.
Karp, Jonathan. "El Al's Tight Security Methods Are Now Envy of Other Airlines." *Wall Street Journal*, September 26, 2001. https://www.wsj.com/articles/SB1001458258397595640.
Kieler, Ashlee. "The Evolution of Airport Security: From Carry-On Dynamite to No Liquids Allowed." *The Consumerist*, January 24, 2014. https://web.archive.org/web/20181214151230/https://consumerist.com/2014/01/24/the-evolution-of-airport-security-from-carry-on-dynamite-to-no-liquids-allowed/.
Koerner, Brendan I. "How Hijackers Commandeered over 130 American Planes." Wired, June 18, 2013. https://www.wired.com/2013/06/love-and-terror-in-the-golden-age-of-hijacking/.

Koerner, Brendan I. *The Skies Belong to Us: Love and Terror in the Golden Age of Hijacking.* New York: Crown, 2013.

Larson, George C. "Moments and Milestones: Perfecting the People Filter." *Smithsonian Magazine*, September 2010. https://www.smithsonianmag.com/air-space-magazine/moments-and-milestones-perfecting-the-people-filter-1490080/.

Latner, Teishan A. "Take Me to Havana! Airline Hijacking, U.S.-Cuba Relations, and Political Protest in Late Sixties' America." *Diplomatic History* 39, no. 1 (January 2015): 16–44. https://www.jstor.org/stable/26376639.

"Legislative Summary—Aviation." John F. Kennedy Presidential Library and Museum. Accessed September 22, 2022. https://www.jfklibrary.org/archives/other-resources/legislative-summary/aviation#:~:text=This%20amendment%20to%20the%20Federal,in%20flight%20in%20air%20commerce.

Lindsey, Robert. "U.S. Is Moving on Two Fronts in Effort to Halt Sharp Increase in Plane Hijacks." *New York Times*, September 5, 1969. https://www.nytimes.com/1969/09/05/archives/us-is-moving-on-two-fronts-in-effort-to-halt-sharp-increase-in.html.

Mallia, Jillian. "35 Years Ago: The EgyptAir Hijacking-Turned-Massacre That Stunned Malta & the World." GuideMalta.com. Accessed November 30, 2022. https://www.guidememalta.com/en/35-years-ago-the-egyptair-hijacking-turned-massacre-that-stunned-malta-the-world.

Mars, Roman (host), and Brendan Koerner (interviewee). "Skyjacking (transcript)." *99% Invisible* (podcast, episode #120), June 23, 2014. https://99percentinvisible.org/episode/skyjacking/transcript/.

Mazzoleni, Nicoletta, and Massimo Catusi. "The Cuban Hijackings: Their Significance and Impact Sixty Years On." *Transport Security International*, October 19, 2018. https://www.tsi-mag.com/the-cuban-hijackings-their-significance-and-impact-sixty-years-on/.

McKinney, David D. "Riding the Planes: Sky Marshals Redefined Airline Security in the 1970s." *Frontline* 5, issue 4 (2013): 40–41. https://www.cbp.gov/sites/default/files/documents/ridingtheplanes.pdf.

Melman, Yossi. "Setting the Record Straight: Entebbe Was Not Auschwitz." *Haaretz*, July 8, 2011. https://www.haaretz.com/2011-07-08/ty-article/setting-the-record-straight-entebbe-was-not-auschwitz/0000017f-da7f-dea8-a77f-de7fcaeb0000.

"Memorandum of Understanding on Hijacking of Aircraft and Vessels and Other Offenses." Department of State, February 13, 1973. https://2001-2009.state.gov/documents/organization/52191.pdf.

Mickolus, Edward R. *Transnational Terrorism: A Chronology of Events, 1968–1979.* Westport, CT: Greenwood.

Moran, Terry (host), and Brian Ross (reporter). "U.S. Security Flaws Post-9/11." ABC News, airdate August 31, 2011. https://www.youtube.com/watch?v=BZaqhqEhvCg.

Naftali, Timothy. *Blind Spot.* New York: Basic Books, 2005.

National Commission on Terrorist Attacks upon the United States. *The 9/11 Commission Report, Executive Summary* (Washington, D.C., 2004). https://www.9-11commission.gov/report/911Report.pdf.

Nixon, Richard M. "Statement Announcing a Program to Deal with Airplane Hijacking." The American Presidency Project, September 11, 1970. https://www.presidency.ucsb.edu/documents/statement-announcing-program-deal-with-airplane-hijacking.

Pearce, David, and Ilan Ziv (writers/directors). "American Experience: Hijacked." Produced by WGBH (PBS), Season 18, Episode 8, airdate February 25, 2006. https://www.pbs.org/wgbh/americanexperience/features/people-involved-and-affected.

Pearson, Erica. "Pan Am Flight 73 Hijacking." *Encyclopædia Britannica*, March 16, 2023. https://www.britannica.com/event/Pan-Am-flight-73-hijacking.

Peck, Ira. *Raid at Entebbe.* New York: Scholastic Books, 1977.

"The PFLP Hijacking of TWA Flight 840." *Association for Diplomatic Studies and Training*, August 10, 2015. https://adst.org/2015/08/the-pflp-hijacking-of-twa-840/.

Podesta, Don. "Terror for Terror's Sake." *Washington Post*, December 1, 1985. https://www.washingtonpost.com/archive/politics/1985/12/01/terror-for-terrors-sake/09a94f88-578d-42f9-a2b6-71543965ce45/.

"Privacy Impact Assessment for the Federal Flight Deck Officer Program." U.S. Department

of Homeland Security, January 10, 2008. https://www.dhs.gov/sites/default/files/publications/privacy_pia_tsa_ffdo.pdf.
Rashba, Gary. "Rescue at Entebbe." *HistoryNet*, September 10, 2022. https://www.historynet.com/rescue-at-entebbe/?f.
"S.39—An Act to Amend the Federal Aviation Act of 1958 to Implement the Convention for the Suppression of Unlawful Seizure of Aircraft; To Provide a More Effective Program to Prevent Aircraft Piracy; and for Other Purposes (Public Law No: 83–366)." 93rd Congress, Senate Commerce Committee and House Interstate and Foreign Commerce Committee (1973–1974), August 5, 1974. https://www.congress.gov/bill/93rd-congress/senate-bill/39/text.
Sartore, Melissa. "In the 1970s, Airport Security Didn't Exist—and the 'Golden Age of Airplane Hijackings' was Born." *Ranker*, March 20, 2020. https://www.ranker.com/list/golden-age-of-plane-hijacking/melissa-sartore.
Schmidt, Dana Adams. "Czechs Insist U.S. Send Back Airmen." *New York Times*, March 25, 1950. https://timesmachine.nytimes.com/timesmachine/1950/03/31/94251809.html?pageNumber=16.
Scott, Erik R. "The Hijacking of Aeroflot Flight 244: States and Statelessness in the Late Cold War." *Past & Present* 243, issue 1 (May 2019): 213–245. https://doi.org/10.1093/pastj/gty044.
Sharkey, Joe. "The Lull Before the Storm for the Nation's Airports." *New York Times*, November 19, 2002. https://www.nytimes.com/2002/11/19/business/business-travel-on-the-road-the-lull-before-the-storm-for-the-nation-s-airports.html.
Sof, Eric. "Hijacking of Lufthansa Flight 181 and Brillian GSC 9 Rescue Operation." *Special Ops Magazine*, March 31, 2022. https://special-ops.org/hijacking-of-lufthansa-flight-181/.
Sussman, Ellen. "GV Woman Recalls Historic 1969 Hijacking." *Green Valley News*, April 30, 2013. https://www.gvnews.com/news/local/gv-woman-recalls-historic-1969-hijacking/article_16fd4f84-a980-11e2-b14e-001a4bcf887a.html.
Tanner, Henry. "German Troops Free Hostages on Hijacked Plane in Somalia; Four Terrorists Killed in Raid." *New York Times*, October 18, 1977. https://www.nytimes.com/1977/10/18/archives/german-troops-free-hostages-on-hijacked-plane-in-somalia-four.html.
Tristam, Pierre. "1970: King Hussein Crushes the PLO and Expels It from Jordan." *ThoughtCo*, July 3, 2019. https://www.thoughtco.com/black-september-jordanian-plo-civil-war-2353168.
"Trusted Travelers Programs." Department of Homeland Security. Accessed December 21, 2022. https://ttp.dhs.gov/.
"TSA PreCheck." Transportation Security Administration. Accessed December 21, 2022. https://www.tsa.gov/precheck.
"12 September 1970—Hijacked Jets Destroyed by Guerrillas." *The Malta Independent*, September 12, 2012. https://www.independent.com.mt/articles/2012-09-12/local-news/12-September-1970---Hijacked-Jets-destroyed-by-guerrillas-315884.
Vargo, Marc E. *The Mossad: Six Landmark Missions of the Israeli Intelligence Agency, 1960–1990*. Jefferson, NC: McFarland, 2015.
"Will Hijack More Planes, Gunman Says." United Press International, November 4, 1968. https://skyjackeroftheday.tumblr.com/post/49258112380/50-raymond-johnson.
Willoughby, Gloria. Personal communication. September 17, 2022.
Within, Richard. "Threat of Strike Raised by Pilots." *New York Times*, November 16, 1972. https://www.nytimes.com/1972/11/16/archives/threat-of-strike-raised-by-pilots-union-presses-demands-for-more.html.

Two

Improvised Explosive Devices and Surface-to-Air Missiles

Although a bad actor may slip a bomb onto a commercial carrier for any number of reasons, domestic terrorism is thought to have been the motive behind the first such incident. It was October 10, 1933, and the aircraft was a Boeing 247, touted in those early days of commercial air travel as the first passenger-friendly airliner. Among the features meant to offer travelers "creature comforts," the ten-seater boasted a restroom and a heated passenger cabin; the aircraft itself was able to reach a speed of 200 miles an hour and a service ceiling of 25,400 feet.[1]

On this rainy autumn night, United Airlines Flight 23, as it was designated, was traveling from Cleveland, Ohio, to Chicago, and it was nearing its destination, Midway Airport. At 9:15 p.m., while flying at an altitude of 1,000 feet over a northern Indiana town (also called Cleveland), it exploded.[2]

"It shot to earth like a blazing comet before the horrified eyes of dozens of farmers and others in the vicinity," reported the *New York Times*, breathlessly.[3] Onlookers, shocked by the sight and sound of the blast, hurried to the wreckage to help the victims, but the inferno kept these would-be rescuers at a distance. However, once the fire was extinguished and the casualties removed, numerous bystanders descended on the scene to rummage for mementos, with one firefighter making off with the plane's propeller. This caused investigators to initially speculate that a faulty airscrew had brought about the tragedy.[4] "We'll never know how much evidence got snatched up by local people who wander around these fields," said Bryan Alaspa.[5] Worsening matters, the wreckage itself was hauled away the next day, United Airlines having sold it for seventy-five dollars to a nearby junk dealer. Of course, this inadvertently stymied the investigation that followed, but it did yield one long-term benefit: law enforcement officers would henceforth be more diligent in protecting the sites of airplane crashes from scavengers and the like, preserving the crime scenes until officials could give the go-ahead to clear them.

In terms of the forensic evidence that *was* obtained in the case, investigators performed microscopic analyses of cloth and metal samples recovered from the debris, and they determined that the explosive device had contained nitroglycerin. Furthermore, they concluded that the IED was hidden in a stack of towels near the plane's midsection, producing a blast that broke the aircraft in half.[6] Although the residents who rushed to the scene described hearing the moans of passengers, all of those who had been on board ultimately died, with two falling from the fragmenting aircraft and the others perishing in the impact and conflagration.[7]

In the end, the investigators were unable to establish a motive for the crime. A gangland-style hit was an early hypothesis, followed by that of labor unrest, which was rampant at the time. Sixty-five years later, a local man who remembered the tragedy, Howard Johnson, recounted his knowledge of the crash and his understanding of the perpetrator. "I guess it had something to do with some labor racketeer because they said ... that someone got on the plane in Cleveland [Ohio] and had a suitcase and then they got off and no one saw them take the suitcase off," he said.[8]

In the three decades that followed, more airline bombings made the news, nearly all of them centering on insurance-fraud schemes, suicides, or the murders of family members. As to the latter, one of the earliest homicides took place on May 7, 1949, on a Philippine Airlines flight. While en route from Daet, Philippines, to Manila, the Douglas C-47B, which was carrying thirteen people, was blown up by a time bomb and plunged into the sea. An inquiry found that two former convicts had devised the plot, the pair having been hired by a man and woman who wished to kill the woman's husband, a passenger on the plane. All of the passengers perished in the incident, while the perpetrators themselves were apprehended, tried, and hanged.

Presumably inspired by the Philippine Airlines incident, a Canadian man named Joseph-Albert Guay and two accomplices followed suit four months later, on September 9, 1949. This time, the aircraft was a Douglas DC-3, and it was designated Canadian Pacific Airlines Flight 108. Three small children and three American industrialists were among the twenty-three people on the aircraft, which was traveling from Montreal to Sept-Îles, Québec. In this act of sabotage, Guay, a jewelry salesman whose wife was on the flight, arranged to have a package, one containing dynamite, loaded into the cargo hold. The reason for his malice: Guay was involved romantically with a teenage girl and wished to remove his wife from the picture. As well, he had taken out a $10,000 life insurance policy on his spouse. Although his murderous scheme succeeded and everyone on

Flight 108 was killed, the authorities eventually collared Guay and his collaborators and a Canadian court sentenced the three of them to death.

Notwithstanding the fact that the culprits in such cases were often apprehended and executed, airline sabotage continued to occur. In the same way that Guay appears to have borrowed his homicidal plot from the bombers of the Philippine airliner, so other perpetrators may have been inspired by Guay's ill-advised actions. "In Los Angeles, in April, 1951," wrote E.J. Kahn, Jr., in *The New Yorker*, "a technician employed in an airplane-parts factory insured the lives of his wife and two children and then attempted to put a suitcase containing a homemade gasoline bomb on a plane they were boarding."[9] Luckily for the woman, her children, and the other passengers and crew on the plane, a cargo handler dropped the package before it could be placed in the hold. Although it burst into flames, no one was killed.

Equally nasty was the sabotage of United Airlines Flight 629 on November 1, 1955, a crime in which a man named Jack Gilbert Graham packed his mother's suitcase for an upcoming flight from Denver to Portland, Oregon. In it, he planted a home-made incendiary device that contained twenty-five sticks of dynamite, which were timed to ignite once the plane was aloft. It turned out that Graham, who later admitted that he despised his mother, had also purchased a $37,500 life insurance policy on her.[10] Unfortunately, all of the forty-four people on the aircraft died in the explosion and crash, while the perpetrator himself was convicted and executed in a Colorado gas chamber.

A lurid act of matricide and insurance fraud, the Graham bombing was widely publicized in its day and became seared into the public mind, and it was revisited each time another in-flight airliner explosion occurred. Finally, after two more commercial airline bombings in the United States in late 1959, law enforcement agencies and aviation officials in 1960 set out to find a solution. While luggage inspections were ruled out because it was assumed that travelers would oppose them, two other measures were considered: metal detectors and fluoroscopes.[11] These possibilities were eventually discarded, too, on the grounds that a metal detector would set off alarms for all manner of metal objects, from electric razors to clocks, while a fluoroscope would not produce a sufficiently useful image. "[I]t only supplies a shadow outline and couldn't detect bomb devices that hadn't been assembled," writes Joy Miller.[12] So it was that airports and airline companies retained their standard procedures for preventing IEDs from making their way onto commercial carriers, although there was a handful of exceptions. The airport serving Akron, Ohio, instructed its staff to report suspicious customers, bags, or parcels to the Federal Bureau of Investigation (FBI) for action.[13] Although it was only a regional initiative, it was an advancement all the same.

Two. Improvised Explosive Devices and Surface-to-Air Missiles 51

As it happened, the FBI would find itself overwhelmed in the coming years as political activism swept across the United States, much of it protesting the racial prejudice that plagued the nation as well as the contentious war being prosecuted in Vietnam. As a feature of this opposition, numerous political extremists in the 1960s crossed the line into domestic terrorism, attempting to force social change by means of bombings and associated forms of intimidation. But while their targets ranged from colleges to military recruitment centers and from residential structures to government offices, they did not bomb commercial airliners. It would be in other parts of the world that the use of IEDs in aviation sabotage would find favor, especially in the Middle East, where political conflicts had long raged.

Not surprisingly, El Al would be a target, and also unsurprising, the company's planes would not fall to such efforts. Even when a bomb exploded in one of its airliner's holds, the crisis was contained. Particularly despicable was a stretch in 1971 in which "mules"—those who smuggle illicit materials across borders—were used to carry bombs onto El Al aircraft. Among the cases were those in which male extremists planted IEDs in their female lovers' luggage without the knowledge of these women.

A report published by the RAND Corporation in 1989 provided details about the various extremist groups that had carried out aviation sabotage, specifically airline bombings, between 1968 and 1988, and the facts were revealing. "Palestinian, Shia, and other Middle East organizations," it noted, "account for 45 percent of the sabotage incidents."[14] Given the white-hot enmity that existed between the State of Israel and the Occupied Palestinian Territories at the time, this is perhaps predictable. The Israeli-Palestinian dispute was known to spark considerable terrorist activity not only by Palestinians but also by entities sympathetic to the Palestinian cause, among them an infamous extremist outfit based in Japan. Commercial airliners, then, became yet another theater for political violence.

Still, despite the Palestinian overrepresentation, few regions of the world were without their share of airline bombers, with Latin America and Asia among those represented. And as one might imagine considering the diversity of terrorist organizations, the bombings were perpetrated for a host of political ends. Of course, the immediate outcome was most often a massive loss of life. "In all, 1,128 persons have died in the past 20 years as a result of bombs going off aboard airliners in flight or in cargo containers on the ground," states the RAND document. "This represents 20 percent of all of the deaths in international terrorist incidents during the past two decades."[15]

As it stands, the largest number of casualties stemming from an in-flight bombing would not be linked to the Israeli-Palestinian conflict but rather to Sikh extremists in Canada. Members of a group identified as Babbar Khalsa, they had as their goal the establishment of an independent Sikh nation on the Indian subcontinent. The group was part of a larger political movement centered in India, one that was responsible for the assassination of Indira Gandhi the previous year. The present terrorist mission was in retaliation for the Indian prime minister's military action against Sikh separatists ("Operation Blue Star").[16] The group's target: an Air India flight slated to fly from Toronto to Mumbai, with Montréal and London as intermediate stops. A Boeing 747, the wide-bodied jet would carry twenty-two crew members and 307 passengers, with eight-two children among the travelers.

The terrorist operation kicked into gear on June 22, 1985, at a Canadian Pacific Air Lines (CP Air) ticket counter in Vancouver, where a ticket agent found herself confronted by a belligerent customer insisting that she tag, or check in, his brown Samsonite suitcase. This was in spite of the fact that he lacked a confirmed ticket and was only on standby. But the line was long, the man was adamant, and the other customers were becoming restless, so the agent accepted his bag and placed it in the CP Air baggage-routing system.[17] Upon arrival in Toronto, the suitcase, having a bomb concealed inside it, would be transferred into the forward cargo hold on Air India Flight 181, which would be re-designated Flight 182 in Montréal.

The explosion occurred at 12:11 a.m., on June 23, 1985, as the aircraft was cruising at an altitude of 31,000 feet over the Atlantic Ocean south of Ireland. The plane simply vanished from the radar screens of air traffic controllers in Shannon. Up to this point, there had been no indications from the aircrew that there were any problems with the jetliner, nor had anyone on the flight deck issued a mayday call.

Hours later, rescue teams located the wreckage at a point in the Atlantic where the depth reaches nearly 7,000 feet and the waters teem with sharks. In the days that followed, experts from France, England, India, and Canada volunteered their services, helping analyze the bodies and debris. Officials soon determined that everyone on the aircraft had perished; fewer than 50 percent of the casualties were recovered. Of those that were retrieved, forensics experts found that the passengers who had been seated at the rear of the plane exhibited no burns or other signs of a blast. "They were not killed by the initial explosion," reported the BBC, "and some may even have survived the terrifying dive into the sea, only to be drowned in the most awful circumstances imaginable."[18] It seemed increasingly apparent that an IED had been the cause of the disaster.

Supporting this hypothesis were findings gleaned from the airliner's black box when it was eventually recovered. The only sounds recorded by the cockpit microphone were those of an undefined thud, followed by a whooshing sound, and then by a human scream, according to the BBC.[19] After weeks of analysis, officials determined that the explosion had indeed been caused by a bomb, one comprised of the traditional elements, meaning a clock, a 12-volt battery, a high-explosive charge, gunpowder, an accelerant, and other components.[20] It blew a hole in the left side of the fuselage, causing rapid decompression. "The aft [rear] portion of the aircraft separated from the forward portion before striking the water," reported the Aviation Safety Network.[21] The incident marked the first time an improvised explosive device had brought down a Boeing 747.

Although no individual or organization claimed responsibility for the attack, Sikh extremists had recently warned of such bombings and were the top suspects. Even so, those who planned and executed the strike were never arrested and prosecuted. "In the immediate aftermath of the bombing, and in the years that followed, the largest, most complex and expensive investigation in Canadian history failed to bring those responsible for the bombing to justice," stated a report by the Canadian government.[22] On the other hand, the man who helped construct the bomb itself, Inderjit Singh Reyat, did plead guilty to manslaughter in 2003 and was sentenced to five years in prison. Reyat had previously been sentenced to ten years for another act of aviation-related sabotage in Japan, which was likely linked to the Air India 182 disaster.

Insofar as the disaster led to improved prevention methods, it spurred officials to better secure aircraft traveling on global routes. "The infiltration of IEDs onto the CP Air flights by means of checked luggage heralded the commencement of a global initiative to introduce hold baggage screening for all baggage being loaded onto international flights," Philip Baum writes. Baum also points out that it was "an initiative that was accelerated following the subsequent destruction of Pan Am flight 103 over Lockerbie in 1988."[23]

To be sure, the tragedy of Flight 103 stands as the most prominent act of airline sabotage that has ever been confirmed. Exploding in midair over a Scottish town during the Christmas holidays, it is the subject of Chapter Six, and for this reason will not be examined at this point. It is important to note, however, that it became a defining moment in sabotage-prevention measures.

"In direct response to the Lockerbie bombing," reported the *New York Times* a dozen years later, "the Government has spent hundreds of millions of dollars paying for the development of new technology, most for screening checked baggage, then buying and installing the new machines at hundreds of airports."[24] As well, the U.S. government mandated the use of computerized systems designed to discern whose carry-on luggage should be screened, required that all potential passengers answer questions to determine if others may have had access to their bags, improved the quality of X-ray screening devices at airports, and tightened the requirements for access to sensitive areas of airports.[25] And although international air carriers were supposed to have already been practicing baggage reconciliation, the Lockerbie bomb, which was concealed in an unaccompanied, uninspected piece of luggage, renewed demands that such procedures be implemented without fail. "[T]he Lockerbie terrorist attack triggered the introduction of the aviation security principle, *'no pax, no bags,'* according to which no baggage can travel if it is not linked to a flying passenger," writes Giacomo Amati.[26] Additional measures intended to keep aircraft free of incendiary devices were also created and applied, some of which, for obvious reasons, were not made public. "The threat of bombings, more than hijackings, now drives airline security," wrote terrorism expert Brian Michael Jenkins after the Lockerbie tragedy.[27]

In reality, bombings would continue into the 1990s, albeit at far lower rates. The prevention methods were working. Of the incidents that did occur, two took place in 1994, with hostility toward Jews and the State of Israel emerging as the common denominator. In the first episode, a Panamanian commuter airliner, Flight 901, crashed in a forest near the coastal city of Colón, killing all twenty-one people on board. Because metal shards were recovered from the passengers' bodies as well as from the wreckage, authorities suspected an IED had produced the disaster. The plane's manifest, moreover, seemed to offer a clue to the motive behind the midair tragedy. "A number of passengers on the flight were reported to have been Jewish businessmen," writes David Gero, "and a Lebanese group was said to have 'hinted' that they were responsible for the attack."[28]

Five months later in January of 1995, another terrorist operation was planned—it was code-named Oplan (operational plan) Bojinka—and it entailed, among other deeds, blowing out of the sky up to a dozen U.S.-owned airliners flying over the Pacific Ocean and the South China Sea. "The plot would involve a team of five bombers who would travel on planes for a particular leg of their journey," writes security expert Paul J. Smith, "plant the bomb, and then exit the plane at the next stop."[29] Eventually, the five perpetrators would end up in Pakistan if all went according to plan. The reason for the operation? It was to be retribution against the United States for its support for the State of Israel. Fortunately, the monstrous plot, which was the work of al-Qaeda and was to have included the assassination of Pope John Paul II, was thwarted. Even so, its first step, which was essentially a trial run, did succeed, and it involved an in-flight bombing on an aircraft traveling the Pacific route.

The target was Philippine Airlines Flight 434, and it was en route from Manila to Tokyo. While the plane was at a cruising altitude of 30,000 feet, a bomb detonated, one that extremists had wrapped in a life vest and stowed under a passenger's seat.[30] It was later discovered that the explosive liquid used in the bomb, nitroglycerin, was smuggled onto the plane in a bottle of saline solution, the type that passengers who wear contact lens often have in their possession when traveling.[31] Sadly, ten people were wounded and another person killed in this "dry run." On the upside, the act of sabotage allowed authorities to uncover and prevent the more destructive multi-plane plot that the terrorists were preparing.

Although more bombings would occur in the 1990s, or at least would be attempted, the airline industry was largely spared this sort of malevolence as the decade progressed. Then came the spectacle of September 11, 2001, and it forever changed the face of aviation security. The sweeping measures that ensued would cause aviation terrorism to drop to exceptionally low levels. The number of attempts would not fall to zero, however.

Innovative IED Methods

The new century would find terrorists and their organizations struggling to concoct ingenious ways to evade the evolving security technology, but it would not be easy for them. Each time that the authorities apprehended a would-be bomber attempting to employ a novel modus operandi, they would promptly and publicly make it known that security forces were now aware of this fresh method of attack and were putting into place supplemental measures to prevent it. Moreover, the TSA, as well as many of its counterparts in other nations, would often make quite a display of these new practices, since publicity was known to play a deterrent role in crime prevention. "It's not just about the measures, it's about the theatre," says John Coyne of the Australian Strategic Policy Institute.[32]

Shoe bomb plot. One terrorist stunt that was stymied on December 22, 2001, illustrates both the inventiveness of the post–9/11 bombmakers and the swiftness of the security community in responding to the extremists' latest creations. It happened on a Boeing 767 traveling from Paris to Miami. Designated American Airlines Flight 63 and carrying 197 passengers and crew members, the jetliner was cruising at 35,000 feet over the Atlantic, roughly two hours into its journey, when the smell of sulfur began wafting through the passenger cabin. The odor seemed to be emanating from a man, Richard Reid, who was seated by a window. A twenty-eight-year-old British citizen, Reid was a convert to Islamic fundamentalism, and he had undergone guerrilla training at al-Qaeda camps in Afghanistan and Pakistan. At six feet, four inches tall, he had an intimidating presence, and his onboard demeanor was unusual—he seemed frazzled and refused to drink or eat on the transatlantic trip.

Tracing the sulfurous scent to Reid, flight attendant Hermis Moutardier approached the man, saw he was holding a match, and reminded him that cigarette smoking was forbidden. Reid complied, but moments later Moutardier spotted him once again hunched over a match; her assumption was that he was determined to smoke. "It got me mad," she said.[33]

It was at this point, as the terrorist looked up at the flight attendant, that Moutardier spied in his lap a pair of basketball shoes with wires attached to them—the shoes were black suede high-tops—and at once she grasped the danger of the situation. Although she did not know it, implanted in the soles of Reid's shoes were the plastic explosive PETN (pentaerythritol tetranitrate) and TATP (triacetone triperoxide), the primary explosive or trigger.[34] Reid was there to obliterate the plane and everyone in it. Suspecting as much, Moutardier grabbed him, the pair wrestled, and Reid heaved her into the aisle. A colleague arrived to help restrain the extremist, but Reid sank his teeth deep into the woman's hand and refused to release it. Now realizing what was happening, other passengers climbed over the seats and overpowered the terrorist.

Considering that the September 11 attacks had happened only three months before, many on the jetliner were primed for another terrorist strike, and anger, as much as fear, became the dominant emotion throughout the cabin. Wasting no time, the passengers and cabin crew secured Reid's hands with plastic cuffs, then trussed up his body with the belts of passengers, headphone cords, tape, and other materials, after which a doctor injected the would-be killer with a sedative retrieved from the aircraft's medical kit. "The passengers then spent two anxious hours taking turns watching Reid while the movie 'Legally Blonde' played in the cabin," reported one source.[35]

In the end, the aircraft was diverted to Boston Logan International Airport, where the FBI literally had to cut Reid out of his seat, so thoroughly had the flight attendants and passengers bound him to it. Forensics analyses subsequently revealed that the shoe bomb did not detonate because Reid, extremely nervous during the flight, had perspired so profusely that it had dampened and thereby deactivated the explosives. His sweat, then, had been a godsend for everyone on board. "[B]omb techs determined that the bomb would have blown a hole in the plane's fuselage and caused the plane to crash if it had detonated," an FBI report stated.[36]

Officials would publicly announce the foiled plot shortly after it occurred as well as enact a procedure whereby all passengers would, effective immediately, be required to remove their shoes for inspection prior to boarding a commercial carrier. By publicizing this new practice, officials were trying to ensure that prospective bombers would know that they would henceforth be detected, arrested, and imprisoned if they undertook to hide explosives in their shoes. Certainly, Richard Reid would not be trying it again any time soon, having received a life sentence without parole for his airborne crime. To date, no further attacks of this type have been reported anywhere in the world.

One year later, in December 2002, the TSA installed explosives-detection systems at U.S. airports. A key feature of the Aviation and Transportation Security Act, this technology guaranteed that all bags traveling on airliners in the United States would be screened for explosives. As well, passengers were required to hand over their laptop computers to TSA agents during their pre-flight inspections. But while these extra measures were indispensable in aviation security in light of the mounting risks, vulnerabilities remained.

Liquid bomb plot. To illustrate, an ambitious scheme that British authorities scotched on August 9, 2006, involved a liquid that would outwardly appear to be ordinary and benign and therefore could pass through security screenings without a second glance. In reality, it would be sufficiently volatile to devastate a fuselage when detonated.

The diabolical al-Qaeda project, which was housed in a nondescript London apartment, would entail several teams of operatives smuggling the liquid onto ten commercial aircraft flying out of Heathrow Airport, specifically on planes owned by American Airlines, Air Canada, and United Airlines. Although the various flights would depart at different times of day, the onboard bombers would trigger their IEDs at the same moment. Some of the planes would explode over the Atlantic Ocean, while others would disintegrate over American cities.

By any measure, the bombs were imaginative. The perpetrators planned to convert AA batteries into makeshift detonators and to insert the innocuous-looking liquid explosive into branded sports-drink bottles that could be carried into a passenger cabin. "The sports drink (500ml of Oasis or Lucozade) was to be emptied out from a small hole in the bottom of the bottle, refilled with explosives by means of [a] syringe, and the hole filled with glue so the drink would appear factory sealed," writes Robert J. Bunker.[37] It was the same type of bomb that extremists had used a year earlier to cause catastrophic blasts on three London Underground trains. Initially, analysts were unsure of, or at least unwilling to acknowledge publicly, the exact composition of the explosive, perhaps to avoid encouraging copy-cat crimes. "Chemists in the Department of Homeland Security (DHS)," wrote David Biello in *Scientific American*, "hinted that it would have been based on peroxides, commonly available as hydrogen peroxide—a household cleaner or bleach."[38]

As it turned out, a cache of al-Qaeda documents, which was unearthed six years later, permitted intelligence analysts to verify that pure hydrogen peroxide had indeed been the terrorists' compound of choice. A written entry in the log of Rashid Rauf, a British al-Qaeda operative, revealed this information. Rauf was a central figure in the plot, and he had stealthily embedded, in a pornographic movie contained on a computer disk, a chronicle of his operational planning. "The discovery that hydrogen peroxide could be colored without losing its explosive properties was a major breakthrough," he wrote, adding that seventeen ounces could bring down a jetliner.[39]

In part because al-Qaeda was now known to be attempting to employ liquids in its sabotage operations, the TSA, in March 2008, increased the number of canine units at federalized airports. As a function of the National Explosives Detection Canine Team Program, some of the dogs were used to check suspicious passengers, while others helped screen cargo that was loaded onto commercial airliners and as well as checked baggage. Having a sense of smell 1,000 greater than that of humans, bomb-sniffing dogs are able to detect not only bombs but also the traces of elements that comprise explosive devices.[40] Expanding the number and uses of these canines no doubt enhanced travelers' safety.

Underwear bomb plot. Efforts to sneak explosives onto jetliners would persist, unfortunately, and would be the aim of Umar Farouk Abdulmutallab, a Nigerian al-Qaeda operative who smuggled, beneath his clothing, a volatile chemical onto Northwest Airlines Flight 253. It was Christmas Day, 2009, and the wide-body Airbus A300 was traveling from Amsterdam to Detroit. On descent into Detroit Metropolitan Airport, Abdulmutallab told those around him that he felt sick, then covered his body with a blanket. His fellow travelers would soon find out what he was doing underneath it.

"There was a pop that sounded like a firecracker," said passenger Syed Jafry.[41] Smoke began to rise from Abdulmutallab's seat as his pant leg and the wall next to him burst into flames. A flight attendant arrived with a fire extinguisher, while passengers set about smothering the blaze with blankets. One of these passengers, a Dutch film director by the name of Jasper Schuringa, intuited what Abdulmutallab had in mind. "Oh, he's trying to blow up the plane," Schuringa recalled thinking to himself.[42] The director subdued the terrorist, following which Schuringa and a male flight attendant walked Abdulmutallab to the first-class section, where they stripped him and hand-cuffed him.

Regarding the IED, it was a powder mixture that contained the plastic explosive PETN, which had been sewn into one side of the would-be bomber's underwear. Concealed a few inches away, in the crotch, was a plastic syringe loaded with chemicals, presumably to inject into the explosive. A potentially lethal plot, it likely would have killed the 278 passengers and twelve crew members had it unfolded as planned.

Once the jetliner was back on the ground, Abdulmutallab found himself headed to a burn unit and later to jail. "I looked him right in the eye, he was in a lot of pain," said a bystander as the terrorist was rolled away on a gurney.[43] The extremist would forever be known as the "Christmas Bomber," while the *New York Post* would dub his airborne blunder the "'Great Balls of Fire' suicide bombing."[44]

It would later be determined that al-Qaeda, as suspected, was responsible for the terrorist operation and that a prominent leader of its Yemen affiliate, Anwar al-Awlaki, had helped Abdulmutallab prepare for what was to have been a "martyrdom mission" or suicide bombing. "Wait until you are in the U.S.," Awlaki reportedly told him, "then bring the plane down."[45] Nineteen months later, a U.S. drone strike would bring down Awlaki instead, a controversial killing that President Barack Obama ordered in response to the Northwest Airlines incident.[46] "[A] leader of the Al Qaeda affiliate in Yemen—gone," Obama announced, unapologetically.[47]

Just as Richard Reid's shoe bomb had failed to detonate properly because he had sweated so profusely that it deactivated the plastic explosive, so too did Abdulmutallab's bodily functions prevent his improvised explosive device from igniting. It seems he had worn the specially-designed underwear during the two weeks prior to traveling to Detroit because he wished to become familiar with them and be able to move about naturally without drawing attention to himself. During that fortnight, however, he did not remove them, and it was later found that he had soiled them and the explosives they held. "Thank goodness for bad hygiene," said Catherine Herridge, television correspondent and an Aspen Security Forum moderator.[48]

Hours after Abdulmutallab's bungled attempt to bomb Flight 253, the TSA publicized the incident and announced that supplemental security measures were being enacted at once. As could be expected, these temporary procedures carried international ramifications, with passengers flying from Britain to the United States, for instance, suddenly facing further restrictions. "Travellers can carry only one piece of hand luggage, including duty-free items, face a pat-down body search before boarding planes and will have to remain in their seats for the final hour before arrival in the US," reported *The Guardian* shortly after the incident.[49] Three months later, Abdulmutallab's effort to hide an IED in his clothing would lead to permanent changes in U.S. security protocols.

In March 2010, the TSA, in addition to requiring more aggressive pat-downs, commenced swabbing random passengers' hands for explosive residue (swabbing was previously confined to carry-on bags) and set about upgrading its "advanced imaging technology" (AIT) units. The organization would eventually install the machines at an estimated 500 airports across the United States. "The units, also known as 'full-body scanners,' are designed to detect non-metallic weapons, explosives and other threats, which could be concealed under layers of clothing and may evade traditional metal detectors," writes journalist Diane Gerace.[50]

By 2017, nearly 1,000 units were operational in American airports, and other nations had likewise installed the innovative technology at their own facilities. Although metal detectors, which can distinguish metal objects inside the body, continued to be used in the United States, the introduction of advanced imaging technology, which can detect both metallic and non-metallic objects outside the body, markedly increased security officers' ability to identify potentially dangerous items carried on a traveler.

A TSA report, one that was presented to the U.S. Congress in 2019, explained how such units operate. "Advanced Imaging Technology (AIT) uses millimeter wave technology to locate anomalies on a passenger's divested body using transmitters that generate millimeter wave electromagnetic energy," the document stated. "This low electromagnetic energy penetrates clothing and detects threats carried on the human body, but bounces off the body. The wave energy then is collected by signal receivers and is used to generate an image."[51]

In a typical scenario, an airline customer stands inside a scanner, and the readings appear on-screen to a security officer. Any irregularity, which theoretically could be an IED, is exhibited on an avatar in the shape of the human body, so that the officer will know precisely where to inspect the person by hand. (In 2022, the TSA announced that it is replacing its gender-based AIT system with one that is gender-neutral. This is in recognition of transgender, nonbinary, and gender-nonconforming passengers and will permit "less invasive screening," explains a TSA press release.[52])

Despite the progress offered by whole-body scanning technologies, which at one time included the use of controversial "backscatter X-ray machines," terrorists persisted in their search for ways to evade airport and airline security measures. Because the widespread usage of full-body scanning units rendered it nearly impossible for a person to carry an intact bomb onto an airliner, extremists had little choice but to pursue more inventive methods that would not be subject to whole-body imaging technology.

Printer cartridge bomb plot. For the Yemen-based terrorist organization AQAP (al-Qaeda in the Arabian Peninsula), a plastic explosive disguised as printer toner seemed to fit the bill. A dry, powdery mixture, toner is used in laser printers, and removing the toner and replacing it with a plastic explosive was the AQAP's strategy.

Two. Improvised Explosive Devices and Surface-to-Air Missiles 61

It was on October 29, 2010, that one of the organization's female operatives entered a shipping office in Yemen's capital city, Sana'a, where she mailed a box containing a Hewlett-Packard HP laser printer to a synagogue in Chicago. Elsewhere in the city, another female operative did the same. Soon, the packages were loaded into cargo planes owned and operated by United Parcel Service (UPS) and FedEx (formerly Federal Express Corporation), both of them American companies.

The explosive devices were intricate, and Western intelligence sources concluded they were built by Ibrahim Hassan al-Asiri, a notorious AQAP bomb-maker who was thought to have constructed the 2009 underwear bomb.[53] "Each printer contained up to 400 grams of white, military-grade explosive PETN in a highly concentrated form, along with a syringe loaded with lead azide, an explosive compound. In addition, the bomb-maker had inserted a tiny, cracked light diode in the lead azide, and connected it to a cellphone circuit board and battery."[54] Like dominoes tumbling, the process would be triggered when the cellphone's alarm clock became activated at a pre-set time. "The diode would then light and warm, thus igniting the lead azide, which would in turn set the PETN on fire—a potentially deadly chain reaction," write Jörg Diehl and Matthias Gebauer.[55] For al-Qaeda, it was simply a matter of waiting for the twin catastrophes to play out and dominate global headlines. But the organization was in for a letdown.

"Within days," writes Chris Shelton, "the two packages advanced through four countries in at least four different airplanes—two of them carrying passengers—before they were intercepted thanks to a last-minute tip from Saudi Arabia's intelligence."[56] British and American officials tracked the explosive cargo to a UPS freight center at an airport in Leicestershire, England, and to another facility in Dubai, where the bombs were deactivated. Analysts speculated that the devices were to have exploded over the United States, one over the East Coast and the other over Chicago.

Soda can bomb. Five years later, another clever device would unfortunately prove to be more successful, shattering a plane chartered by a large group of Russians. Metrojet Flight 9268 was traveling from the Egyptian resort town of Sharm el-Sheikh to Russia, when a sweeping act of violence killed all of the 224 people on board, including seventeen Russian children. "According to our experts," said Alexander Bortnikov, chief of Russia's security service, "a homemade explosive device equivalent to 1 kilogram of TNT went off onboard, which caused the plane to break up in the air, which explains why the fuselage was scattered over such a large territory."[57] The wreckage of the Airbus A321–200 was strewn across seven square miles of the Sinai Desert.

In short order, the Islamic State of Iraq and Syria (ISIS) claimed responsibility for the attack and published photos of the alleged IED in

Dabiq, its online propaganda magazine. The bomb's design was similar to that which al-Qaeda had planned to use in its thwarted 2006 "liquid bomb" plot, in that a plastic explosive was purportedly inserted into a soft-drink can through a hole in the base. The photo also displayed a crudely constructed detonator and a switch. In terms of the ground strategy, three ISIS suicide bombers ostensibly managed to compromise security officers at the Egyptian airport, then smuggled onto the jet the components of the bomb. Once the plane was airborne, the men assembled it. "Russia said explosives weighing up to 1 kilogram, a little more than 2 pounds, brought down Metrojet 9268, which means ISIS' claim it used a bomb the size of a soda can is plausible," CNN reported.[58]

Russia, it should be pointed out, had previously dispatched troops to Syria to help in the fight against the Islamic State, and ISIS subsequently claimed that, for this reason, it had targeted the Metrojet carrying Russian civilians. In retaliation for the in-flight bombing, Russia ramped up its airstrikes in Syria and, for safety reasons, suspended commercial air travel to and from Egypt for more than two years. Other international air carriers were likewise reticent. The Egyptian tourism industry suffered a staggering loss of revenue from foreign travelers and businesses also expressing safety concerns.

That said, aviation safety continued to be an issue far beyond Egypt, and understandably so, as was demonstrated once again on February 2, 2016. On this day, a terrorist succeeded in smuggling a new type of IED onto Daallo Airlines Flight 159, which was traveling from the Somalian cities of Mogadishu to Djibouti. Shortly after the aircraft departed from Aden Adde International Airport, the bomber, who selected a seat that would cause the maximum amount of damage, detonated the device. Although the flight attendants reeled from the onboard explosion, which blew a hole in the fuselage, they nevertheless managed to herd the passengers to the rear of the cabin. Meanwhile, the pilot struggled to return the crippled airliner to Aden Adde airport. Against the odds, he succeeded, with only one passenger dying in the attack, namely, the bomber. It was later concluded that two airport workers likely collaborated with the terrorist by ensuring that the IED made it through the airport's X-ray machine undetected. Seventy-two hours later, one of these men died under mysterious circumstances when his vehicle blew up.[59]

The bomb in the Mogadishu case was of particular interest to aviation security agencies since it had been integrated into a laptop computer. The existence of such IEDs had long spooked the U.S. security community. "The explosive device built into a laptop computer … was 'sophisticated,'" said an investigator in the case, "and got past X-ray machines at the Mogadishu airport."[60] Naturally, the TSA, which had required its agents to cursorily examine laptop computers as far back as 2002, was apprehensive about this recent development. And the organization became even more focused on the matter in 2017, when the Israeli intelligence community shared disturbing information it had hacked from ISIS bomb-makers in Syria. "That was how the United States learned that the terrorist group [Islamic State] was working to make explosives that fooled airport X-ray machines and other screening by looking exactly like batteries for laptop computers," reported David E. Sanger and Eric Schmitt.[61] Intelligence officers further learned that ISIS was not alone: al-Qaeda in the Arabian Peninsula, al Shabaab, and the former al-Qaeda in Syria were likewise experimenting with laptop bombs.[62]

The Islamic State's advancements in this area revealed that it had become more knowledgeable about what the various technologies at Western airports could, and could not, detect. And this meant they could construct IEDs to defeat them. Middle Eastern bomb-makers, for instance, invented explosive devices known as "thin bombs" that were capable of sailing, unnoticed, through conventional screening technology. "They are so thin the X-ray machines can't see them," said John Halinski, formerly a TSA administrator.[63]

For such reasons, the United States, in March 2017, enacted a ban affecting flights departing from ten nations in the Middle East and North Africa. Prohibited from passenger cabins were laptop computers and any other consumer electronics larger than a cellphone. "Under the new restrictions, the electronic devices—many of which have lithium ion batteries—will now be carried in the cargo deck of the airplane, underneath the passenger cabin," reported CNN's Barbara Starr and Rene Marsh.[64] In that the restrictions were politically controversial as well as ill-conceived—a terrorist bomber could simply board a plane to the United States from a nation not covered by the ban—it was lifted four months later. In its place, the TSA, in July 2017, instituted an all-embracing policy that would require travelers to place their electronic devices, other than cellphones, in bins for screening.

Body cavity and implanted bombs. As it became more difficult for terrorists to conceal explosive mechanisms in their clothing and luggage, their attention turned to the human body itself. As countless drug smugglers can attest, the practice of concealing illicit items in a body cavity is not a new one, and terrorist entities, rather predictably, began experimenting with the practice.

This may, or may not, have been the case when Fadhel al-Maliki, a thirty-five-year-old Iraqi man, was flagged in 2007 by airport security officers at Los Angeles International Airport (LAX) owing to his atypical behavior. Al-Maliki was extremely anxious and perspiring profusely, and his condition prompted the officers to subject him to a secondary screening.

In the course of it, he set off a metal detector. "Al-Maliki, a former security guard, told screeners that he knew what had triggered the alarm and proceeded to remove items from his rectum, including a rock, chewing gum and thin wire filament," reported the *Los Angeles Times*.[65] News reports varied, however, and it has been suggested that the items were actually a magnet, putty, and wire.[66] Without delay, the LAX team alerted a bomb squad as well as involved the FBI and HAZMAT technicians. Al-Maliki, for his part, claimed to be innocent, explaining that the rock (or magnet) in his rectum kept him calm, but federal agents remained concerned that it may have been a "dry run" for a body-cavity IED. "Ultimately, it was determined that al-Maliki had broken no laws, no matter how suspicious or bizarre his actions, and he was not charged for any crimes," writes Robert Bunker.[67] It may be of significance that al-Maliki had previously been taken into custody on suspicion of possessing an unspecified destructive device, but the charges were dropped.[68]

More worrisome perhaps than cavity bombs are explosive devices, or their components, that are surgically implanted into the human body. In 2010, Western intelligence agencies picked up chatter emerging from AQAP, chatter centering on the prospects of imbedding explosives in its operatives. Reportedly, it was the widespread use of full-body scanners at airports that prompted the terrorist outfit to consider surgical methods.[69] In response, the TSA notified passengers that they could henceforth anticipate closer scrutiny, including more aggressive pat-downs, prior to boarding, especially at overseas airports offering flights to destinations within the United States.

The reasoning behind implanted IEDs is sound. Colombian drug smugglers have previously attempted to implant narcotics in their bodies, and there is no reason the practice could not be adapted for more violent purposes. Referred to as "body packing," it would entail, in a terrorist mission, sealing an explosive in plastic, then implanting it inside an operative's buttocks, abdomen, or breasts. "In order for it to work, there would need to be a detonation device," says explosives expert James B. Crippin, "and it's conceivable that if the explosive was implanted in a woman's breast, the detonator could be underneath the breast so that all the operative would have to do is press downward."[70] Alternatively, "a syringe containing a different chemical could be jammed into the plastic bag, triggering an explosion," write Keith Johnson and Siobhan Gorman.[71] Doing so would be feasible in that syringes are allowed on airliners if accompanied by medication and checked by security officers.

To date, no IED implants are known to have been used in a terrorist strike involving an aircraft. As to their continued prevention, neither an AIT unit nor a metal detector are capable of detecting explosive materials

Two. Improvised Explosive Devices and Surface-to-Air Missiles 65

inside the body, so the TSA's solution has been to underscore the importance of behavioral scrutiny—that is, more rigorous examinations of travelers who seem suspicious. In this regard, the organization has educated airport security teams about the potential indicators of an implanted item that a TSA officer might encounter when performing a pat-down. A passenger may experience soreness or discomfort in the region of an implanted explosive, for instance, or may exhibit bulging or swelling in that area. Useful, too, is the practice of swabbing an individual's skin and clothing for traces of nitroglycerin and other residues. "When dealing with explosives, it's very hard not to have some kind of residue that gets on your clothing," says one security expert.[72] Of course, explosives-sniffing dogs may also prove quite useful in such circumstances.

All in all, the measures that the TSA has enacted to protect passengers and crew on airliners have proven to be remarkably effective, with in-flight bombings, as well as skyjackings, dropping to near-zero levels. Although security protocols may be somewhat intrusive and time-consuming, the result, in terms of the lives that have been saved, would appear to warrant their usage. That said, critics continue to raise concerns about the TSA's all-encompassing role at American airports and about the potential risks its protocols may pose to travelers' privacy rights. In response, the organization continues to assess and upgrade its procedures.

Of note, the TSA has as one its goals the integration and streamlining of security procedures, including identity verification, at airport checkpoints. The aim is to make the screening process a more user-friendly experience for travelers in terms of being quicker, simpler, and less invasive. "No slowing down, no dropping your bag, and an automation of security procedures," the TSA states.[73]

To this end, the organization is actively testing emergent technologies, among them new forms of biometric (identity) verification. These include facial recognition technologies, iris scanning systems, fingerprinting, and more. All of these have become especially useful in the era of Covid-19, since they do not require close human contact. Furthermore, it is anticipated that a traveler's face will soon become the person's boarding pass. "Many of the latest biometric developments use facial recognition, which the National Institute of Standards and Technology recently found is at least 99.5 percent accurate, rather than iris-scanning or fingerprints," writes Elaine Glusac.[74]

The TSA has also announced that U.S. airports will be using advanced equipment nationwide starting in 2023, equipment designed to make it unlikely that travelers will be required to empty their carry-on bags for inspection by federal agents. The aim, once again, is both to accelerate the screening process and to make it more discreet. With the new tools, a carry-on bag will move through a computed-tomography machine (CT or CAT scan) that has three-dimensional capabilities; the result was that a TSA agent can view the bag's contents from all angles. "Like existing CT technology used for checked baggage, the machines create such a clear picture of a bag's contents that computers can automatically detect explosives, including liquids," states a TSA document.[75] A suspicious liquid may then be subjected to a "black box" process at a checkpoint—the TSA will not reveal how the machine operates—in which the liquid is placed in a closed compartment and analyzed chemically to ensure it contains no components of an explosive. Collectively, these and related advancements are expected to ensure improved prevention of IEDs on aircraft as well as a better pre-flight experience for passengers.

While commercial airliners are steadily gaining protection from bombings and hijackings, terrorist attacks are still a concern. As we have noted, when security measures evolve, extremist entities respond by upgrading their strategies to keep pace with or even surpass them. Among the enduring risks: a weapon, such as a surface-to-air missile, targeting a commercial airliner.

Surface-to-Air Missiles

More than fifty civilian aircraft have been the targets of missiles since 1973, nearly half of them in southern Africa, mainly Angola.[76] While this figure is unsettling, it should not be taken to mean that commercial carriers are unusually vulnerable to such attacks. For the most part, the conditions in which missiles have downed civilian planes have been rather specific and are the type of circumstances that rarely confront the average air traveler. "Attacks have almost exclusively taken place in active war zones," writes Michael Ashkenazi and his associates at the Bonn International Center for Conversion. "The threat to civil aviation outside conflict zones may thus be less grave than assumed."[77] In a war zone, a nation's military may mistake a civilian plane for an enemy aircraft or it may assume that the aircraft is contributing to the conflict by transporting, overtly or covertly, supplies or troops. In contrast, on those infrequent occasions when a missile has destroyed a commercial carrier in a conflict-free region, it has often been the work of a terrorist entity intentionally orchestrating the act of violence as a means of making a political statement.

In terms of the weapons that extremists have deployed in such assaults, they have entailed "man-portable air-defense systems," or MANPADS, of which there are three broad categories. The version that terrorists are likely to possess is the infrared (IR) type, a shoulder-fired missile that targets an aircraft's exhaust plume or other heat source. "The most commonly used MANPADS in attacks against civilian aircraft have been from the Strela family, which are the most widely proliferated systems in the world," writes Ashkenazi and his colleagues.[78] The heat-seeking Strela missiles, which have the advantage of being light weight, were originally manufactured by the Soviet Union for its military and thereafter produced by Russia.

The second type of MANPADS are "command line of sight" (CLOS) projectiles. When deploying this missile, an operator visually guides it to the target. This stands in contrast to the third type, a "beam rider," in which a laser-guided, shoulder-fired missile travels along a light beam to its airborne mark.

Despite the advantages of MANPADS, such as their portability and their increasing affordability on the black market, they do have limitations. Most problematic is their ceiling, which ranges from 18,000 to 20,000 feet. Due to this drawback, they cannot reach an airliner that is traveling at cruising altitude, or 33,000 to 42,000 feet. They are instead constrained to low-flying, slow-moving aircraft, including helicopters. Even so, a terrorist group that is determined to bring down an airliner may lock onto it during takeoff or landing when its altitude is low. "[D]eparting aircraft with heavy fuel loads operating at high engine power, often along predefined departure routes, may be particularly vulnerable and can be targeted up to 30 miles away from the airport before they climb above the effective range of shoulder-fired SAMs [surface-to-air missiles]," says Bartholomew Elias, an aviation security specialist.[79] Certainly it is true that terrorists, when they have successfully struck commercial aircraft, have usually done so a few minutes after their targets have become airborne.

Previous Hostile Attacks

In terms of the history of violent actions against commercial aircraft, regardless of the perpetrator, the first recorded incident took place on August 24, 1938, and involved machine-gun fire. The war between Japan and China was at its height—the Second Sino-Japanese War—and the aerial mission was an attempt by the Japanese to assassinate the Chinese president's son, who was erroneously believed to be on the plane.

In this episode, the small airliner, a DC-2, was operated by China National Aviation Corporation (CNAC) and was carrying eighteen passengers and crew. The journey was to be a long one, more than 700 miles, from Hong Kong to the Chinese city of Chungking (Chongqing). Only twenty minutes into the flight, a Japanese air patrol consisting of five biplanes charged at the CNAC airliner, causing its pilot to force-land by a river. But the Japanese pilots did not stop; they continued their pursuit, flying lower and strafing the commercial carrier. "Bullets clipped through the DC-2 fuselage," writes Gregory Crouch, "and a woman yelped inside."[80] In all, fifteen passengers and crew were killed in the assault.

Official aircraft. Non-commercial flights carrying government officials or NGO personnel have also been the casualties of in-flight strikes, among them a United Nations plane, a DC-6, that was transporting UN Secretary-General Dag Hammarskjöld. Crashing in the African nation of Rhodesia (today Zambia) in 1961, it was during Hammarskjöld's politically-fraught task in the region. It is suspected that a guerrilla operation was the cause of the tragedy.

In another episode, the Polisario Front, a nationalist liberation outfit operating in the western Sahara Desert, shot down a research aircraft, the *Polar*, which was returning from Antarctica. All of the passengers and crew were killed.

And on January 15, 1973, at the Leonardo da Vinci International Airport in Rome, an assassination plot was set into motion by the Palestinian terrorist group Black September. The intended victim: Israeli prime minister Golda Meir, who had come to the Vatican for an official visit with Pope Paul VI. Afterward, she would be boarding the Boeing 707 for her return to Tel Aviv. Fortunately, the assassination attempt was foiled, and the State of Israeli's aircraft was unharmed.[81]

Commercial aircraft. Throughout the remainder of the Seventies, both lawful and unlawful entities continued exploring the use of portable air-defense weapons. "During the 1970s, nonstate armed groups (NSAGs) began to use MANPADS in civil wars and other conflicts of varying intensity in such countries as Angola and Mozambique," states a report from the RAND Corporation. "North Vietnamese forces also resorted to MANPADS use, downing an Air Vietnam DC-4 in 1975."[82]

The first MANPADS attack on a commercial airliner that was not in a war zone occurred on September 3, 1978, in Zambia. Designated Air Rhodesia Flight 825, the ill-fated plane was carrying fifty-six people and was on a domestic run, traveling from Kariba to Salisbury. Five minutes after take-off, while its altitude was still low, the pilot issued a distress call, reporting to the tower that a missile had taken out the right inboard engine. The Vickers Viscount landed, albeit in flames, in the scrub nearly forty miles away. Although eighteen passengers and crew managed to survive the fiery ordeal, guerrillas representing the ZIPRA (Zimbabwe People's Revolutionary Army) arrived shortly thereafter and murdered ten of them on the spot.

Pleased with the successful mission, a team from ZIPRA decided to replicate the horror three months later, when they blasted out of the sky another Air Rhodesia aircraft. Also traveling from Kariba to Salisbury on February 12, 1979, the plane was designated Flight 827, and the perpetrators used the same type of projectiles that had been deployed in the earlier attack, namely, two Strela-2 (SA-7) surface-to-air missiles. All fifty passengers and crew on board died in the incident.

Seven years would pass before political extremists would turn once again to missiles to obliterate a large passenger plane in flight, this time a Sudan Airways carrier traveling from Malakal to Khartoum, Sudan. In this operation, the Fokker Friendship aircraft was blown out of the sky by a rebel group, the Sudan People's Liberation Army (SPLA), using a Strela-2 antiaircraft missile to impact the airliner's right engine. "The plane then vanished in a ball of fire," writes Margaret Rogg.[83] The reason for the midair attack, which happened on August 16, 1986, was to dissuade Sudan Airways from flying its airliners over the southern part of the nation. Fifty-seven passengers and three crew members perished.

Even more passengers and crew would lose their lives on July 17, 1996, when TWA Flight 800 exploded over water near Long Island, New York. The Boeing 747 had departed from JFK International Airport twelve minutes earlier and was flying at a comparatively low altitude of 13,700 feet. In this controversial episode, 258 people on the ground, in boats, and in nearby aircraft reported watching as a streak of bright light soared from the ground to the airliner, followed by a series of midair explosions. Lengthy and costly government investigations ensued, but the investigators were purportedly unable to pinpoint what had sparked the explosion in the airliner's center fuel tank. The official conclusion: an unspecified mechanical malfunction had initiated the deadly chain of events. Because radar and satellite data refuted much of the investigations' findings, however, and since a large number of eyewitnesses, aviation experts, and specialists who had taken part in the formal inquiries continued to insist it was a missile strike, the incident has remained contentious. The intriguing case of TWA 800 is examined in Chapter Four.

A couple of years later, a terrorist organization would again strike a commercial carrier, and it would happen off the Sri Lankan coast. The date was September 29, 1998, and the target was Lion Air Flight 602. A Soviet-made Antonov An-24 turboprop, it was following a domestic route, departing from the city of Jaffna and bound for Colombo. Fifteen minutes after takeoff, a missile struck the plane, with the pilot contacting the control tower to report that the passenger cabin was depressurizing. The plane's altitude was 8,000 feet. Minutes later, the aircraft crashed into the sea, killing all fifty-five people on board in an attack that was ascribed to a Sri Lankan separatist organization, the Liberation Tigers of Tamil Eelam

(LTTE). The group's motive was retaliation, Lion Air having transported soldiers for the Sri Lankan military. Ironically, all of the passengers on the doomed aircraft turned out to be Tamils—that is, members of the indigenous ethnic group for which the LTTE was seeking independence.

After the extraordinary events of September 11, 2001, missile attacks on large passenger planes declined substantially, presumably due to tightened security measures around the world. Even so, there would be an attempt the following year, when al-Qaeda would make use of the surface-to-air missiles it had come to possess. Among them were Stinger anti-aircraft missiles that the U.S. military had previously supplied to the Mujahideen in Afghanistan.[84]

It happened on November 28, 2002, when the terrorist organization set out to destroy an Israeli-registered Boeing 757. Designated Arkia Israeli Airlines Flight 582, the plane had previously been used to transport Israeli prime minister Ariel Sharon, and now it was on a routine weekly flight from Mombasa, Kenya, to Tel Aviv. Because its schedule and flight path were common knowledge, it appeared to be an easy mark. Accordingly, shortly after wheels up, two Strela-2 missiles raced toward the plane. Both of them missed.

Despite the fact that its plan had flopped, al-Qaeda's bold attempt served as a wakeup call, one that would have wide-ranging and lasting repercussions. "Today they fired missiles at Israeli planes, tomorrow they'll fire missiles at U.S. planes, British planes, planes from every state," railed Benjamin Netanyahu, the Israeli foreign minister at the time.[85] The incident was also felt in Washington, D.C. "Unlike the prior attacks on jet airliners that occurred in war torn areas, the Mombasa attack was clearly a politically motivated attack," wrote Bartholomew Elias in a report for the Department of Homeland Security. "That fact, coupled with already heightened concerns over aviation security in the aftermath of the September 11, 2001 terrorist attacks, has made the shoulder-fired missile threat a key issue for homeland security."[86]

As things stood, a sizable number of weapons had fallen into the hands of terrorists, a large share having been abandoned by American military forces in South Central Asia and the Middle East. "In all, the United States left behind more than $7 billion worth of weapons and equipment when it left Afghanistan," writes Jack Detsch in *Foreign Policy*.[87] Also troubling, the weapons included heat-seeking Stinger missiles, at least 100 of them, according to defense analyst Thomas Withington.[88] Other sources have put the number as high as 500 Stingers.[89] Due to the al-Qaeda incident in Kenya, then, plus the fact that thousands of black-market MANPADS were known to be in the hands of a numerous terrorist entities, the federal government spent three years studying the emergent risks and brainstorming

Two. Improvised Explosive Devices and Surface-to-Air Missiles 71

potential solutions. On February 16, 2006, its conclusions were delivered in a document titled "Homeland Security: Protecting Airliners from Terrorist Missiles."[90]

The prospective interventions outlined in the report centered on aircraft, airports, and governments. "[A] menu of options may be considered," the document stated, "including installing infrared (IR) countermeasures on aircraft; modifying flight operations and air traffic control procedures; improving airport and regional security; and strengthening missile non-proliferation efforts."[91] While elements of these options were considered and adopted, however, the first recommendation was discarded, namely, the installation of sophisticated antimissile technology on commercial carriers.

On the face of it, it seems rather obvious that antimissile defense systems could be useful on airliners, since the technology is effective at low altitudes when planes are most susceptible to attack from the ground. Then, too, such countermeasures could be beneficial to those commercial planes serving airports that are situated in conflict zones or that have substandard or inconsistent security operations.

But there are drawbacks. For one thing, certain types of missiles are capable of escaping detection by onboard defense systems. For another, the projected cost is steep. Onboard countermeasures would carry a $1 million to $3 million price tag per aircraft, which would be prohibitive for a fleet of airliners, especially for a small company. In addition, integrating the equipment into the aircraft, furnishing specialized training for aircrews, and providing ongoing maintenance would further compound the expense. For these and other reasons, the DHS offered a modified recommendation, one that entailed installing missile countermeasures only on those airliners that travel to high-risk locations. Again, though, the recommendation was shelved.

The Israeli company El Al was the first commercial airline in the world to mount antimissile technology on its fleet of planes, beginning in 2004. Two other Israeli airlines, Arkia and Israir, later installed the equipment on their own planes.

In its initial form, El Al fitted its planes with Doppler radar systems, positioning the antennae at four different points on each aircraft. When an incoming heat-seeking missile was detected, the airliner would release flares to attract and misdirect the projectile. Known as "Flight Guard," the system appeared to be both sensible and feasible, but it ran into opposition from the FAA and the governments of Switzerland and other European nations. Their apprehensions were that the technology might create false alarms near airports or that the flares might constitute fire hazards over land.

Undaunted, El Al continued using the Flight Guard system while attempting to address the above concerns, for instance by clarifying that the flares used a special substance that burns at low temperatures. Then, in 2013, the company began fitting its Boeing 737–800s with a more advanced technology, one akin to that used by the Israeli Air Force.[92] On commercial and civilian aircraft, including helicopters, it is known as the "C-MUSIC" system, which is an acronym for "Commercial-Multi Spectral Infrared Countermeasure."[93] A fully-automated process that notifies the pilot after it has nullified a threat, the C-MUSIC system is composed of a radar device emplaced on the bottom of the plane. "If any missiles come in the radar of the aircraft, within seconds a powerful laser beam is then fired accurately at the missile causing it to be deflected away from the aircraft," reports *AIRLIVE*.[94] More precisely, the C-MUSIC system, which is pod-mounted on the lower rear section of the fuselage, directs a laser at the "seeker" or sensor, which is the heat-seeking component of the missile, and this jams it. What is more, the system can continue jamming other incoming projectiles. "With a laser system, you have unlimited rounds you can dispense against threats," says Jong K. Lee.[95] The cost of the antimissile defense system is estimated to be $1.2 million per aircraft.

While no nation's airlines other than those of Israel have installed these types of countermeasures on their fleets of passenger planes, missile strikes continue to be a worry of carrier companies. It is a concern that dates back to November 22, 2003, when Iraqi insurgents in Baghdad targeted an Airbus A300. A cargo plane operated by DHL Express, it was struck on the left wing shortly after takeoff by an old surface-to-air missile manufactured in the former Soviet Union. The pilot was able to land the Airbus safety a few minutes later, but its hydraulic system was mangled. As it happened, the insurgents who launched the attack videotaped it, presumably to demonstrate their proficiency to their funding sources as well as to inspire others to join their cause. "I guess the point here is obviously getting these tapes out has a very, very good propaganda value," said national security analyst Peter Bergen.[96] If that were the plan, though, it fizzled, since news organizations did not report the name of the group.

Since that time, cargo planes have not been targeted in troubling numbers, but the possibility remains a concern for companies like FedEx, UPS, and DHL, which travel to airports in conflict zones or to regions that are susceptible to terrorist activity. It is for this reason that FedEx, to safeguard its new line of aircraft, the Airbus A321–200s, petitioned the United States government in 2022 for authorization to install antidefense technology on these planes. If approved, it will be the first line of U.S.-registered commercial carriers to acquire this capability.

Two. Improvised Explosive Devices and Surface-to-Air Missiles

The odds of an airliner being destroyed by a surface-to-air missile remain low at this time, but as we have noted, terrorist organizations persist in their efforts to circumvent preventive strategies. If missile strikes on commercial carriers were to increase in number, airline companies (and their governments) would likely reconsider the costly but effective practice of equipping their airliners with antimissile defense systems. For now, however, securing airport perimeters is still one of the most preferred, and comparatively cost-effective, means of reducing the probability of such attacks. As we shall see in Chapter Three, the perimeter strategy is intended to block a terrorist entity's access to property that could be used to stage a missile strike on departing or arriving commercial airliners.

Notes

1. Bryan R. Swopes, "10 October 1933," *This Day in Aviation*, accessed December 27, 2022, https://www.thisdayinaviation.com/.
2. "Seven Die as Plane Crashes in Flames," *New York Times*, October 11, 1933, https://timesmachine.nytimes.com/timesmachine/1933/10/11/99936550.html?pageNumber=1.
3. "Seven Die as Plane Crashes in Flames."
4. Howard Johnson, "Interview with Howard Johnson," Westchester Public Library Oral History Project, August 13, 1999, http://www.duneacres.org/Archives/Aviation.pdf.
5. Phil Rogers, "80 Years Later, Plane Bombing Remains a Mystery," NBC Chicago, October 8, 2013, https://www.nbcchicago.com/news/local/80-years-later-plane-bombing-remains-a-mystery/1964534/.
6. Philip Baum, *Violence in the Skies: A History of Aircraft Hijacking and Bombing* (West Sussex, England: Summersdale, 2016).
7. "Seven Die as Plane Crashes in Flames."
8. "Interview with Howard Johnson," 7.
9. E.J. Kahn, Jr., "It Has No Name," *The New Yorker*, November 7, 1953, https://www.newyorker.com/magazine/1953/11/14/it-has-no-name.
10. Gary Brown, "The Monday After: Airline Bombings in '50s Led to Tighter Security," *CantonRep.com | The Repository*, January 26, 2010, https://www.cantonrep.com/story/news/politics/elections/county/2010/01/26/the-monday-after-airline-bombings/42211630007/.
11. Gary Brown, "The Monday After."
12. Gary Brown, "The Monday After."
13. Gary Brown, "The Monday After."
14. Brian Michael Jenkins, *The Terrorist Threat to Commercial Aviation* (Santa Monica, CA: RAND Corporation, 1989), 9, https://www.rand.org/pubs/papers/P7540.html.
15. Brian Michael Jenkins, "The Terrorist Threat to Commercial Aviation," 6.
16. "The Kanishka Bombing, 20 years on Lest We Forget," *The Tribune* (India), July 10, 2005, https://www.tribuneindia.com/2005/20050710/spectrum/main1.htm.
17. Chris Summers, "Deadly Puzzle Remains a Mystery," BBC News, March 16, 2005, http://news.bbc.co.uk/2/hi/americas/4344051.stm.
18. Chris Summers, "Deadly Puzzle Remains a Mystery."
19. Chris Summers, "Deadly Puzzle Remains a Mystery."
20. Philip Baum, *Violence in the Skies*.
21. "Air India Flight 181/182," Flight Aviation Safety Network, accessed January 6, 2023, https://aviation-safety.net/database/record.php?id=19850623-2.
22. "The Government of Canada Response to the Commission of Inquiry into the Investigation of the Bombing of Air India Flight 182," *Public Safety Canada*, July 27, 2022, https://www.publicsafety.gc.ca/cnt/rsrcs/pblctns/rspns-cmmssn/index-en.aspx.
23. Philip Baum, *Violence in the Skies*, 181.
24. Matthew L. Wald, "Long Before Verdict, Lockerbie Changed Airport Security," *New

York Times, January 31, 2001, https://www.nytimes.com/2001/01/31/world/long-before-verdict-lockerbie-changed-airport-security.html.

25. Matthew L. Wald, "Long Before Verdict, Lockerbie Changed Airport Security."
26. Giacomo Amati, "FBI Arrest 1988 Lockerbie Bombing Suspect," *Simple Flying*, accessed January 5, 2023, https://simpleflying.com/fbi-arrest-1988-lockerbie-bombing-suspect/.
27. Brian Michael Jenkins, "The Terrorist Threat to Commercial Aviation," 6. https://www.rand.org/pubs/papers/P7540.html.
28. David Gero, *Flights of Terror: Aerial Hijack and Sabotage Since 1930* (Somerset, England: Haynes Publishing, 2009), 72.
29. Paul J. Smith, "Transnational Terrorism and the al Qaeda Model: Confronting New Realities," *Parameters* 32, no. 2 (2002), 33, https://press.armywarcollege.edu/parameters/vol32/iss2/13/.
30. David Gero, *Flights of Terror*.
31. David Biello, "Liquid Explosives Linked to Terror Plot," *Scientific American*, August 10, 2006, https://www.scientificamerican.com/article/liquid-explosives-linked/.
32. Emily Clark, "How Has the Global Terror Threat Shaped Airline Security and Just How Confident Can You Be?" ABC News (Australian Broadcasting Corp.), July 30, 2017, https://www.abc.net.au/news/2017-07-30/how-terror-incidents-have-shaped-global-airline-security/8757450.
33. Cathy Booth Thomas, "Courage in the Air," *TIME Magazine*, September 1, 2002, https://web.archive.org/web/20100604162640/http://www.time.com/time/covers/1101020909/aattendants.html.
34. Pam Belluck, with Kenneth Chang, "A Nation Challenged: The Investigation; Shoes Were a 'Homemade Bomb,' F.B.I. Agent Says," *New York Times*, December 29, 2001, https://www.nytimes.com/2001/12/29/us/a-nation-challenged-the-investigation-shoes-were-a-homemade-bomb-fbi-agent-says.html.
35. New York Daily News Staff, "Richard C. Reid, the Shoe Bomber, Was Subdued by Flight Attendants and Passengers in 2001," *New York Daily News*, December 21, 2016, https://www.nydailynews.com/news/world/shoe-bomber-subdued-flight-attendants-passengers-2001-article-1.934624.
36. "History: Richard Reid's Shoes," FBI, accessed October 22, 2022, https://www.fbi.gov/history/artifacts/richard-reids-shoes.
37. Robert J. Bunker, "The Projected Al Qaeda Use of Body Cavity Suicide Bombs against High Value Targets," *Los Angeles County Terrorism Early Warning Group—GroupIntel Network*, March 2011. https://nation.time.com/wp-content/uploads/sites/8/2011/07/bunker-groupintel_bodycavitybombs.pdf.
38. David Biello, "Liquid Explosives Linked to Terror Plot."
39. Nic Robertson, Paul Cruickshank, and Tim Lister, "Document Shows Origins of 2006 Plot for Liquid Bombs on Planes," CNN, April 30, 2012, https://www.cnn.com/2012/04/30/world/al-qaeda-documents/index.html.
40. Ronnie Garrett, "Explosives Detection Goes to the Dogs," *Airport Improvement Magazine*, May–June 2011, https://airportimprovement.com/article/explosives-detection-goes-dogs#:~:text=The%20success%20of%20the%20Transportation,it%20was%20set%20to%20detonate.
41. Anahad O'Connor and Eric Schmitt, "Terror Attempt Seen as Man Tries to Ignite Device on Jet," *New York Times*, December 25, 2009, https://www.nytimes.com/2009/12/26/us/26plane.html.
42. Scott Shane and Eric Lipton, "Passengers' Quick Action Halted Attack," *New York Times*, December 26, 2009, https://web.archive.org/web/20101201060215/http://www.nytimes.com/2009/12/27/us/27plane.html.
43. Jennifer Dixon and Jim Schaefer, "Northwest Bomb Attempt: Response Was Botched in Aftermath of Flight 253 Landing," *Detroit Free Press*, September 10, 2014, https://www.freep.com/story/news/nation/2014/09/10/underwear-bomber-nwa-253/15392267/.
44. Michael Grabell, "U.S. Government Glossed Over Cancer Concerns as It Rolled Out Airport X-Ray Scanner," *ProPublica*, November 1, 2011, https://www.propublica.org/article/u.s.-government-glossed-over-cancer-concerns-as-it-rolled-out-airport-x-ray.
45. Scott Shane, "Inside Al Qaeda's Plot to Blow Up an American Airliner," *New York*

Two. Improvised Explosive Devices and Surface-to-Air Missiles

Times, February 22, 2017, https://www.nytimes.com/2017/02/22/us/politics/anwar-awlaki-underwear-bomber-abdulmutallab.html.

46. John Yoo, "From Gettysburg to Anwar al-Awlaki," *Wall Street Journal*, October 3, 2011, https://www.wsj.com/articles/SB10001424052970204226204576603114226847494.

47. Scott Shane, "The Lessons of Anwar al-Awlaki," *New York Times*, August 27, 2015, https://www.nytimes.com/2015/08/30/magazine/the-lessons-of-anwar-al-awlaki.html.

48. Catherine Herridge (moderator), "Aspen Security Forum: TSA—Toward a Risk-Based Approach to Aviation Security," Aspen Institute, July 24, 2014, https://www.aspensecurityforum.org/2014-videos.

49. "Flight Terror Suspect Abdulmutallab Charged with Trying to Blow Up Jet," *The Guardian*, December 27, 2009, https://www.theguardian.com/world/2009/dec/27/us-terror-flight-abdulmutallab-charged.

50. Diane Gerace, "A Look at How Airport Security Has Evolved Post-9/11," Philadelphia International Airport, accessed January 15, 2022, https://www.phl.org/newsroom/911-security-impact.

51. "Use of Advanced Imaging Technology at Checkpoints—Fiscal Year 2019 Report to Congress," Transportation Security Administration, May 10, 2019, https://www.dhs.gov/sites/default/files/publications/tsa_-_use_of_advanced_imaging_technology_at_checkpoints.pdf.

52. "TSA Announces Measures to Implement Gender-Neutral Screening at Its Checkpoints," Transportation Security Administration, March 31, 2022, https://www.tsa.gov/news/press/releases/2022/03/31/tsa-announces-measures-implement-gender-neutral-screening-its.

53. Mark Hosenball, "Trump Confirms Al Qaeda Bomb-Maker, Mastermind of 'Underwear Bomber' Attempt and Other Attacks, Is Dead," Reuters, October 10, 2019, https://www.reuters.com/article/uk-usa-yemen-militant-idUKKBN1WP1YM.

54. Jörg Diehl and Matthias Gebauer, "Communications Error Enabled Explosive Package to Go Unchecked," *Der Spiegel*, November 11, 2010, https://www.spiegel.de/international/germany/german-security-lapse-communications-error-enabled-explosive-package-to-go-unchecked-a-728565.html.

55. Jörg Diehl and Matthias Gebauer, "Communications Error Enabled Explosive Package to Go Unchecked."

56. Chris Shelton, "Looking Back: The Printer Cartridge Bomb Plot," MSA Security, https://www.msasecurity.net/security-and-counterterrorism-blog/looking-back-the-printer-cartridge-bomb-plot.

57. News Desk, "Russia Says Bomb Downed Passenger Plane in Egypt," *PBS News Hour*, November 17, 2015, https://www.pbs.org/newshour/world/russia-says-bomb-downed-passenger-plane-in-egypt.

58. Jason Hanna, Michael Martinez, and Jennifer Deaton, "ISIS Publishes Photo of What It Says Is Bomb That Downed Russian Plane," CNN, November 13, 2015, https://www.cnn.com/2015/11/18/middleeast/metrojet-crash-dabiq-claim/index.html.

59. Robert Kriel and Paul Cruickshank, "Source: 'Sophisticated' Laptop Bomb on Somali Plane Got through X-Ray Machine," CNN, February 12, 2016, https://www.cnn.com/2016/02/11/africa/somalia-plane-bomb/index.html.

60. Robert Kriel and Paul Cruickshank, "Source: 'Sophisticated' Laptop Bomb on Somali Plane Got through X-Ray Machine."

61. David E. Sanger and Eric Schmitt, "U.S. Cyberweapons, Used against Iran and North Korea, Are a Disappointment against ISIS," *New York Times*, June 12, 2017, https://www.nytimes.com/2017/06/12/world/middleeast/isis-cyber.html.

62. David E. Sanger and Eric Schmitt, "U.S. Cyberweapons, Used against Iran and North Korea, Are a Disappointment against ISIS."

63. Alan Levin, "Race to Prevent Airline Terror Turns to Laptops, Thin Bombs," Bloomberg, May 16, 2017, https://www.bloomberg.com/news/articles/2017-05-16/race-to-prevent-airline-terror-turns-to-laptops-thin-bombs#xj4y7vzkg.

64. Barbara Starr and Rene Marsh, "AQAP Trying to Hide Explosives in Laptop Batteries, Official Says," CNN, March 22, 2017, https://edition.cnn.com/2017/03/21/politics/electronics-ban-devices-explosives-intelligence/.

65. Andrew Blankstein, "LAX Passenger Hides Objects in His Body; Bomb Squad Called," *Los Angeles Times*, March 7, 2007, https://www.latimes.com/archives/la-xpm-2007-mar-07-me-lax7-story.html.
66. Robert J. Bunker, "The Projected Al Qaeda Use of Body Cavity Suicide Bombs against High Value Targets."
67. Robert J. Bunker, "The Projected Al Qaeda Use of Body Cavity Suicide Bombs against High Value Targets."
68. Robert J. Bunker, "The Projected Al Qaeda Use of Body Cavity Suicide Bombs against High Value Targets."
69. Eileen Sullivan, "TSA Warning Describers Surgically Implanted Bombs," Associated Press, July 7, 2011, https://www.csmonitor.com/USA/Latest-News-Wires/2011/0707/TSA-warning-describes-surgically-implanted-bombs.
70. Eileen Sullivan, "TSA Warning Describers Surgically Implanted Bombs."
71. Keith Johnson and Siobhan Gorman, "Bomb Implants Emerge as Airline Terror Threat," *Wall Street Journal*, July 7, 2011, https://www.wsj.com/articles/SB10001424052702303365804576429741400016376.
72. Brian Knowlton and Nicola Clark, "U.S. Adds Body Bombs to Concerns on Air Travel," *New York Times*, July 6, 2011, https://www.nytimes.com/2011/07/07/world/07security.html.
73. "Remembering the Past, Informing the Future," Transportation Safety Administration, accessed January 26, 2023, https://www.tsa.gov/sites/default/files/mission_hall_exhibit_final_508.pdf.
74. Elaine Glusac, "Your Face Is, or Will Be, Your Boarding Pass," *New York Times*, December 7, 2021, https://www.nytimes.com/2021/12/07/travel/biometrics-airports-security.html.
75. "Computed Tomography," National Transportation Administration, accessed January 25, 2023, https://www.tsa.gov/computed-tomography#:~:text=Advantages%20of%20CT&text=Like%20existing%20CT%20technology%20used,the%20bag%20during%20checkpoint%20screening.
76. Sean M. Zeigler, Alexander C. Hou, Jeffrey Martini, Daniel M. Norton, Brian Phillips, Michael Schwille, Aaron Strong, and Nathan Vest, "Acquisition and Use of MANPADS against Commercial Aviation," RAND Corp., 2019, https://www.rand.org/content/dam/rand/pubs/research_reports/RR4300/RR4304/RAND_RR4304.pdf.
77. Michael Ashkenazi, Princess Mawuena Amuzu, Jan Grebe, Christof Kögler, and Marc Kösling, "Brief 47: MANPADS—A Terrorist Threat to Civilian Aviation?" Bonn International Center for Conversion, February 2013, https://www.files.ethz.ch/isn/160759/BICC_brief_47.pdf.
78. Michael Ashkenazi, Princess Mawuena Amuzu, Jan Grebe, Christof Kögler, and Marc Kösling, "Brief 47: MANPADS."
79. Bartholomew Elias, "Homeland Security: Protecting Airliners from Terrorist Missiles," Congressional Research Service, February 16, 2006, https://www.everycrsreport.com/reports/RL31741.html.
80. Gregory Crouch, *China's Wings: War, Intrigue, Romance, and Adventure in the Middle Kingdom during the Gold Age of Flight* (New York: Bantam, 2012), p. 157.
81. Sean M. Zeigler, Alexander C. Hou, Jeffrey Martini, Daniel M. Norton, Brian Phillips, Michael Schwille, Aaron Strong and Nathan Vest, "Acquisition and Use of MANPADS against Commercial Aviation."
82. Sean M. Zeigler, Alexander C. Hou, Jeffrey Martini, Daniel M. Norton, Brian Phillips, Michael Schwille, Aaron Strong and Nathan Vest, "Acquisition and Use of MANPADS against Commercial Aviation."
83. Margaret L. Rogg, "Sudanese Airliner with 60 on Board Downed by Missile," *New York Times*, August 18, 1986, https://www.nytimes.com/1986/08/18/world/sudanese-airliner-with-60-on-board-downed-by-missile.html.
84. Martin Landauer, "The Threat from MANPADS," Royal United Services Institute for Defence and Security Studies, November 14, 2007, https://rusi.org/publication/threat-manpads.
85. "Attacked Plane Lands in Tel Aviv," CNN, airdate November 28, 2002, https://edition.cnn.com/2002/WORLD/africa/11/28/kenya.plane/.

86. Bartholomew Elias, "Homeland Security: Protecting Airliners from Terrorist Missiles."
87. Jack Detsch, "The U.S. Left Billions Worth of Weapons in Afghanistan," *Foreign Policy*, April 28, 2022, https://foreignpolicy.com/2022/04/28/the-u-s-left-billions-worth-of-weapons-in-afghanistan/.
88. Thomas Withington, "Stung by Stingers," *Bulletin of the Atomic Scientists*, May/June 2003, https://journals.sagepub.com/doi/pdf/10.2968/059003005.
89. Bartholomew Elias, "Homeland Security: Protecting Airliners from Terrorist Missiles."
90. Bartholomew Elias, "Homeland Security: Protecting Airliners from Terrorist Missiles."
91. Bartholomew Elias, "Homeland Security: Protecting Airliners from Terrorist Missiles."
92. Arie Egozi, "PARIS: El Al Fields First C-MUSIC Protected 737," *Flight Global*, June 19, 2013, https://www.flightglobal.com/paris-el-al-fields-first-c-music-protected-737/110243.article.
93. Arieh O'Sullivan, "Israeli Tech Uses Lasers to Protect Civilian Aircraft," *Jerusalem Post*, October 6, 2011, https://www.jpost.com/defense/israeli-tech-uses-lasers-to-protect-civilian-aircraft#:~:text=Mike%20Yanuv%20of%20El%2DOp,civilian%20air%20liners%20in%20Israel.
94. "How Works Anti-Missile Defense System on El Al Commercial Aircraft?" *AIRLIVE*, October 8, 2020, https://airlive.net/how-works-anti-missile-defense-system-on-el-al-commercial-aircraft/.
95. Michael Goldstein, "FedEx to Protect Planes from Man-Portable Missile Launchers with Anti-Missile Lasers," *Forbes*, January 18, 2022, https://www.forbes.com/sites/michaelgoldstein/2022/01/18/fedex-plans-to-protect-its-pilots-and-planes-with-anti-missile-lasers/?sh=10c122041107.
96. David Ensor and CNN Staff, "Tape Purports to Show Missile Attack on Cargo Jet," CNN, November 26, 2003, https://edition.cnn.com/2003/WORLD/meast/11/25/sprj.irq.missile.tape/index.html.

Bibliography

"Air India Flight 181/182." Flight Aviation Safety Network. Accessed January 6, 2023. https://aviation-safety.net/database/record.php?id=19850623-2.
Amati, Giacomo. "FBI Arrest 1988 Lockerbie Bombing Suspect." *Simple Flying*, December 11, 2022. https://simpleflying.com/fbi-arrest-1988-lockerbie-bombing-suspect/.
Ashkenazi, Michael, Princess Mawuena Amuzu, Jan Grebe, Christof Kögler, and Marc Kösling. "Brief 47: MANPADS—A Terrorist Threat to Civilian Aviation?" *Bonn International Center for Conversion*, February 2013. https://www.files.ethz.ch/isn/160759/BICC_brief_47.pdf.
"Attacked Plane Lands in Tel Aviv." CNN, airdate November 28, 2002. https://edition.cnn.com/2002/WORLD/africa/11/28/kenya.plane/.
Baum, Philip. *Violence in the Skies: A History of Aircraft Hijacking and Bombing*. West Sussex, England: Summersdale, 2016.
Belluck, Pam, with Kenneth Chang. "A Nation Challenged: The Investigation; Shoes Were a 'Homemade Bomb,' F.B.I. Agent Says." *New York Times*, December 29, 2001. https://www.nytimes.com/2001/12/29/us/a-nation-challenged-the-investigation-shoes-were-a-homemade-bomb-fbi-agent-says.html.
Biello, David. "Liquid Explosives Linked to Terror Plot." *Scientific American*, August 10, 2006. https://www.scientificamerican.com/article/liquid-explosives-linked/.
Blankstein, Andrew. "LAX Passenger Hides Objects in His Body; Bomb Squad Called." *Los Angeles Times*, March 7, 2007. https://www.latimes.com/archives/la-xpm-2007-mar-07-me-lax7-story.html.
Brown, Gary. "The Monday After: Airline Bombings in '50s Led to Tighter Security." *CantonRep.com | The Repository*. January 26, 2010. https://www.cantonrep.com/story/

news/politics/elections/county/2010/01/26/the-monday-after-airline-bombings/42211630007/.

Bunker, Robert J. "The Projected Al Qaeda Use of Body Cavity Suicide Bombs against High Value Targets." *Los Angeles County Terrorism Early Warning Group—GroupIntel Network*, March 2011. https://nation.time.com/wp-content/uploads/sites/8/2011/07/bunker-groupintel_bodycavitybombs.pdf.

Clark, Emily. "How Has the Global Terror Threat Shaped Airline Security and Just How Confident Can You Be?" ABC News (Australian Broadcasting Corp.), airdate July 30, 2017. https://www.abc.net.au/news/2017-07-30/how-terror-incidents-have-shaped-global-airline-security/8757450.

"Computed Tomography." National Transportation Administration. Accessed January 25, 2023. https://www.tsa.gov/computed-tomography#:~:text=Advantages%20of%20CT&text=Like%20existing%20CT%20technology%20used,the%20bag%20during%20checkpoint%20screening.

Crouch, Gregory. *China's Wings: War, Intrigue, Romance, and Adventure in the Middle Kingdom during the Gold Age of Flight.* New York: Bantam, 2012.

Detsch, Jack. "The U.S. Left Billions Worth of Weapons in Afghanistan." *Foreign Policy*, April 28, 2022. https://foreignpolicy.com/2022/04/28/the-u-s-left-billions-worth-of-weapons-in-afghanistan/.

Diehl, Jörg, and Matthias Gebauer. "Communications Error Enabled Explosive Package to Go Unchecked." *Der Spiegel*, November 11, 2010. https://www.spiegel.de/international/germany/german-security-lapse-communications-error-enabled-explosive-package-to-go-unchecked-a-728565.html.

Dixon, Jennifer, and Jim Schaefer. "Northwest Bomb Attempt: Response Was Botched in Aftermath of Flight 253 Landing." *Detroit Free Press*, September 10, 2014. https://www.freep.com/story/news/nation/2014/09/10/underwear-bomber-nwa-253/15392267/.

Egozi, Arie. "PARIS: El Al Fields First C-MUSIC Protected 737." *Flight Global*, June 19, 2013. https://www.flightglobal.com/paris-el-al-fields-first-c-music-protected-737/110243.article.

Elias, Bartholomew. "Homeland Security: Protecting Airliners from Terrorist Missiles." *Congressional Research Service*, February 16, 2006. https://www.everycrsreport.com/reports/RL31741.html.

Ensor, David, and CNN Staff. "Tape Purports to Show Missile Attack on Cargo Jet." CNN, November 26, 2003. https://edition.cnn.com/2003/WORLD/meast/11/25/sprj.irq.missile.tape/index.html.

"Flight Terror Suspect Abdulmutallab Charged with Trying to Blow Up Jet." *The Guardian*, December 27, 2009. https://www.theguardian.com/world/2009/dec/27/us-terror-flight-abdulmutallab-charged.

Garrett, Ronnie. "Explosives Detection Goes to the Dogs." *Airport Improvement Magazine*, May–June 2011. https://airportimprovement.com/article/explosives-detection-goes-dogs#:~:text=The%20success%20of%20the%20Transportation,it%20was%20set%20to%20detonate.

Gerace, Diane. "A Look at How Airport Security Has Evolved Post-9/11." Philadelphia International Airport. Accessed January 15, 2022. https://www.phl.org/newsroom/911-security-impact.

Gero, David. *Flights of Terror: Aerial Hijack and Sabotage Since 1930.* Somerset, England: Haynes Publishing, 2009.

Glusac, Elaine. "Your Face Is, or Will Be, Your Boarding Pass." *New York Times*, December 7, 2021. https://www.nytimes.com/2021/12/07/travel/biometrics-airports-security.html.

Goldstein, Michael. "FedEx to Protect Planes from Man-Portable Missile Launchers with Anti-Missile Lasers." *Forbes*, January 18, 2022. https://www.forbes.com/sites/michaelgoldstein/2022/01/18/fedex-plans-to-protect-its-pilots-and-planes-with-anti-missile-lasers/?sh=10c122041107.

"The Government of Canada Response to the Commission of Inquiry into the Investigation of the Bombing of Air India Flight 182." *Public Safety Canada*, July 27, 2022. https://www.publicsafety.gc.ca/cnt/rsrcs/pblctns/rspns-cmmssn/index-en.aspx.

Grabell, Michael. "U.S. Government Glossed Over Cancer Concerns as It Rolled Out

Airport X-Ray Scanner." *ProPublica*, November 1, 2011. https://www.propublica.org/article/u.s.-government-glossed-over-cancer-concerns-as-it-rolled-out-airport-x-ray.

Hanna, Jason, Michael Martinez, and Jennifer Deaton. "ISIS Publishes Photo of What It Says Is Bomb That Downed Russian Plane." CNN, November 13, 2015. https://www.cnn.com/2015/11/18/middleeast/metrojet-crash-dabiq-claim/index.html.

Herridge, Catherine (moderator). "Aspen Security Forum: TSA—Toward a Risk-Based Approach to Aviation Security." Aspen Institute, July 24, 2014. https://www.aspensecurityforum.org/2014-videos.

"History: Richard Reid's Shoes." FBI. Accessed October 22, 2022. https://www.fbi.gov/history/artifacts/richard-reids-shoes.

Hosenball, Mark. "Trump Confirms Al Qaeda Bomb-Maker, Mastermind of 'Underwear Bomber' Attempt and Other Attacks, Is Dead." Reuters, October 10, 2019. https://www.reuters.com/article/uk-usa-yemen-militant-idUKKBN1WP1YM.

"How Works Anti-Missile Defense System on El Al Commercial Aircraft?" *AIRLIVE*, October 8, 2020. https://airlive.net/how-works-anti-missile-defense-system-on-el-al-commercial-aircraft/.

Jenkins, Brian Michael. "The Terrorist Threat to Commercial Aviation." Santa Monica, CA: RAND Corporation, 1989. https://www.rand.org/pubs/papers/P7540.html.

Johnson, Howard. "Interview with Howard Johnson." Westchester Public Library Oral History Project, August 13, 1999. http://www.duneacres.org/Archives/Aviation.pdf.

Johnson, Keith, and Siobhan Gorman. "Bomb Implants Emerge as Airline Terror Threat." *Wall Street Journal*, July 7, 2011. https://www.wsj.com/articles/SB10001424052702303365804576429741400016763.

Kahn, E.J., Jr. "It Has No Name." *The New Yorker*, November 7, 1953. https://www.newyorker.com/magazine/1953/11/14/it-has-no-name.

"The Kanishka Bombing, 20 years on Lest We Forget." *The Tribune* (India), July 10, 2005. https://www.tribuneindia.com/2005/20050710/spectrum/main1.htm.

Knowlton, Brian, and Nicola Clark. "U.S. Adds Body Bombs to Concerns on Air Travel." *New York Times*, July 6, 2011. https://www.nytimes.com/2011/07/07/world/07security.html.

Kriel, Robert, and Paul Cruickshank. "Source: 'Sophisticated' Laptop Bomb on Somali Plane Got through X-Ray Machine." CNN, February 12, 2016. https://www.cnn.com/2016/02/11/africa/somalia-plane-bomb/index.html.

Landauer, Martin. "The Threat from MANPADS." Royal United Services Institute for Defence and Security Studies, November 14, 2007. https://rusi.org/publication/threat-manpads.

Levin, Alan. "Race to Prevent Airline Terror Turns to Laptops, Thin Bombs." Bloomberg, May 16, 2017. https://www.bloomberg.com/news/articles/2017-05-16/race-to-prevent-airline-terror-turns-to-laptops-thin-bombs#xj4y7vzkg.

New York Daily News Staff. "Richard C. Reid, the Shoe Bomber, Was Subdued by Flight Attendants and Passengers in 2001." *New York Daily News*, December 21, 2016. https://www.nydailynews.com/news/world/shoe-bomber-subdued-flight-attendants-passengers-2001-article-1.934624.

News Desk. "Russia Says Bomb Downed Passenger Plane in Egypt." *PBS News Hour*, November 17, 2015. https://www.pbs.org/newshour/world/russia-says-bomb-downed-passenger-plane-in-egypt.

O'Connor, Anahad, and Eric Schmitt, "Terror Attempt Seen as Man Tries to Ignite Device on Jet." *New York Times*, December 25, 2009. https://www.nytimes.com/2009/12/26/us/26plane.html.

O'Sullivan, Arieh. "Israeli Tech Uses Lasers to Protect Civilian Aircraft." *Jerusalem Post*, October 6, 2011. https://www.jpost.com/defense/israeli-tech-uses-lasers-to-protect-civilian-aircraft#:~:text=Mike%20Yanuv%20of%20El%2DOp,civilian%20air%20liners%20in%20Israel.

"Remembering the Past, Informing the Future." Transportation Safety Administration. Accessed January 26, 2023. https://www.tsa.gov/sites/default/files/mission_hall_exhibit_final_508.pdf.

Robertson, Nic, Paul Cruickshank, and Tim Lister. "Document Shows Origins of 2006 Plot for Liquid Bombs on Planes." CNN, April 30, 2012. https://www.cnn.com/2012/04/30/world/al-qaeda-documents/index.html.

Rogers, Phil. "80 Years Later, Plane Bombing Remains a Mystery." NBC Chicago, October 8, 2013. https://www.nbcchicago.com/news/local/80-years-later-plane-bombing-remains-a-mystery/1964534/.

Rogg, Margaret L. "Sudanese Airliner with 60 on Board Downed by Missile." *New York Times*, August 18, 1986. https://www.nytimes.com/1986/08/18/world/sudanese-airliner-with-60-on-board-downed-by-missile.html.

Sanger, David E., and Eric Schmitt. "U.S. Cyberweapons, Used against Iran and North Korea, Are a Disappointment against ISIS." *New York Times*, June 12, 2017. https://www.nytimes.com/2017/06/12/world/middleeast/isis-cyber.html.

"Seven Die as Plane Crashes in Flames." *New York Times*, October 11, 1933. https://timesmachine.nytimes.com/timesmachine/1933/10/11/99936550.html?pageNumber=1.

Shane, Scott. "Inside Al Qaeda's Plot to Blow Up an American Airliner." *New York Times*, February 22, 2017. https://www.nytimes.com/2017/02/22/us/politics/anwar-awlaki-underwear-bomber-abdulmutallab.html.

Shane, Scott. "The Lessons of Anwar al-Awlaki." *New York Times*, August 27, 2015. https://www.nytimes.com/2015/08/30/magazine/the-lessons-of-anwar-al-awlaki.html.

Shane, Scott, and Eric Lipton. "Passengers' Quick Action Halted Attack." *New York Times*, December 26, 2009. https://web.archive.org/web/20101201060215/http://www.nytimes.com/2009/12/27/us/27plane.html.

Shelton, Chris. "Looking Back: The Printer Cartridge Bomb Plot." MSA Security. https://www.msasecurity.net/security-and-counterterrorism-blog/looking-back-the-printer-cartridge-bomb-plot.

Smith, Paul J. "Transnational Terrorism and the al Qaeda Model: Confronting New Realities." *Parameters* 32, no. 2 (2002). https://press.armywarcollege.edu/parameters/vol32/iss2/13/.

Starr, Barbara, and Rene Marsh. "AQAP Trying to Hide Explosives in Laptop Batteries, Official Says." CNN, March 22, 2017. https://edition.cnn.com/2017/03/21/politics/electronics-ban-devices-explosives-intelligence/.

Sullivan, Eileen. "TSA Warning Describers Surgically Implanted Bombs." Associated Press, July 7, 2011. https://www.csmonitor.com/USA/Latest-News-Wires/2011/0707/TSA-warning-describes-surgically-implanted-bombs.

Summers, Chris. "Deadly Puzzle Remains a Mystery." BBC News, March 16, 2005. http://news.bbc.co.uk/2/hi/americas/4344051.stm.

Swopes, Bryan R. "10 October 1933." *This Day in Aviation*. Accessed December 27, 2022. https://www.thisdayinaviation.com/.

Thomas, Cathy Booth. "Courage in the Air." *TIME Magazine*, September 1, 2002. https://web.archive.org/web/20100604162640/http://www.time.com/time/covers/1101020909/aattendants.html.

"TSA Announces Measures to Implement Gender-Neutral Screening at Its Checkpoints." Transportation Security Administration, March 31, 2022. https://www.tsa.gov/news/press/releases/2022/03/31/tsa-announces-measures-implement-gender-neutral-screening-its.

"Use of Advanced Imaging Technology at Checkpoints—Fiscal Year 2019 Report to Congress." TransportationSecurity Administration, May 10, 2019. https://www.dhs.gov/sites/default/files/publications/tsa_-_use_of_advanced_imaging_technology_at_checkpoints.pdf.

Wald, Matthew L. "Long Before Verdict, Lockerbie Changed Airport Security." *New York Times*, January 31, 2001. https://www.nytimes.com/2001/01/31/world/long-before-verdict-lockerbie-changed-airport-security.html.

Withington, Thomas. "Stung by Stingers," *Bulletin of the Atomic Scientists,* May/June 2003. https://journals.sagepub.com/doi/pdf/10.2968/059003005.

Yoo, John. "From Gettysburg to Anwar al-Awlaki." *Wall Street Journal*, October 3, 2011. https://www.wsj.com/articles/SB10001424052970204226204576603114226847494.

Zeigler, Sean M., Alexander C. Hou, Jeffrey Martini, Daniel M. Norton, Brian Phillips, Michael Schwille, Aaron Strong, and Nathan Vest. "Acquisition and Use of MANPADS against Commercial Aviation." RAND Corp., 2019. https://www.rand.org/content/dam/rand/pubs/research_reports/RR4300/RR4304/RAND_RR4304.pdf.

Three

Conventional Assaults and Cyberattacks on Airports and Airliners

The principal reason that a terrorist may select an airport as a target is because it is much easier to gain access to such a facility than, say, to a Boeing 787. Anyone can enter one. Then, too, an array of nationalities will likely be present in an international airport at any given moment, meaning that travelers from numerous countries may be impacted by a single terrorist strike. The result: the act of violence becomes a magnet for the global media. That said, nearly all of those who have taken part in airport offensives have been arrested, wounded, or killed, suggesting that their organizations weigh the value of such high-profile targets to be worth the costs to their operatives. In one early episode, which was conducted at the Munich-Reim Airport in West Germany, a shuttle bus was in the killers' crosshairs in a massacre that reverberated around the world.

It was in the late afternoon on February 10, 1970, when three commandos, rather than hijacking or sabotaging a commercial carrier, took a simpler, safer, and cheaper route by assaulting a busload of unarmed passengers who were about to board El Al Flight 435. The plane had traveled from Tel Aviv to Munich, and soon it would be departing for London. As to the perpetrators, they were pro–Palestinian militants who represented two groups: an entity calling itself the Action Organization for the Liberation of Palestine and the Democratic Popular Front for the Liberation of Palestine (DPFLP), a spinoff of the PFLP. Armed with submachine guns and a grenade, two of the men were Jordanian and the other one Egyptian.

The operation kicked off when the shuttle, which was holding fifteen passengers, prepared to leave the terminal for the airliner. The lead commando stood up and pulled a grenade from his jacket pocket. Instantly, however, he found himself overpowered by Uri Cohen, an El Al pilot, who was also on the shuttle and recognized what was happening. In a swift yet decisive confrontation, one that slightly harmed the pilot, Cohen succeeded in sparing the passengers from the brunt of the blast. Not so lucky was the man who pulled the pin. "The Arab terrorist had his hand blown off when the grenade exploded," reported the Jewish Telegraphic Agency.[1]

Resuming the attack, the two remaining commandos commenced firing into the bus, killing a thirty-two-year-old engineer from Haifa, Israel. Eight others were wounded in the maelstrom, some of them critically. Among the latter was the Israeli actress and peace activist Hanna Maron, who required a leg amputation.

Of course, the fact that the unprovoked assault was directed at El Al customers was not lost on the Israeli leadership. "An act of cowardice perpetrated by people who are incapable of fighting on or within the frontiers of Israel," is how Ezer Weizman, Israel's minister of transport and future president characterized it.[2] Within minutes, police apprehended the perpetrators. Hospitalized for their injuries, the men were subsequently imprisoned, although seven months later they would be released as part of the Dawson Field hostage-exchange agreement.

Not surprisingly, the violence visited upon the passengers of the Munich shuttle would not be a one-off. More the opposite. "It was an event that opened a series of attacks on Israeli aircraft and flights, which occurred in airports in Israel and around the world during the 1970s," reported the Israeli news source YNET.[3]

One such offensive took place three years later when pro–Palestinian militants embarked on a shooting spree at the Leonardo da Vinci International Airport. The Rome facility was not their ultimate target, though. The bloodshed inside the terminal was merely the opening salvo in the extremists' strategy to gain access to the tarmac and two airliners.

So it was that the team of terrorists, having assembled in a transit lounge on the afternoon of December 17, 1973, walked through the airport with their carry-on luggage, comporting themselves as carefree travelers. The all-male group headed for the security barrier, the section of the airport that contained the search booths and metal detectors through which all passengers had to pass before boarding an aircraft. "A few steps before reaching the security fence," writes Paul Hofmann, "they reportedly pulled submachine guns out of their hand luggage and starting firing, rushing forward."[4] Some of the gunmen shot at Italian police officers, while others sprinted outside to a Pan Am airliner. Firing into the Boeing 707's passenger cabins, they also hurled grenades and a phosphorus bomb. The attack, which was intended to gain the release of two Palestinian prisoners in Athens, would progress to the hijacking of a nearby Lufthansa airliner twenty-two minutes later.

In other assaults, the perpetrators have selected targets that were positioned solely within international airports. They have homed in on airline ticket counters, for instance, in an attempt to infer the customers' national origins and liquidate them. In these incidents, vendors selling airfare for carriers based in Israel and its ally, the United States, have been the principal targets.

The deadliest episode of this type was a coordinated strike on ticket counters in Rome and Vienna, which transpired on December 27, 1985. In the Rome offensive, four guerrillas belonging to the Abu Nidal Organization armed themselves with rifles and grenades, then swallowed simulants. Arriving at Leonardo da Vinci International Airport, they strode to the El Al and Trans World Airlines ticket counters and commenced firing on customers waiting in line. Killed were thirteen civilians and three terrorists, with another seventy-five people wounded. The ANO had ordered the extremists to single out the El Al ticket counter, claiming its clientele would include Israeli soldiers in disguise. This was untrue, of course, and was meant to motivate the shooters. As an afterthought, the gunmen added the TWA counter to the offensive on the assumption that its clientele would consist of Americans as well as Israelis. Investigators would learn that the terrorists had further planned to hijack an El Al airliner to Tel Aviv, one loaded with Israelis, then blow it up over the city in a suicide mission. When the guerrillas came face to face with an intimidating contingent of security and police officers at the Rome facility, however, they ditched this aspect of the plan.

Coinciding with the Rome operation, three additional Abu Nidal gunmen arrived at the Vienna (Schwechat) International Airport and opened fire on customers awaiting service—once again, at an El Al ticket counter. Three civilians and one terrorist died, while another thirty people were wounded. Although the airport in Frankfurt, West Germany, was to have been attacked as well, it was dropped from the plan at the eleventh hour.

Besides shootings, airports have also been the site of bombings. In one episode, a massive explosion rocked a section of the Kimpo Airport in Seoul, South Korea, on September 14, 1986. It happened six days before the start of the Asian Games, or Asiad, which the country was set to host. "The blast, according to the authorities, may have occurred inside a metal garbage can placed by one of the many large tinted glass plates that enclose the building," reported Clyde Haberman.[5] Five people perished in the ordeal and thirty-six more were wounded; most of those who died or sustained serious injuries were located near a taxi stand outside the terminal. Although the killers were never formally identified, South Korean officials attributed the violence to operatives working for the North Korean government. Presumably, the purpose of the crime was to disrupt the forthcoming Asian Games.

Near the city of Reus, Spain, a decade later, this strategy was repeated, but by a different group and for a different reason. Members of Euskadi Ta Askatasuna (ETA), a Basque separatist group, planted an explosive device in a garbage can located in a passenger lounge at Tarragona International Airport. The date was July 21, 1996, and the ETA phoned airport officials shortly before the device was set to discharge, warning them of the impending explosion. Unfortunately, the security officers did not have sufficient time to evacuate the 1,000-plus people in the terminal. Thirty-three people were injured, mostly British tourists, although their nationality was not an issue for the perpetrators. Rather, the ETA's focus was on a struggle for a sovereign Basque homeland, and the British tourists just happened to be situated near the explosive device at the time of detonation.

Shortly after the attack, officials beefed up security, hiring more security officers and implementing supplemental safety measures. "Among them [was] the removal of airport trash cans," reported Al Goodman, "like the one where the bomb was hidden."[6]

Unfazed, the ETA would persist in committing indiscriminate violence, subsequently bombing the Santander Airport in Estella, a port in northern Spain and a popular tourist resort. Planting the explosive device in an airport parking lot, an ETA spokesperson, once again, phoned officials to warn them about the forthcoming blast. While the police were able to evacuate the parking lot, thereby saving lives, the discharge itself was far from benign. "There is extensive material damage," said a police officer on the scene.[7] In addition to the structural damage, a dozen vehicles were incinerated in the conflagration.

As could be expected, the year 2001 would be a watershed in airport security. Yet even before the ghastly events of September 11, the year had witnessed another attack at an air facility, this one in Kashmir, India. The date was January 17, and the site was Sheikh Ul Alam International Airport. "The battle," writes Barry Bearak, "began when guerrillas dressed in the regulation camouflage of the Indian paramilitary arrived at a security cordon outside the airport, where departing passengers have their baggage screened and searched."[8] Gunmen opened fire on the police in a one-hour shootout that would spread to two airport shops, killing eleven bystanders and three law enforcement officers in the process. All six of the assailants, who represented the Pakistan-based militant organization Lashkar-e-Toiba, would also die in the assault. The group was opposed to Indian rule in Kashmir, and its objective was to intimidate the existing leadership.

Several months later, and in response to the al-Qaeda attacks at the World Trade Center and the Pentagon, the U.S. government evaluated the vulnerability of domestic airports and put into place new measures to better protect them from terrorist operations. Besides creating the Transportation

Security Administration and federalizing airport security, supplemental actions included restricted parking near the airports' drop-off and pick-up zones; a greater security presence in the facilities' secondary and peripheral structures; enhanced training of security officials in behavioral profiling practices; and heightened surveillance throughout the facilities, including attention to unauthorized articles and loiterers on the premises. The number of special-security patrols in airports was also doubled; the visibility of such patrols, which sometimes included canines, was considered a deterrent in itself. As well, the vetting systems used to select employees were reevaluated and improved, while the quality of airports' security programs was to be assessed more often, both overtly and covertly, in order to gauge the perceptiveness and efficiency of security personnel. Some airports went even further, exploring innovative ways to redesign their physical structures so as to better prevent, or withstand, terrorist attacks. Such options included relocating airport parking lots a greater distance from terminals themselves and eliminating multi-level parking garages that could be vulnerable to vehicle bombs.

Even as American airports became better fortified in the twenty-first century, those in the European Union (EU) diverged widely in their capacities to avert acts of terror. In the main, this was because the EU required all of the airports in its member nations to comply with a uniform set of security standards, but only in those areas located behind the airports' security checkpoints. As to the remaining areas—those not behind checkpoints—the EU allowed each country to decide whether, and how, to protect them. And herein lay the problem. An act of barbarity committed at a Belgian airport is instructive in this regard.

In 2016, the airport that served Brussels was widely viewed as lacking proper, reliable security protocols and suitable personnel. Even its own security division was critical of the company that operated the facility, arguing that the airport was exposed at a time and place when it could well become a terrorist target. It was a fair point. Brussels, in a sense, served as a symbol of western Europe, as it was the headquarters of the European Union and hosted national leaders from across the continent throughout the year. At the same time, the Belgian capital was also home to one of the largest concentrations of Muslims in Europe, which included a number of Islamist extremists. Most lived in the Molenbeek district, located a stone's throw away from EU headquarters. And the juxtaposition of these contrasting elements contributed to a certain tension in the capital city. It was in this context that the Brussels Airport, along with a metro station, came under assault by Islamic State terrorists on March 22, 2016, in what Radio France Internationale deemed "the worst-ever attacks in the de facto capital of the European Union."[9]

On an ordinary Tuesday at 7:55—morning rush hour—three members of ISIS walked into the Brussels Airport in Zaventem, Belgium, carrying three suitcases that contained nail bombs. The nails had been added to intensify the carnage, acting as shrapnel. Once inside the building, the men fanned out across the departure hall, and three minutes later two of them detonated their explosive devices, obliterating the structure's interior. (Investigators could not determine why the third IED had not been denotated.) Then, one hour later, a fourth accomplice set off a bomb at the Maelbeek Metro Station. In these coordinated mass murders, thirty-two people died, together with the four terrorists, while another 340 people were injured, nearly 20 percent of them critically. The official response was immediate.

At the national level, the Belgian government deployed 18,000 troops to areas of concern as well as initiated aggressive police action aimed at detecting and shutting down terrorist cells across the country. "The Belgian police have carried out several hundred raids, detentions, and stops and searches," reported Human Rights Watch, with the organization proceeding to question the methods used in some of the law enforcement operations.[10] In all, seventy-two people were indicted on terror-related counts and another forty-three were convicted.[11]

At the Brussels Airport itself, an analysis of the ISIS bombing revealed that no security measures had been in place at the terminal's entrance; there had been nothing to prevent, or even discourage, the bombers. It was further discovered that the Brussels Airport Company had received a request to construct a security checkpoint at the entrance in December 2015—three months before the terrorist attack—but had declined due to the costs involved.[12]

After the ISIS strike, the police division at Brussels Airport, still worried about the situation, penned an open letter pointing out the continuing dangers.[13] One issue for the police was the fact that non-travelers were permitted access to the departure hall and other areas of the terminal without being subject to any type of scrutiny. Another was that the airport's vetting and hiring procedures were dubious, especially for baggage handlers and others having access to the restricted areas. It seems that the airport had knowingly hired numerous workers with criminal backgrounds.[14] In time, these and other problems, such as bureaucratic incompetence, were acknowledged and addressed in part, although not to everyone's satisfaction.

As could be expected, the terrorist operation in Brussels had an impact on international airports in other nations. Several countries, among them the United States, reassessed their own protocols and subsequently boosted security at domestic airports. And while bombings and shootings at airports have not occurred on a major scale in recent years, the situation could, of course, change at any moment. Certainly, security operations at air facilities are frequently being challenged, and sometimes in unforeseen ways.

The Impact of Covid-19 on Air Security

In 2020, for instance, coronavirus disease, particularly Covid-19, swept the globe and impacted countless aspects of daily life. Although virtually all businesses were affected, the outbreak bore down especially hard on the airline industry due to the sharply reduced demand for air travel. Among the costs of the contagion: sixty-four airlines had filed for bankruptcy or shuttered their operations by the spring of 2023, among them mainstays like Alitalia, at one time Italy's flag carrier.

In terms of the pandemic's effects on airport facilities in the United States, public health experts warned that the heavily-trafficked venues were risky and called for stringent precautions to ensure travelers' safety. "Scientists say airports are more dangerous than airplanes," Christopher Elliott wrote early in the pandemic, "at least when it comes to your chances of being infected with the coronavirus."[15] The reason was because international airports teemed with people from myriad nations who congregated for hours on end, often clustering at ticket counters, security checkpoints, and baggage carousels. Furthermore, a considerable number of these travelers did not appear to fully understand the nature and mechanisms of SARS-CoV-2, the pathogen that causes the respiratory ailment, and therefore disregarded, or only sporadically complied with, masking requirements and related practices designed to reduce the spread of infection. Yet even those travelers who did wear masks were placed at risk on occasion, since the TSA insisted that face coverings be removed at airport checkpoints so that security officers could match the individuals' faces with their identification photos. At this critical moment in the boarding process, then, protection from terrorism outflanked protection from the virus, a prioritization that displeased a number of public health authorities.[16] On this point, a solution was offered by advocates of iris recognition technology (i.e., "iris scanning"), who made the case that the biometric procedure, which involves only the surface of the eye, could confirm a traveler's identity while also adhering to coronavirus prevention measures.[17] To date, however, it is facial recognition technology that is fast becoming the preference of airports, not ocular-based biometric authentication.

The pandemic also witnessed a dismaying rise in travelers who refused to abide by the new procedures that were put into place on airliners and at airports, commonsense practices that were designed to help prevent infection with the potentially lethal virus. All too often, such individuals not only failed to comply but were also belligerent in the process. During a seven-month period in 2021, for instance, the TSA processed 4,102 reports of Covid-related disputes, while the FAA, a few months later, received an additional 3,500 documented occurrences.[18] At times, the resources needed to monitor and manage disruptive outbursts of this sort, combined with the other pandemic-related duties being shouldered by TSA and airport personnel, competed for the time and attention of those whose responsibilities centered on detecting and dealing with potential terrorist threats.

As of this writing, the Covid-19 virus, having infected more than 757 million people and caused the deaths of nearly seven million of them, appears to be ebbing.[19] At the same time, many airports around the world have begun phasing in advanced technologies that entail little or no human contact, while also ensuring security in airports and on airliners. Though several major airports, prior to the coronavirus outbreak, had begun putting into service these innovative measures, the global health emergency spotlighted their value and hastened their implementation. "Just as aviation security changed after 9/11," writes Larry Anderson, "the COVID-19 crisis is expected to lead to a paradigm shift to create a safer and more secure environment."[20] Indeed, it is already in progress. If dangerous variants of SARS-CoV-2 emerge and threaten the population once again, or if a unique pathogen materializes and poses a grave health threat, airports will be better able to weather them, and with less disruption and risk to travelers, TSA staff, and facility employees. Regarding airport security measures, their effectiveness is expected to increase as more facilities transition to the sophisticated screening and surveillance technologies that continue to be developed.

CYBERATTACKS ON AIRPORTS AND COMMERCIAL AIRLINERS

As airports and airliners become better protected from conventional terrorist operations, the focus of aviation security experts has expanded to encompass the prospect of cyberattacks. The overarching advantage of exchanging an AK-47 for a computer keyboard is obvious: the latter does not require the perpetrator to be present at a targeted site. The person could conceivably devise and execute the attack from the other side of the world, and with little or no risk to life and limb. And whereas a conventional terrorist operation may impact hundreds, even thousands, of lives, a single cyberattack could affect millions, especially if directed at a nation's infrastructure. If the attempt were to fail, the perpetrator would have lost nothing but time and effort. But if it were to succeed, the cyber operation could result in massive damage and countless deaths, while bestowing upon the extremist organization the full attention of the global media.

As it stands, a marked difference exists between the types of cyberattacks that have been, and continue to be, directed at airports, and those that cybersecurity experts fear could be directed at airliners in flight. To date, cybercriminals who have targeted airports and airline offices have sought to access private information, disrupt the facilities' operations, or both. Data harvesting hacks have been frequent, hacks in which airline customers' personal information is stolen, then sold, on the dark web. In such cases, the tactics have ranged from phishing schemes to ransomware infiltrations. Cybercriminals aiming to disrupt or freeze airport operations have often accomplished it through denial-of-service attacks.

"'Denial of service' or 'DoS' describes the ultimate goal of a class of cyberattacks designed to render a service inaccessible," explains the National Cyber Security Centre in London. "DoS events are often brought about by a service's underlying systems being overloaded."[21] Some DoS actions fall into a subcategory known as Distributed Denial of Service (DDoS) attacks, defined as efforts "to interfere with normal operations of an online service (such as a website or app) by overwhelming it with repeated automated requests for data from multiple sources."[22] By overwhelming and thus temporarily paralyzing online activities, including digital transactions, DoS and DDoS strategies are capable of inflicting considerable harm on an airport or airline company.

One early DDoS attack targeted LOT Polish Airlines in 2015, causing 1,400 passengers to be stranded in Warsaw. This was only the beginning of the air-related cybercrime spree, however, with such strikes quickly growing in number, reach, and destructiveness. On October 10, 2022, for instance, a band of Russian hackers, dubbed "Killnet," launched a sweeping DDoS operation that brought down the public-facing websites of more than a dozen U.S. airports, including those in Chicago, Los Angeles, New York, Atlanta, Des Moines, and Denver. Although the perpetrators did not gain entry into vital air traffic control systems, their actions nevertheless created havoc for airports and airline passengers from coast to coast. With respect to the group's motive, Killnet, based in the Russian Federation, is thought to have had political motives. "The group 'Killnet' has been active since the beginning of the war in Ukraine," reported ABC News, "targeting Ukrainian allies and recently claiming credit for taking down government websites in the U.S."[23]

Subsequent cyber crimes have been even bolder and more detrimental. Between August 21 and September 5, 2018, British Airways was the target of a sophisticated cyber assault in which the perpetrators gained access to the personal data of 429,000 customers.[24] The information included the customers' names, street and email addresses, and credit card data, including CVCs (card verification codes). "The theft of data was the result of a Magecart attack," writes Eduard Kovacs, "where the cybercriminals plant malicious code on the website of a company in an effort to steal information provided by its customers."[25] More specifically, when unsuspecting users enter their information on online forms as they conduct financial transactions, it is "skimmed" and channeled to a Magecart collection server. "Skimmed credit cards are then sold on the dark web for $5 to $30 each and subsequently used to steal money," reports *Sansec*.[26] For the British Airways security breach, British authorities announced that the airline would be fined £183 million ($230 million), but this amount was eventually lowered to £25 million ($20 million). A fraction of the original amount, the fine did not include any compensation for the customers who were directly affected by the crime. Accordingly, 16,000 customers of British Airways filed, and ultimately settled, a class action suit against the company.

By far, the largest breach of this type was suffered by the Hong Kong–based Cathay Pacific Airlines, which experienced repeated malware attacks between March and October of 2018. One of them locked 500 Cathay employees out of their accounts. A more devastating one harvested user data. As an estimated 9,400,00 customers conducted online transactions with the airline, their personal information was stolen, including passport numbers, credit card data, birthdates, phone numbers, street and email addresses, flight numbers and dates, and identity card numbers. Not compromised, fortunately, were flight operations and safety systems. "It is quite clear that contraventions aside, Cathay adopted a lax attitude toward data governance, which fell short of the expectation of its affected passengers and the regulator," said Stephen Kai-yi Wong, Office of the Privacy Commissioner for Personal Data, Hong Kong.[27] The airline was fined $700,000.

Even in the absence of a malicious actor, confidential data may still be endangered if an airport lacks stringent security protocols. An incident at London's Heathrow Airport is illustrative. "In 2017," writes Stéphane Prevost, "UK's Heathrow airport was criticized for its negligence in protecting confidential information: one of the employees of the airport is said to have lost a USB key containing 76 folders and more than 1,000 confidential files relating to the identity of passengers, the routes taken by official members of the British government, and information related to the airport's surveillance cameras and runways."[28] Worsening matters, the USB key was neither encrypted nor password-protected. By chance, someone found it and returned the key to the authorities.

The fact is, formal cybersecurity assessments of airports around the globe have uncovered serious vulnerabilities in the overwhelming majority of them. Frequent flaws have included outdated, exploitable software, a lack of encryption and firewall protections, vulnerabilities in public clouds used for data storage, and the exposure of private information on the dark web.[29] All the while, malicious actors prowl the cybersphere, rummaging for, and acting upon, such weaknesses. "The cyberthreat is always moving," says Mike Vanguardia, a cybersecurity engineer for Boeing.[30]

While cybercrimes directed at airports have impeded the continuity of day-to-day operations and jeopardized customers' personal data, far more chilling is the prospect of a cyberterror attack directed at an airliner in flight. For several years, this scenario has been a genuine concern in cybersecurity circles.

"Cyberterrorism is the convergence of cyberspace and terrorism," says Dorothy E. Denning, a professor of computer science at Georgetown University. "It refers to unlawful attacks and threats of attacks against computers, networks and the information stored therein when done to intimidate or coerce a government or its people in furtherance of political or social objectives. Further, to qualify as cyberterrorism, an attack should result in violence against persons or property, or at least cause enough harm to generate fear."[31]

Vulnerability to cyberterrorism was the subject of a study conducted by IOActive, an information security service, which uncovered serious failings in commonly used satellite terminals. "Critical design flaws have been discovered in the firmware of popular satellite land equipment that could allow attackers to hijack and disrupt communications links to ships, airplanes, military operations, industrial facilities, and emergency services," writes Kelly Jackson Higgins.[32] "The vulnerabilities included what would appear to be backdoors, hardcoded credentials, undocumented and/or insecure protocols, and weak encryption algorithms," the report revealed.[33] By compromising vital systems from an external site, it is conceivable that an extremist entity could, in fact, commandeer and redirect an aircraft.

The Disappearance of Malaysia Airlines 370

The prospect of a terrorist entity seizing control of an airliner from a remote location came into public discourse following the disappearance of Malaysia Airlines Flight 370 (MH370) on March 8, 2014. The aircraft was a Boeing 777, and it carried 239 people. At 12:41 a.m., it departed from Kuala

Lumpur, Malaysia, bound for Beijing, China. Thirty-nine minutes later, as the aircraft was leaving Malaysian airspace and entering that of Vietnam, its transponder stopped transmitting a signal, radio communications ceased, and MH370 vanished from the radar screens of air traffic controllers in Malaysia. Although it had momentarily appeared on Vietnamese radar, it abruptly disappeared from it as well. The military, however, was temporarily able to track the plane, with the radar readings indicating that an aircraft, presumably MH370, was moving southwesterly toward the Malay Peninsula. A subsequent analysis of satellite data suggested that the aircraft thought to be MH370 may have remained in flight for a total of seven hours. It would not be located.

As could be expected when a Boeing 777 disappears, conjecture ruled the day, and it ran the gamut from the reasonable to the ridiculous. "On the internet," writes William Langewiesche, "you will find claims that the airplane has been found intact in the Cambodian jungle, that it was seen landing in an Indonesian river, that it flew into a time warp, that it was sucked into a black hole."[34] Other explanations would claim that MH370 was abducted by extraterrestrials, was liquidated for transporting politically-sensitive cargo, or was the outcome of a covert Russian plot designed to divert attention away from its invasion and annexation of Crimea that was underway at the time.[35]

The official story is that someone in the heavily-fortified cockpit flew the airliner southward until it ran out of fuel, then crashed it into the Indian Ocean. Lending credence to this hypothesis are pieces of shattered debris that purportedly began washing up onshore five months later, thousands of miles to the west of the proposed crash site. French judicial authorities, who participated in the case, analyzed some of this wreckage and determined "with certainty" that at least one piece of debris, a flaperon, came from MH370.[36] The wreckage was retrieved from the beaches of Réunion, Mauritius, Mozambique, Madagascar, and Tanzania, which is consistent with Indian Ocean currents.

Of significance as well, the Australian Transport Safety Board (ATSB), which also participated in the investigations, examined the hard drive of a flight simulator located in the captain's home. Programmed into it were thousands of simulations to different parts of the world; one model was "initially similar" to that of MH370.[37] Many investigators, along with the mass media, jumped on this new disclosure, regarding it as suspicious, if not incriminating. This is despite the fact that the ATSB made it clear that the course programmed into the captain's home simulator did not align precisely with the satellite data denoting MH370's apparent flight path. Rather, the journey of the ill-fated jetliner came to an end 900 miles to the northwest of the simulated flight.[38]

THREE. *Conventional Assaults and Cyberattacks* 93

A second hypothesis is that a mechanical failure or onboard fire forced the aircrew to shut down the airliner's electrical systems, hence the abrupt silence. Of course, either of these crises could have caused the aircraft to crash into the sea. But while the premise of a fire, in particular, seems plausible at first glance, it does not explain how a burning airliner could remain airborne for up to seven hours, assuming that the satellite data are accurate, and why the debris showed no signs of fire damage.

Still another proposition, a popular one in certain quarters, is that MH370 was being flown to the island of Diego Garcia, situated 2,100 miles southwest of Kuala Lumpur in the Indian Ocean. A British-controlled atoll, Diego Garcia is home to a vital, and highly secretive, U.S. military base, whose strategic location in the middle of the ocean guarantees it immense security. Among other activities, the base serves as a platform from which the U.S. launches military operations in the Middle East.

According to this scenario, the U.S. military shot down MH370 before the aircraft could deliberately crash into, or perhaps land at, the base at Diego Garcia. "This theory was deemed credible after it was discovered that the island landing strip was programmed into the MH370 pilot's home flight simulator," writes Lauren Piette.[39] Then, too, residents of the Maldives, a group of islands situated 725 miles north of Diego Garcia, reported watching as a large airliner sailed overhead at a relatively low altitude on the night of the event, the color of its markings the same as those of Malaysia Airlines. Once again, though, the wreckage showed no signs of fire damage or shrapnel from a missile strike. Moreover, the pilot's flight simulation to Diego Garcia was merely one of thousands programmed into his home equipment.

Lastly, and pertinent to the topic of cyberterrorism, a number of aviation and cybersecurity experts have offered the unnerving possibility that a terrorist entity working from a remote location—or, alternatively, on board MH370 in its electronics bay—may have seized control of the plane by means of a sophisticated hacking operation. Although the information the Malaysian government has chosen to make public suggests that the perpetrator, for reasons unknown, flew MH370 to the southern Indian Ocean and crashed it, the notion of a remote-control cyber operation continues to be deliberated, partly because such a feat, although improbable, is theoretically possible all the same.

In 2006, the U.S. Patent and Trademark Office granted a patent to Boeing for a remarkable technology through which the company could take control of its airliners in flight.[40] "Boeing patented a remote control system using a computer placed inside or outside the aircraft," says Marc Dugain, the former CEO of Proteus Airlines.[41] In the event of a hijacking, the technology would be indispensable in that it would return control of the aircraft to the manufacturer. Stephen J. Wright, an expert in aviation and aeronautical engineering, has described it as "an uninterruptable (control) landing system that can be activated from the ground or in the air, to be able to take over the control of the aircraft to land at a designated airfield, taking over from the occupants of the aircraft." Wright adds, "[t]he system foreseen is said to be *uninterruptable*, meaning the Automatic Control System 'control box' that interfaces with all the aircraft systems would need to have its own power source and supply, and that once it has been activated, the aircraft must land."[42] Airbus has a similar version of the technology.

In the MH370 case, the principal Malaysian investigation confirmed that the Boeing 777 was capable of accommodating the remote-control system but implied that it had not been installed on this particular plane.[43] On this point, numerous officials have cast doubt on the integrity of the Malaysian inquiry, among them the Malaysian prime minister, Mahathir Bin Mohamad. "I think something has happened which some people might know but are not telling," Mohamed said in a 2019 interview on CNN.[44] "In 2006, Boeing was given permission to take over a plane in flight," the prime minister continued. "I'm not accusing Boeing, but the capacity to take over planes in flight is available and somebody might use it, maybe not Boeing, maybe somebody else."[45]

One thing is certain: the conjecture will persist, with questions, doubts, and rumors churning until the airliner is found, if ever. Those who are convinced that a cover-up is in place may never be swayed. When wreckage from the airliner was discovered, numerous skeptics insisted it had been planted. Others have expressed doubts about the lack of surveillance in the region, questioning how the United States' advanced military intelligence apparatus at Diego Garcia could fail to detect a stray Boeing 777 flying for seven hours over the Indian Ocean. To be sure, suspicions will linger. It is important to bear in mind, however, that there is no publicly available evidence indicating that a terrorist entity, either at a remote location or in the electronics bay of the plane itself, seized control of Malaysia Airlines Flight 370. That said, the prospect of a commercial carrier being the focus of a cyber operation remains a valid one; it had already happened in the United States.

Factual Hackings of Airliners

The first incident in which a person hacked into a domestic airliner in flight occurred on May 15, 2015, and, although it was unconfirmed at the time, the episode was quickly picked up by news services from coast to coast. The man in question was a highly regarded cybersecurity specialist

THREE. Conventional Assaults and Cyberattacks

who had cofounded a cybersecurity firm. "[A] security researcher who conducted penetration-testing and research for a living," writes Kim Zetter, he was purportedly troubled by airliners' vulnerability to cyberattacks.[46] In the recent past, he had sought to convince the FBI that the in-flight entertainment system (IFE) on an airliner could be hacked, specifically those manufactured by Panasonic and Thales.[47] Susceptible aircraft purportedly included the Airbus A320 and Boeing 737 and Boeing 757.[48] The researcher would also tell the FBI, in 2015, that he had hacked into such aircraft up to twenty times between 2011 and 2014.[49]

The reason for his 2015 conversation with the FBI stemmed from an incident on April 15 of that year, when the security researcher flew from Chicago to Syracuse on United Airlines Flight 3642. While the Boeing 737 was in flight, he posted, jokingly, on social media about hacking the plane. As a result, the United Airlines Cyber Security Division notified the FBI, whose agents met him at the Syracuse airport to interview him and examine his laptop computer and flash drives.

In the accompanying search warrant, the researcher's modus operandi was outlined.[50] To commence his hacking operation, he told the FBI that he would begin by prying open the casing of an in-flight entertainment module situated beneath the passenger seat in front of him, following which he would connect an ethernet cable linking the IFE to his laptop computer. "He then connected to other systems on the airplane network after he exploited/gained access to, or 'hacked' the IFE system," reads the search warrant. "He stated that he then overwrote code on the airplane's Thrust Management Computer while aboard a flight."[51] Most disturbing, the researcher told the FBI that he had once activated the plane's "climb" command, affecting one of its engines and thereby sending the airliner into a sideways movement.[52]

The Boeing Company, for its part, took issue with this account, releasing a statement that challenged the man's claims. "In-flight entertainment (IFE) systems on commercial airplanes are isolated from flight and navigation systems," asserted the Boeing document.[53] Not only are the IFE systems sequestered from other systems, the statement added, but the aircraft also has multiple navigational options available to the pilots, any changes to which must be approved by them. United Airlines also refuted the claims and banned the security researcher from its flights.[54] He was not charged with a crime.

Significantly, the Government Accounting Office, in the midst of this drama, released its analysis of the Federal Aviation Administration's cybersecurity operations. "Modern aircraft are increasingly connected to the internet," the report stated. "This interconnectedness can potentially provide unauthorized remote access to aircraft avionics systems."[55]

After acknowledging that commercial carriers can indeed be targeted for cyberattacks from a remote site, the GAO offered several recommendations to help better protect the traveling public from cybercriminals and cyberterrorists.

The U.S. Department of Homeland Security also conducted research on the subject in 2016. The team was headed by Dr. Robert Hickey, Aviation Program Manager in the Cyber Security Division, DHS Science and Technology Directorate. Members included academic and industry figures associated with the Massachusetts Institute of Technology, QED Secure Solutions, and the Pacific Northwest National Laboratory (U.S. Department of Energy). The aircraft used in the study was a Boeing 757, and it was situated on the ground at Atlantic City International Airport in New Jersey. The results were obtained quickly, and they were indisputable.

"We got the airplane on the 19th of September 2016, [and] two days later I was successful in accomplishing a remote, non-cooperative, penetration," Hickey reported.[56] Using materials that could pass through airport security, the researcher employed radio-frequency communications to hack into the plane's systems. No one in the study had physical contact with the airliner.[57]

By Hickey's own account, many experts in the field seemed indifferent to his accomplishment, asserting that they already knew airliners could be hacked.[58] Others were stunned, however, among them airline pilots. In any event, the aircraft's manufacturer, as before, issued a statement intended to reassure the flying public. "While the research was alarming, showing how future terrorists could take over planes using technology alone," writes Jason Murdock, "Boeing stressed at the time there was 'no hack of the airplane's flight control systems.'"[59]

Two years later, a top cybersecurity researcher, Ruben Santamarta, reportedly hacked an aircraft as well, but on this occasion the plane was airborne. Santamarta was the man whose team had conducted the satellite-vulnerability study mentioned earlier, and now he stated that, from the ground, he had hacked into the communications systems of an aircraft in flight.[60] Among the vulnerabilities that Santamarta exposed were backdoors, insecure protocols that would allow hackers to access data, and misconfigured networks that could, among other problems, allow firewall breaches. Associated cyberthreats included the ability for a malicious actor to take over the aircraft's Wi-Fi and SATCOM (Satellite Communications) equipment, and, in the case of the latter, potentially control the transmissions and change the position of antennae.[61]

In 2020, Santamarta turned his attention to the Boeing 787—the "Dreamliner"—which is Boeing's most highly-networked, electronic-enabled commercial aircraft and a unique one in important respects.

"Instead of physically separating the networks that can be accessed from the outside world—such as the inflight entertainment system or radios the plane uses to communicate maintenance data—all the networks come together in the core network cabinet," writes Max Eddy.[62] Once again, Santamarta's research exposed a host of flaws, some of which tend to be difficult to detect and correct, such as buffer overruns, integer overflows, and memory corruption.[63] On this point, Santamarta and his team were not alone in their concerns. "Boeing 787 Dreamliner jets, as well as Airbus A350 and A380 aircraft, have Wi-Fi passenger networks that use the same network as the avionics systems of the planes, raising the possibility that a hacker could hijack the navigation system or commandeer the plane through the in-plane network," writes Kim Zetter, citing a GAO report.[64] Both Boeing and Airbus maintain that their commercial airliners are safe, that flights have not been impacted by any of the purported flaws, and that their planes' security is continuously being assessed and strengthened.[65] To date, there have been no confirmed penetrations of an airliner's avionics or flight control system.

Cyberterrorism and ADS-B Technology

More troubling to cybersecurity experts is the threat associated with Automatic Dependent Surveillance-Broadcast (ADS-B) technology, which, as of 2020, the Federal Aviation Administration has required on domestic aircraft traveling in most airspace over the forty-eight contiguous U.S. states. The FAA's purpose in mandating this conversion to ADS-B, which supplements ground-based radar with satellite positioning, is to furnish both pilots and air traffic controllers with a keener representation of the situation in the air. Now in use around the world, ADS-B technology will replace ground radar as the principal tracking method in the United States.[66]

The transition to ADS-B began in 2011, when the FAA predicted a colossal surge in air travel in the coming decades, one that promised to overwhelm airports. It therefore set about creating and executing a sweeping new approach known as the Next Generation Air Transportation System (NextGen).[67] "Rather than slightly upgrading an aging infrastructure, the FAA and its partners have implemented major new technologies and capabilities, which is leading to a new way of managing air traffic known as Trajectory-Based Operations (TBO)," states the FAA.[68] "The Next Generation Air Transportation System (NextGen) is the FAA's multibillion-dollar program to modernize the U.S. National Airspace System (NAS). Recognized as one of the most ambitious infrastructure projects in U.S. history,

NextGen aims to increase the safety, efficiency, capacity, predictability, and resiliency of American aviation."[69]

Unlike the ground-based radar that has long been employed at airports, ADS-B, a NextGen program, is a satellite navigational technology that uses GPS (Global Positioning System) to ascertain the exact location of aircraft in flight. And its merits are plentiful. More precise and reliable than radar, it is not affected by weather conditions, it enhances pilots' situational awareness, and it increases the capacity of airspace. Also, an aircraft's position is displayed instantly, whereas radar can take up to twelve seconds to update.[70] And ADS-B opens up more areas for air traffic controllers to surveil. By furnishing them with the latitude-longitude positions of aircraft in real time, it allows ATCs to track and provide services to aircraft flying in areas where line-of-sight radar is not possible or at best dicey, such as at low altitudes, in mountainous regions, and over large bodies of water, such as the Gulf of Mexico.[71] Then, too, a missing airplane can be found more rapidly and reliably, since the system enables an aircraft to be tracked within thirty feet of its location.

It should be noted that there are two types of ADS-B services—"In" and "Out"—and it is only the latter that the FAA requires on aircraft traveling in U.S. airspace. The FAA has no plans to mandate the "In" service.[72]

An airplane that is equipped with "Out" continuously broadcasts its identity, airframe dimensions, position, altitude, and velocity to air traffic controllers as well as to other aircraft. The FAA retains all of this information for a period of six months.[73] An airplane equipped with the "In" counterpart is able to receive this same data. It affords the pilot a cockpit display on which can be seen the positions of other aircraft in the area, along with temporary flight restrictions and a plethora of other information that previously was available only to those on the ground.

In terms of security issues, they stem from the fact that an aircraft equipped with ADS-B is linked to a satellite in low earth orbit, to other aircraft in the air, and to a ground-based system. Information is exchanged via radio signals. Collectively, this constitutes a cyber-physical system whose interconnectedness has, from the start, generated considerable apprehension in the cybersecurity community as well as segments of the aviation community. And their concerns are understandable. Among the technology's shortcomings: ADS-B signals are neither encrypted nor authenticated, and unless a user arranges for special provisions, aircraft data are publicly accessible. "This means anyone can purchase a receiver (often for less than $100) and then begin seeing information including aircraft ID, altitude, latitude, longitude, bearing, and speed," writes Kellyn Wagner Ramsdell.[74]

With regard to the various methods of cyberattack, Jon C. Haass and his colleagues at Embry-Riddle Aeronautical University have identified several strategies.⁷⁵ They include signal jamming, message injections, message modifications, message deletions, and eavesdropping.⁷⁶ Jamming the GPS signals to an aircraft can result in a denial-of-service situation, while the insertion of false messages can produce a host of other problems depending on the information being broadcast. "Message injection involves injecting spurious messages into the air-traffic communication system," write Haass and his associates. "This is possible because ADS-B messages are unencrypted, combined with the fact that the source of the message is not authenticated."⁷⁷ Spoofing attacks, in particular, can easily be conducted against an unprotected ADS-B service; this is an intrusion in which the perpetrator introduces, for instance, a fake aircraft or phantom ground facility or otherwise fabricates or replicates signals. Not surprisingly, it has been demonstrated repeatedly that spoofing can be a very effective form of attack. "Global Positioning System (GPS) spoofing has been used to send a hovering drone into an unplanned dive and to steer a yacht off course," write Mark Psiaki and Todd Humphreys.⁷⁸ Still other malicious deeds center on manipulating information to alter an aircraft's trajectory. And, of course, there is the disturbing prospect of a virtual hijacking.⁷⁹

Although the FAA does not require encryption or authentication for ADS-B Out transmissions, it has offered solutions, of sorts, to those worried about privacy issues. Certainly, there were, and still are, many who voice such concerns in the fields of cybersecurity, general aviation, business, and the military. In the case of the latter, the military made it known to the FAA that the ADS-B Out on its aircraft was broadcasting information that an enemy could exploit, most notably classified aircraft position data.⁸⁰ It was the same issue that the Government Accountability Office examined in 2018, releasing its findings in a report to Congress titled "Urgent Need for DOD and FAA to Address Risks and Improve Planning for Technology That Tracks Military Aircraft."⁸¹ Concluding that ADS-B Out broadcasts offered far too much information about military activities in the air, the report led to a new FAA ruling the following year. It did not, however, entail encryption or authentication. Instead, the 2019 ruling permits a military aircraft, when necessary and upon authorization by the FAA, to temporarily switch off ADS-B Out. Belatedly, the FAA recognized and stated in official documents that military pilots "need the ability to terminate the transmission signal when conducting sensitive national defense, homeland security, intelligence and law enforcement missions that could be compromised by transmitting real time identification and positional flight information over ADS–B."⁸²

Since privacy issues have also been expressed by those who own, operate, or are otherwise involved with civilian aircraft, including companies that wish to ensure that their employees' air travel remains confidential, the FAA has offered a solution similar to that negotiated with the military. While the ADS-B Out service must continue to broadcast all of the flight information, the aircraft's owner may apply in advance for a temporary, alternate aircraft address—in effect, an alias or pseudonym.[83]

As to the possibility of a cyberattack on an airliner in flight, one inflicted by a terrorist entity exploiting the vulnerabilities in the ADS-B Out service, an FAA communications officer has suggested that such an intrusion would be relatively minor and manageable. The officer also explained that additional protections exist, pointing to the "redundancies and independent backup capabilities" that are integrated into the current air traffic system.[84] Then, too, it has been stressed that ADS-B information does not exist in isolation, that it can be checked against other data, such as radar, for corroboration.[85] All the same, cybersecurity specialists, both civilian and military, continue to explore encryption strategies designed to contend with the lack of authentication and encryption on aircraft traveling in United States airspace, thereby lessening the chances of an in-flight cyberterror attack. Of course, it remains the task of other nations to ensure that their own ADS-B–equipped aircraft are also protected from cyberterrorism if worldwide air travel is to be deemed truly safe.

As it stands, terrorism in its varied manifestations will no doubt persist and will continue being committed chiefly by individuals or groups who feel they must resort to shocking acts of inhumanity for their voices to be heard. In terms of terrorist operations that explicitly target airliners in order to inflict mass casualties and produce social chaos, such attempts will likely persist, despite the fact that assaults on commercial carriers are less inclined to succeed than was the case in past decades. This is attributable, of course, to the impressive arsenal of safeguards that are now in place to avert acts of air piracy, sabotage, and related offenses. Still, such tools must be assessed frequently and upgraded as necessary, and novel forms of attack that terrorist entities have yet to conceive must be anticipated to the extent that it is possible to do so.

Notes

1. "Arab Terrorists Attack El Al Passengers; Pilot Disregards Own Safety to Save Others," *Jewish Telegraphic Agency* (JTA), February 11, 1970, https://www.jta.org/archive/arab-terrorists-attack-el-al-passengers-pilot-disregards-own-safety-to-save-others.

2. "West German Government Condemns Arab Terrorist Attack on El Al Airlines," *Jewish Telegraphic Agency* (JTA), February 12, 1970, https://www.jta.org/archive/west-german-government-condemns-arab-terrorist-attack-on-el-al-airline.

3. "Over the Bacha Valley," *YNET—Yedioth Ahronoth*, February 6, 2007, https://www.ynet.co.il/articles/0,7340,L-3361439,00.html.

4. Paul Hofmann, "Arab Guerrillas Kill 31 in Rome during Attack on U.S. Airliner, Take Hostages to Athens, Fly On," *New York Times*, December 18, 1973, https://www.nytimes.

com/1973/12/18/archives/arab-guerrillas-kill-31-in-rome-during-attack-on-us-airliner-take.html.

5. Clyde Haberman, "5 Dead, 36 Hurt in an Explosion at Seoul Airport," *New York Times*, September 15, 1986, https://www.nytimes.com/1986/09/15/world/5-dead-36-hurt-in-an-explosion-at-seoul-airport.html.

6. Al Goodman, "After Bomb in Airport, Spain Tightens Security," *New York Times*, August 4, 1996, https://www.nytimes.com/1996/08/04/travel/after-bomb-in-airport-spain-tightens-security.html.

7. "Santander Airport Car Bomb Blast," CNN, July 27, 2003, https://www.cnn.com/2003/WORLD/europe/07/27/spain.blast/.

8. Barry Bearak, "11 Are Killed as Militants Attack Kashmir Airport," *New York Times*, January 17, 2001, https://www.nytimes.com/2001/01/17/world/11-are-killed-as-militants-attack-kashmir-airport.html.

9. RFI Staff, "Belgium Airport to Reopen with Tighter Security," Radio France Internationale, April 2, 2016, https://www.rfi.fr/en/europe/20160402-belgium-airport-reopen-tighter-security.

10. Human Rights Watch Staff, "Grounds for Concern: Belgium's Counterterror Responses to the Paris and Brussels Attacks," Human Rights Watch, November 3, 2016, https://www.hrw.org/report/2016/11/03/grounds-concern/belgiums-counterterror-responses-paris-and-brussels-attacks.

11. Human Rights Watch Staff, "Grounds for Concern."

12. Dan Bilefsky, "Brussels Attacks Renew Criticism of Security at Europe's Airports," *New York Times*, March 31, 2016, https://www.nytimes.com/2016/04/01/world/europe/brussels-attacks-airport-security.html.

13. Dan Bilefsky, "Brussels Attacks Renew Criticism of Security at Europe's Airports."

14. Dan Bilefsky, "Brussels Attacks Renew Criticism of Security at Europe's Airports."

15. Christopher Elliott, "Traveling for the Holidays? Here's How to Avoid Contracting COVID-19 at the Airport," *USA Today*, December 18, 2020, https://www.usatoday.com/story/travel/advice/2020/12/18/how-avoid-being-infected-COVID-19-airport/6505537002/.

16. Robert Mackey, "Despite Omicron Risk, TSA Still Require Travelers to Remove Masks at Airport Checkpoints," *The Intercept*, January 4, 2022, https://theintercept.com/2022/01/04/ignoring-omicron-risk-tsa-still-requires-travelers-remove-masks-airport-checkpoints/.

17. Robert Mackey, "Despite Omicron Risk, TSA Still Require Travelers to Remove Masks at Airport Checkpoints."

18. Robert Mackey, "Despite Omicron Risk, TSA Still Require Travelers to Remove Masks at Airport Checkpoints."

19. World Health Organization, "WHO Coronavirus (COVID-19) Dashboard," World Health Organization, accessed on February 27, 2023, https://covid19.who.int/?mapFilter=deaths.

20. Larry Anderson, "Will Airport Security's Pandemic Measures Lead to Permanent Changes?" Security Informed, accessed March 6, 2023, https://www.securityinformed.com/insights/airport-security-pandemic-measures-lead-permanent-co-1519898497-ga-sb.1619523671.html?utm_source=SSc%20International%20Edition&utm_medium=Redirect&utm_campaign=International%20Redirect%20Popup.

21. "Denial of Service (DoS) Guidance," National Cyber Security Centre, Government Communications Headquarters (GCHQ), March 16, 2016, https://www.ncsc.gov.uk/collection/denial-service-dos-guidance-collection.

22. "Distributed Denial of Service," Merriam-Webster Dictionary Online, accessed March 2, 2023, https://www.merriam-webster.com/dictionary/distributed%20denial%20of%20service.

23. Josh Margolin, Sam Sweeney and Quinn Owen, "Cyberattacks Reported at U.S. Airports," ABC News, October 10, 2022, https://abcnews.go.com/Technology/cyberattacks-reported-us-airports/story?id=91287965.

24. Will Horton, "Cathay Pacific Faulted for Data Breach, but Hackers' Objective Unclear," *Forbes*, June 6, 2019, https://www.forbes.com/sites/willhorton1/2019/06/06/cathay-pacific-faulted-for-data-breach-but-hackers-objective-unclear/?sh=12c5db867068.

25. Eduard Kovacs, "British Airways Settles Class Action Over 2018 Data Breach,"

Security Week, June 6, 2021, https://www.securityweek.com/british-airways-settles-class-action-over-2018-data-breach/.

26. "What Is Magecart? History, Cases, Taxonomy, and Prevention," *Sansec*, February 4, 2023, https://sansec.io/docs/what-is-magecart.

27. Will Horton, "Cathay Pacific Faulted for Data Breach, but Hackers' Objective Unclear."

28. Stéphane Prevost, "Ten Major Cyberattacks against the Airport Industry," *Stormshield*, July 26, 2022, https://www.stormshield.com/news/ten-major-cyberattacks-against-the-airport-industry/.

29. CBR Staff Writer, "Flying Blind: 70% of Airport Websites Contain Vulnerabilities," *Tech Monitor*, January 31, 2020, https://techmonitor.ai/technology/cybersecurity/airport-cybersecurity.

30. Greg Freiherr, "Will Your Airliner Get Hacked?" *Smithsonian Magazine*, February 2021, https://www.smithsonianmag.com/air-space-magazine/will-your-airliner-get-hacked-180976752/.

31. Dorothy E. Denning (witness), "Statement of Dr. Dorothy E. Denning," House Special Oversight Panel on Terrorism [H.A.S.C. No. 106–52], May 23, 2000, https://irp.fas.org/congress/2000_hr/00-05-23denning.htm.

32. Kelly Jackson Higgins, "Satellite Communications Wide Open to Hackers," *Dark Reading*, April 17, 2014, https://www.darkreading.com/vulnerabilities-threats/satellite-communications-wide-open-to-hackers.

33. Ruben Santamarta, "A Wake-Up Call for SATCOM Security," *IOActive*, April 17, 2014, https://ioactive.com/pdfs/IOActive_SATCOM_Security_WhitePaper.pdf.

34. William Langewiesche, "What Really Happened to Malaysia's Missing Airplane," *The Atlantic*, July 1, 2019, https://www.theatlantic.com/magazine/archive/2019/07/mh370-malaysia-airlines/590653/.

35. Rozanna Latiff, "New MH370 Probe Shows Controls Manipulated, but Mystery Remains Unsolved," Reuters, July 30, 2018, https://www.reuters.com/article/us-malaysiaairlines-mh370/new-mh370-probe-shows-controls-manipulated-but-mystery-remains-unsolved-idUSKBN1KK0I9.

36. BBC Staff, "MH370: Reunion Wing Debris 'Certainly' from Missing Flight," BBC, September 3, 2015, https://www.bbc.co.uk/news/world-asia-34145127.

37. Tom Westbrook, "Report on MH370 Finds 'Initially Similar' Route on Pilot's Flight Simulator," Reuters, October 2, 2017, https://www.reuters.com/article/us-malaysia-airlines-mh370/report-on-mh370-finds-initially-similar-route-on-pilots-flight-simulator-idUSKCN1C8090.

38. Tom Westbrook, "Report on MH370 Finds 'Initially Similar' Route on Pilot's Flight Simulator."

39. Lauren Piette, "Inside Diego Garcia: The Most Mysterious U.S. Naval Base," *Veteran Life*, accessed January 3, 2023, https://veteranlife.com/military-history/diego-garcia/.

40. Eric D. Brown, et al., Inventors; The Boeing Company, Assignee. "System and Method for Automatically Controlling a Path of Travel of a Vehicle," United States Patent Office, United States Patent No. U.S. 7, 142, 971, B2, issued November 27, 2006, https://patentimages.storage.googleapis.com/a4/0e/05/00279b428d65dc/US7142971.pdf.

41. France 24 Staff, "French Ex-Airline Boss Claims Cover-Up on MH370," France 24, December 18, 2014, https://www.france24.com/en/20141218-dugain-malaysia-airlines-mh370-disappearance-diego-garcia-cover-up.

42. Stephen J. Wright, *Aviation Safety and Security: Utilizing Technology to Prevent Aircraft Fatality* (Boca Raton, Florida: CRC Press, 2021), 164.

43. Stephen J. Wright, *Aviation Safety and Security*.

44. Richard Quest (host) and John Defterios (reporter), "Malaysian Prime Minister: MH370 May Have Been Hacked," *Quest Means Business* (CNN), airdate June 24, 2019, https://youtu.be/TAD0gS7MZt8.

45. Richard Quest (host) and John Defterios (reporter), "Malaysian Prime Minister: MH370 May Have Been Hacked."

46. Kim Zetter, "Feds Say That Banner Researcher Commandeered a Plane," *Wired*, May 15, 2015, https://www.wired.com/2015/05/feds-say-banned-researcher-commandeered-plane/.

47. Tim Brown, "Investigation into Claims Planes Hacked Through Entertainment System," *The Manufacturer*, May 18, 2015, https://www.themanufacturer.com/articles/investigation-into-claims-planes-hacked-through-entertainment-system/.
48. Tim Brown, "Investigation into Claims Planes Hacked Through Entertainment System."
49. Elizabeth Weise, "FBI: Computer Expert Briefly Made Plane Fly Sideways," *USA Today*, May 16, 2015, https://www.usatoday.com/story/tech/2015/05/16/chris-roberts-fbi-plane-hack-one-world-labs/27448335/.
50. Mark S. Hurley, "Application for a Search Warrant: Case No. 5:15-MJ-00154 (ATB)," United States District Court for the Northern District of New York, April 17, 2015, https://www.wired.com/wp-content/uploads/2015/05/Chris-Roberts-Application-for-Search-Warrant.pdf.
51. Mark S. Hurley, "Application for a Search Warrant: Case No. 5:15-MJ-00154 (ATB)," 12.
52. Mark S. Hurley, "Application for a Search Warrant: Case No. 5:15-MJ-00154 (ATB)."
53. Tim Brown, "Investigation into Claims Planes Hacked through Entertainment System."
54. Associated Press, "Security Expert Banned from ALL United Flights After Boasting He Knew How Hack into Aircraft Controls and Bring the Plane Down," *Daily Mail*, April 20, 2015, https://www.dailymail.co.uk/news/article-3046272/Security-Researcher-banned-United-flight-tweeted-systems-hacked.html.
55. "Air Traffic Control: FAA Needs a More Comprehensive Approach to Address Cybersecurity as Agency Transitions to NextGen," Government Accountability Office, April 14, 2015, https://www.gao.gov/products/gao-15-370.
56. Calvin Biesecker, "DHS Led Team Demonstrates That Commercial Aircraft Can Be Remotely Hacked," *Defense Daily*, November 8, 2017, https://www.defensedaily.com/dhs-led-team-demonstrates-commercial-aircraft-can-remotely-hacked/cyber/.
57. Calvin Biesecker, "DHS Led Team Demonstrates That Commercial Aircraft Can Be Remotely Hacked."
58. Calvin Biesecker, "DHS Led Team Demonstrates That Commercial Aircraft Can Be Remotely Hacked."
59. Jason Murdock, "In-Flight Airplanes Can Now Be Hacked from the Ground, Cyber Expert Warns," *Newsweek*, June 6, 2018, https://www.newsweek.com/flight-airplanes-can-now-be-hacked-ground-cyber-expert-warns-962420.
60. Jason Murdock, "In-Flight Airplanes Can Now Be Hacked from the Ground, Cyber Expert Warns."
61. Ruben Santamarta, "White Paper: Last Call for SATCOM Security," *IOActive*, August 2018, https://i.blackhat.com/us-18/Thu-August-9/us-18-Santamarta-Last-Call-For-Satcom-Security-wp.pdf.
62. Max Eddy, "Security Researcher Says He Cracked 787 Airliner, but Boeing, FAA Disagree," *PC Magazine*, August 8, 2019, https://www.pcmag.com/news/security-researcher-says-he-cracked-787-airliner-but-boeing-faa-disagree.
63. Ruben Santamarta, "White Paper: Arm IDA and Cross Check: Reversing the 787's Core Network," *IOActive*, August 7, 2019, https://ioactive.com/arm-ida-and-cross-check-reversing-the-787s-core-network/.
64. Kim Zetter, "Hackers Could Commandeer News Planes through Passenger Wi-Fi," *Wired*, April 15, 2015, https://www.wired.com/2015/04/hackers-commandeer-new-planes-passenger-wi-fi/.
65. Kim Zetter, "Hackers Could Commandeer News Planes Through Passenger Wi-Fi."
66. "ADS-B Out Explained," Textron Aviation, accessed March 14, 2023, https://txtav.com/en/journey/articles/articles/adsb-out-explained#:~:text=ADS%2DB%20allows%20equipped%20aircraft,known%20as%20ADS%2DB%20In.
67. "Next Generation Air Transportation System (NextGen)," Federal Aviation Administration, accessed February 25, 2023, https://www.faa.gov/nextgen.
68. "Next Generation Air Transportation System (NextGen)," Federal Aviation Administration.
69. "Next Generation Air Transportation System (NextGen)," Federal Aviation Administration.

70. Federal Aviation Administration, "ADS-B Benefits," FAA website, last updated April 15, 2022, https://www.faa.gov/air_traffic/technology/equipadsb/capabilities/benefits.
71. Tom Hoffmann, "To 'B' Or Not To 'B,'" FAA Safety Briefing, July 1, 2020, https://medium.com/faa/to-b-or-not-to-b-e9db6ee6e065.
72. "ADS-B Privacy—Frequently Asked Questions," Federal Aviation Administration, March 1, 2023, https://www.faa.gov/air_traffic/technology/equipadsb/resources/faq.
73. "ADS-B Privacy—Frequently Asked Questions."
74. Kellyn Wagner Ramsdell, "Few Answers for ADS-B Security Concerns," *International Aviation News Online*, accessed on March 15, 2023, https://www.ainonline.com/aviation-news/business-aviation/2018-02-14/few-answers-ads-b-security-concerns.
75. Jon C. Haass, J. Philip Craiger and Gary C. Kessler, "A Framework for Aviation Cybersecurity," NAECON 2018—IEEE National Aerospace and Electronics Conference, 2018, doi: 10.1109/NAECON.2018.8556747.
76. Jon C. Haass, J. Philip Craiger and Gary C. Kessler, "A Framework for Aviation Cybersecurity."
77. Jon C. Haass, J. Philip Craiger and Gary C. Kessler, "A Framework for Aviation Cybersecurity," 135.
78. Mark L. Psiaki and Todd E. Humphreys, "GNSS Spoofing and Detection," *Proceedings of the IEEE* 104, no. 6 (June 2016), 1258, doi: 10.1109/JPROC.2016.2526658.
79. Jon C. Haass, J. Philip Craiger and Gary C. Kessler, "A Framework for Aviation Cybersecurity."
80. David Walsh, "The Latest on U.S. Military Aircraft ADS-B Security Concerns," *Aviation Today*, April 6, 2018, https://www.aviationtoday.com/2018/04/06/latest-us-military-aircraft-ads-b-security-concerns/.
81. "Homeland Defense: Urgent Need for DOD and FAA to Address Risks and Improve Planning for Technology That Tracks Military Aircraft (GAO-18-177)," Government Accountability Office, accessed March 15, 2023, https://www.gao.gov/assets/gao-18-177.pdf.
82. "Federal Aviation Administration: Revision to Automatic Dependent Surveillance-Broadcast (ADS-B) Out Equipment and Use Requirement," *Federal Register* 84, no. 138 (July 18, 2019), 34281, https://www.govinfo.gov/content/pkg/FR-2019-07-18/pdf/2019-15248.pdf.
83. "ADS-B Privacy," Federal Aviation Administration, accessed March 1, 2023, https://www.faa.gov/air_traffic/technology/equipadsb/privacy.
84. David Walsh, "The Latest on U.S. Military Aircraft ADS-B Security Concerns."
85. Kellyn Wagner Ramsdell, "Few Answers for ADS-B Security Concerns."

Bibliography

"ADS-B Out Explained." Textron Aviation. Accessed March 14, 2023. https://txtav.com/en/journey/articles/articles/adsb-out-explained#:~:text=ADS%2DB%20allows%20equipped%20aircraft,known%20as%20ADS%2DB%20In.
"ADS-B Privacy." Federal Aviation Administration. Accessed March 1, 2023. https://www.faa.gov/air_traffic/technology/equipadsb/privacy.
"ADS-B Privacy—Frequently Asked Questions." Federal Aviation Administration. Accessed March 1, 2023. https://www.faa.gov/air_traffic/technology/equipadsb/resources/faq.
"Air Traffic Control: FAA Needs a More Comprehensive Approach to Address Cybersecurity as Agency Transitions to NextGen." Government Accountability Office, April 14, 2015. https://www.gao.gov/products/gao-15-370.
Anderson, Larry. "Will Airport Security's Pandemic Measures Lead to Permanent Changes?" Security Informed. Accessed March 6, 2023. https://www.securityinformed.com/insights/airport-security-pandemic-measures-lead-permanent-co-1519898497-ga-sb.1619523671.html?utm_source=SSc%20International%20Edition&utm_medium=Redirect&utm_campaign=International%20Redirect%20Popup.
"Arab Terrorists Attack El Al Passengers; Pilot Disregards Own Safety to Save Others." Jewish Telegraphic Agency (JTA), February 11, 1970. https://www.jta.org/archive/arab-terrorists-attack-el-al-passengers-pilot-disregards-own-safety-to-save-others.

Associated Press. "Security Expert Banned from ALL United Flights after Boasting He Knew How Hack into Aircraft Controls and Bring the Plane Down." *Daily Mail*, April 20, 2015. https://www.dailymail.co.uk/news/article-3046272/Security-Researcher-banned-United-flight-tweeted-systems-hacked.html.
BBC Staff. "MH370: Reunion Wing Debris 'Certainly' from Missing Flight." BBC, September 3, 2015. https://www.bbc.co.uk/news/world-asia-34145127.
Bearak, Barry. "11 Are Killed as Militants Attack Kashmir Airport." *New York Times*, January 17, 2001. https://www.nytimes.com/2001/01/17/world/11-are-killed-as-militants-attack-kashmir-airport.html.
Biesecker, Calvin. "DHS Led Team Demonstrates That Commercial Aircraft Can Be Remotely Hacked." *Defense Daily*, November 8, 2017. https://www.defensedaily.com/dhs-led-team-demonstrates-commercial-aircraft-can-remotely-hacked/cyber/.
Bilefsky, Dan. "Brussels Attacks Renew Criticism of Security at Europe's Airports." *New York Times*, March 31, 2016. https://www.nytimes.com/2016/04/01/world/europe/brussels-attacks-airport-security.html.
Brown, Eric D., et al., Inventors; The Boeing Company, Assignee. "System and Method for Automatically Controlling a Path of Travel of a Vehicle." United States Patent Office, United States Patent No. U.S. 7, 142, 971, B2, issued November 27, 2006. https://patentimages.storage.googleapis.com/a4/0e/05/00279b428d65dc/US7142971.pdf.
Brown, Tim. "Investigation into Claims Planes Hacked Through Entertainment System." *The Manufacturer*, May 18, 2015. https://www.themanufacturer.com/articles/investigation-into-claims-planes-hacked-through-entertainment-system/.
CBR Staff Writer. "Flying Blind: 70% of Airport Websites Contain Vulnerabilities." *Tech Monitor*, January 31, 2020. https://techmonitor.ai/technology/cybersecurity/airport-cybersecurity.
"Denial of Service (DoS) Guidance." National Cyber Security Centre, Government Communications Headquarters (GCHQ), March 16, 2016. https://www.ncsc.gov.uk/collection/denial-service-dos-guidance-collection.
Denning, Dorothy E. (witness). "Statement of Dr. Dorothy E. Denning." House Special Oversight Panel on Terrorism [H.A.S.C. No. 106–52], May 23, 2000. https://irp.fas.org/congress/2000_hr/00-05-23denning.htm.
"Distributed Denial of Service." Merriam-Webster Dictionary Online. Accessed March 2, 2023. https://www.merriam-webster.com/dictionary/distributed%20denial%20of%20service.
Eddy, Max. "Security Researcher Says He Cracked 787 Airliner, but Boeing, FAA Disagree." *PC Magazine*, August 8, 2019. https://www.pcmag.com/news/security-researcher-says-he-cracked-787-airliner-but-boeing-faa-disagree.
Elliott, Christopher. "Traveling for the Holidays? Here's How to Avoid Contracting COVID-19 at the Airport." *USA Today*, December 18, 2020. https://www.usatoday.com/story/travel/advice/2020/12/18/how-avoid-being-infected-covid-19-airport/6505537002/.
"Federal Aviation Administration: Revision to Automatic Dependent Surveillance-Broadcast (ADS–B) Out Equipment and Use Requirement." *Federal Register* 84, no. 138 (July 18, 2019): 34281. https://www.govinfo.gov/content/pkg/FR-2019-07-18/pdf/2019-15248.pdf.
France 24 Staff. "French Ex-Airline Boss Claims Cover-Up on MH370." France 24, December 18, 2014. https://www.france24.com/en/20141218-dugain-malaysia-airlines-mh370-disappearance-diego-garcia-cover-up.
Freiherr, Greg. "Will Your Airliner Get Hacked?" *Smithsonian Magazine*, February 2021. https://www.smithsonianmag.com/air-space-magazine/will-your-airliner-get-hacked-180976752/.
Goodman, Al. "After Bomb in Airport, Spain Tightens Security." *New York Times*, August 4, 1996. https://www.nytimes.com/1996/08/04/travel/after-bomb-in-airport-spain-tightens-security.html.
Haass, Jon C., J. Philip Craiger and Gary C. Kessler. "A Framework for Aviation Cybersecurity." NAECON 2018—IEEE National Aerospace and Electronics Conference (2018): 132–136. doi: 10.1109/NAECON.2018.8556747.
Haberman, Clyde. "5 Dead, 36 Hurt in an Explosion at Seoul Airport." New York Times,

September 15, 1986. https://www.nytimes.com/1986/09/15/world/5-dead-36-hurt-in-an-explosion-at-seoul-airport.html.

Higgins, Kelly Jackson. "Satellite Communications Wide Open to Hackers." *Dark Reading*, April 17, 2014. https://www.darkreading.com/vulnerabilities-threats/satellite-communications-wide-open-to-hackers.

Hoffmann, Tom. "To 'B' Or Not To 'B.'" FAA Safety Briefing, July 1, 2020. https://medium.com/faa/to-b-or-not-to-b-e9db6ee6e065.

Hofmann, Paul. "Arab Guerrillas Kill 31 In Rome during Attack on U.S. Airliner, Take Hostages to Athens, Fly On." *New York Times*, December 18, 1973. https://www.nytimes.com/1973/12/18/archives/arab-guerrillas-kill-31-in-rome-during-attack-on-us-airliner-take.html.

"Homeland Defense: Urgent Need for DOD and FAA to Address Risks and Improve Planning for Technology That Tracks Military Aircraft (GAO-18-177)." Government Accountability Office. Accessed March 15, 2023. https://www.gao.gov/assets/gao-18-177.pdf.

Horton, Will. "Cathay Pacific Faulted for Data Breach, but Hackers' Objective Unclear." *Forbes*, June 6, 2019. https://www.forbes.com/sites/willhorton1/2019/06/06/cathay-pacific-faulted-for-data-breach-but-hackers-objective-unclear/?sh=12c5db867068.

Human Rights Watch Staff. "Grounds for Concern: Belgium's Counterterror Responses to the Paris and Brussels Attacks." Human Rights Watch, November 3, 2016. https://www.hrw.org/report/2016/11/03/grounds-concern/belgiums-counterterror-responses-paris-and-brussels-attacks.

Hurley, Mark S. "Application for a Search Warrant: Case No. 5:15-MJ-00154 (ATB)." United States District Court for the Northern District of New York, April 17, 2015. https://www.wired.com/wp-content/uploads/2015/05/Chris-Roberts-Application-for-Search-Warrant.pdf.

Kovacs, Eduard. "British Airways Settles Class Action Over 2018 Data Breach." *Security Week*, June 6, 2021. https://www.securityweek.com/british-airways-settles-class-action-over-2018-data-breach/.

Langewiesche, William. "What Really Happened to Malaysia's Missing Airplane." *The Atlantic*, July 1, 2019. https://www.theatlantic.com/magazine/archive/2019/07/mh370-malaysia-airlines/590653/.

Latiff, Rozanna. "New MH370 Probe Shows Controls Manipulated, but Mystery Remains Unsolved." Reuters, July 30, 2018. https://www.reuters.com/article/us-malaysiaairlines-mh370/new-mh370-probe-shows-controls-manipulated-but-mystery-remains-unsolved-idUSKBN1KK0I9.

Mackey, Robert. "Despite Omicron Risk, TSA Still Require Travelers to Remove Masks at Airport Checkpoints." *The Intercept*, January 4, 2022. https://theintercept.com/2022/01/04/ignoring-omicron-risk-tsa-still-requires-travelers-remove-masks-airport-checkpoints/.

Margolin, Josh, Sam Sweeney and Quinn Owen. "Cyberattacks Reported at U.S. Airports." ABC News, October 10, 2022. https://abcnews.go.com/Technology/cyberattacks-reported-us-airports/story?id=91287965.

Murdock, Jason. "In-Flight Airplanes Can Now Be Hacked from the Ground, Cyber Expert Warns." *Newsweek*, June 6, 2018. https://www.newsweek.com/flight-airplanes-can-now-be-hacked-ground-cyber-expert-warns-962420.

"Next Generation Air Transportation System (NextGen)." Federal Aviation Administration. Accessed February 25, 2023. https://www.faa.gov/nextgen.

"Over the Bacha Valley." *YNET—Yedioth Ahronoth*, February 6, 2007. https://www.ynet.co.il/articles/0,7340,L-3361439,00.html.

Piette, Lauren. "Inside Diego Garcia: The Most Mysterious U.S. Naval Base." *Veteran Life*. Accessed January 3, 2023. https://veteranlife.com/military-history/diego-garcia/.

Prevost, Stéphane. "Ten Major Cyberattacks against the Airport Industry." *Stormshield*, July 26, 2022. https://www.stormshield.com/news/ten-major-cyberattacks-against-the-airport-industry/.

Psiaki, Mark L., and Todd E. Humphreys. "GNSS Spoofing and Detection." *Proceedings of the IEEE* 104, no. 6 (June 2016): 1258-1270. doi: 10.1109/JPROC.2016.2526658.

Quest, Richard (host) and John Defterios (reporter). "Malaysian Prime Minister: MH370

May Have Been Hacked." *Quest Means Business* (CNN), airdate June 24, 2019. https://youtu.be/TAD0gS7MZt8.
Ramsdell, Kellyn Wagner. "Few Answers for ADS-B Security Concerns." *International Aviation News Online*. Accessed March 15, 2023. https://www.ainonline.com/aviation-news/business-aviation/2018-02-14/few-answers-ads-b-security-concerns.
RFI Staff. "Belgium Airport to Reopen with Tighter Security." Radio France Internationale, April 2, 2016. https://www.rfi.fr/en/europe/20160402-belgium-airport-reopen-tighter-security.
Santamarta, Ruben. "White Paper: Arm IDA and Cross Check: Reversing the 787's Core Network." *IOActive*, August 7, 2019. https://ioactive.com/arm-ida-and-cross-check-reversing-the-787s-core-network/.
Santamarta, Ruben. "White Paper: Last Call for SATCOM Security." *IOActive*, August 2018. https://i.blackhat.com/us-18/Thu-August-9/us-18-Santamarta-Last-Call-For-Satcom-Security-wp.pdf.
"Santander Airport Car Bomb Blast." CNN, July 27, 2003. https://www.cnn.com/2003/WORLD/europe/07/27/spain.blast/.
Walsh, David. "The Latest on U.S. Military Aircraft ADS-B Security Concerns." *Aviation Today*, April 6, 2018. https://www.aviationtoday.com/2018/04/06/latest-us-military-aircraft-ads-b-security-concerns/.
Weise, Elizabeth. "FBI: Computer Expert Briefly Made Plane Fly Sideways." *USA Today*, May 16, 2015. https://www.usatoday.com/story/tech/2015/05/16/chris-roberts-fbi-plane-hack-one-world-labs/27448335/.
"West German Government Condemns Arab Terrorist Attack on El Al Airlines." Jewish Telegraphic Agency (JTA), February 12, 1970. https://www.jta.org/archive/west-german-government-condemns-arab-terrorist-attack-on-el-al-airline.
Westbrook, Tom. "Report on MH370 Finds 'Initially Similar' Route on Pilot's Flight Simulator." Reuters, October 2, 2017. https://www.reuters.com/article/us-malaysia-airlines-mh370/report-on-mh370-finds-initially-similar-route-on-pilots-flight-simulator-idUSKCN1C8O9O.
"What Is Magecart? History, Cases, Taxonomy, and Prevention." *Sansec*, February 4, 2023. https://sansec.io/docs/what-is-magecart.
World Health Organization, "WHO Coronavirus (COVID-19) Dashboard." World Health Organization. Accessed on February 27, 2023. https://covid19.who.int/?mapFilter=deaths.
Wright, Stephen J. *Aviation Safety and Security: Utilizing Technology to Prevent Aircraft Fatality*. Boca Raton, Florida: CRC Press, 2021.
Zetter, Kim. "Feds Say That Banner Researcher Commandeered a Plane." *Wired*, May 15, 2015. https://www.wired.com/2015/05/feds-say-banned-researcher-commandeered-plane/.
Zetter, Kim. "Hackers Could Commandeer News Planes through Passenger Wi-Fi." *Wired*, April 15, 2015. https://www.wired.com/2015/04/hackers-commandeer-new-planes-passenger-wi-fi/.

Part II

Case Studies

Four

Up in the Air
The Controversy of TWA Flight 800

It was sunset on Long Island, and the cool evening air was luring residents and sightseers alike to the restaurants, piers, and beaches for which the area was renowned. Drawing enthusiasts, too, was Long Island Sound, which was dotted with pleasure craft in spite of the dimming sky. And then, far above this placid scene, the unthinkable happened: TWA Flight 800 exploded in midair and plummeted into the Atlantic, with all of the jetliner's passengers and crew perishing in what would prove to be the deadliest airline disaster in U.S. history. As to the trio of investigations that ensued, they would acquire a notoriety of their own, and even today they stand as the most controversial and contentious inquiries ever conducted into a domestic airline incident on American soil. To be sure, accusations of wrongdoing were rampant, not only from those with a predilection for conspiracy theories, but also from among the top echelon of the aviation industry.

"During the course of my 42-year career as an investigator, the investigation of TWA Flight 800 was the only case in which I witnessed deception, lies and corruption on the parts of investigators and their management," Henry F. Hughes would swear in an affidavit presented to the Office of Special Counsel. "The extraordinary measures to which the NTSB, FBI and CIA went to falsify and distort witness statements or accounts of what occurred, to alter and hide physical evidence and to mount a false public relations campaign to misinform the public, was unconscionable."[1]

Henry F. Hughes was neither a rookie nor a kook. His title was senior accident investigator, National Transportation and Safety Board (NTSB), and it was he who oversaw the meticulous reconstruction of the demolished TWA jetliner in a former Grumman aircraft hangar. Hughes also served as chairman of the Airplane Interior Documentation Group, a team that identified, examined, and documented the myriad interior components from the doomed aircraft that navy divers retrieved from the crash site. By all accounts, his role in the Flight 800 investigation was a major one. It was therefore stunning when he subsequently complained, publicly, of malfeasance. And Hughes was not alone in voicing such allegations; a number of his colleagues at both the FBI and NTSB expressed grave concerns about the investigation's integrity as well.

As it stands, the tragedy of Flight 800, which occurred on July 17, 1996, is perhaps best known for a stunning incongruity: 258 men and women on or near Long Island, New York—people of all ages and from all walks of life—reported watching as a streak of light (or two or three streaks of light depending on the observers' locations), approached a passenger-filled Boeing 747, which exploded several seconds later.[2] Of these bystanders, nearly a hundred added that the light originated at ground level and soared upward to the aircraft, with more than three dozen people further describing condensation trails, or contrails, behind the brightly-lit object. As could be expected, many thought they were looking at a surface-to-air missile. In the ensuing set of investigations, however, the FBI, CIA, and NTSB discounted these witness reports as misperceptions, insisting that none of the observers had, in fact, seen what they described. And it is largely because of this chasm—the scores of credible and consistent eyewitness accounts versus the investigators' across-the-board dismissal of them—that the TWA 800 catastrophe remains one of the paramount mysteries in modern air travel. It is also why numerous experts in the aviation community believe the government's investigations were deeply flawed or perhaps worse, that they were designed to eclipse the true origin of the event—a missile strike—for political or economic reasons.

In this chapter, the intriguing case of Flight 800 is revisited, together with the federal investigations it prompted, and the prolonged and provocative disputes that arose from them. Among the latter are the official challenges brought by two organizations, ARAP (Associated Retired Aviation Professionals) and the TWA 800 Project, both of which contested the federal agencies' procedures and conclusions. The aim is to furnish a rich, accurate, and nuanced understanding of the horrific human tragedy that commenced as the sun set off the shores of Long Island.

The Political Milieu

The political climate was tense in the United States in the weeks leading up to the incident. President Bill Clinton was running for reelection in the upcoming November contest, and the scandal-plagued politician was adamant that no unforeseen events be allowed to upset his anticipated victory. Given recent happenings, he had reason to worry.

A few weeks earlier, Ramzi Ahmed Yousef was put on trial in New York City, and the proceedings, which commenced on May 26, 1996, were expected to last for months. A Pakistani terrorist, Youssef was the architect of the 1993 bombing of the World Trade Center, a spectacular act of violence that wounded more than a thousand people and killed six others. Then, in 1994, Yousef, who was still at large, planted a bomb on Philippine Airlines Flight 434, again bringing suffering and death to innocents. But on this particular day, he was facing a jury for a new offense. "Today Mr. Yousef—almost certainly not his real name—stands in Federal Court in lower Manhattan on charges that he and his accomplices plotted to blow up American jetliners in Asia, as many as 11 in a single day," the *New York Times* reported.[3] Understandably, the city, along with domestic airline companies, were on edge as the legal proceedings got underway, with authorities taking the precautionary measure of issuing a terrorism alert.

Days later, several terrorist groups held a summit in Tehran, after which a U.S. military installation in Saudi Arabia was targeted for a devastating attack. The date was June 25, 1996, three weeks before the TWA tragedy, and members of the Iranian-backed Saudi Hezbollah al-Hejaz terrorist group drove a tanker trunk loaded with 20,000 pounds of explosives into a U.S. Air Force barracks, known as Khobar Towers, in Dhahran, Saudi Arabia. In this strike that damaged or leveled half a dozen high-rise buildings, nearly 600 people were injured and 19 American soldiers were killed. A blood-stained victory for Hezbollah (some speculate that al-Qaeda was also involved), the bombing handed political ammunition to Clinton's rival, ammunition that threatened to dent the president's prospects for reelection.

It was also during this period that the 1996 Summer Olympics were preparing to launch in Atlanta. Visitors from around the globe were pouring into Hartsfield–Jackson Atlanta International Airport, with 170,000 athletes and spectators expected to descend on the southern city in a matter of days.

So it was that Clinton and his security team in the nation's capital were monitoring this trifecta of events—the terrorist trial in Manhattan, the terrorist attack in Saudi Arabia, and the forthcoming Olympics in Atlanta—in what was a tense period for the White House. The administration was acutely aware that the eyes of the world were upon the United States at this moment and that circumstances were ripe for exploitation by hostile actors. It has long been known that those who aspire to commit cinematic acts of political violence seek out precisely such conditions, and it was for this reason that terrorism had now become a dominant concern at the White House. "A terrorist attack on America would have spoiled the Olympics about to get underway in Atlanta and created tons of negative publicity, making Clinton seem vulnerable and weak," writes columnist and author Bret Burquest.[4]

The threat ratcheted up even further on the cusp of the Olympic Games, when an Israeli intelligence officer, one whose job was to covertly monitor the communications and activities of terrorist groups in the Middle East, contacted U.S. intelligence figures in Tel Aviv. The officer warned that Islamist extremists were planning to strike an American aircraft. "The threat of sabotage or a hijacking was analysed and considered serious enough for us to pass on to the Americans," the source stated.[5]

In July as well, a terrorist organization known as the Movement of Islamic Change (also known as "Islamic Movement for Change"), which some assumed to be either an incarnation or a façade of al-Qaeda, delivered a more direct threat to the United States. It was this group, which opposed the American military presence in Saudi Arabia, that had bombed a three-story U.S. military building in Riyadh seven months earlier, killing five soldiers and wounding 60 civilians and service members. "It was like an earthquake," recalled one resident.[6] Regarding the group's current threat, it was faxed to an Arabic language newspaper in Beirut on July 17, 1996, with the CIA and State Department promptly translating the message and verifying its authenticity. And the warning was ominous. "[T]omorrow morning we will strike the Americans in a way they do not expect," it read in part, "and it will be very surprising to them."[7] It was eight hours later, against this backdrop of vicious attacks and plausible threats, that hundreds of people on and around Long Island witnessed a ghastly spectacle in the sky.

Long Island, New York

The day was winding down, the winds were calm, and the temperature was 72 degrees. The local weather station on Westhampton Beach was registering scattered clouds with a light haze. At Docker's Restaurant in East Quogue, a local woman was poised on a deck, where she busily snapped photographs at a Republican fundraiser. Twenty miles to the west of her, a wedding was underway on a beach near the town of Moriches and a handful of the guests were videotaping the ceremony. Elsewhere on this slice of Long Island, hundreds more residents and visitors, for myriad reasons, were out of doors.

Offshore, meanwhile, Coast Guard patrol boats plied the waters alongside pleasure craft and fishing boats. According to an FBI report, also operational in the area were a trio of U.S. Navy nuclear submarines and the USS

Normandy, an Aegis cruiser, one of the most powerful and efficient warships in the world.⁸ Then, too, a steady string of airliners was taking to the air from John F. Kennedy International Airport, traveling on eastbound routes that would take them to Europe and beyond.

Among these commercial carriers was Trans World Airlines (TWA) Flight 800. Captain Ralph Kevorkian, a 58-year-old Californian and career pilot who had worked for the airline for 36 years, was at the controls. On this flight to Charles de Gaulle Airport in Paris, he would be joined by, and have his work monitored by, Steven Snyder, a 57-year-old check airman and captain. Also comprising the crew would be the flight engineer and his trainee, ages 62 and 24, respectively.

At JFK, the jetliner, which had just arrived from Athens, refueled, then waited on the apron for two and a half hours in an unscheduled delay. During this interval, two of its three air conditioning packs—"packs" is an acronym for "pressurization and air conditioning kits"—remained in operation to ensure passenger comfort, a procedure that is not uncommon for commercial airliners.

Finally, at 8:00 p.m., the cockpit voice recorder (CVR) picked up the sound of the cockpit door closing, meaning the aircraft was preparing to taxi to the runway. Nineteen minutes later, the Boeing 747 became airborne, according to data retrieved from the CVR and flight data recorder (FDR), or "black box."

The airliner was carrying 230 people. In addition to the cockpit crew, 14 flight attendants were on board, along with 19 off-duty TWA pilots, flight engineers, and flight attendants. As to the remaining 193 passengers, they ranged in age from eight to 81 years and represented a broad swath of the population. Among them were a composer, a physicist, two architects, a seamstress, a waitress and mother of four, and a fashion photographer. Also on the flight: the wife of renowned jazz saxophonist Wayne Shorter, husband and wife anesthesiologists, a high school secretary, a French hockey player, an Italian cloth merchant, and an ABC-TV executive producer. At least 14 children were on board as well, some of whom were traveling unaccompanied, their loved ones awaiting them at the airport in Paris.

At 8:26 p.m., air traffic control instructed Flight 800, which was now roughly 20 miles south of East Moriches, a hamlet on Long Island's South Shore, to maintain an altitude of 13,000 feet. Comparatively low, this flight level was assigned to prevent a collision between the jetliner and another plane that was flying above it on a perpendicular course. Three minutes later, the CVR recorded Kevorkian remarking to his co-pilot, "Look at that crazy fuel flow indicator there on number four … see that?"⁹ A technical glitch—Kevorkian did not sound troubled by it. The air traffic controller handling the flight next advised the pilot to commence climbing to 15,000 feet, after which 50 seconds passed without the cockpit crew voicing any problems or concerns. It appeared to be an ordinary flight until the aircraft reached 13,700 feet. "The CVR then recorded a 'very loud sound' for a fraction of a second," reads the investigative report. "At 8:31, the CVR recording ended."[10] (More precisely, 20:31:12:26.) Those in the control tower would later state that they had no further contact with TWA 800.

Fifty-three miles away from the last known position of Flight 800, Mike Wire and a team of engineers and electrical experts were working on Beach Lane Bridge in Westhampton Beach.[11] A millwright and U.S. Army veteran, Wire propped his arm on the guardrail and glanced toward the coastline when, he recalled, "cheap fireworks" caught his attention.[12] He quickly realized they were not pyrotechnics, however. In an interview with federal investigators, Wire described the spectacle as "a white light that was traveling skyward from the ground at approximately a 40° angle."[13] Reaching its apex, Wire said it curved and vanished. "Then I saw what appeared to be an explosion, it expanded into a large fireball, and then I watched the aircraft [TWA Flight 800] in flames descend from the fireball and fall to the sea, breaking up as it fell."[14]

During this same period and approximately six miles from the last known position of the TWA airliner, an airborne flight crew in a Black Hawk (H-60) search-and-rescue helicopter watched as two events materialized in front of them separated in time by a few seconds. The men comprising the crew were members of the New York Air National Guard, a reserve module of the U.S. Air Force, and they were on a routine training exercise. Although Major Frederick "Fritz" Meyer was the aircraft's commander, the co-pilot, Christian (Chris) Baur, was at the controls.[15]

At approximately 8:30 p.m., Meyer was scanning the sky through the windshield, looking for another aircraft that was reported to be in the helicopter's traffic pattern. His own helicopter was at an altitude of 250 feet, and his attention was fixed on the sky ahead of it. It was at this moment that he observed the two occurrences, both of them involving explosions.

In Meyer's statement to investigators, he described the first event, which he sought to understand and explain based on his military experience. "[I]n front of me and slightly to my left of dead front I saw a streak of light in the sky," he said, "[a]nd my reaction when I saw it was, what the hell is that?" He continued, "[I]t was red-orange in color.... And about one to two seconds after that I saw a second, and possibly a third, explosion. Now, these were hard explosions. This looked like flak."[16]

Flak, of course, is anti-aircraft fire, so it is understandable that Meyer did not observe any features of a jumbo jet. "I saw no airframe," he said.[17] The veteran aviator, in subsequent discussions, would be more explicit when recounting his observations. "It was definitely a rocket motor," he would say. "What I saw explode was definitely ordnance."[18] It "looked like flak in the sky—and I've seen a lot of flak—ours and theirs."[19]

It is true that Meyer had considerable firsthand knowledge of anti-aircraft fire, having served as a combat helicopter pilot during the Vietnam War, where he carried out rescue operations. In his meeting with investigators, he described the types of explosions he had witnessed in Southeast Asia and highlighted the ways in which anti-aircraft fire looks unlike, say, an explosion at a fuel storage facility. Both the color and speed of such explosions, he explained, are different.[20] And what Meyer saw in the skies off the coast of Long Island during the first set of explosions, he maintained, looked like a weapon.[21]

He next recounted the second incident: the ensuing catastrophe. "So, [after] the streak of light, I saw the explosion about one to two seconds [later]. And then, from that approximate position emanated this fireball, which was a soft explosion. And it was definitely petroleum."[22]

So whereas Meyer asserted that the features of the first set of "hard explosions" pointed to anti-aircraft fire, he concluded that the "soft explosion" that followed it, the one that generated the immense fireball and culminated in a "lake of fire" in the ocean, was the ignition of petroleum or a petroleum product—presumably, the petroleum-based fuel contained in an aircraft.[23] Meyer and Baur were soon able to confirm that portions of a jet-liner had fallen into the ocean as they approached the flaming debris and assessed the nightmarish scene that stretched out beneath them.

In a separate meeting with officials, the co-pilot, Chris Baur, recounted his own experience. "I was flying the aircraft," he said. "And for whatever reason, I looked up and saw what I thought was an incendiary device."[24] Baur continued, "The device that—I saw—there was an object that came from the left. And it appeared to be like—like, a white-hot.... It came from the left and went to the right. And it made the object on the right explode."[25]

At a later point in the interview, Baur returned to the blazing object he had watched, the one that had purportedly triggered the massive fireball. "[T]he things that stand out in my mind was this object ... that had a white phosphorous kind of flame ... or whatever you want to call it—coming out of it striking another object."[26]

Other witnesses to the extraordinary phenomena were in boats, some of them fishing, others partying or simply relaxing. From different vantage points in the ocean or nearby inlets and bays, they reported a similar spectacle: a bright light (or two or three lights) soaring upward, traveling for a few seconds and occasionally zigzagging until attaining a high altitude. In some accounts, the light or lights then arced or descended somewhat, again depending upon the viewer's location. These witnesses next observed an explosion, or two or three explosions, and moments later watched as a massive fireball erupted and fell into the ocean. The final blast was so intense as to pulverize the jetliner, with the expanding sphere of debris appearing as a cloud on weather-radar systems in the region.

Still other witnesses were landbound and strolling along a beach, jogging in a park, driving along a highway, or fishing from a dock. Most described seeing only an immense fiery sphere—that is, the explosion of TWA 800. It was so immense that its radiance caught their attention even if they were facing another direction. Yet some of these landbound individuals reported seeing an unusual object in the sky immediately before the mammoth explosion. They described watching a point, or points, of bright light, which some initially thought to be a bottle rocket or perhaps a comet, travel upward and then across the sky, followed seconds later by a tremendous explosion. Some also described the ascending object as having a tail. Additionally, a portion of witnesses, again depending on their locations, described an ear-splitting noise similar to a sonic boom after the final, grand explosion.

Then there were those who watched from above, specifically from 21,000 feet. At least three passengers on USAir Flight 217 were looking out of their windows, one of them a 12-year-old boy, Adam Coletti, who was traveling with his mother. From his window, Coletti looked out upon an unlikely sight from this altitude: the shape of a boat with a wake trailing behind it. The youth turned to his mother, who was seated across the aisle, and told her what he had seen, but when Coletti turned back and glanced out the window again, all he could see was the color red. "I'm not sure if it exploded then, or if I turned again and looked back," he said, "but it was 10 to 15 seconds after I saw the red that I saw the explosion."[27] The boy added that the blast extended upward from the boat-shaped figure he had initially observed.[28]

Fellow passenger Dwight Brumley, who, like Coletti, was seated on the right side of the plane, was gazing out a window as well. A navy master chief, Brumley had served in the military since 1972 and had acquired considerable training and experience in numerous aspects of warfare. Holding a degree in education with a specialization in mathematics, the 44-year-old Brumley had served on guided-missile battleships and was experienced in both electronic warfare and missile launches. Topping off his credentials, he held a top-secret security clearance.

In an affidavit, Brumley stated that, as his flight was nearing Long Island, he watched as what appeared to be a small aircraft with blinking lights fly comparatively slowly, from right to left, a few hundred feet beneath USAir 217.[29] In all likelihood, the aircraft he observed was a P-3 Orion, a four-engine military airplane used for maritime surveillance and anti-submarine warfare. Then, 20 to 30 seconds later, a streak of bright light caught Brumley's eye. It "appeared to be some kind of flare," he said.[30] Ascending and moving faster than USAir 217, it overtook the plane. Ten seconds later as he continued watching the luminous object, Brumley caught sight of two small explosions separated in time by a couple of seconds, followed by a colossal inferno.[31] Since TWA 800 had been beneath and ahead of USAir 217 and thus out of his line of sight before the explosion, Brumley was unaware that it had become the ball of fire. Another passenger, James Nugent, who was seated behind the navy officer, likewise observed the spectacle. "Did you see that too?" he asked Brumley.[32]

Reaction and Recovery

At the site of the crash, meanwhile, the surface of the ocean had become a mantle of fire, with flames leaping 50 feet into the air. In short order, three National Guard cutters and six helicopters raced to the scene in an attempt to rescue survivors. Many more left from the Boston area, and scores of civilian boats promptly joined the effort. Piloted by Long Islanders, their watercraft ranged from lobster boats to yachts.

But there was a mystery vessel as well. Shortly before the lethal event in the sky, a handful of eyewitnesses spotted an unfamiliar white boat in the ocean, 20 to 30 feet long. Evidently, it had been in the area for two or three days, was unfamiliar to those who lived and boated in the area, and remained in the ocean even during a storm. What is puzzling is that, while military and civilian vessels were hurrying to the site of the tragedy, this boat was leaving the area of the crash. Furthermore, no one on the vessel contacted the authorities to report the fiery, midair occurrence, not even in the days afterward when government officials, soliciting witness accounts, promoted a special telephone line that had been set up exclusively for this purpose.

Bolstering the locals' descriptions of the unfamiliar white boat and its incongruous course was radar data, which federal investigators, for whatever reason, initially withheld from the public and from formal accounts of the catastrophe.[33] According to *The Observer*, the two entities nearest to TWA 800 in its final moments were the military's P-3 Orion surveillance aircraft and the white boat. As the TWA plane plunged into the ocean, the vessel fled the area at a speed of 30 knots, or roughly 35 miles an hour. "Radar data for the next 20 minutes showed the mystery boat heading on a beeline out to sea, on a south-southwest course, even as other boats rushed to the crash to try to help out," writes Philip Weiss.[34] Incommunicado in the midst of a crisis and suspicious in its dodge to open waters, the vessel has never been identified.

In Washington, D.C., Bill Clinton had just returned to the White House after a campaign appearance and was about to settle into his living quarters when news of the disaster arrived. The White House chief of staff, Leon Panetta, was notified at 9:45 p.m., and he, in turn, relayed the information to the president at 10:00 p.m.[35] In a 2006 interview, Anthony Lake, Clinton's national security advisor, revealed that the immediate assumption was that a terrorist attack had brought down the plane.[36] As is standard procedure, the NTSB launched an inquiry into the crash. At 1:25 a.m., however, less than five hours after the tragedy, it was announced that the FBI's Joint Terrorism Task Force–New York Police Department would, in fact, also be investigating, since the authorities believed the event was likely a criminal act, not an accident.[37]

The Clinton administration took further action as well. "Within hours of the TWA explosion," says CNN's Jim Polk, "security officials were meeting at the White House to discuss possible bombing raids as retaliation, once they knew who might be responsible."[38]

To this end, the Clinton administration provided the Mossad with the flight manifest of TWA 800 and asked the Israeli intelligence agency to check the list of passengers for anyone suspected of having connections to extremist organizations.[39] It was an astute request; Flight 800, until a few months earlier, routinely flew to Tel Aviv after landing in Paris, meaning that a terrorist attack may have been planned for those Israelis on the flight who were returning to their homeland. Potentially relevant as well, an El Al plane was supposed to have been in the precise airspace where the TWA exploded and crashed, but the Israeli aircraft's departure had been delayed. Some wondered if the El Al aircraft had been the intended target.

As these events were unfolding in the capital, a vigorous effort remained underway in the dark waters off the shore of Long Island to locate and rescue survivors. Unfortunately, none were being found. By all accounts, the situation seemed hopeless, and the rescuers, both military and civilian, were overwhelmed. Contributing to the sense of urgency, medical authorities warned that hypothermia would set in within a matter of hours owing to the ocean temperature. Haste was crucial in such situations.

Regarding the nature of the victims' injuries, some of the bodies recovered in the 20-mile stretch of debris displayed burn damage, while many others had no burns at all. It would be 16 days before navy divers located the pilot's body, which, as it happened, was still strapped to his cockpit seat at the bottom of the Atlantic. In contrast, many passengers' bodies were no longer secured to their seats or, for that matter, intact.

"Most of the people we saw—or a fair amount of them—seemed to be decapitated," said Chris Baur, co-pilot of the helicopter that was first to arrive on the scene. "There was [sic] double amputees; indicative of sudden stoppage," he added.[40]

The Suffolk County medical examiner, Charles Wetli, subsequently analyzed the fatalities and elaborated on the injuries. "It's like a car smashing into a brick wall at 400 m.p.h.," he said.[41] "First of all, massive facial and head injuries from hitting the seat in front of them and then a secondary whiplash backward which basically was going to sever all function [sic] of the brain stem," he explained.[42] Death was instantaneous. Wetli proceeded to offer his opinion on what brought down the jetliner, which broke apart at 13,700 feet, then exploded a few seconds later after falling to 9,000 feet. The physician believed that an act of terrorism, one involving an incendiary device, was the cause.[43]

To hold the fatalities, a makeshift morgue was set up in East Moriches, Long Island, but soon was replaced by a much larger one at an air national guard hangar in Westhampton. At JFK, in the meantime, airport officials, together with representatives of Trans World Airlines and the American Red Cross, set to work providing the victims' loved ones with lodging and grief counseling. Similar services were offered at Charles de Gaulle Airport.

As an emergency measure, the Federal Aviation Administration (FAA) set about heightening security at American airports, particularly JFK in New York and Dulles in Washington, D.C. In Atlanta, where the opening ceremonies of the Olympics were only hours away, officials worked overtime to protect Hartsfield–Jackson International Airport and reassure both the public and the International Olympic Committee (IOC) of the airport's safety. "We have been informed," the director general of the IOC told the Associated Press, "that security measures have been tightened in connection with everything related to flights, airport procedure and control."[44] By all accounts, the Atlanta airport had become a veritable fortress.

Mangling the Message

As the sun rose the morning after the explosion and crash of Flight 800, U.S. government officials began appearing before the cameras to field questions about the catastrophe and to keep the American people abreast of developments in the ill-fated aircraft's retrieval. In light of the voluminous number of witnesses who reported watching a bright object, or objects, zero in on the jetliner, the principal question was whether a terrorist attack had brought down the plane. A dutiful press set about offering answers.

"Investigators Suspect Explosive Device as Likeliest Cause of Crash of Flight 800," proclaimed the *New York Times* on July 19, 1996.[45] The same day, competing newspapers emphasized TWA's history of being targeted by terrorists, or, alternatively, they analyzed the disaster's financial impact on the airline.[46] But even as media reports heralded the prospect of a terrorist act, statements issued by the Clinton administration and federal agencies struggled to tamp down such talk. "There was the usual amount of official anti-speak," writes journalist Walter Goodman.[47] The upshot: the media's early, breathless accounts of a probable terrorist strike and the government's opposing "anti-speak" led to public confusion at a moment when the citizenry, most of all the victims' loved ones, yearned for solid, reliable information. And such conflicted messaging existed not only between the media and the government; the government's own communications were in themselves inconsistent, ambiguous, and contradictory. Such topsy-turvy messaging commenced within hours of the crash, when the White House denied that a terrorist organization had threatened an attack on American interests.

"A top Clinton administration official said late last night that no warnings were received from any group," *Newsday* reported the morning after the crash.[48] A comforting assertion, it was nevertheless false. In the Middle East and Washington, D.C., it was already known that the Movement of Islamic Change, the aforementioned terrorist group that had bombed American military housing in Saudi Arabia, had issued a threat only eight hours before the TWA explosion and crash. When this subject was broached, however, the U.S. State Department spokesperson, Nicolas Burns, brushed it aside. Conceding that a message in Arabic had indeed declared that a terrorist strike on an American entity was imminent, Burns stressed that it did not identify the target. "It had no specific threats in it whatsoever," he said, "certainly nothing pertaining to the crash."[49] Of course, terrorist threats, so as to retain the element of surprise, virtually never announce their targets in advance. Noteworthy, too, was the fact that Burns did not mention the warning Israel had relayed to the United States earlier in the month: to reiterate, that Israeli intelligence had intercepted communications from an Islamist terror organization that revealed a credible threat to an American aircraft.

As for terrorist communications following the TWA tragedy, the *London Times* reported soon after the catastrophe that the Movement of Islamic Change had since claimed credit for it, and, moreover, that an Iranian official had served as the newspaper's source on the matter.[50] In response, the White House chief of staff, Leon Panetta, called a press conference during which he stated unequivocally that no person or organization had taken credit for the TWA disaster.[51]

Furthering the confusion, Janet Reno, the U.S. attorney general, next revealed that two groups had indeed claimed responsibility and they had done so within 48 hours of the crash.[52] Yet even this disclosure was imprecise. At least three entities sought to take credit for the downing of Flight 800. One was the aforementioned Movement of Islamic Change and another was an Islamist extremist in Florida. It was a third set of threats that most concerned the White House, though: a set comprised of the supporters of Ramzi Ahmed Yousef, the terrorist who was on trial in Manhattan at the moment.[53] "[O]fficials discounted the specific declaration of responsibility, but did not rule out the possibility that someone in Mr. Yousef's loosely connected terrorist circle of Islamic, anti–American veterans of the Afghan war against Soviet forces might have played a part—given their past record of terrorist acts and known efforts to attack airliners," reported David Johnston.[54]

Regarding communications with the TWA jetliner itself, communications that might help determine whether the catastrophe was due to pilot error, mechanical problems, or a terrorist device such as a bomb or missile, the government's position was that, in the final moments of Flight 800, the CVR recorded "a brief fraction-of-a-second sound" and abruptly fell silent.[55] The pilot, it was pointed out, did not issue a distress call. Yet this account was undercut by a disclosure from a highly reliable source. A Coast Guard cutter patrolling the waters off Long Island on the evening of the tragedy picked up a two-word message—"Mayday, mayday!"—immediately before TWA 800 exploded and crashed into the ocean, according to Commandant Robert E. Kramek.[56] An admiral with a flawless tenure in the military, it was Kramek who would lead the local Coast Guard's search and rescue operation for the passengers and crew of the downed plane. (The Coast Guard's First District Command Center in Boston would be in charge of the overall operation itself.) And although the "mayday" transmission could not be definitively tied to Flight 800, the TWA airliner was the only aircraft or vessel known to be in a life-or-death situation at 8:31 p.m. in the Long Island area.

Of perhaps the greatest significance was the government's position on the "missile theory" and the conflict between its public messaging and private deliberations. The day after the crash, Bill Clinton released a statement lamenting the deaths of all of the jetliner's 230 passengers and crew, and he touched on the question that was on everyone's mind. "We do not know what caused this tragedy," the president declared from the podium in the White House Briefing Room. "I want to say that again: We do not know as of this moment what caused this tragedy."[57] Clinton seemed to be trying to quell the conjecture that was raging internationally about a bomb or missile having destroyed the airliner, the latter powered by the scores of eyewitness accounts.

Even more strident was White House Press Secretary Mike McCurry. Speaking on behalf of the Clinton administration, McCurry publicly insinuated that the missile hypothesis was ludicrous. "Asked about speculation that the plane may have been hit by a surface-to-air missile," writes Terrence Hunt, "McCurry replied, 'There is no American official with half a brain who ought to be speculating on anything of that nature.'"[58]

In point of fact, the White House, as noted earlier, did believe a terrorist operation was the probable cause of the TWA 800 disaster, even to the point of planning military action in retaliation. According to Clinton's national security advisor, the administration immediately considered Iran to be the number-one suspect, not in the least because of the Khobar Towers bombing in Saudi Arabia three weeks earlier.[59] The powers that be also thought that a projectile, not a bomb, had most likely produced the colossal explosion. "[T]here was widespread speculation in the C.S.G. [Counterterrorism Security Group] that it had been shot down by a shoulder-fired missile from the shore," Lawrence Wright revealed in *The New Yorker*.[60] Notably, the C.S.G. is composed of members of the National Security Council, the Central Intelligence Agency, and the departments of Defense, Justice, and State—in other words, the most informed people in a national security emergency.

Furthermore, the C.S.G. was not alone in its partiality toward the missile hypothesis. "Government officials, both civil and criminal, said they were seriously examining the possibility that a missile struck the plane, because of an apparent [radar] blip on the screen before the explosion," *Newsday* reported.[61]

Fueling concern about the possibility of such a weapon bringing down the airliner, it was well known that the CIA, in the 1980s, had armed the Taliban in Afghanistan with hundreds of heat-seeking Stinger missiles for the Taliban's fight against Soviet forces. "We were handing them out like lollipops," said an American intelligence officer.[62] Then, in the wake of the Soviet withdrawal from Afghanistan in 1989, the CIA made a concerted effort to track down and buy back the weapons, but the project failed in spite of Congress having earmarked $65 million for it.[63] So it was that, in 1996, the year of the TWA explosion, an estimated six hundred Stingers remained unaccounted for. "Some of the missing missiles ended up in the hands of terrorists, insurgents, and hostile governments as far away as North Korea and Sri Lanka," writes Matthew Schroeder in *Foreign Policy* magazine.[64] They also made their way to Iran, Qatar, and Croatia.

At this juncture, federal law enforcement figures set about trying to discourage speculation about a shoulder-fired missile causing the crash; one argument was that the jetliner's altitude of 13,700 feet placed it above the ceiling of most such weapons.[65] While this observation was accurate, it did not address the fact that some shoulder-fired missiles *could* reach a maximum altitude of 20,000 feet, well within the range of Flight 800.

Moreover, new types of projectiles had been ingeniously designed specifically to destroy high-flying aircraft, meaning those traveling above 20,000 feet. Accordingly, the missile hypothesis continued to circulate.

The Friendly Fire Imbroglio

Within weeks of the crash, the traditional media began reporting on yet another possibility, a version of the missile hypothesis that was dominating internet discussion groups and radio talk shows. The gist: the U.S. Navy accidentally blasted the plane out of the sky while conducting missile tests off the shores of Long Island. In short order, it would become obvious that this "friendly fire" scenario had overstepped a boundary. By proposing that the Navy caused the disaster and was hiding its culpability, the friendly-fire hypothesis received a volatile reaction from federal officials, who were at once indignant and inordinately defensive. Among them was James Kallstrom, the assistant director of the FBI, who denounced the hypothesis on September 17, 1996. "It's an outrageous allegation," he railed, even as he conceded that he did not know what caused the airliner to ignite and crash.[66] Although virtually everyone believed, correctly, that the plane's center wing fuel tank (CWT) had exploded at some point, the question remained as to what triggered the blast itself, a mechanical problem or a criminal act. The friendly-fire hypothesis therefore persisted despite officials' admonitions, catapulting to international attention after a man by the name of Richard Russell made contact with Pierre Salinger about the matter.

Richard Russell was an army veteran who had served as a military photographer during the Korean War. Afterward, he became a pilot for United Airlines, a position he held for thirty-five years. On occasion, he also investigated aircraft accidents for the Air Line Pilots Association, where he served as the western regional safety coordinator. Russell was presented with the organization's Air Safety award for his contributions.[67] In terms of Flight 800, Russell found it puzzling from the outset. "I knew there was something wrong," he stated in an affidavit, "and could not understand why the Pentagon was announcing the demise of a civilian airliner crash unless the military was involved."[68]

In the aftermath of the tragedy, a high-level source in the federal government reportedly sent Russell a document that was said to contain proof that a Navy-launched missile had struck TWA 800.[69] After discussing the potentially incriminating information with eleven colleagues, Russell, in September 1996, arranged to furnish Pierre Salinger with it.

A distinguished figure at the time, Salinger had served as White House press secretary for two presidents, John F. Kennedy and Lyndon B. Johnson.

Subsequent to this, he was appointed Paris bureau chief of ABC News, and eventually he anchored *ABC World News Tonight* from the company's Manhattan studios. The recipient of a Peabody Award, Salinger was vice chairman of a high-powered public relations firm in Washington, D.C., when Russell, through intermediaries, provided him with the aforementioned document. Five weeks later, Salinger acted on it.

On November 7, 1996, at a global aviation conference in Cannes, France, Salinger went on record with a claim that the U.S. Navy had inadvertently brought down Flight 800 during missile tests off Long Island, adding that he was in possession of a document that substantiated it.[70] "The original document was written by an American but it was given to me by someone in French intelligence in Paris," Salinger said.[71] The former press secretary believed it shed light on how the accident had occurred. "Salinger said the document showed the Navy was testing missiles off the coast of New York, and had been told [civilian] planes would be flying higher than 21,000 feet," reported Jocelyn Noveck.[72] As mentioned earlier, TWA 800 was temporarily flying at 13,700 feet because another airliner was in the airspace above it. While Salinger did not identify the source of his material, he did allow that the document was originally leaked by a person in the U.S. Secret Service.[73] Dated August 22, it was uploaded to the internet a few weeks later, although it is not known by whom. Salinger offered to share his copy with the FBI.[74]

In short order, the brunt of the U.S. government came to the fore. In response to Salinger's allegations, the Secret Service, the Navy, the Federal Bureau of Investigation, and the National Transportation Safety Board called a joint press conference in New York City on November 9, 1996. A collective front, its attitude was defensive and its message hostile. "[W]e deplore these unfortunate and irresponsible statements," exclaimed Jim Hall, head of the NTSB.[75] "We have looked at this thoroughly," interjected the FBI's James Kallstrom, "and we have absolutely not one shred of evidence that it happened or it could have happened."[76] The most startling moment of the emotional and unruly event occurred when a reporter asked Kallstrom if the Navy was facing a conflict of interest, since it was now a suspect in the TWA crash and yet was participating in the salvage operation and investigation. By several accounts, Kallstrom was visibly unnerved by the fact that the journalist had referred to the U.S. Navy as "a suspect."[77] And so Kallstrom went ballistic, shouting, "Remove him!"[78] At once, two men seized the reporter and hustled him out of the room, after which Kallstrom stated that it was "highly, highly, highly, highly, highly unlikely" that friendly fire was the cause of the crash.[79]

Entering the fray, a Navy spokesperson from the Pentagon stated that only two military entities were in the Long Island area on the night of the disaster, neither of which could have shot down the airliner. One was the

P-3 Orion anti-submarine aircraft, which does not carry missiles, and the other was the USS *Normandy*, a warship that does carry missiles, but it was said to be out of range of the TWA jetliner. In addition, it was reported that the *Normandy*'s radar was set on low power that evening, thus limiting its range.[80] An inspection of the ship's log, however, did not support the Navy's claim that the ship's radar was set on low power.[81]

Concerning other inaccuracies, the FBI and the Pentagon would acknowledge that there were in fact other Navy vessels in the area when Flight 800 went down. Among them were three submarines: the USS *Wyoming*, a nuclear-powered ballistic missile vessel; the USS *Trepang*, a nuclear-powered "fast attack" submarine; and the USS *Albuquerque*, a fast-attack vessel that contained a vertical launch system. All were within a short distance of the location in which the disintegrating jetliner would hurtle into the ocean. Reversing its position on another issue, the Navy would also acknowledge that it had been conducting military exercises—"war games"—on the night of the crash.[82]

The fact is, the FAA's air traffic control logs revealed that sizable sectors of the airspace off the coast of Long Island were closed to civilian air traffic due to active military operations. "A large area within twelve miles of where Flight 800 exploded not only was active, off-limits to nonmilitary aircraft, and considered dangerous to civilian air traffic, but another large area normally off-limits to the military had been reserved for navy operations," writes journalist and editor David E. Hendrix. "The Navy P-3 Orion anti-submarine aircraft that was almost over Flight 800 at the time the jetliner exploded was headed for the special zone for a hide-and-seek game with the nuclear submarine USS *Trepang*."[83] Such about-faces and belated disclosures shook the public's trust in the government's assertions about the military's actions on the night of the disaster.

That said, the traditional U.S. media nevertheless closed ranks alongside the federal government in what appeared to be a campaign to quash the friendly-fire hypothesis and discredit the former White House press secretary for proposing it. This was unlike the French media, which kept alive Salinger's allegations and persisted in discussing them. Then, too, there was one instantly positive aspect to Salinger's provocative claim and it involved Trans World Airlines itself: the company's stock rose nearly 20 percent after his accusation, presumably because, if correct, it promised to absolve the airline of financial responsibility for the crash.[84]

In February 1997, Richard Russell's sources furnished him with more material, most important a videotape of a radar readout allegedly showing an object merging with the airliner.[85] "The tape showed a non-beacon target in close proximity to TWA 800 just prior to the [airliner] indicating a loss of a transponder signal," Russell stated in his affidavit.[86]

Russell forwarded the materials to Salinger, who in turn loaned them to *Paris Match*, the French news magazine. At the periodical's behest, a team of experts analyzed the radar images. After reviewing the results, *Paris Match*, in an article co-written by Salinger and dated March 13, 1997, publicly endorsed the friendly-fire hypothesis. "He and his co-authors in *Paris Match* said that the Navy has concealed the truth of the TWA 800 crash to cover up a top-secret new missile that violates the long-standing SALT I arms control treaty," reported *Salon*.[87] The Strategic Arms Limitation Treaty I (SALT I) was the anti-ballistic missile accord signed in 1972 by Richard Nixon and Leonid Brezhnev.

Evidently, the missile that Salinger and his informants were alluding to was the infamous "continuous rod missile," a diabolical weapon that is capable of slicing through an airliner in flight.[88] The explosive warhead, in such a missile, is sheathed in a cannister of steels rods fused end to end. When detonated, the weapon's diameter of destruction expands dramatically, with a ring of steel reaching and slashing through airliners at higher altitudes. It was a continuous-rod missile that brought down Malaysian Airlines Flight 17 in 2014. "When the warhead explodes," explains journalist Julian Morgans, "the bars expand into a zig-zag shaped ring, slicing through the plane's fuselage."[89] As for Flight 800, a journalist and participant at Salinger's 1997 press conference pointed out that "sixteen passengers have no heads," suggesting that a continuous-rod missile had lacerated not only the jetliner but the passengers as well.[90]

Posthaste, the FBI attacked both Salinger and his assertions, yet again declaring his charges to be wrong and reckless.[91] It was at this point that federal agents traveled to Richard Russell's home in Daytona Beach and confiscated his duplicate of the radar tape. "Russell says the FBI would denounce the tape as a phony," reported United Press International.[92] As it turned out, the FBI did not make a case that the images were faked, but it did contend that the radar blip was the P-3 flying overhead rather than a missile. Like many other aspects of the TWA disaster, it was an interpretation that was met with public doubt, and so the hypothesis remained that the U.S. military, during war games off the coast of Long Island, shot down the commercial airliner by mistake.

The more detailed version of events claims that the U.S. Navy fired three missiles that were supposed to target and destroy a common military target, a drone, while the P-3 flying overhead was to monitor the faux attack. Instead, the missiles locked onto the relatively low-flying TWA jetliner that had unexpectedly entered the airspace. Those who support this scenario point to a fax that was intercepted, entirely by accident, by a Long Island resident, a fax revealing that the FBI had contacted a maker of drones used by the military, Teledyne Ryan in San Diego, because Navy divers had recovered drone debris in the TWA wreckage.[93] In the fax, Teledyne Ryan engineers were providing written information, along with a diagram of the company's product, to help the FBI better determine the drone's origin. Publicly, however, the FBI flatly rejected the drone hypothesis, stating there were none missing in the military's East Coast arsenal. "No damage in this airplane was caused by a drone," James Kallstrom added, even though no one had suggested that the drone had damaged the plane or even made contact with it.[94] As noted earlier, the airliner was simply mistaken for the drone in this scenario.

Distressing for Pierre Salinger, meanwhile, was the barrage of attacks on his credibility, including the false charge that he had gotten his information about Flight 800 from an anonymously-sourced post on the internet. A computer neophyte in 1996, Salinger refuted the accusation in a letter to the *New York Times*. "I had never been on the Internet," he wrote, "and did not get the information from that source."[95] Salinger further emphasized that some of his materials about the disaster had still not been posted online. All the same, the rumor about his internet usage stuck and became known derogatorily as the "Pierre Salinger Syndrome." And it is still with us today. "A gullible person who believes everything he or she reads on the Internet, even if these defy the rules of common sense, is believed to be suffering from the Pierre Salinger syndrome," reads a definition on the Techslang website.[96] (The website clarifies that the association with Salinger was spurious.) Still, the one-time press secretary did himself no favors by releasing, prematurely, information about the TWA catastrophe and voicing accusations against the U.S. military based solely on single-sourced, unconfirmed material. So it was that, partly by exposing and exploiting the weaknesses in Salinger's reportorial methods, the FBI, Pentagon, and White House were able to largely discredit, in the public mind, the friendly-fire hypothesis itself. Unfortunately, the Salinger episode helped eclipse the other premise that a shoulder-fired missile had caused the TWA crash, terrorists having used such weapons to blast large aircraft in flight in the past.[97] Concerning Salinger himself, until his death on October 16, 2004, he remained convinced that it was the U.S. Navy that had shot down the jetliner.

Investigations and Political Interference

As internet users and the media pondered the cause of the tragedy, two federal agencies took on the disaster with multimillion-dollar investigations. The NTSB led one of them, an extensive aviation study, while the

FBI led the second, which was conducted by more than a thousand agents and designed to unearth evidence of criminal activity. In addition, the Bureau of Alcohol, Tobacco, and Firearms (ATF) carried out an auxiliary inquiry that was performed by three certified fire investigators.

To provide materials for examination, the NTSB and the FBI, in a collaborative arrangement, oversaw the retrieval of the shattered jetliner and the reconstruction of the fuselage, center wing fuel tank, and wing structure. Amassing three hundred tons of wreckage, the salvaging process took fifteen months to complete.[98] In the end, 96 percent of the plane was recovered.

The reassembly was undertaken in a hangar at Long Island's Calverton Executive Airpark, where a considerable portion of the wreckage was reconstructed and examined by May 1997. Standing three stories tall and filling the cavernous building, "Jetosaurus Rex," as the workers nicknamed it, was not the first airliner to be rebuilt in this fashion.[99] Other planes, or portions of them, had also been reconstituted, most famously Pan Am 103, which a terrorist bomb demolished over Lockerbie, Scotland. In terms of the mock-up of TWA 800, it was touted as an example of governmental transparency at a moment when the Clinton administration and other federal agencies were fending off charges of undue secrecy in revealing what was known about the disaster. "If the Government wanted to just sweep [the TWA crash] under the rug, we would never have insisted on building the mock-up," said the FBI's James Kallstrom, who was leading the bureau's investigative team.[100]

The ATF Investigation

The first inquiry to conclude was that of the ATF, which released its findings in a report dated January 20, 1997, six months after the crash. The Bureau of Alcohol, Tobacco, and Firearms, in an ancillary role, was to deliver the results to the Federal Bureau of Investigation, but it gave them to other entities as well and without the bureau's knowledge.[101] Not surprisingly, this led to ill feelings.

As to the findings, the ATF stated that an undetermined technical problem had caused Flight 800's central fuel tank to explode and emphasized that its trio of investigators had uncovered no evidence of an incendiary device. But while the report essentially ruled out a terrorist act or a friendly-fire incident, the inquiry's procedures and therefore its findings were problematic. The fact is, the ATF wrapped up its investigation and disseminated its conclusions at a time when several tons of the jetliner were still entrenched on the ocean floor and numerous casualties remained in the waters off Long Island. Indeed, the last body would not be pulled from the Atlantic for another six months. Accordingly, critics rejected the inquiry's findings as premature and therefore meaningless. "The report was sophomoric in its science and in its writing," protested the FBI's Kallstrom.[102] "To reach the conclusion that [the TWA crash] was not criminal, with tons of wreckage still in the water, after we gave our word to victims' families that we were going to do everything possible, well, we weren't at 70 percent of doing everything possible," he said.[103] Kallstrom proceeded to denounce as "an extraordinary violation of investigative protocol" the ATF's issuance of a conclusion without the entirety of evidence having been examined, coupled with its handover of information to other agencies.[104] Furthermore, he voiced his concern that, if his FBI team were ultimately to determine that terrorists had in fact caused the TWA 800 crash, the perpetrators' defense attorneys could use the ATF's document to undermine the prosecution's argument.[105]

In a decision that would come back to haunt him, Kallstrom, troubled by the ATF report, did not immediately forward it to the NTSB. He did within forty-eight hours, though, only to discover that the ATF had already furnished the safety board with a copy through a back channel.[106] To some, the ATF's actions smacked of politics, especially since the report's conclusions coincided neatly with a new airline security plan the White House Commission on Aviation Safety and Security was set to deliver to the Oval Office in three weeks.

This high-level working group was created in response to the TWA disaster. It was under the leadership of Vice President Al Gore and its purpose was to review existing regulations and propose enhanced security measures that would better protect airlines and their passengers. To this end, the commission released an interim report on September 9, 1996, seven weeks after the Flight 800 disaster, which recommended twenty changes, some of them quite sweeping. For this reason, the document proved to be a bitter pill for airline bigwigs, unnerved, as they were, by the estimated one-billion-dollar price tag. Lobbying feverishly against the proposed upgrades—and, quite controversially, donating half a million dollars to the Clinton-Gore reelection campaign at this time—airline executives appeared to succeed in persuading the commission to backpedal on some of the tougher, costlier measures. And so it was that the working group's final set of proposals, a watered-down version of the original, was scheduled to be presented to President Clinton in February 1997. But there was a hitch: the commission fully expected its recommendations to trigger the ire of airline passengers' organizations, which were predicted to dismiss them as anemic and insufficient. Now, however, the commission could cite the ATF's rejection of a terrorism-related incident to justify its own weakening of the safety measures, according to John B. Roberts II, author and producer of the PBS public affairs program *The McLaughlin Group*.[107] And indeed, critics were quick to call attention to the fact that the ATF report came at the ideal moment to help the White House commission defend its retreat from its more rigorous and expensive safety and security recommendations.

Adding to the skepticism, during a subsequent Senate hearing in which the ATF's findings were a key topic, the White House study group's final recommendations as well as the airline industry's exquisitely-timed Clinton-Gore campaign donation were both off-limits during the otherwise wide-ranging discussion. As could be expected, this exclusion further fueled suspicions, especially since it was no secret that Vice President Gore had long enjoyed a cozy relationship with the commercial airline business. Even so, there is no tangible proof of an association between the ATF's rejection of criminal activity in the TWA 800 case and the White House Commission on Aviation Safety and Security Commission's softened security recommendations.

The FBI Investigation

Turning to the sixteen-month inquiry that the Federal Bureau of Investigation conducted, one scouring the wreckage and flight records and amassing 700 interviews with witnesses, it was beset with problems from the outset. According to his colleagues in the bureau, James Kallstrom, as chief of the investigative team, was convinced that terrorists had brought down the airliner using an incendiary device, and he was openly antagonistic to suggestions that a friendly-fire incident or mechanical malfunction may have produced the catastrophe.[108] It was a surprise, then, when he appeared at a press conference at the conclusion of the FBI's investigation on November 18, 1997, to announce that "no evidence has been found that would indicate a criminal act was the cause of the tragedy of Flight 800."[109] Striking, too, was the fact that Kallstrom announced his retirement from the FBI only twenty-three days later. "I don't leave because I want to," he said, "but it is time for me to think about other responsibilities."[110]

Truth be told, the assistant director's stretch during the TWA investigation was marked by political infighting, rival interests, and plausibly undue influence from forces outside the bureau. Throughout the FBI's investigation, Kallstrom's efforts to prove that terrorists destroyed the jetliner frustrated those government officials and lawmakers who were insistently advancing the mechanical malfunction explanation. Senator Chuck Grassley, for one, had long promoted the notion that a technical glitch had triggered the TWA explosion, and he was noticeably displeased by the FBI's painstaking search for a criminal component. In view of that, the senator announced an inquiry into the FBI's handling of the investigation. A months-long probe, it would culminate in a Senate hearing on May 10, 1999, one branded a publicity stunt by its critics. Significantly, the Senate panel did not allow Kallstrom, the top figure in the matter, to testify at the hearing, according to the former FBI assistant director himself.[111]

Among Grassley's complaints was the fact that Kallstrom had delayed forwarding the ATF's conclusory report of January 20, 1997, to the NTSB, the early report that essentially exonerated terrorists and the U.S. military of causing the TWA catastrophe. Yet an official representing the FBI stood firm, maintaining that Kallstrom had sent the ATF document within a day or two of receiving it. Moreover, Kallstrom had affixed to it his complaints about the three fire investigators' hasty conclusions as well as the ATF's violation of the agreement with the FBI concerning the document's distribution.[112] The official then produced physical copies of these documents, yet Grassley continued to insist that Kallstrom had failed to act promptly.

The senator further asserted that he himself was in possession of "a March 1997 report sent to the FBI by the deputy director of the CIA, concluding that there was 'absolutely no evidence' of a missile attack."[113] It seemed that the Republican lawmaker was agitated because both the ATF and CIA had, early on, told Kallstrom and his FBI team that a terrorist operation or military error did not cause the TWA tragedy, yet the bureau continued collecting and analyzing potential evidence of a bomb or missile attack as additional segments of the wreckage, along with human casualties, were pulled from the ocean. It may be pertinent that the handwritten notes of an ATF official, in reference to Kallstrom's negative reaction to his agency's premature conclusions, said, "Kallstrom upset with [the ATF] report, locks him into eliminating missile."[114] It is conceivable that Kallstrom felt the ATF and CIA were deliberately pressuring him into adopting the more benign, non-criminal hypothesis of the disaster.

And Grassley leveled still more accusations. He charged Kallstrom and the FBI of holding so tightly to the possibility of a criminal act that their sixteen-month search for evidence had allowed the popular notions of a friendly-fire incident and a terrorist attack to persist in the public arena. In response, a high-level FBI official refuted Grassley's attempt to paint the bureau's work on the case as excessive. "That is what we are there for," said Lewis Schiliro of the FBI's New York division.[115] Schiliro's stance was clear: professional thoroughness is a virtue, not a shortcoming, if truth is the objective. And indeed, public speculation about the TWA disaster was not the FBI's responsibility, nor was it a viable reason for the bureau to rush its criminal probe into the event.

Such testimony notwithstanding, and much to the indignation of the FBI's workforce, Grassley proceeded to attack the bureau's proficiency. "I think that the public was ill-served by the FBI in the TWA Flight 800 investigation and I intend to make sure that this type of investigation does not take place again," raged the senator.[116] Once again promoting the mechanical defect explanation, Grassley attempted to shut down further discussion of the source of the Flight 800 disaster. "In a hearing that [appeared] designed solely to get newspaper headlines, Grassley pronounced TWA 800 a closed case," wrote John Roberts II.[117] Of course, it was not within the senator's power to close the case, and so it proceeded.

While Grassley claimed to take offense at Kallstrom's and the FBI's relentless search for evidence of a criminal act, as well as their purported turf wars with other agencies, others were critical of the bureau's final report itself. Among their concerns, they were puzzled by the Central Intelligence Agency's involvement in it. And it is true, the CIA did help the FBI assemble its presentation, the one ruling out illicit activity and thus implicitly supporting the notion of a malfunction causing the plane's center wing fuel tank to detonate. While not an impossibility, the odds of such an occurrence were estimated to be one in twelve million.[118]

Regarding the CIA's role, it was on the second day of the FBI investigation that a bureau official contacted the Central Intelligence Agency and asked that it devise a video, one demonstrating that eyewitnesses to the disaster had not seen a projectile soar upward to TWA 800 and trigger an explosion.[119] The request came from John O'Neill, the FBI's director of counterterrorism. It remains unknown why he did not assign his own FBI staff to create the video; certainly, the bureau possessed the facilities for a project of this nature. Whatever the reason, the suitability of the CIA's insertion into the FBI's investigation, and particularly the predetermined nature of its ten-month task, was widely questioned once its participation became public knowledge.

So it was that the FBI handed over to the CIA the bureau's eyewitness descriptions, with the Central Intelligence Agency promptly putting them under its microscope. Irregularities in the investigative process reportedly ensued.[120]

In the FBI's original round of interviews, eighty agents questioned more than 700 people who had watched the Flight 800 explosion, among them numerous witnesses who described seeing a bright light in the sky or two or three lights, depending on the individual's location, a few seconds before the airliner ignited. Of the latter group, 96 percent stated that the light originated at ground level and rose to the elevation of TWA 800. It was this shared observation that the CIA now had in its crosshairs.

As it happened, the squad of FBI agents who conducted the initial interviews did not record, verbatim, the eyewitnesses' accounts. Instead, the agents wrote in their notebooks, in their own words, summaries of the interviewees' descriptions of events. But now, as the CIA was preparing to devise a video characterizing the ascending-light observations as erroneous, it instructed the FBI to re-interview a small number of eyewitnesses, most notably those who had furnished the soundest accounts of the soaring light being a possible projectile. (The CIA itself did not interview any of the eyewitnesses.) The FBI's undertaking would prove to be tainted, however, as the bureau was confronted with a series of grave allegations after its agents had purportedly carried out their supplemental visits.

According to some of the witnesses who succeeded in gaining access to the FBI's writeups of their second and third interviews, the bureau had doctored their statements.[121] In other instances, witnesses said the FBI's final report claimed they had been re-interviewed when, in fact, there had been no such interviews. Additional allegations consisted of bureau agents pressuring eyewitnesses to withdraw their original accounts.

Taken aback by these developments was retired commander William S. Donaldson. A former nuclear weapons targeting officer for NATO and a decorated Navy pilot during the Vietnam War, Donaldson had also served as an aircraft crash investigator during his long and distinguished military career. So it was that the retired commander dispatched a complaint to the director of the FBI, Louis Freeh, the man who oversaw the work of James Kallstrom and John O'Neil. "Multiple witnesses tell me agents on rare second and third visits to persons who saw ascending objects tried to get the witnesses to change their original stories," Donaldson wrote. "Many of these people are now afraid of and disgusted with their own government."[122] Donaldson would proceed to monitor the TWA investigations for the next four years, becoming a leading voice, an increasingly skeptical one, in discussions of the federal government's integrity in the case.

Based on the bureau's eyewitness reports, including those the FBI or the CIA allegedly modified, the Central Intelligence Agency dispatched a memo to Kallstrom in the spring of 1997 stating there was "absolutely no evidence" that a missile had taken down Flight 800.[123] It was this memo to which Chuck Grassley alluded during the Senate hearing on the FBI investigation. As the bureau had requested, the CIA also created a narrated video that detailed the airliner's explosion and crash, a fifteen-minute production through which it sought to prove that the eyewitnesses had not seen a bright light travel from ground level to the airliner's location. The video was positioned to be the closing exhibit at the FBI press conference in which Kallstrom would declare that the bureau had uncovered no evidence of criminal activity in America's worst airline disaster. As such, the short film was to stand as the FBI's final word on Flight 800. To expand its reach and ensure its impact, the video was also aired on national television in 1997, the American public being the target audience.

But this was not the end of it. Despite public calls for openness, the FBI persuaded the NTSB to prohibit the eyewitnesses from testifying before Congress in an upcoming hearing even though the safety board had already planned for these individuals to talk to lawmakers. The FBI and NTSB further refused to release the eyewitnesses' written accounts, notwithstanding the fact that some of these people had explicitly asked that their descriptions be made available to the public. Thus, owing in large part to the constraints placed on the eyewitnesses, the CIA's video presentation would, for the next two to three years, remain the most visible and authoritative explanation of the cause of Flight 800's destruction.

In terms of the video's specifics, it consisted of an animated re-creation of TWA 800 igniting at 13,700 feet, with the narrator explaining that the aircraft's nose cone, which is part of the forward fuselage, plummeted into the ocean when the plane exploded. The voice-over further claimed that, after the spectacular blast, the jetliner's main body traveled forward and upward, its speed remaining the same as before the explosion. Only when it rose to 17,000 feet did it purportedly start to descend. Importantly, the video posited that it was this post-explosion ascent of 3,200 feet, coupled with the flaming fuel that was presumably pouring downward as the damaged body of the plane moved upward, that the eyewitnesses had seen in the sky, not a missile. In this way, the CIA's explanation changed both the time and place of the observers' sightings. Rather than a bright light (or lights) appearing several seconds *before* the TWA 800 explosion, the video claimed the observers saw the light *after* the plane exploded. And instead of the light originating at ground level and arcing upward to a high altitude, the video posited that the observers had first seen the light appear at an altitude of 13,700 to 17,000 feet. This would place its point of origin more than three miles above the earth.

Reaction to the video was mixed. The traditional media accepted its premises uncritically and broadcast them widely, while numerous eyewitnesses and those in the academic and scientific communities rejected the video outright. In the main, critics dismissed it as a standard CIA disinformation project designed to jettison the sightings of scores of observers, the goal being to remove the missile hypothesis from further consideration. "[O]ne of the most spectacular and successful deceptions ever visited on the American people," is how writer Jack Cashill and his coauthor, journalist and former police officer James Sanders, referred to the intelligence agency's production.[124]

Other appraisals were more specific. Members of the scientific community pointed out that the large portion of the airliner's fuselage, following the enormous blast that split the plane in half, would not have continued traveling forward at the same speed and ascending; doing so would violate the laws of physics. Instead, the body of the plane would have lost speed and plunged into the ocean immediately after the explosion, as did the plane's nose cone. Confirming this proposition were radar readings from before, during, and after the plane ignited, data showing that all parts of the plane began falling to earth immediately. There was no further forward movement. In the ensuing days, the NTSB would publicly release these and radiolocation readings.

It would later be learned that the CIA had encountered turmoil within its own ranks about its decision to promote its ascending-fuselage scenario, also known as the "zoom-climb scenario," with an internal memo noting that the jetliner's proposed path in the video deviated sharply from the actual trajectory as established by radar data.[125] All the same, the CIA pushed forward with its version of events, while attempting to bolster its position by asserting that Boeing engineers supported the agency's assertions about the aircraft and its destruction. Boeing took issue, however, distancing itself from the controversial video on the same day it was exhibited. A press release by Boeing explained that its engineers were in the dark about the data the CIA had used to prepare its video production, adding that the company had merely supplied the intelligence agency with general information about its 747–131 aircraft.[126] As well, the aerospace company bestowed final authority on those people who had actually watched the TWA disaster transpire in real time. "The video's explanation of the eyewitness observations can best be assessed by the eyewitnesses themselves," the press release stated.[127]

More discrepancies soon came to light. The FBI's Kallstrom, for instance, to add credibility to the video that was now under fire, told the victims' families that eyewitnesses had watched the film and found its explanation of events to be believable. But his claim was troublesome. "Almost a year later, in an interview with Dr. Tom Stalcup ... Kallstrom admitted that the eyewitnesses had *not* screened the CIA video prior to its release."[128] They had also objected to its content.

In the end, it appeared to many observers that the CIA and FBI had worked in tandem to sway public opinion about the tragedy's probable cause and in the direction of manufacturing an explanation that removed a missile from consideration, either friendly-fire or terrorist-related. This does not mean that a mechanical malfunction did not take down the airliner, simply that the two organizations, for whatever reasons, appeared to coordinate, synchronize, and promote an explanation of events that was not in line with observational, radar, or satellite data.

NTSB Investigation

The final, overarching investigation would cost American taxpayers forty million dollars and take four years to complete, throughout which the National Transportation and Safety Board, bedeviled by skeptics outside of the organization, would repeatedly broadcast its impartiality. Indeed, six months into the inquiry, Jim Hall, head of the NTSB, insisted that his team was unbiased, that it had not prematurely ruled out any causes of the TWA 800 catastrophe. "All three theories—a bomb, a missile or mechanical failure—remain," he said.[129] It would only be at the end of the massive investigation that he would finally lay to rest two of the theories, and he would do so brusquely.

The NTSB aired its conclusions during a televised briefing on August 22, 2000, in Washington, D.C. (The final NTSB report would be adopted on August 23, 2000.) While members of the public, among them eyewitnesses to the Flight 800 explosion and family members of the victims, were allowed to attend the briefing in person, they were not permitted to participate.

It was only eighteen minutes into the six-hour presentation that Hall, presiding over the proceedings, set out to preempt discussion of the missile and bomb theories even though he and his team had not yet laid out their findings. "I know at the outset that many believe the crash of Flight 800 was caused by a criminal act," Hall told the audience, "and for many, the events of the times—the ongoing court trials and the aftermath of the World Trade Center bombings in New York and the heightened concern about terrorism at the 1996 Olympic Games in Atlanta—tend to lend a certain credence to the notion."[130] The NTSB director then proceeded to reject the bomb and missile theories by pointing to the FBI's earlier criminal investigation, the one that purportedly found no evidence of malice.

"Despite this finding by our nation's law enforcement agency, the Federal Bureau of Investigation," said Hall, "some have urged the Safety Board to assume, in effect, a law enforcement role to prove or disprove their assertion that the crash of Flight 800 was the result of a bomb or a missile." Distinguishing between the FBI's mandate and that of the NTSB, he clarified the latter's role: "Our focus is safety."[131]

Lastly, Hall shamed those outside of the organization who had voiced concerns about its transparency in the investigative process. "It is unfortunate that a small number of people pursuing their own agendas have persisted in making unfounded charges of a government coverup in this investigation," the NTSB director stated. "These people do a grievous injustice to the many dedicated individuals, civilian and military, who have been involved in this investigation."[132]

Four. Up in the Air

Regarding the safety board's conclusion, it was precisely what supporters and critics of the organization had predicted: the NTSB determined that an unidentified factor, probably a short circuit, triggered a chain of events on TWA 800 that culminated in its explosion and crash. Of course, the 341-page report contained considerably more detail: "The National Transportation Safety Board determines that the probable cause of the TWA flight 800 accident was an explosion of the center wing fuel tank (CWT), resulting from ignition of the flammable fuel/air mixture in the tank," read the report. "The source of ignition energy for the explosion could not be determined with certainty, but, of the sources evaluated by the investigation, the most likely was a short circuit outside of the CWT that allowed excessive voltage to enter it through electrical wiring associated with the fuel quantity indication system."[133]

Put another way, the NTSB team did not know what initiated the jetliner's explosion but was asserting that it was probably a combination of faulty wiring and a defective fuel-quantity probe. The team posited that a crack in the wiring's insulation had released a high-voltage charge that, in turn, caused a defective fuel-quantity probe inside an empty fuel tank to spark and ignite the vapors.[134] "We cannot be certain that this occurred," said Bernard Loeb, director of the NTSB's Office of Aviation Safety, "but of all of the ignition scenarios that we considered, this scenario is the most likely."[135]

The critical weakness in the NTSB's conclusion was immediately apparent, and critics wasted no time pointing it out: there was no evidence of either faulty wiring or faulty fuel-quantity probes. During the painstaking recovery of the airliner, the fuel-quantity probes were retrieved, tested rigorously, and determined to be functioning normally. Moreover, divers recovered 90 percent of the aircraft's wiring—nearly 160 miles of it—and none of it was damaged. All of the insulation was intact.[136] For the NTSB's conclusion to be plausible, then, it would mean that any supporting evidence was still underwater and would probably never to be recovered, a state of affairs that skeptics noted was convenient for the safety board.

Curiously, the NTSB offered the reverse explanation for the presence of explosive residues that investigators discovered in three different parts of the aircraft. These fluids and compounds had previously caused Kallstrom's team at the FBI to consider it highly probable that a missile had taken down Flight 800. As already noted, however, the Bureau would ultimately reject, very publicly, this possibility.

In terms of the residues' composition, analyses revealed the presence of nitroglycerin and pentaerythritol tetranitrate (PETN), both of which are commonly found in missiles and bombs. The third sample consisted of RDX, shorthand for "cyclotrimethylenetrinitramine," and it was especially concerning. "[S]enior investigators identified the substance as RDX, a major ingredient of Semtex, a plastic explosive developed in Czechoslovakia that has become a favorite of terrorist bombers," reported the *New York Times*.[137]

In its final report, however, the NTSB, while conceding that it could not account for these chemical traces, rejected them as evidence of an incendiary device. "Despite being unable to determine the exact source of the trace amounts of explosive residue found on the wreckage, the lack of any corroborating evidence associated with a high-energy explosion indicates that these trace amounts did not result from the detonation of a high-energy explosive device on TWA flight 800," reads the NTSB report. "Accordingly, the Safety Board concludes that the in-flight breakup of TWA flight 800 was not initiated by a bomb or a missile strike."[138] In response, critics contended that there was no legitimate reason for traces of these fluids and compounds to be detected on the jetliner, particularly the two principal components of Semtex and that their presence, in and of itself, pointed to a probable criminal operation.

After Hall and his staff concluded their presentation, the press relayed the NTSB's findings to an attentive public. The case of TWA 800 was now officially closed, although the myriad allegations that arose during the investigations would not be forgotten or, for that matter, abandoned.

CHALLENGES TO THE OFFICIAL STORY

The FBI and NTSB, in particular, would find accusations of wrongdoing dogging them well into the twenty-first century, most notably charges of evidence tampering, noncompliance, and obstruction. In an affidavit filed in 2003, for instance, a man by the name of Richard Speers described the barriers he encountered in his interactions with the FBI during its investigation. A former pilot for TWA, Speers had also served as a project manager at General Electric Aircraft Engines, a safety engineer at Aeroquip Corporation, and an aircraft accident investigator. In the Flight 800 inquiries, TWA and the Air Line Pilots Association (ALPA) appointed him their official TWA/ALPA representative and investigator in the case.

In his sworn statement, Speers said the FBI permitted him to watch, albeit only in the presence of a bureau agent, videotapes of underwater search and salvage operations that had been carried out in the debris field. And it was while Speers was viewing what should have been continuous footage of the subaquatic explorations in the Atlantic that he detected an irregularity: at least one of the tapes had been altered.

"[W]e're watching these videotapes of the bottom of the ocean and I notice that the time clock stops in a given run," he stated. To the FBI agent monitoring him, Speers said, "I want to see the unedited version."[139] The agent denied that the recordings had been edited; Speers continued pushing for the original tapes. "No," the agent finally said.[140] The TWA/ALPA representative was stunned.

Other investigators described similar occurrences at other locations. At Calverton hangar, where pieces of the jetliner's wreckage were identified and labeled and where the plane itself was reassembled and analyzed, those present, including investigators assigned to the case, recounted moments when nearly everyone on-site was ordered to leave the premises for a period of time before being allowed to return. The reason given for such abrupt retreats: "national security."[141] To aviation professionals on the scene, it was a mystery as to why secrecy at the national-security level would be invoked in an inquiry centering on a commercial—that is, a civilian—airliner.

Also at the Calverton hangar, those who were working after hours reported watching as unidentified individuals removed pieces of TWA 800's wreckage from the darkened hangar in the middle of the night, potentially a criminal act. In another episode, a police investigator reported seeing passengers' seat numbers being switched, surreptitiously, from their correct placements to other locations in the demolished aircraft.[142] Segments of the wreckage were also mislabeled. And in still another instance, an FBI member was caught pounding a portion of bent metal—a piece of evidence—to alter its shape.[143] For such reasons, surveillance cameras were installed at the facility during the second month of the project.

As could be expected given these and other procedural irregularities, several people involved in the plane's reconstruction began to harbor doubts about the mission's integrity and objectives. Perhaps the most concerned was Henry F. Hughes, the man in charge. Quoted at the beginning of this chapter, Hughes was the highly-regarded senior accident investigator at the NTSB who headed up the mammoth rebuilding operation and who later recounted, in a sworn statement to the Office of Special Counsel, his knowledge of malfeasance during the Flight 800 inquiries. Highly unsettling, the ostensible misdeeds included "evidence tampering, altering of evidence, official intimidation, failure to follow established rules and protocols and the omission of expert testimony."[144] As Hughes was a principal member of the NTSB investigative team, his charges carried considerable weight. As for his own conclusion about the origin of the Flight 800 explosion, he was unambiguous: "The witness statements, the physical evidence and other facts clearly show there was an explosion external to the aircraft, not the center wing fuel tank," he said.[145]

Compatible with Hughes' assessment was that of the International

Association of Machinists and Aerospace Workers (IAMAW), which played a role in determining the sequence of events that culminated in TWA 800's destruction. The IAMAW became aware of a rumor sweeping across the capital in 1997, namely, that federal investigators were planning to attribute the jetliner's midair breakup to a fuel tank explosion. This ruffled the IAMAW, since its investigators had, by this point, determined that the eruption of the center wing fuel tank was not the initiating event and they had conveyed this finding to the FBI and NTSB.

"It appears to the IAMAW that a major event may have occurred on the left side of the aircraft," the organization's final report stated. "The center fuel tank did explode [but] its explosion was as the result of the aircraft breakup. The initial event caused a structural failure in the area of Flight Station 854 to 860, lower left side of the aircraft. A high-pressure event breached the fuselage and the fuselage unzipped due to the event. The [center fuel tank] explosion was a result of this event."[146]

Remarkably, the IAMAW's report also contained a grievance against the Federal Bureau of Investigation. "We feel that our expertise was unwelcome and not wanted by the FBI," read the statement. "The threats made during the first two weeks were unwarranted and are unforgettable!"[147] Other than noting the purported harassment, the document did not provide any details about the targets or methods of the bureau's intimidation efforts.

It was also in 1997, while the NTSB's investigation was still underway, that nine distinguished men from the military and aviation communities united to form the Associated Retired Aviation Professionals (ARAP). Their mission was to conduct their own inquiry into the TWA tragedy. The reason such elite figures came together—it was three years before the safety board would publicly announce its conclusion—is because the NTSB chairperson had published a letter in the *Wall Street Journal* at this early point, one in which he implied that his organization would determine that a mechanical failure had caused the center wing fuel tank to trigger the disaster. Similar to the premature conclusion that the Bureau of Alcohol, Tobacco, and Firearms had reached in its inquiry, the NTSB likewise appeared to have settled on a cause of the Flight 800 disaster at least three years before its investigators had analyzed the evidence. A reversal of the investigative process by which the entirety of evidence is examined and a conclusion is then drawn, it was one of the problems in the NTSB's approach to the tragedy that troubled the Associated Retired Aviation Professionals.

The head of ARAP was retired commander William S. Donaldson, and it was he, as noted earlier in this chapter, who protested to the FBI director about the bureau's agents reportedly pressuring eyewitnesses to withdraw or alter their accounts of the catastrophe. Among the ARAP's other members was the former chairman of the Joint Chiefs of Staff, Admiral Thomas Moore. Also onboard were Rear Admiral Mark Hill, Brigadier General Ben Partin, Commander Bruce Valley, and Dr. Gregory Harrison, a specialist in fire investigations. Captain Al Mundo, a career pilot who was in the doomed airliner's cockpit during the preceding leg from Athens to New York City, was a member as well, along with Captain Howard Mann, a former TWA pilot and accident investigator with expertise in interpreting aircraft data.

For financial and professional support, ARAP turned to two bodies. One was Accuracy in Media, the nonprofit watchdog organization, which financed much of the group's work. The other was the Flight 800 Independent Researchers Association (FIRO), another autonomous organization that was likewise examining the calamity. Tom Stalcup, a doctoral candidate in physics at Florida State University, presided over FIRO, which would share its expertise with ARAP.

Over a two-year period, ARAP and FIRO reassessed the existing materials and acquired new evidence about the midair tragedy. Among other actions, the allied organizations analyzed previously undisclosed radar readings and performed further studies of the FDR data. The contents of the flight data recorder readouts, in particular, would lead to a far different picture of the final moments of TWA 800.

Originally, the NTSB claimed that readings from the jetliner's flight data recorder ceased at precisely 20:31:12:26 due to a power failure. Yet the specialists at ARAP and FIRO discovered that the data stream did not end at this moment, that there was, in fact, more data being registered afterward.[148] It was a point the NTSB would eventually concede.

"On the last page of actual data taken from the FDR's magnetic tape," writes journalist Robert Davey, the readings reveal "a flight thrown into chaos, with values that fluctuate wildly from those recorded just a second earlier."[149] Specifically, the FDR readouts pointed to a devastating event occurring on the lower left side of the plane. "Altitude, airspeed, angle of attack, G force, Pitch and Roll sensors all agree," reads the ARAP document, which yielded other important measurements as well.[150] It turned out that the NTSB had not analyzed this critical information about the airliner's pitch, vertical acceleration, airspeed, heading, altitude, and other critical aspects of the flight that had been registered at the end of the FDR recording. Instead, its analysts had drawn a line through the data that continued entering the FDR after the 20:31:12:26 point, omitting it from their assessments. When confronted, the safety board claimed that the FDR on TWA 800 had probably recorded over data from an earlier flight, which is why its analysts had discarded it from consideration. It was an explanation that critics ridiculed, since it would mean that an earlier Boeing 747 had exploded and crashed in flight. This had not happened, of course. Disconcerting, too, it was discovered that the NTSB had expunged even more of the streaming data prior to sharing it with journalists.[151]

In a separate set of analyses, those that ARAP and FIRO conducted on the cockpit voice recorder, the findings were commensurate with the results from the flight data recorder. It will be recalled that an earlier examination of the CVR revealed an earsplitting sound immediately before the device stopped recording. The ARAP and FIRO teams were able to demonstrate that this sound lasted 105 milliseconds. The organizations' acoustics experts subsequently determined that it was precisely this amount of time that was required for a shock wave, one caused by a critical event on the lower left section of a Boeing 747, to clear the length of the aircraft and then be picked up by the recorder in the cockpit.[152]

In terms of the ARAP's overall conclusion, it concurred with those of other non-governmental investigative teams. "There is no evidence that the Center Wing Fuel Tank of TWA Flight 800 exploded due to mechanical failure as the initiating event," the ARAP document stated.[153] "Eyewitness testimony and forensic evidence in the Debris Field and the Flight Data Recorder fully support a missile engagement of the TWA flight 800. TWA Flight 800 was destroyed by an airbursting anti-aircraft missile."[154]

As to the perpetrator, the report stated that its investigators found no indications of a friendly-fire mishap. "The preponderance of evidence strongly points to a hostile attack by enemies of the United States."[155]

In that the ARAP considered the TWA 800 disaster to be the act of a foreign government or terrorist organization, the subject naturally turned to the U.S. government's response to it. In this regard, ARAP was unsparing in its disapproval of what it viewed as the Clinton administration's calculated misrepresentation of the tragic episode. "Based on the fact that TWA Flight 800 was the likely target of a State Sponsored terrorist attack, which is an Act of War, and the fact that the Administration has covered up this act for political expediency prior to the 1996 election, the Congress should do one or more of the following: (a) Hold Congressional Hearings into the cause of the crash of TWA Flight 800. (b) Request the Justice Department appoint an Independent Counsel to investigate."[156] Congress rejected both requests.

Fellow independent investigators who were seeking the Flight 800 materials would encounter problems of their own, their efforts stymied through methods both legal and illegal. One such person was Graeme Sephton, a telecommunications engineer with expertise in radar interpretation and a member of FIRO who struggled for years to obtain materials related to the disaster. In the course of his efforts, he filed seven requests through the Freedom of Information Act (FOIA), all of which were initially or permanently met with protracted delays or rejections.

In 1998, for instance, the NTSB, in cooperation with the FBI, generated a medical forensic report drawn from the autopsies of the TWA 800 casualties, a document intended to shed light on the nature and survivability of the passengers' injuries. A potentially pivotal finding contained in this report revealed that, during the post-mortems, foreign bodies were extracted from eighty-nine of the victims. While a tremendous explosion could propel virtually any type of item into a passenger, if a missile had caused the blast, the autopsies could be expected to reveal fragments of it. On this issue, Dr. Wetli, the Long Island medical examiner who assessed the TWA 800 casualties, did in fact extract metal fragments from many of the bodies. "[T]he victims' x-rays light up like Christmas Trees [sic] from metal contamination," Wetli said, and he used the word "shrapnel" to refer to the fragments.[157] To assess these objects further, the FBI, which monitored the post-mortems, took possession of them and transferred the items to its own labs for analysis.[158] At this juncture, a mystery emerges.

On June 24, 1998, Sephton filed a FOIA request for the written results of the analyses, but the FBI/NTSB claimed they had "no written documents containing analysis of the foreign objects."[159] An incredulous Sephton pointed out that such analyses and documentation would have been essential to determining the survivability of the victims' injuries, a key purpose of the medical forensic report itself. After a court intervened, the FBI did release to Sephton a handful of pages, and then five years later, after further court intervention, a trove supposedly containing the foreign-object analyses. "Amazingly, of the almost six hundred pages of records that the FBI sent ... only one contains any analysis of the foreign bodies located on the victims," reads a document cited in one of Sephton's legal challenges.[160]

On March 5, 2005, the telecommunications engineer again sought access to the full set of documents (*Graeme Sephton v. F.B.I.*, 2005).[161] The judge began by summarizing events up to that point. "The FBI's halting response to the plaintiff's requests has exacerbated an already excruciating situation and undoubtedly deepened the mistrust felt by the grieving families who have supported this FOIA initiative," said the judge. "The families deserved better from their government."[162] In the end, however, the court rejected Sephton's request for additional documents, the judge asserting that he accepted the FBI's claim that it had no further information about the metal fragments embedded in the passengers' bodies.[163]

Still other independent researchers zeroed in on the "zoom-climb scenario"— that is, the claim that the body of TWA 800, after the explosion, continued traveling forward at the same speed while ascending more than three thousand feet. Among them was Glen Schulze, a specialist in magnetic tape-recording systems, with additional expertise in CVR and FDR analysis. Besides his contractual work for the CIA and the U.S. Naval

Research Labs, Shulze had also worked at NASA in the area of tape recording and telemetry engineering. Among his credits in the American space program, he had contributed to both the Apollo and Skylab projects.

Schulze, acting on a request from a TWA 800 victim's family, obtained and reviewed the CVR and FDR tapes of Flight 800 together with the NTSB's analyses of them. His studies of these recordings soon led to a disturbing discovery. Schulze, like previous investigators, determined that FDR data was missing at the very end of the recording—four seconds of it—which was arguably the most critical and potentially revealing moment in the catastrophe. "It is my strong belief that the NTSB cannot release the FDR accident tape from FL 800 for the purpose of independent read-out and analysis without revealing their complicity in tampering with this most important piece of [the] TWA FL 800 accident investigation," he said.[164] In a sworn statement, Schulze reprimanded the NTSB. "[T]he review of the evidence and the attendant analyses that I have been able to perform," he protested, were "greatly limited by a high level of clandestine censorship of these tapes invoked by the NTSB."[165]

Despite the devices' truncated readouts, Schulze was nevertheless able to reach at least one conclusion as it pertained to the CIA's animated video, and it rebutted the agency's hypothesis. "I find no corroborating evidence whatsoever of a Zoom-Climb phase of the disintegrating Flight 800's Boeing 747 aircraft from the NTSB evidence derived from these two most important tapes," he wrote.[166] Many years later, Schulze would publicly reject the NTSB's narrative of an onboard, internal blast (i.e., center-wing fuel tank explosion) having caused the disaster. "What I believe at this point is that it ... was not an internal explosion," he told the press.[167]

The zoom-climb hypothesis was an issue for retired Captain Ray Lahr as well. A former Navy Air Corps member and a United Airlines pilot for thirty-two years, Lahr was the man who invented what would become known as the Jeppesen navigation computer for use in flight planning.

In the retired captain's judgment, the zoom-climb hypothesis was utterly implausible, and he was certain that he could demonstrate its fallacy by inspecting the materials used to generate it. By showing that Flight 800 could not have continued traveling forward after the blast, let alone ascending 3,200 feet, he reasoned that the NTSB would have no recourse but to revise its conclusions.

To this end, Lahr, after having had his efforts to obtain the relevant materials obstructed, initiated a FOIA-related lawsuit on November 6, 2003, one in which the defendants were the NTSB and the CIA. Soon, however, the CIA made a game-changing claim: it now asserted that it had actually used a National Security Agency (NSA) computer program to formulate the zoom-climb hypothesis. Lahr therefore acted on this rather troubling development. "Ray [Lahr] added the NSA as a defendant," writes John H. Clarke, "and thereafter argued that this spy Agency [NSA] was tasked, in bad faith, only to avoid disclosure under the FOIA, as courts cannot order disclosure of NSA records."[168] That is to say that Lahr suspected the CIA of taking refuge behind the more formidable NSA owing to the latter's considerable protection from Freedom of Information Act requests.

To support the retired captain's case, Lahr's legal team submitted twenty-nine affidavits as part of the documentation, with the affiants consisting of independent experts as well as investigators who had participated in the FBI and NTSB inquiries. Among them were Tom Stalcup, Graeme Sephton, James Speers, Glen Schulze, Dwight Brumley, Fred Meyer, and James Sanders, all of whom have been discussed in this chapter.

On August 31, 2006, the case went before a judge, who summarized Lahr's allegations of inappropriate action by government agencies and reiterated Lahr's request for access to the materials used to originate the zoom-climb hypothesis. The question to be resolved was whether Lahr's legal argument satisfied the requirements for him to continue his pursuit of the CIA, NSA, and NTSB materials.

In large measure, the court ruled in his favor. "[T]he Court finds that, taken together, this evidence is sufficient to permit Plaintiff [Lahr] to proceed based on his claim that the government acted improperly in its investigation of Flight 800, or at least performed in a grossly negligent fashion," said the judge. Turning to the common good, the judge added, "the public interest in ferreting out the truth would be compelling indeed."[169] For this reason, the court ruled that the federal agencies must hand over some, although not all, of the materials Lahr was seeking. In October of the same year, the court added more items to be made available to him.

Unfortunately for Lahr, he would not receive the packet he needed most, namely, the data and computer program used to arrive at the zoom-climb hypothesis. This is because the NSA won its argument that the software and data were exempt from the Freedom of Information Act. According to court documents, a senior NSA official submitted an affidavit to justify why this critical packet was protected. "[T]he program is used to analyze foreign weapons," the official divulged. The official then laid out "specific reasons why release of the program, including the data inputs, would put the agency's sources and methods at risk."[170] Faced with this assertion of national security, the judge had little choice but to rule in the NSA's favor, meaning that Lahr would not be in a position to refute the CIA's explanation of the Flight 800 explosion.[171]

Despite the persistent stonewalling, rejections, and claims of lost or misplaced documents by government agencies, some of those who served as investigators in the FBI and NTSB inquiries, along with an assortment of interested parties outside of the federal government, kept alive the public conversation. Their stated intention was to discern the actual cause of the Flight 800 disaster, a cause that, at one point, 40 percent of the American citizenry believed was being withheld from the public.[172]

Andrew Danziger was one of those who rejected the federal government's narrative. A pilot for Barack Obama during the 2008 presidential campaign, Danziger had flown international routes for fourteen years as the captain of Boeing 757 and 767 jetliners. Several years after the TWA 800 disaster, he spoke for many career pilots in voicing his deep skepticism of the NTSB's conclusions. "There's hardly an airline pilot among the hundreds I know who buys the official explanation—that it was a fuel-tank explosion—offered by the National Transportation Safety Board," he said.[173]

Besides explaining why fuel tanks on transatlantic jetliners simply do not explode in midair, Danziger also discussed elements of the TWA catastrophe that, he maintained, signaled a classic missile strike. And he noted, like others before him, what appeared to be attempts by the FBI, in particular, to suppress potential evidence of a hostile attack. For instance, Danziger revealed that segments of the airliner's external skin had been pierced from the outside inward, so-called "spike-tooth" fractures that are a signature of missile strikes. Further, he drew attention to the fact that on-site investigators, when they discovered these indentations, set about photographing them as protocol dictates, but that FBI officials ordered them to stop.[174] It was one of many disconcerting interventions by the FBI and NTSB that remained fresh in the minds of Danziger and others who questioned the agencies' methods and conclusions.

So it was that a group of men and women would prepare a final appeal for government transparency into the historic catastrophe. Time had passed, new information had come to light, and the leadership at the relevant federal agencies had changed. To those who considered the investigative practices in the government's probes to have been insupportable, it seemed the proper time to revisit the case.

Petition to Reconsider and Amend

On June 18, 2013, the TWA 800 Project petitioned the National Transportation Safety Board to reevaluate its investigation and to incorporate into the review several pieces of evidence that had since emerged. "The Petitioners," began the twenty-four-page document, "which include investigators from the original National Transportation Safety Board (NTSB) investigation, family members of crash victims, former airline crash investigators, and concerned scientists, hereby request Reconsideration and Modification of the National Transportation Safety Board's Findings and Determination of the Probable Cause for the Crash of TWA Flight 800."[175] It added, "This petition is based upon new and material evidence and analyses that refute the NTSB's original findings."[176]

The document referenced twenty eyewitness interview summaries that the FBI had conducted but withheld from the NTSB and the public.[177] Supplementary materials consisted of unexamined explosive residue from other sections of the aircraft, new and updated analyses of FAA radar readouts, and studies of the inward-penetrating holes, or spike-tooth fractures, that had been discovered on the airliner's skin. The petition further asked that the NTSB assess the full, verbatim testimony of "airborne military witnesses" to the Flight 800 explosion—that is, the National Guard flight crew that described watching "ordnance" arc toward the airliner immediately before Flight 800 exploded—since the FBI had also withheld these officers' complete, original statements from the safety board.[178] Arguably, the latter interviews yielded the most accurate and informative first-person accounts the FBI had in its possession.

Dovetailing with this request was a ninety-minute documentary released on American television on November 17, 2013, the seventeenth anniversary of the tragedy. Titled *TWA Flight 800*, it was the creation of Tom Stalcup, the indefatigable physicist who had studied the TWA disaster from the beginning, and Kristina Borjesson, a journalist and recipient of an Edward R. Murrow Award and an Emmy Award for her investigative reportage at CBS News.[179] The film contained interviews with independent analysts as well as those who had participated in the Flight 800 investigations, among them NSTB senior investigator Henry Hughes, TWA/ALPA investigator James Speer, and medical examiner Charles Wetli. The documentary's principal claim: three "proximity missiles," a type of weapon that is designed to explode within a predetermined distance of its target, brought down Flight 800. (Inexplicably, the NTSB had chosen not to consider the possibility of proximity missiles in its investigation.) Like the petition, the film called for reopening the inquiry, with the document and documentary constituting a one-two punch aimed at getting the safety board and the public onboard.

On the whole, the film was well received by the public and commended for its scientific integrity. "This isn't crackpot conspiracy theory stuff," wrote Neil Genzlinger in the *New York Times*, "the documentary is as serious and somber as its title."[180] Even so, the film would be misrepresented and disparaged by the same entities that had long sought to block or discourage challenges to the NTSB's conclusions about the calamity.

Regarding the petition to the National Transportation Safety Board, one year later the organization would act on it, and it would be a letdown to those hoping the NTSB's new leadership would reopen the investigation. But the safety board was resolute. "The federal agency," reported NBC News, "stands by its conclusion that the explosion that downed the jet on July 17, 1996, near John F. Kennedy Airport in New York was an accident, caused when fuel in a wing tank ignited."[181]

As for the reassembled aircraft, it was moved in 2003 to Ashburn, Virginia, where it was used to train first responders and accident investigators. In 2021, the decision was made to decommission the shattered plane, while digitally preserving components of it by means of 3D laser scanning. Even though the aircraft itself is no longer in existence, however, the controversy over the cause of the disaster remains.

Consequences

For some who argue that a terrorist strike likely produced the catastrophe, there is an especially unsettling upshot, one that involves the human and political costs of the U.S. government having failed to publicly acknowledge and address what may have amounted to an act of war. Among the penalties: a lack of preparedness for future assaults on American soil.

Political scientist Yossef Bodansky spoke to this issue in 1999, a time when it was common knowledge in the nation's capital that the NTSB would likely attribute the TWA explosion to a mechanical malfunction. It was a conclusion he rejected. A former senior consultant to both the Department of Defense and the Department of State, Bodansky was director of the Congressional Task Force on Terrorism and Unconventional Warfare when the TWA 800 tragedy transpired. Studying the disaster and comparing the evidence to that of Pan Am Flight 103, which had been the target of a terrorist bombing over Lockerbie, Scotland, Bodansky was convinced that an act of terrorism was behind the TWA explosion. Furthermore, he connected the timing of the horrific episode to the founding of Hezbollah International a few months earlier in 1996, an organization in which Osama bin Laden was granted a top role.

"The significance of this organization for the prevailing terrorist threat was demonstrated in its first strikes: the bombing of the U.S. barracks in Khobar, Saudi Arabia; the downing of TWA 800; and the assassination of a U.S. intelligence officer in Cairo," Bodansky wrote.[182] The political scientist painted this trio of attacks as Hezbollah's declaration of power, a demonstration that threatened future violence against the United States if the nation did not alter its course in the Middle East.

Four. Up in the Air

On this topic, a number of critics came to regard the Flight 800 explosion as a precursor to the September 11 attacks in Manhattan and Washington, D.C., ostentatious acts of political brutality that perhaps could have been prevented if more stringent security measures had been put in place on airliners and in airports. Democratic senator Bob Kerry of Nebraska, for one, addressed the problem of airline and airport security shortly after the 9/11 atrocities. Informed and articulate, the senator had served as vice chairman of the Senate Intelligence Committee from 1995 to 1999, the period during which the TWA disaster occurred and was investigated by federal agencies. In two interviews on national television, Kerry alluded to the TWA explosion while speaking about the need for the United States to beef up its anti-terrorism measures. "I served on the intelligence committee up until last year," the senator said on CNN on the evening of September 11, 2001, "and I can remember after the bombings of the embassies, after TWA 800, we went through this flurry of activity talking about it, but not really doing the hard work of responding."[183]

It was a view that Dick Morris also expressed. Morris was a former advisor to the Clinton White House and chief strategist of the president's 1996 reelection campaign at the time of the Flight 800 tragedy. "The true cause of the crash has never been established," Morris wrote in his 2004 book about the Clinton years, *Because He Could*.[184] Critical of the former president's response to terrorist threats, Morris added that Clinton "fell short of making our air traffic system safe."[185]

In a similar vein, Judith Miller of the *New York Times* pointed out that the White House dragged its feet in enacting robust anti-terrorism measures prior to the September 11 attacks. "Progress was slow," she wrote, "particularly after federal investigators determined that the crash of T.W.A. Flight 800 resulted from a mechanical flaw, not terrorism."[186]

Today, the mechanical-malfunction explanation, despite the years of controversy, persists as the final word on the Flight 800 tragedy, the NTSB's forty-million-dollar, four-year investigation carrying the imprimatur of the United States government. And while it is true that the NTSB investigation, like the allied ATF and FBI inquiries, was flawed in certain respects, it nevertheless employed some of the most reputable figures in domestic aviation and forensic science in its search for the origins of the Flight 800 explosion and crash. Then, too, the NTSB's public messaging about the cause of the disaster has proven to be resolute, consistent, and closed to debate. Consequently, the public largely accepts its official conclusion, that of a glitch sparking a series of events that brought down the jetliner.

In the opposite corner are those who question or reject outright this explanation, professionals and laypersons who have studied the evidence and found themselves unable to accept a technical anomaly as the cause of the Flight 800 disaster. In part because they openly challenge the official narrative, many of these individuals have, and will continue to be, branded as cranks, attention seekers, or conspiracy theorists prone to cherry-picking inconsistencies in the government's complex, sweeping investigations. And without a renewal of the NTSB investigation, which is highly improbable, no further information will be forthcoming in support of the missile hypothesis—information that would vindicate the critics. It is for this reason that a number of skeptics regard the situation as a victory for officialdom. "Flight 800 is just a fuck-you to the world," says physicist Tom Stalcup. "'Look what we can really get away with.'"[187]

Notes

1. Henry F. Hughes, "Affidavit of Henry F. Hughes," Associated Retired Aviation Professionals—The Flight 800 Investigation, June 26, 2014, https://twa800project.files.wordpress.com/2014/10/final-final-revised-affidavit.pdf.
2. Martin C. Evans, "LIers Still Haunted by Lessons, Legacy of TWA Flight 800," *Newsday*, July 11, 2016, https://www.newsday.com/long-island/liers-still-haunted-by-lessons-legacy-of-twa-flight-800-1.12029236.
3. Christopher S. Wren, "Charged as Terror Master, Surrounded by Mysteries," *New York Times*, May 29, 1996, https://www.nytimes.com/1996/05/29/nyregion/charged-as-terror-master-surrounded-by-mysteries.html.
4. Bret Burquest, "TWA Flight 800," *Bret Burquest, Hermit in the Land of Ark*, July 18, 2008, https://bret1111.blogspot.com/2008/07/twa-flight-800.html.
5. SCMP Reporter, "USA Warned of Terrorist Threat," *South China Morning Post*, July 22, 1996, https://www.scmp.com/article/167838/usa-warned-terrorist-threat
6. "Ambassador: Car Bomb Destroyed Military Building," CNN, November 13, 1995, http://edition.cnn.com/WORLD/9511/saudi_blast/11am/.
7. *"Searching for Answers: Probers Focus on Possibility of Bomb or Missile; Toll at 230,"* Newsday, July 19, 1996, https://www.pulitzer.org/winners/staff-39.
8. Jack Cashill, *TWA 800: The Crash, the Cover-Up, the Conspiracy* (New York: Regnery, 2016).
9. National Transportation Safety Board, *Aircraft Accident Report: In-Flight Breakup over the Atlantic Ocean Trans World Airlines Flight 800 Boeing 747-131, N93119, Near East Moriches, New York July 17, 1996*; Aircraft Accident Report NTSB/AAR-00/03 (Washington, D.C.: NTSB, August 23, 2000), 2, https://www.ntsb.gov/investigations/AccidentReports/Reports/AAR0003.pdf.
10. National Transportation Safety Board, *Aircraft Accident Report: In-Flight Breakup*, 3.
11. Jack Cashill, *TWA 800*.
12. National Transportation Safety Board, *Aircraft Accident Report: In-Flight Breakup*.
13. National Transportation Safety Board, *Aircraft Accident Report: In-Flight Breakup*.
14. Mike Wire, "TWA 800: What the CIA Did to Mike Wire, Witness 571," *American Thinker*, June 9, 2016, https://www.americanthinker.com/articles/2016/06/twa_800_what_the_cia_did_to_witness_571_mike_wire.html.
15. Jack Cashill, *TWA 800*.
16. Frederick Meyer, "Interview Transcript" (Appendix O), January 11, 1997, *Witness Group Chairman's Factual Report (DCA96MA070)*, National Transportation Safety Board, Washington, D.C., February 9, 2000, https://twa800.com/witnesscd/AppendixO.pdf.
17. Frederick Meyer, "Interview Transcript," 34.
18. Jack Cashill, *TWA 800*, 26.
19. Michael K. Hull, "The Downing of TWA 800—Part 2—Major Meyer Speaks Out,"

Patch, June 26, 2013. https://patch.com/new-york/newcity/the-downing-of-twa-800--part-2--major-meyer-speaks-out.
20. Frederick Meyer, "Interview Transcript."
21. Frederick Meyer, "Interview Transcript," 8.
22. Frederick Meyer, "Interview Transcript," 19.
23. Frederick Meyer, "Interview Transcript," 19.
24. Christian Baur, "Interview Transcript" (Appendix N), January 11, 1997, *Witness Group Chairman's Factual Report (DCA96MA070), National Transportation Safety Board*, Washington, D.C., February 9, 2000, 4, https://twa800.com/witnesscd/AppendixN.pdf.
25. Christian Baur, "Interview Transcript," 5–6.
26. Christian Baur, "Interview Transcript," 17.
27. Robert Davey, "Still Bearing Witness," *Village Voice*, July 17, 2001, https://www.villagevoice.com/2001/07/17/still-bearing-witness/.
28. Robert Davey, "Still Bearing Witness."
29. Dwight Brumley, "Affidavit of Mr. Dwight Brumley" (Exhibit P, June 16, 2003), *Lahr vs. National Transportation and Safety Board*, U.S. District Court, C.D. California, August 31, 2006, https://twa800.com/lahr/affidavits/p-dwight-brumley.pdf.
30. Gannett News Service, "TWA 800 Crash Witnesses Ally, Request Federal Hearing," *Quad-City Times*, July 18, 2000, https://qctimes.com/article_569a52e6-94e5-5855-ad1b-e9329e9278a4.html.
31. Gannett News Service, "TWA 800 Crash Witnesses Ally."
32. Jack Cashill and James Sanders, *First Strike: TWA Flight 800 and the Attack on America* (Nashville: WND Books, 2003), p. 8.
33. Philip Weiss, "Radar Shows 'Getaway Boat' Fleeing Flight 800 Crash," *The Observer*, July 12, 1999, https://observer.com/1999/07/radar-shows-getaway-boat-fleeing-flight-800-crash/.
34. Philip Weiss, "Radar Shows 'Getaway Boat.'"
35. Associated Press, "Federal Crash Investigators to be Sent to Crash Scene," Associated Press News, July 17, 1996, https://apnews.com/article/c14490da2b096cb5699130ef3187ec7e.
36. Jim Polk, "U.S. Focused on Iran after TWA 800 Explosion," CNN, July 17, 1996, https://www.cnn.com/2006/U.S./07/12/twa.terrorism/index.html.
37. Philip Dioniato, "229 Perish in Jet Crash: Coast Guard Says No Survivors Are Found," *Newsday*, July 18, 1996, https://www.pulitzer.org/winners/staff-39.
38. Jim Polk, "U.S. Focused on Iran."
39. "*CIA Asks Mossad to Check Passenger List On Ill Fated Airliner*," *The Irish Times*, July 23, 1996, https://www.irishtimes.com/news/cia-asks-mossad-to-check-passenger-list-on-ill-fated-airliner-1.69871.
40. Christian Baur, "Interview Transcript," 17.
41. Joseph A. Kirby and Tribune Staff Writer, "Coroner: TWA Victims Died at Once," *Chicago Tribune*, August 9, 1996, https://www.chicagotribune.com/news/ct-xpm-1996-08-09-9608090267-story.html.
42. Don Phillips, "*TWA Probers Shift Hunt For Jet's Center Fuel Tank*," *Washington Post*, August 8, 1996, https://www.washingtonpost.com/archive/politics/1996/08/20/twa-probers-shift-hunt-for-jets-center-fuel-tank/edad65bc-673f-4fdd-9788-40f7fda2233e/.
43. "'*Phenomenal Whiplash' Killed Most in Mid Air*," *The Irish Times*, August 8, 1996, https://www.irishtimes.com/news/phenomenal-whiplash-killed-most-in-mid-air-1.78371#:~:text=MOST%20of%20the%20230%20people,examiner%20(coroner)%20said%20yesterday.
44. Alice Reid, "FAA Seeks to Soothe Passengers," *Washington Post*, July 19, 1996, https://www.washingtonpost.com/archive/politics/1996/07/19/faa-seeks-to-soothe-passengers/dfbeeedd-3c4d-4a08-9887-bcd6b2c9fa6d/.
45. Matthew Purdy, "Explosion Aboard T.W.A. Flight 800: The Overview; Investigators Suspect Explosive Device as Likeliest Cause for Crash of Flight 800," *New York Times*, July 19, 1996, https://www.nytimes.com/1996/07/19/nyregion/explosion-aboard-twa-flight-800-overview-investigators-suspect-explosive-device.html.
46. Suzanne Wooton, "Impact on TWA May Hinge on Cause, Firm Not Financially Secure Despite Turnaround: Tragedy of Flight 800," *Baltimore Sun*, July 18, 1996, https://www.baltimoresun.com/news/bs-xpm-1996-07-19-1996201054-story.html.

47. Walter Goodman, "Explosion Aboard T.W.A. Flight 800: Television; Crash Coverage Is Fed by 24-Hour Guesswork," *New York Times*, July 19, 1996, https://www.nytimes.com/1996/07/19/nyregion/explosion-aboard-twa-flight-800-television-crash-coverage-fed-24-hour-guesswork.html.
48. Philip Dioniato, "229 Perish in Jet Crash."
49. Richard A. Serrano and Marc Lacey, "U.S. Probing for Sabotage in Fiery Explosion of Jumbo Jet," *Los Angeles Times*, July 19, 1996, https://www.latimes.com/archives/la-xpm-1996-07-19-mn-25715-story.html.
50. Bret Burquest, "TWA Flight 800."
51. Jim Polk, "U.S. Focused on Iran after TWA 800 Explosion."
52. David Johnston, "The Crash of Flight 800: The Possibilities; Tips, Leads and Theories Are Flooding In," *New York Times*, July 21, 1996, https://www.nytimes.com/1996/07/21/nyregion/crash-flight-800-possibilities-tips-leads-theories-are-flooding.html.
53. David Johnston, "The Crash of Flight 800."
54. David Johnston, "The Crash of Flight 800."
55. Matthew L. Wald, "The Fate of Flight 800: The Data; Record of Quick Destruction: Briefest Sound, Then Silence," *New York Times*, July 26, 1996, https://www.nytimes.com/1996/07/26/nyregion/fate-flight-800-data-record-quick-destruction-briefest-sound-then-silence.html.
56. "Bodies, Debris Recovered from TWA Crash Site," CNN Interactive, July 18, 1996, http://www.cnn.com/U.S./9607/18/twa2/.
57. William Jefferson Clinton, "Remarks on the Aircraft Tragedy in East Moriches, New York, and an Exchange with Reporters," The American Presidency Project—UC Santa Barbara, July 18, 1996, https://www.presidency.ucsb.edu/documents/remarks-the-aircraft-tragedy-east-moriches-new-york-and-exchange-with-reporters.
58. Terrence Hunt, "Don't Rush to Conclude Terrorism, Clinton Says," Associated Press News, July 18, 1996, https://apnews.com/article/4fe55c42e12821bdd8c7c2590d5c5d20.
59. Jim Polk, "U.S. Focused on Iran."
60. Lawrence Wright, "The Counter-Terrorist," *The New Yorker*, January 6, 2002, https://www.newyorker.com/magazine/2002/01/14/the-counter-terrorist.
61. "Searching for Answers: Probers Focus on Possibility of Bomb or Missile," *Newsday*.
62. Christopher Woody, "'A Fighting War with the Main Enemy': How the CIA Helped Land a Mortal Blow to the Soviets in Afghanistan 32 Years ago," *Business Insider*, October 2, 2018, https://www.businessinsider.com/32-year-anniversary-of-first-stinger-missile-use-in-afghanistan-2018-9.
63. Christopher Woody, "'A Fighting War with the Main Enemy.'"
64. Matthew Schroeder, "Stop Panicking about the Stingers," *Foreign Policy*, July 28, 2010, https://web.archive.org/web/20170802165612/https://foreignpolicy.com/2010/07/28/stop-panicking-about-the-stingers/.
65. Matthew Purdy, "Explosion Aboard T.W.A. Flight 800."
66. Pat Milton, "Friendly Fire Theory Called 'Outrageous Allegation," Associated Press News, September 17, 1996, https://apnews.com/article/41b96be891af069563a03e2ad8dd8ad1.
67. "Obituaries: Richard Denver 'Dick' Russell," *Daytona Beach News Journal*, April 1, 2021, https://www.legacy.com/obituaries/news-journalonline/obituary.aspx?n=richard-denver-russell-dick&pid=198231210&fhid=24276.
68. Richard Russell, "Affidavit of Richard Russell" (Exhibit M, January 2, 2003), *Lahr vs. National Transportation and Safety Board*, U.S. District Court, C.D. California, August 31, 2006, 1, https://www.twa800.com/lahr/affidavits/m-richard-russell.pdf.
69. Richard Russell, "Affidavit of Richard Russell."
70. Jocelyn Noveck, "Report: TWA Jet Blasted by Navy," Associated Press, November 8, 1996, https://www.sfgate.com/news/article/Report-TWA-jet-blasted-by-Navy-3113688.php.
71. Pat Milton, "FBI Denies Newsman's Claim Navy Missile Shot Down TWA Flight 800," Associated Press News, November 8, 1996, https://apnews.com/article/7411e8c7cc0a61445574074924828dc8.
72. Jocelyn Noveck, "Report: TWA Jet Blasted by Navy."

73. Jocelyn Noveck, "Report: TWA Jet Blasted by Navy."
74. Jocelyn Noveck, "Report: TWA Jet Blasted by Navy."
75. Anne Swardson and Serge F. Kovaleski, "Misguided Missile?" *Washington Post*, November 9, 1996, https://www.washingtonpost.com/archive/lifestyle/1996/11/09/misguided-missile/a6efeece-7c5e-49a8-ab43-b1cbdf2927bb/.
76. Elaine Ganley, "Navy Missile Shot Down Plane, Ex-newsman Says," Associated Press, November 8, 1996, https://journaltimes.com/news/national/navy-missile-shot-down-plane-ex-newsman-says/article_3990083c-afaf-54d4-8819-04b28ebb3b29.html.
77. Kristina Borjesson, "Did U.S. Gov't Lie about TWA Flight 800 Crash? Ex-Investigators Seek Probe as New Evidence Emerges," *Democracy Now*, June 20, 2013, https://www.democracynow.org/2013/6/20/did_us_govt_lie_about_twa.
78. Kristina Borjesson, ed., *Into the Buzzsaw: Leading Journalists Expose the Myth of a Free Press* (Amherst, New York: Prometheus Books, 2002), p. 110.
79. Kristina Borjesson, "Did U.S. Gov't Lie about TWA Flight 800 Crash?"
80. Pat Milton, "FBI Denies Newsman's Claim Navy Missile Shot Down TWA Flight 800."
81. Kristina Borjesson, ed., *Into the Buzzsaw*.
82. David E. Hendrix, "Coal Mine Canaries," in *Into the Buzzsaw: Leading Journalists Expose the Myth of a Free Press*, edited by Kristina Borjesson (Amherst, New York: Prometheus Books, 2002).
83. David E. Hendrix, "Coal Mine Canaries," 158.
84. Jocelyn Noveck, "Report: TWA Jet Blasted by Navy."
85. Jeffery Reid, "'Pierre Salinger Syndrome' and the TWA 800 Conspiracies," CNN, July 17, 1996. https://www.cnn.com/2006/U.S./07/12/twa.conspiracy/.
86. Richard Russell, "Affidavit of Richard Russell," p. 2.
87. Mark Hunter, "The Buffoon Brigade," *Salon*, March 26, 1997, https://www.salon.com/1997/03/26/news_355.
88. Associated Press, "France—Allegations That Missile Hit Flight TWA 800," Associated Press Archive, March 13, 1997, http://www.aparchive.com/metadata/youtube/925e51cb7221b87184e572c32d3f3053.
89. Julian Morgans, "Know Your Missiles," *Vice*, July 28, 2014, https://www.vice.com/en/article/8gdvw4/know-your-missiles.
90. Associated Press, "France—Allegations That Missile Hit Flight TWA 800."
91. Mark Hunter, "The Buffoon Brigade."
92. "Feds Take Alleged Missile Video," United Press International Archives, March 11, 1997, https://www.upi.com/Archives/1997/03/11/Feds-take-alleged-missile-video/8458858056400/.
93. Robert Davey, "How Did Flight 800 Blow Up?" *Village Voice*, March 3, 1998, https://www.villagevoice.com/1998/03/03/how-did-flight-800-blow-up/.
94. Robert Davey, "How Did Flight 800 Blow Up?"
95. Pierre Salinger, "Internet and Flight 800 (Op-Ed.)," *New York Times*, August 22, 1997, https://www.nytimes.com/1997/08/22/opinion/l-internet-and-flight-800-734802.html.
96. "What Is the Pierre Salinger Syndrome?" *Techslang*, accessed May 4, 2022, https://www.techslang.com/definition/what-is-the-pierre-salinger-syndrome/.
97. John B. Roberts II, "The Ongoing Dissent over TWA 800," *The American Spectator*, August 1999, http://twa800.com/news/as-8-99.htm.
98. NASA Safety Center, "Fire in the Sky," *Systems Failures Case Studies* 5, issue 1 (January 2011), 1, https://sma.nasa.gov/docs/default-source/safety-messages/safetymessage-2011-01-09-twa800inflightbreakup.pdf?sfvrsn=6fae1ef8_4.
99. Don van Natta, Jr., "Reconstructing T.W.A. 800," *New York Times*, May 11, 1997, https://www.nytimes.com/1997/05/11/magazine/reconstructing-twa-800.html.
100. Don van Natta, Jr., "Reconstructing T.W.A. 800."
101. John B. Roberts II, "The Ongoing Dissent over TWA 800."
102. John B. Roberts II, "The Ongoing Dissent over TWA 800."
103. Matthew L. Wald, "Investigators Describe a Stubborn F.B.I. at Hearing on Jet Explosion," *New York Times*, May 11, 1999, https://www.nytimes.com/1999/05/11/nyregion/investigators-describe-a-stubborn-fbi-at-hearing-on-jet-explosion.html.
104. "Administrative Oversight of the Investigation of TWA Flight 800 (Senate Hearing

106-534)," U.S. Senate Subcommittee on Administrative Oversight and the Courts, Committee on the Judiciary, May 10, 1999, https://www.govinfo.gov/content/pkg/CHRG-106shrg65055/html/CHRG-106shrg65055.htm.
105. Edward Walsh, "FBI Probe of TWA Crash Criticized," *Washington Post*, May 11, 1999, https://www.washingtonpost.com/wp-srv/national/longterm/twa/twa.htm.
106. John B. Roberts II, "The Ongoing Dissent over TWA 800."
107. John B. Roberts II, "The Ongoing Dissent over TWA 800."
108. John B. Roberts II, "The Ongoing Dissent over TWA 800."
109. Juan González, "Did U.S. Gov't Lie about TWA Flight 800 Crash? Ex-Investigators Seek Probe as New Evidence Emerges," *Democracy Now*, June 20, 2013, https://www.democracynow.org/2013/6/20/did_us_govt_lie_about_twa.
110. "FBI's Kallstrom, Who Led TWA Probe, to Retire," *Washington Post*, December 10, 1997, https://www.washingtonpost.com/archive/politics/1997/12/10/fbis-kallstrom-who-led-twa-probe-to-retire/0ec613bb-623b-493b-9826-dd992f148541/.
111. Matthew L. Wald, "Investigators Describe a Stubborn F.B.I. at Hearing on Jet Explosion."
112. Matthew L. Wald, "Investigators Describe a Stubborn F.B.I. at Hearing on Jet Explosion."
113. Frank Pelligrini, "FBI Grilled over Role in TWA 800 Probe," *TIME Magazine*, May 10, 1999, http://content.time.com/time/printout/0,8816,24519,00.html#.
114. *Administrative Oversight of the Investigation of TWA Flight 800, Day 1.*
115. *Administrative Oversight of the Investigation of TWA Flight 800, Day 1.*
116. *Administrative Oversight of the Investigation of TWA Flight 800, Day 1.*
117. John B. Roberts II, "The Ongoing Dissent over TWA 800."
118. John B. Roberts II, "The Ongoing Dissent over TWA 800."
119. Jack Cashill and James Sanders, *First Strike*.
120. Jack Cashill and James Sanders, *First Strike*.
121. Jack Cashill and James Sanders, *First Strike*.
122. Jack Cashill and James Sanders, *First Strike*, p. 144.
123. Frank Pelligrini, "FBI Grilled over Role in TWA 800 Probe."
124. Jack Cashill and James Sanders, *First Strike*, p. 142.
125. TWA Flight 800 Documentary Team, "Rebuttal of CIA Video about TWA Flight 800," The TWA 800 Project, July 16, 2014, https://www.youtube.com/watch?v=IyluFVxqBlo&t=159s.
126. *Lahr v. National Transportation Safety Board*, "United States District Court, C.D. California, No. CV 03-8023 AHM (RZx), Plaintiff's Opposition to CIA's Motion for Partial Summary Judgment," October 31, 2005, 18, https://www.cia.gov/readingroom/docs/DOC_0001251752.pdf.
127. "Boeing's Press Release after the Release of the CIA Video," The TWA 800 Project, accessed January 21, 2021, https://twa800.com/news/boeing11-18-97.htm.
128. Kristina Borjesson, ed., *Into the Buzzsaw*, 138.
129. Christine Negroni, "Six Months Later, Still No Answer to TWA Flight 800 Mystery," CNN, January 17, 1977, http://www.cnn.com/U.S./9701/17/twa/index.html.
130. National Transportation and Safety Board, "TWA Flight 800 Crash, Final NTSB Report, Day 1," C-SPAN, airdate August 22, 2000, https://www.c-span.org/video/?158913-1/twa-800-crash-final-report-day-1.
131. National Transportation and Safety Board, "TWA Flight 800 Crash, Final NTSB Report, Day 1."
132. National Transportation and Safety Board, "TWA Flight 800 Crash, Final NTSB Report, Day 1."
133. *National Transportation Safety Board, Aircraft Accident Report: In-Flight Breakup*, 308.
134. Andrew Danziger, "Former Obama Pilot: TWA Flight 800 Was Not Blown Up by a Faulty Fuel Tank; It Was Shot Down. I'll Always Believe That, and Here's Why," *New York Daily News*, April 15, 2015, https://www.nydailynews.com/new-york/obama-pilot-twa-flight-800-shot-article-1.2186329.
135. Ramon Lopez, "TWA 800 Crash Report Puts Faulty Wiring as Main Cause,"

FlightGlobal, August 28, 2000, https://www.flightglobal.com/twa-800-crash-report-putsfaulty-wiring-as-main-cause-/33916.article.
    136. Andrew Danziger, "Former Obama Pilot: TWA Flight 800 Was Not Blown Up by a Faulty Fuel Tank."
    137. Don van Natta, Jr., "More Traces of Explosive in Flight 800," *New York Times*, August 31, 1996, https://www.nytimes.com/1996/08/31/nyregion/more-traces-of-explosive-in-flight-800.html.
    138. National Transportation Safety Board, Aircraft Accident Report: In-Flight Breakup, 259.
    139. James Speers, "Affidavit of James Speers (June 18, 2003)," *Lahr vs. National Transportation and Safety Board*, U.S. District Court, C.D. California, 4, http://twa800.com/lahr/affidavits/l-james-speer.pdf.
    140. James Speers, "Affidavit of James Speers," p. 5.
    141. Jack Cashill, *TWA 800: The Crash, the Cover-Up, the Conspiracy*.
    142. Jack Cashill, *TWA 800: The Crash, the Cover-Up, the Conspiracy*.
    143. *Lahr v. National Transportation Safety Board*, "United States District Court, C.D. California, No. CV 03-8023 AHM (RZx), 453 F. Supp. 2d 1153 (C.D. Cal. 2006), Decided Aug 31, 2006," https://casetext.com/_print/doc/lahr-v-national-transp-safety-bd?_printInclude Highlights=false&_printIncludeKeyPassages=false&_printIsTwoColumn=true&_printEmail=&_printHighlightsKey=#922443fe-c44c-4939-aad1-87b4f10ead56-fn49.
    144. Henry F. Hughes, "Affidavit of Henry F. Hughes," p. 45.
    145. Henry F. Hughes, "Affidavit of Henry F. Hughes," p. 17.
    146. International Association of Machinists and Aerospace Workers, AFL-CIO, CLC, "Analysis and Recommendations Regarding T.W.A. Flight 800," IAMAW District Lodge 142, July 17, 1996, http://twa800.com/iamaw/iamaw.pdf.
    147. International Association of Machinists and Aerospace Workers (IAMAW), "Analysis and Recommendations Regarding TWA Flight 800."
    148. International Association of Machinists and Aerospace Workers (IAMAW), "Analysis and Recommendations Regarding TWA Flight 800."
    149. Robert Davey, "High-ranking Military Officers, Independent Investigators, Pilots, and Eyewitnesses Believe a Missile Destroyed TWA Flight 800," *Village Voice*, July 21, 1998, https://www.villagevoice.com/1998/07/21/high-ranking-military-officers-independent-investigators-pilots-and-eyewitnesses-believe-a-missle-destroyed-twa-flight-800/.
    150. William S. Donaldson in cooperation with ARAP, "Interim Report on the Crash of TWA Flight 800 and the Actions of the NTSB and the FBI," Cmdr. William S. Donaldson and Associated Retired Aviation Professionals, July 17, 1988, p. 25, http://twa800.com/report/final.pdf.
    151. William S. Donaldson in cooperation with ARAP, "Interim Report on the Crash of TWA Flight 800."
    152. William S. Donaldson in cooperation with ARAP, "Interim Report on the Crash of TWA Flight 800."
    153. William S. Donaldson in cooperation with ARAP, "Interim Report on the Crash of TWA Flight 800," 121.
    154. William S. Donaldson in cooperation with ARAP, "Interim Report on the Crash of TWA Flight 800," 121.
    155. William S. Donaldson in cooperation with ARAP, "Interim Report on the Crash of TWA Flight 800," 121.
    156. William S. Donaldson in cooperation with ARAP, "Interim Report on the Crash of TWA Flight 800," 124.
    157. William S. Donaldson in cooperation with ARAP, "Interim Report on the Crash of TWA Flight 800."
    158. Ray Lahr, "Ten-Year Commemoration of TWA Flight 800." Ray Lahr, July 17, 2006, https://web.archive.org/web/20130202015649/http://raylahr.entryhost.com/tenyearcommemoration.php.
    159. Graeme Sephton, "Affidavit of Graeme Sephton, PE, RCDD (July 31, 2003)," *Lahr vs. National Transportation and Safety Board*, U.S. District Court, C.D. California, August 31, 2006, http://twa800.com/lahr/affidavits/aa-graeme-sephton.pdf.

160. *Graeme Plaintiff v. Federal Bureau of Investigation, Defendant*, United States District Court, D, Massachusetts, March 29, 2005, https://www.casemine.com/judgement/us/5914b679add7b04934779064.
161. *Graeme Plaintiff v. Federal Bureau of Investigation, Defendant*.
162. *Graeme Plaintiff v. Federal Bureau of Investigation, Defendant*.
163. *Graeme Plaintiff v. Federal Bureau of Investigation, Defendant*.
164. Michael A. Hamann, "An Open Letter to CNN," Associated Retired Aviation Professionals—The TWA 800 Investigation, July 13, 2001, http://twa800.com/letters/hamann-8-13-01.htm.
165. Glen H. Schulze, "Affidavit (Glen H. Schulze, February 4, 2003)," *Lahr vs. National Transportation and Safety Board*, U.S. District Court, C.D. California, August 31, 2006, http://twa800.com/lahr/affidavits/bb-glen-schulze.pdf..
166. Glen H. Schulze, "Affidavit (Glen H. Schulze, February 4, 2003)."
167. Staff Report, "Local Man Seeks Truth in Flight 800 Crash," *Williamsport Sun-Gazette*, June 22, 2013, https://www.sungazette.com/news/top-news/2013/06/local-man-seeks-truth-in-flight-800-crash/.
168. John H. Clarke, "NTSB Clears Up TWA 800 Conspiracy Theory?" Ray Lahr, July 8, 2013, http://raylahr.com/ntsb-clears-up-twa-800-conspiracy-theory.php.
169. *Lahr v. National Transportation Safety Board*.
170. *Lahr v. National Transportation Safety Board*.
171. *Lahr v. National Transportation Safety Board*.
172. Shane Miller, "Conspiracy Theories: Public Arguments as Coded Social Critiques: A Rhetorical Analysis of the TWA Flight 800 Conspiracy Theories," *Argumentation and Advocacy* 39, no. 1 (2002), https://doi.org/10.1080/00028533.2002.11821576.
173. Andrew Danziger, "Former Obama Pilot: TWA Flight 800 Was Not Blown Up by a Faulty Fuel Tank."
174. Andrew Danziger, "Former Obama Pilot: TWA Flight 800 Was Not Blown Up by a Faulty Fuel Tank."
175. The TWA 800 Project, "Petition for the Reconsideration and Modification of the National Transportation Safety Board's Findings and Determination of the Probable Cause for the Crash of TWA Flight 800," The TWA 800 Project, June 18, 2013, https://twa800project.files.wordpress.com/2013/06/petition-final.pdf.
176. The TWA 800 Project, "Petition for the Reconsideration and Modification."
177. The TWA 800 Project, "Petition for the Reconsideration and Modification."
178. The TWA 800 Project, "Petition for the Reconsideration and Modification."
179. Kristina Borjesson (writer/director), "TWA Flight 800," Epix Entertainment, LLC, airdate July 17, 2013.
180. Neil Genzlinger, "Leaving No Survivors but Many Questions," *New York Times*, July 16, 2013, https://www.nytimes.com/2013/07/17/arts/television/twa-flight-800-examines-a-1996-tragedy.html.
181. Brian Williams and Tom Costello, "NTSB Refuses to Reopen TWA Flight 800 Crash Probe," NBC News, https://www.nbcnews.com/news/us-news/ntsb-refuses-reopen-twa-flight-800-crash-probe-n147051.
182. Yossef Bodansky, *Bin Laden: The Man Who Declared War on America* (Rocklin, California: Forma, 1999), p. 152.
183. John Kerry (interviewee), "Larry King Live: American Under Attack," CNN, airdate September 11, 2001, https://www.youtube.com/watch?v=AmdkcVr-K1s.
184. Dick Morris and Eileen McGann, *Because He Could* (New York: Harper Perennial, 2004), p. 111.
185. Dick Morris and Eileen McGann, *Because He Could*, p. 111.
186. Judith Miller, "A Nation Challenged: The Response; Planning for Terror but Failing to Act," *New York Times*, December 30, 2001, https://www.nytimes.com/2001/12/30/us/a-nation-challenged-the-response-planning-for-terror-but-failing-to-act.html.
187. Adrianne Jeffries, "TWA Flight 800: A Long-Runing Conspiracy Theory Makes It to National Television," *The Verge*, July 17, 2013, https://www.theverge.com/2013/7/17/4529196/twa-flight-800-a-long-running-conspiracy-theory-makes-it-to-national-television.

Bibliography

"Administrative Oversight of the Investigation of TWA Flight 800 (Senate Hearing 106-534)." U.S. Senate Subcommittee on Administrative Oversight and the Courts, Committee on the Judiciary, May 10, 1999. https://www.govinfo.gov/content/pkg/CHRG-106shrg65055/html/CHRG-106shrg65055.htm.

"Ambassador: Car Bomb Destroyed Military Building." CNN, November 13, 1995. http://edition.cnn.com/WORLD/9511/saudi_blast/11am/.

Associated Press. "France—Allegations That Missile Hit Flight TWA 800." Associated Press Archive, March 13, 1997. http://www.aparchive.com/metadata/youtube/925e51cb7221b87184e572c32d3f3053.

Associated Press. "Federal Crash Investigators to be Sent to Crash Scene." Associated Press News, July 17, 1996. https://apnews.com/article/c14490da2b096cb5699130ef3187ec7e.

Baur, Christian. "Interview Transcript" (Appendix N), January 11, 1997. *Witness Group Chairman's Factual Report (DCA96MA070), National Transportation Safety Board*, Washington, D.C., February 9, 2000. https://twa800.com/witnesscd/AppendixN.pdf.

Bodansky, Yossef. *Bin Laden: The Man Who Declared War on America*. Rocklin, California: Prima Publishing, 1999.

"Bodies, Debris Recovered from TWA Crash Site." CNN Interactive, July 18, 1996. http://www.cnn.com/U.S./9607/18/twa2/.

"Boeing's Press Release after the Release of the CIA Video." The TWA 800 Project, accessed January 21, 2021. https://twa800.com/news/boeing11-18-97.htm.

Borjesson, Kristina. "Did U.S. Gov't Lie about TWA Flight 800 Crash? Ex-Investigators Seek Probe as New Evidence Emerges." *Democracy Now*, June 20, 2013. https://www.democracynow.org/2013/6/20/did_us_govt_lie_about_twa.

Borjesson, Kristina, ed. *Into the Buzzsaw: Leading Journalists Expose the Myth of a Free Press*. Amherst, New York: Prometheus Books, 2002.

Borjesson, Kristina (writer/director). "TWA Flight 800." Epix Entertainment, LLC, airdate July 17, 2013.

Brumley, Dwight. "Affidavit of Mr. Dwight Brumley" (Exhibit P, June 16, 2003). *Lahr vs. National Transportation and Safety Board*, U.S. District Court, C.D. California, August 31, 2006. https://twa800.com/lahr/affidavits/p-dwight-brumley.pdf.

Burquest, Bret. "TWA Flight 800." *Bret Burquest, Hermit in the Land of Ark*, July 18, 2008. https://bret1111.blogspot.com/2008/07/twa-flight-800.html.

Cashill, Jack. *TWA 800: The Crash, the Cover-Up, the Conspiracy*. New York: Regnery, 2016.

Cashill, Jack, and James Sanders. *First Strike: TWA Flight 800 and the Attack on America*. Nashville: WND Books, 2003.

"CIA Asks Mossad to Check Passenger List on Ill Fated Airliner." *The Irish Times*, July 23, 1996. https://www.irishtimes.com/news/cia-asks-mossad-to-check-passenger-list-on-ill-fated-airliner-1.69871.

Clarke, John H. "NTSB Clears Up TWA 800 Conspiracy Theory?" Ray Lahr, July 8, 2013. http://raylahr.com/ntsb-clears-up-twa-800-conspiracy-theory.php.

Clinton, William Jefferson. "Remarks on the Aircraft Tragedy in East Moriches, New York, and an Exchange with Reporters." The American Presidency Project—UC Santa Barbara. July 18, 1996. https://www.presidency.ucsb.edu/documents/remarks-the-aircraft-tragedy-east-moriches-new-york-and-exchange-with-reporters.

Danziger, Andrew. "Former Obama Pilot: TWA Flight 800 Was Not Blown Up by a Faulty Fuel Tank; It Was Shot Down. I'll Always Believe That, and Here's Why." *New York Daily News*, April 15, 2015. https://www.nydailynews.com/new-york/obama-pilot-twa-flight-800-shot-article-1.2186329.

Davey, Robert. "How Did Flight 800 Blow Up?" *Village Voice*, March 3, 1998. https://www.villagevoice.com/1998/03/03/how-did-flight-800-blow-up/.

Davey, Robert. "High-Ranking Military Officers, Independent Investigators, Pilots, and Eyewitnesses Believe a Missile Destroyed TWA Flight 800." *Village Voice*, July 21, 1998. https://www.villagevoice.com/1998/07/21/high-ranking-military-officers-independent-investigators-pilots-and-eyewitnesses-believe-a-missile-destroyed-twa-flight-800/.

Davey, Robert. "Still Bearing Witness." *Village Voice*, July 17, 2001. https://www.villagevoice.com/2001/07/17/still-bearing-witness/.
Dioniato, Philip. "229 Perish in Jet Crash: Coast Guard Says No Survivors Are Found." *Newsday*, July 18, 1996. https://www.pulitzer.org/winners/staff-39.
Donaldson, William S., in cooperation with ARAP. "Interim Report on the Crash of TWA Flight 800 and the Actions of the NTSB and the FBI." TWA 800 Project, July 17, 1998. http://twa800.com/report/final.pdf.
Evans, Martin C. "LIers Still Haunted by Lessons, Legacy of TWA Flight 800." *Newsday*, July 11, 2016. https://www.newsday.com/long-island/liers-still-haunted-by-lessons-legacy-of-twa-flight-800-1.12029236.
"FBI's Kallstrom, Who Led TWA Probe, to Retire." *Washington Post*, December 10, 1997. https://www.washingtonpost.com/archive/politics/1997/12/10/fbis-kallstrom-who-led-twa-probe-to-retire/0ec613bb-623b-493b-9826-dd992f148541/.
"Feds Take Alleged Missile Video." United Press International Archives, March 11, 1997. https://www.upi.com/Archives/1997/03/11/Feds-take-alleged-missile-video/8458858056400/.
Ganley, Elaine. "Navy Missile Shot Down Plane, Ex-newsman Says." Associated Press, November 8, 1996. https://journaltimes.com/news/national/navy-missile-shot-down-plane-ex-newsman-says/article_3990083c-afaf-54d4-8819-04b28ebb3b29.html.
Gannett News Service. "TWA 800 Crash Witnesses Ally, Request Federal Hearing." *Quad-City Times*, July 18, 2000. https://qctimes.com/article_569a52e6-94e5-5855-ad1b-e9329e9278a4.html.
Genzlinger, Neil. "Leaving No Survivors but Many Questions." *New York Times*, July 16, 2013. https://www.nytimes.com/2013/07/17/arts/television/twa-flight-800-examines-a-1996-tragedy.html.
González, Juan. "Did U.S. Gov't Lie about TWA Flight 800 Crash? Ex-Investigators Seek Probe as New Evidence Emerges." *Democracy Now*, June 20, 2013. https://www.democracynow.org/2013/6/20/did_us_govt_lie_about_twa.
Goodman, Walter. "Explosion Aboard T.W.A. Flight 800: Television; Crash Coverage Is Fed by 24-Hour Guesswork." *New York Times*, July 19, 1996. https://www.nytimes.com/1996/07/19/nyregion/explosion-aboard-twa-flight-800-television-crash-coverage-fed-24-hour-guesswork.html.
Graeme Plaintiff v. Federal Bureau of Investigation, Defendant. United States District Court, D, Massachusetts, March 29, 2005. tps://www.casemine.com/judgement/us/5914b679add7b04934779064.
Hamann, Michael A. "An Open Letter to CNN." Associated Retired Aviation Professionals—The TWA 800 Investigation, July 13, 2001. http://twa800.com/letters/hamann-8-13-01.htm.
Hendrix, David E. "Coal Mine Canaries." In *Into the Buzzsaw: Leading Journalists Expose the Myth of a Free Press*, edited by Kristina Borjesson, 151–173. Amherst, New York: Prometheus Books, 2002.
Hughes, Henry F. "Affidavit of Henry F. Hughes." Associated Retired Aviation Professionals—The Flight 800 Investigation, June 26, 2014. https://twa800project.files.wordpress.com/2014/10/final-final-revised-affidavit.pdf.
Hunt, Terrence. "Don't Rush to Conclude Terrorism, Clinton Says." Associated Press News, July 18, 1996. https://apnews.com/article/4fe55c42e12821bdd8c7c2590d5c5d20.
Hunter, Mark. "The Buffoon Brigade." *Salon*, March 26, 1997. https://www.salon.com/1997/03/26/news_355/.
International Association of Machinists and Aerospace Workers, AFL-CIO, CLC. "Analysis and Recommendations Regarding T.W.A. Flight 800." IAMAW District Lodge 142, July 17, 1996. http://twa800.com/iamaw/iamaw.pdf.
Jeffries, Adrianne. "TWA Flight 800: A Long-Running Conspiracy Theory Makes It to National Television." *The Verge*, July 17, 2013. https://www.theverge.com/2013/7/17/4529196/twa-flight-800-a-long-running-conspiracy-theory-makes-it-to-national-television.
Johnston, David. "The Crash of Flight 800: The Possibilities; Tips, Leads and Theories Are Flooding In." *New York Times*, July 21, 1996. https://www.nytimes.com/1996/07/21/nyregion/crash-flight-800-possibilities-tips-leads-theories-are-flooding.html.

Four. Up in the Air 161

Kerry, John (interviewee). "Larry King Live: American Under Attack." CNN, airdate September 11, 2001. https://www.youtube.com/watch?v=AmdkcVr-K1s.
Kirby, Joseph A., and Tribune Staff Writer. "Coroner: TWA Victims Died at Once." *Chicago Tribune*, August 9, 1996. https://www.chicagotribune.com/news/ct-xpm-1996-08-09-9608090267-story.html.
Lahr v. National Transportation Safety Board. "United States District Court, C.D. California, No. CV 03-8023 AHM (RZx), 453 F. Supp. 2d 1153 (C.D. Cal. 2006), Decided Aug 31, 2006." https://casetext.com/_print/doc/lahr-v-national-transp-safety-bd?_printInclude Highlights=false&_printIncludeKeyPassages=false&_printIsTwoColumn=true&_printEmail=&_printHighlightsKey=#922443fe-c44c-4939-aad1-87b4f10ead56-fn49.
Lahr v. National Transportation Safety Board. "United States District Court, C.D. California, No. CV 03-8023 AHM (RZx), Plaintiff's Opposition to CIA's Motion for Partial Summary Judgment." October 31, 2005. https://www.cia.gov/readingroom/docs/DOC_0001251752.pdf.
Lahr, Ray. "Ten-Year Commemoration of TWA Flight 800." Ray Lahr, July 17, 2006. https://web.archive.org/web/20130202015649/http://raylahr.entryhost.com/tenyearcommemoration.php.
Lopez, Ramon. "TWA 800 Crash Report Puts Faulty Wiring as Main Cause." *FlightGlobal*, August 28, 2000. https://www.flightglobal.com/twa-800-crash-report-putsfaulty-wiring-as-main-cause-/33916.article.
Meyer, Frederick. "Interview Transcript" (Appendix O), January 11, 1997. *Witness Group Chairman's Factual Report (DCA96MA070), National Transportation Safety Board*, Washington, D.C., February 9, 2000. https://twa800.com/witnesscd/AppendixO.pdf.
Miller, Judith. "A Nation Challenged: The Response; Planning for Terror but Failing to Act." *New York Times*, December 30, 2001. https://www.nytimes.com/2001/12/30/us/a-nation-challenged-the-response-planning-for-terror-but-failing-to-act.html.
Milton, Pat. "Friendly Fire Theory Called 'Outrageous Allegation." Associated Press News, September 17, 1996. https://apnews.com/article/41b96be891af069563a03e2ad8dd8ad1.
Milton Pat. "FBI Denies Newsman's Claim Navy Missile Shot Down TWA Flight 800." Associated Press News, November 8, 1996. https://apnews.com/article/7411e8c7cc0a61445574074924828dc8.
Miller, Shane. "Conspiracy Theories: Public Arguments as Coded Social Critiques: A Rhetorical Analysis of the TWA Flight 800 Conspiracy Theories." *Argumentation and Advocacy*, 39, no. 1 (2002): 40–56. https://doi.org/10.1080/00028533.2002.11821576.
Morgans, Julian. "Know Your Missiles." *Vice*, July 28, 2014. https://www.vice.com/en/article/8gdvw4/know-your-missiles.
Morris, Dick, and Eileen McGann. *Because He Could*. New York: Harper Perennial, 2004.
NASA Safety Center. "Fire in the Sky." *Systems Failures Case Studies* 5, issue 1 (January 2011): 1–4. https://sma.nasa.gov/docs/default-source/safety-messages/safetymessage-2011-01-09-twa800inflightbreakup.pdf?sfvrsn=6fae1ef8_4.
National Transportation Safety Board. *Aircraft Accident Report: In-Flight Breakup over the Atlantic Ocean Trans World Airlines Flight 800 Boeing 747-131, N93119, Near East Moriches, New York July 17, 1996; Aircraft Accident Report NTSB/AAR-00/03*. Washington, D.C.: NTSB, August 23, 2000. https://www.ntsb.gov/investigations/AccidentReports/Reports/AAR0003.pdf.
National Transportation and Safety Board. "TWA Flight 800 Crash, Final NTSB Report, Day 1." C-SPAN, airdate August 22, 2000. https://www.c-span.org/video/?158913-1/twa-800-crash-final-report-day-1.
Negroni, Christine. "Six Months Later, Still No Answer to TWA Flight 800 Mystery." CNN, January 17, 1977. http://www.cnn.com/U.S./9701/17/twa/index.html.
Noveck, Jocelyn. "Report: TWA Jet Blasted by Navy." Associated Press, November 8, 1996. https://www.sfgate.com/news/article/Report-TWA-jet-blasted-by-Navy-3113688.php.
Null, Michael N. "The Downing of TWA 800—Part 2—Major Meyer Speaks Out." *Patch*, June 26, 2013. https://patch.com/new-york/newcity/the-downing-of-twa-800--part-2--major-meyer-speaks-out.
"Obituaries: Richard Denver 'Dick' Russell." *Daytona Beach News Journal*, April 1, 2021. https://www.legacy.com/obituaries/news-journalonline/obituary.aspx?n=richard-denver-russell-dick&pid=198231210&fhid=24276.

Pelligrini, Frank. "FBI Grilled over Role in TWA 800 Probe." *TIME Magazine*, May 10, 1999. http://content.time.com/time/printout/0,8816,24519,00.html#.

"'Phenomenal Whiplash' Killed Most in Mid Air." *The Irish Times*, August 8, 1996. https://www.irishtimes.com/news/phenomenal-whiplash-killed-most-in-mid-air-1.78371#:~:text=MOST%20of%20the%20230%20people,examiner%20(coroner)%20said%20yesterday.

Phillips, Don. "TWA Probers Shift Hunt for Jet's Center Fuel Tank." *Washington Post*, August 8, 1996. https://www.washingtonpost.com/archive/politics/1996/08/20/twa-probers-shift-hunt-for-jets-center-fuel-tank/edad65bc-673f-4fdd-9788-40f7fda2233e/.

Polk, Jim. "U.S. Focused on Iran after TWA 800 Explosion." CNN, July 17, 1996. https://www.cnn.com/2006/U.S./07/12/twa.terrorism/index.html.

Purdy, Matthew. "Explosion Aboard T. W. A. Flight 800: The Overview; Investigators Suspect Explosive Device as Likeliest Cause for Crash of Flight 800." *New York Times*, July 19, 1996. https://www.nytimes.com/1996/07/19/nyregion/explosion-aboard-twa-flight-800-overview-investigators-suspect-explosive-device.html.

Reid, Alice. "FAA Seeks to Soothe Passengers." *Washington Post*, July 19, 1996. https://www.washingtonpost.com/archive/politics/1996/07/19/faa-seeks-to-soothe-passengers/dfbeeedd-3c4d-4a08-9887-bcd6b2c9fa6d/.

Reid, Jeffery. "'Pierre Salinger Syndrome' and the TWA 800 Conspiracies." CNN, July 17, 1996. https://www.cnn.com/2006/U.S./07/12/twa.conspiracy/.

Roberts, John B., II. "The Ongoing Dissent over TWA 800." *The American Spectator*, August 1999. http://twa800.com/news/as-8-99.htm.

Russell, Richard. "Affidavit of Richard Russell" (Exhibit M, January 2, 2003). *Lahr vs. National Transportation and Safety Board*, U.S. District Court, C.D. California, August 31, 2006: 1–3. https://twa800.com/lahr/affidavits/m-richard-russell.pdf.

Salinger, Pierre. "Internet and Flight 800 (Op-Ed.)." *New York Times*, August 22, 1997. https://www.nytimes.com/1997/08/22/opinion/l-internet-and-flight-800-734802.html.

Schroeder, Matthew. "Stop Panicking about the Stingers." *Foreign Policy*, July 28, 2010. https://web.archive.org/web/20170802165612/https://foreignpolicy.com/2010/07/28/stop-panicking-about-the-stingers/.

Schulze, Glen H. "Affidavit (Glen H. Schulze, February 4, 2003)." *Lahr vs. National Transportation and Safety Board*, U.S. District Court, C.D. California, August 31, 2006. http://twa800.com/lahr/affidavits/bb-glen-schulze.pdf.

SCMP Reporter. "USA Warned of Terrorist Threat." *South China Morning Post*, July 22, 1996. https://www.scmp.com/article/167838/usa-warned-terrorist-threat.

"Searching for Answers: Probers Focus on Possibility of Bomb or Missile; Toll at 230." *Newsday*, July 19, 1996. https://www.pulitzer.org/winners/staff-39.

Sephton, Graeme. "Affidavit of Graeme Sephton, PE, RCDD (July 31, 2003)." *Lahr vs. National Transportation and Safety Board*, U.S. District Court, C.D. California, August 31, 2006. http://twa800.com/lahr/affidavits/aa-graeme-sephton.pdf.

Serrano, Richard A., and Marc Lacey. "U.S. Probing for Sabotage in Fiery Explosion of Jumbo Jet." *Los Angeles Times*, July 19, 1996. https://www.latimes.com/archives/la-xpm-1996-07-19-mn-25715-story.html.

Speers, James. "Affidavit of James Speers (June 18, 2003)." *Lahr vs. National Transportation and Safety Board*, U.S. District Court, C.D. California. http://twa800.com/lahr/affidavits/l-james-speer.pdf, p. 4.

Staff Report, "Local Man Seeks Truth in Flight 800 Crash," *Williamsport Sun-Gazette*, June 22, 2013. https://www.sungazette.com/news/top-news/2013/06/local-man-seeks-truth-in-flight-800-crash/.

Swardson, Anne, and Serge F. Kovaleski. "Misguided Missile?" *Washington Post*, November 9, 1996. https://www.washingtonpost.com/archive/lifestyle/1996/11/09/misguided-missile/a6efeece-7c5e-49a8-ab43-b1cbdf2927bb/.

TWA Flight 800 Documentary Team. "Rebuttal of CIA Video about TWA Flight 800." *The TWA 800 Project*, July 16, 2014. https://www.youtube.com/watch?v=IyluFVxqBlo&t=159s.

The TWA 800 Project. "Petition for the Reconsideration and Modification of the National Transportation Safety Board's Findings and Determination of the Probable Cause for the

Crash of TWA Flight 800." The TWA 800 Project, June 18, 2013. https://twa800project.files.wordpress.com/2013/06/petition-final.pdf.
Van Natta, Don, Jr. "Reconstructing T.W.A. 800." *New York Times*, May 11, 1997. https://www.nytimes.com/1997/05/11/magazine/reconstructing-twa-800.html.
Van Natta, Don, Jr. "More Traces of Explosive in Flight 800." *New York Times*, August 31, 1996. https://www.nytimes.com/1996/08/31/nyregion/more-traces-of-explosive-in-flight-800.html.
Wald, Matthew L. "Investigators Describe a Stubborn F.B.I. at Hearing on Jet Explosion." *New York Times*, May 11, 1999. https://www.nytimes.com/1999/05/11/nyregion/investigators-describe-a-stubborn-fbi-at-hearing-on-jet-explosion.html.
Wald, Matthew L. "The Fate of Flight 800: The Data; Record of Quick Destruction: Briefest Sound, Then Silence." *New York Times*, July 26, 1996. https://www.nytimes.com/1996/07/26/nyregion/fate-flight-800-data-record-quick-destruction-briefest-sound-then-silence.html.
Walsh, Edward. "FBI Probe of TWA Crash Criticized." *Washington Post*, May 11, 1999. https://www.washingtonpost.com/wp-srv/national/longterm/twa/twa.htm.
Weiss, Philip. "Radar Shows 'Getaway Boat' Fleeing Flight 800 Crash." *The Observer*, July 12, 1999. https://observer.com/1999/07/radar-shows-getaway-boat-fleeing-flight-800-crash/.
"What Is the Pierre Salinger Syndrome?" *Techslang*. Accessed May 4, 2022. https://www.techslang.com/definition/what-is-the-pierre-salinger-syndrome/.
Williams, Brian, and Tom Costello. "NTSB Refuses to Reopen TWA Flight 800 Crash Probe." NBC News, airdate June 19, 2013. https://www.nbcnews.com/news/us-news/ntsb-refuses-reopen-twa-flight-800-crash-probe-n147051.
Wire, Mike. "TWA 800: What the CIA Did to Mike Wire, Witness 571." *American Thinker*, June 9, 2016. https://www.americanthinker.com/articles/2016/06/twa_800_what_the_cia_did_to_witness_571_mike_wire.html.
Woody, Christopher. "'A Fighting War with the Main Enemy': How the CIA Helped Land a Mortal Blow to the Soviets in Afghanistan 32 Years ago." *Business Insider*, October 2, 2018. https://www.businessinsider.com/32-year-anniversary-of-first-stinger-missile-use-in-afghanistan-2018-9.
Wooton, Suzanne. "Impact on TWA May Hinge on Cause, Firm Not Financially Secure Despite Turnaround: Tragedy of Flight 800." *Baltimore Sun*, July 18, 1996. https://www.baltimoresun.com/news/bs-xpm-1996-07-19-1996201054-story.html.
Wren, Christopher S. "Charged as Terror Master, Surrounded by Mysteries." *New York Times*, May 29, 1996. https://www.nytimes.com/1996/05/29/nyregion/charged-as-terror-master-surrounded-by-mysteries.html.
Wright, Lawrence. "The Counter-Terrorist." *The New Yorker*, January 6, 2002. https://www.newyorker.com/magazine/2002/01/14/the-counter-terrorist.

Five

Over the Skies of Russia
The 2004 Black Widow Attacks

"Siberia Airlines is sorry to confirm that on Tuesday, August 24th [2004], the aircraft carrying out flight #1407 Moscow-Sochi disappeared from the radar screens approximately at 23:00 (Moscow time)."[1] So reads the terse statement released by Siberia Airlines, or Sibir, the largest commercial carrier in Russia. While the company's announcement was distressing, even more disturbing was the fact that the Sibir jet was not the only airliner to disappear from radar at 11:00 p.m. over Russia. A regional airliner, Volga-AviaExpress Flight 1303, had shared its fate.

It was on a clear summer night that the two domestic flights departed from the same terminal at Domodedovo International Airport in Moscow. Both were believed to be carrying Russian passengers exclusively. The first to take off, at 9:35 p.m., was the Siberia Airlines jet, which was traveling to the Black Sea resort of Sochi, located 850 miles to the south. Departing nearly an hour later, at 10:30 p.m., was the Volga-AviaExpress plane. It was one of only six aircraft comprising the fleet, and the company's general director was piloting it. Destination: the city of Volgograd, formerly known as Stalingrad, which is situated in southern Russia on the Volga River.

As it happened, the Volga-AviaExpress flight was the first to vanish from radar screens. A routine trip up to that moment, the plane was cruising at 26,600 feet over the village of Buchalki in the Tula Oblast, a hundred miles south of Moscow. (In Russia, an oblast is similar to a province or comparable administrative division in other nations.) Villagers witnessing the incident described the plane as exploding in midair.[2] Others, inside their homes, heard the calamity. "I thought it was a thunderstorm," said Nikolai Gorokhov, "then there was a very long-drawn-out roar and then everything died out."[3] As dawn broke the next morning, first responders sighted the wreckage strewn in a field of tall grass, the plane's tail section

FIVE. Over the Skies of Russia

lying a half mile away from the fuselage. The aircraft, a Tupolev 134, had carried forty-four passengers and crew, none of whom survived.

At nearly the same moment that the Volga-AviaExpress plane exploded, the Siberia Airlines jet, which was now 500 miles south of it, blew up as well. An onlooker recounted watching as a flash of red illuminated the night sky, followed seconds later by a prolonged rumbling. "I cannot explain," said resident Aleksander Zalchenko, "but it was a long explosion in the sky."[4]

A Tupolev 154, the Sibir plane was cruising at 39,700 feet over the Rostov Oblast when it exploded and crashed in a remote area. So isolated was the region that it took first responders nine hours to locate the twenty-five-mile expanse of wreckage. As expected, there were no survivors among the forty-six passengers and crew.

At once, Russian president Vladimir Putin, who was vacationing by the Black Sea, acknowledged the twin crashes and announced publicly that he was returning to Moscow to assemble a commission to investigate them. Not lost on reporters was the fact that Putin had recently faced stinging criticism for his failure to return expeditiously to the capital in the wake of another domestic disaster. The president further ordered the Russian government to transfer pre-flight checks and other components of airport security to the Ministry of the Interior, suggesting that terrorism was suspected, and he directed the Federal Security Service (FSB), the principal successor to the Soviet-era KGB, to contribute to the inquiries.

Three days later, investigators retrieved the airliners' flight data recorders (FDRs) and cockpit voice recorders (CVRs) for analysis, even as the FSB informed the media that, in all likelihood, terrorism was not the cause of the tragedies. "As of now, no signs of [a] terrorist attack were found on the sites of crashes of the Tu-134 and Tu-154 planes," said Sergei Ignatchenko, an FSB spokesperson. Ignatchenko made it a point to state that neither of the impact sites showed evidence of bombings, specifically.[5] He further implied that violations of air safety regulations, such as ground personnel neglecting to maintain the aircraft as required, were probably the cause of the explosions. Not surprisingly given the FSB's questionable position on the matter, political analysts assumed it was a case of Putin not wanting Russia to appear vulnerable, that conceding that terrorists had successfully attacked Russian properties on Russian soil would make him look ineffectual as the guardian of the nation's interests.[6] Analysts outside of Russia, however, politically unfettered, were quite vocal in asserting that terrorism was the most plausible explanation for the dual disasters. They stressed that the odds of two Russian airliners carrying Russian passengers, departing from the same terminal at the same airport, then exploding at the same time, were immense. "The timing indicates that this is probably a coordinated attack," said Rafi Ron, the chief of security at Tel Aviv's Ben Gurion Airport.[7]

So it was that the Russian government subsequently acknowledged that investigators had indeed detected an organic compound, hexogen, in both planes' debris. "Hexogen, when mixed with nitroglycerin, forms a plastic explosive similar to C4," writes Ryan Chilcote, "and [had] been used by Chechen rebels in attacks on Russian soil in the past."[8] Among these gruesome assaults were suicide bombings carried out at Russian schools and theaters, on buses and trains, and at rock festivals and military installations. However, Chechen bombers had never before targeted a commercial aircraft. If the Volga-AviaExpress and Siberia Airlines explosions proved to be the work of Chechen separatists, it would denote a worrisome shift in tactics, namely a progression to those employed by Palestinian and Islamist extremists in the Middle East.

The issue at the heart of the Russian airliner attacks dated back to the 1700s, a recent manifestation of the blood-soaked struggle between Russia and Chechnya. As the historical record reveals, Russia had long sought to reign over Chechnya, a region situated near the Caspian Sea, but Chechnya had steadfastly resisted. In the course of the conflict, Russia, in particular, was ruthless, at one point forcibly deporting Chechens to Siberia and Central Asia as well as executing them en masse. Russia's periodic genocide of the Chechen people is well documented.

Alas, the struggle persists today, which is explicable in light of the history and characteristics of those who populate the rugged region. "Chechens are a culturally and ethnically distinct people who settled in the mountainous areas of the North Caucasus thousands of years ago," write political scientists Tanya Narozhna and W. Andy Knight. "Their social structure has been organized around self-contained clans and tribes, based on religious cohesion and tight family links."[9] Possessing a unique and vibrant heritage, the region's inhabitants refuse to be assimilated into Russia but seek instead to preserve and protect their autonomy and cultural distinctiveness. Unfortunately, some Chechen separatist groups in the twenty-first century have resorted to unimaginable acts of violence against Russian civilians in this ongoing fight against Russian rule. And while the United States has expressed its support for moderate, nonviolent Chechen separatists, the U.S. government has made it clear that it does not endorse the brutal actions of Chechen extremists.[10]

In the case of the Russian aircraft explosions of 2004, each was the product of a "Black Widow." An unconventional brand of terrorist, black widows are Chechen female suicide bombers, and they are notorious for eliciting fear and delivering death to innocents.

Chechen Female Suicide Bombers

Mia Bloom is a political scientist whose research on this topic has brought to light four factors that appear to dispose women to commit such obscene acts of destruction and self-destruction. "[W]omen across a number of conflicts and in several different terrorist groups tend to be motivated by one or several of the four Rs: *revenge, redemption, relationship*, and *respect*," Bloom writes. "*Revenge* for the death of a close family member is most often cited as the key factor that inspired a woman to get involved in the first place."[11]

Among the female suicide bombers in Chechnya, this is no doubt the case, a considerable portion of whom lost their husbands, lovers, brothers, or other family members in the struggle with Russia, hence the term "black widow." They wear full-length black hijabs that conceal bomb belts, their attire reinforcing the sobriquet. Yet some Chechen women have other reasons for conducting acts of mass murder, such as feeling they are acting in self-defense. "These women, particularly the wives of the mujahedeen who were martyred, are being threatened in their homes, their honor [is] being threatened," said Agu al-Walid, the late rebel leader.[12] Then there are those who have an intense need to avenge their homeland; to "even the score" is considered an honorable deed in Chechen tradition. Whatever the motive, though, it is important to understand that such women are typically acting on their own agency; they are neither drugged nor manipulated, as some Russian theorists would have it. "[T]hey are self-recruited on the basis of seeking a means of enacting social justice, revenge, and warfare against what they perceive as their nation's enemy," write Anne Speckhard and Khapta Akhmedova.[13]

Social scientists Speckhard and Akhmedova conducted an illuminating study of thirty-four Chechen suicide bombers, twenty-six of whom were women. Among other issues, the researchers addressed the question of mental health. "[N]one of the Chechen suicide bombers in our sample had a serious personality disorder prior to deciding to join a terror group," they state. "No less important," the researchers add, "is that all individuals within the sample had experienced deep personal traumatization, and evidence of symptoms of post-traumatic stress disorder and dissociative phenomena as a result of direct personal traumatization were present in the entire sample."[14] For the women, the traumas included the deaths of husbands or one or more family members and were a powerful, if not a decisive, factor in their decision to enter the fray.[15]

And lastly, completing the terrorists' transformations, Chechen separatist groups stand ready to absorb such women, groups that offer a smooth transition into structured violence. Since the 1980s, a similar process has been observed in female suicide bombers in Lebanon, Syria, Iraq, Turkey, Sri Lanka, and Israel.

A Decade of Suicide Strikes

In modern-day Chechnya, the first suicide operation was perpetrated on June 7, 2000, ten months into a fresh Russian-Chechen war. In this inaugural strike, a pair of Chechen females, sixteen-year-old Luiza Magdomadova and twenty-one-year-old Khava Barayeva, detonated a truck bomb at a military facility in Alkhan-Yurt, Chechnya. Although figures vary, the explosion is reported to have killed up to two dozen people, among them Russian soldiers.[16] Sergei Yastrzhembsky, a Kremlin spokesperson, highlighted the fact that the two bombers also "were blown to bits."[17]

Because the brazen strike on the Russian military installation brought international attention to the Chechen cause, separatist leader Shamil Basayev set about adopting suicide bombing as the signature practice in the organization he had created. It was formed in 1999 and dubbed the Riyad-us Saliheen Brigade of Martyrs. Its membership ranged from twenty to fifty people at any given time, and it would become the deadliest Chechen separatist group of the era. In the early years of the twenty-first century, the organization increasingly moved toward Islamism and jihadism due largely to the material support it began receiving from al-Qaeda.[18] It was, in effect, a marriage of convenience. As for its suicide bombers, introducing them into its ranks yielded many benefits as well as bolstered the reputation that Basayev was fast developing as "a mastermind of spectacular and brutal terrorist actions," in the words of journalist Jonathan Steele.[19]

As it stands, the benefits of a terrorist organization utilizing suicide bombers—of either sex—are significant, especially for those groups that have limited funds. Human bombers require little or no training; they leave behind no evidence, since it is destroyed in the blast; and they are cost-effective compared to actual armaments.

The reason Basayev initially turned his attention to Chechen women in particular—he personally recruited and trained scores of them—hinged partly on demographic realities. In the *Joint Force Quarterly*, Alisa Stack-O'Connor, an expert on the subject of female terrorists, discussed the mounting shortage of male extremists at the time.[20] "[T]he number of men available for terrorist operations [had] been reduced by outward labor migration, a lack of male volunteers, and arrests, harassment, and investigations of men," she noted.[21] It is beyond dispute that a sizable number of Chechen men were seized, interrogated, imprisoned, and "disappeared" during the protracted conflict. Yet there was another reason Basayev enlisted women.

Early on, the separatist leader recognized that women's suicide attacks tended to be deadlier than those of men and thus more rewarding for the organization. Relevant to this subject, an examination of Chechen suicide missions found that, on average, female bombers killed twenty-one people in each of their attacks, whereas Chechen male bombers killed only thirteen, or 30 percent fewer.[22] And this difference between the sexes is important, not least because an enhanced kill rate translates into marketability. "[T]he more effective a suicide attack is," explains Caitlin Toto, "the more money a terrorist organization will receive from outside donors."[23] In Basayev's calculations, then, black widows were deemed a strategic investment.

In regard to the factors that contribute to the heightened success of female bombers, they include the fact that women, as a whole, are seldom equated with mass murder and can therefore blend in at the heavily-trafficked venues that terrorist groups typically select as their targets. Then, too, they can modify their appearance more easily and credibly than their male counterparts. "The ability to conceal themselves and avoid suspicion," write Reed Wood and Jakana Thomas, "make female bombers and combatants more effective and lethal combatants."[24] Women may, for instance, take advantage of traditional gender expectations by hiding improvised explosive devices (IEDs) in such a way as to dissuade male security agents from performing hands-on searches. "[T]he IED is often disguised under a woman's clothing to make her appear pregnant," writes Mia Bloom, "and so beyond suspicion or reproach."[25] And in other ways as well, female bombers may concoct measures that, while reflecting their cultures and customs, help them deflect attention and avoid suspicion.

Here it is worth noting that despite black widows' effectiveness compared to that of male suicide bombers, terrorist operations that utilize both sexes often assign tasks to the women that are conventionally associated with their gender. In Shamil Basayev's organization, this was certainly the case at times, with the militant leader ascribing roles to females that were nurturing and maternal, while handing authority and control to the men in the same operation.

An attack that Basayev engineered from afar on October 23, 2002, is illustrative. During a stage performance at Dubrovka Theatre in Moscow, forty-one Chechen terrorists, twelve of them women, stormed into the auditorium and took hostage 912 people.[26] The terrorists' demand was the same as in previous attacks, namely that Russia commit to a troop withdrawal from Chechnya.

On the matter of sex roles, the bombs used in the operation were strapped to the bodies of the female terrorists only. No male terrorists were doomed from the start. Another difference involved the roles of men and women during the group's occupation of the theater. "[T]he men took care of the explosives and intimidation, while the women distributed medical supplies, blankets, water, chewing gum, and chocolate," writes Bloom.[27] "One hostage reported that the women acted more like nuns ministering to the sick than terrorists."[28] Perhaps the most important difference, however, centered on the four-pound bomb belts strapped to the women. "[T]hey did not control the detonators—the men retained control of the remotes," says Bloom.[29]

In the end, the remote controls would be irrelevant, since Russian soldiers would put a stop to the madness. Fifty-seven hours after the standoff commenced, Russian special forces released into the building a narcotic gas, one thought to have been concocted by the FSB. Assumed to be carfentanyl, the drug, which is up to one hundred times more potent than fentanyl, rendered the militants and audience members insentient.[30] In the melee that ensued, Russian soldiers killed nearly all of the Chechen terrorists, with 120 hostages perishing as well.[31]

While attacks like those at the Dubrovka Theatre were perpetrated by mixed teams of male and female operatives, roughly half of all Chechen suicide bombings under Basayev's leadership were performed exclusively by women. Such was the case two years after the Dubrovka affair, when the pair of black widows introduced at the outset of this chapter carried out the midair attacks on Siberia Airlines Flight 1407 and Volga-AviaExpress Flight 1303.

Fire in the Sky

When the two women—the black widows—made the critical decision to carry out the airline attacks, they were living in the war-torn city of Grozny, the predominantly Muslim capital of the Chechen Republic in Russia. Roommates, they shared their lodgings with a pair of other women, all four of whom worked as vendors at a nearby marketplace. Like many dwellings in the devastated city, their apartment, which they rented for thirty dollars a month, was a hovel. "The windows were glassless and covered with plastic film," reports *The Guardian*, "and they slept on two beds that were little more than blankets stacked on top of boxes."[32]

Destitution was nothing new for Amanta Nagayeva, the thirty-year-old operative who would obliterate the Volga-AviaExpress airliner. She was born into poverty in Tevzani, a once-peaceful Chechen village in the South Caucasus. Her father, to better provide for the family, eventually secured a job in the town of Roston, then relocated his wife and children to the farm on which he worked. There, the Nagayevas lived and slept in a single room. At the age of fifteen, Amanta quit school.³³

It was on April 21, 2001, when she was twenty-seven years old, that Amanta lost her adult brother Uvais to the Russians. At a get-together at a friend's home, a gathering at which he and Amanta were present, Russian soldiers rushed into the house and seized the men without warning or explanation. Amanta would never hear from Uvais again.³⁴

The second black widow in the airliner attacks was named Satsita Dzhebirkhanova. Less is known about her, but it has been established that she was thirty-four years old, a divorcée, and had also lost a brother. An Islamic court judge, he had been killed a few years earlier.³⁵ It was Satsita who would carry a bomb onto the Siberia Airlines flight.

Insofar as it can be determined, neither Amanta nor Satsita had previously taken part in the Chechen separatist movement. For that matter, Amanta had never flown on an airplane prior to the day of her suicide mission.

The operation commenced one summer morning as Amanta and Satsita boarded a bus for an unknown destination. Their families assumed the pair was bound for the Azerbaijan capital of Baku, since they traveled to Baku quite regularly to acquire merchandise for their stalls at the marketplace. Accompanying them were their two roommates: Rosa Nagayeva, who was Amanta's younger sister, and Mariyam Tavurova, a friend of Satsita. Although the four women's movements on that day have not been substantiated, it is believed they boarded a plane in the Caspian seaport of Makhachkala, three hours east of Grozny, for a flight to the Russian capital.

Upon arrival at Domodedovo Airport in Moscow at 7:45 p.m., the women suddenly found themselves detained by law enforcement officers. "It is not unusual," notes the *Irish Examiner*, "for Chechens to be stopped by police in Moscow for questioning."³⁶ The fact that the women were travelling as a group in black hijabs and without tickets may have prompted extra precautions by law enforcement, however, especially since the Chechen presidential elections were only five days away. The atmosphere was taut, by all accounts, and terrorist activity was on the rise in both Russia and Chechnya.

"Police officers confiscated their passports," writes journalist Jill Dougherty, "and handed them over to a police captain responsible for anti-terrorist operations for a further check."³⁷ Focusing on Amanta and Satsita because they were the ones traveling by air, the police released Rosa and Mariyam. Now it became the responsibility of Mikhail Artamonov, an airport police captain, to ensure that Amanta and Satsita were subjected to background checks, body searches, and baggage inspections. As it happened, Satsita had no bags to inspect.

Up to this point, the airport security protocols had been effective, particularly the profiling procedures. A risk had been identified, and the proper steps taken. What is more, the security measures may have foiled the terrorist plot if the police captain had done his job. Instead, Artamonov released the black widows without performing any of the obligatory body searches, baggage inspections, or background checks.

What happened next is unclear, although it has been speculated that Basayev's group may have stationed accomplices in Domodedovo Airport, their assignment being to deliver detonators and bombs to the perpetrators. It *is* known that the black widows, no longer in possession of their identification papers, approached a ticket scalper by the name of Armen Arutyunov who agreed to arrange passage for them on Volva-AviaExpress and Siberia Airlines flights.[38] The women gained his trust by pretending they were involved in drug trafficking.

The cost to eliminate ninety human lives would prove to be cheap, with the black widows paying Arutyunov, in rubles, the equivalent of $69 and $103 for their tickets. In turn, Arutyunov bribed an airline official, Nikolai Korenkov, who was in charge of passenger and ticket registration. To permit the women to board the planes, Arutyunov slipped the equivalent of $35 to the official. "Corruption is endemic in post–Soviet Russia," notes C.J. Chivers, "infecting virtually all spheres of life."[39] Domodedovo Airport was no exception.

It was now that the two terrorists encountered a glitch: the Volga-AviaExpress airliner was scheduled to depart that evening, whereas the Sibir flight was slated for the next day. The women knew, of course, that after the first airliner was blown up, Russian officials would tighten security measures at once, alerting aircraft and airports across the nation. The upshot: the second bombing, the one that set for the next day, would almost certainly be prevented. For this reason, Satsita persuaded Arutyunov to return to the airline official and secure a spot for her on Siberia Airlines Flight 1407 that same evening. And so, two minutes before the boarding process was completed, the official scribbled a note on Satsita's ticket directing that she be admitted to Flight 1407. Not long after, the two airliners erupted in flight and crashed.

Hypotheses and Certainties

Investigators initially considered the possibility that at least one of the aircraft, the Siberia Airlines plane, may have had a specific target—Vladimir Putin's location—since its destination was Sochi, where he vacationing. In that the odious events of September 11 had been seared into the public mind, it was thought that the Chechen terrorists may have been attempting to duplicate a key feature of the infamous al-Qaeda attack. Lending support to this notion, the Sibir flight was delayed by one hour at Domodedovo Airport. If the explosive device did contain a timing mechanism that was pre-set for Sochi, it would have activated before the airliner could reach the Black Sea resort. And indeed, the plane did explode before reaching Sochi.

It was this prospect—the use of timers—that investigators quickly seized upon, since the bombs had detonated nearly simultaneously. One premise held that the IEDs had been concealed in the black widows' checked-in baggage and were triggered by timing mechanisms at the pre-programmed moment.[40] An alternative version proposed that, rather than timers, operatives on the ground had activated the bombs using cell phone signals. In either case, investigators did not rule out the possibility that the two women may not have known they were transporting explosive devices, that they had been duped. Of course, when it was discovered that Satsita had been traveling without checked-in baggage, this line of thought was abandoned.

Another hypothesis introduced ground personnel into the plot. Such workers, who range from baggage handlers to those involved in inflight catering, may enjoy unrestricted access to aircraft. In this scenario, ground workers from Sibir and Volga-AviaExpress, workers who were sympathetic to the Chechen cause or susceptible to bribery, planted the IEDs in the passenger cabins. Once the planes were aloft, the black widows, by means of cell phones or remote controls, activated the bombs.

Still another hypothesis proposed that Amanta and Satsita had strapped the bombs onto themselves and manually triggered them at 11:00 p.m., the agreed-upon hour. Bearing in mind that the airport staff had neglected to search the women, it will probably never be known where they acquired the IEDs or when they attached them to their bodies. This explanation, in light of the available evidence, appears to be the most plausible.

In terms of what investigators were able to establish about the terrorists' modi operandi, they determined that both women selected seats at the rear of the passenger cabins and evidently on the same side of the aircraft. Support for this notion came from Siberia Airlines, which had a record of Satsita's seating assignment. Located on the right-hand side of the cabin, it was near the rear restrooms.

It was a similar situation for Amanta, although it seems that she may have actually entered the rear restroom just before the bomb's detonation. This assumption, that the explosion occurred within a walled compartment, was bolstered by the conditions of the casualties. Only one corpse with burn tissue was recovered from the Volga-AviaExpress wreckage.[41] It was further observed that the passengers' remains from both aircraft were largely intact, supporting the hypothesis that the explosive devices were located in close proximity to the terrorists' bodies. Then, too, the airliners' tails had broken off, strongly suggesting explosions toward the rear of the airliners.

The commission that Putin appointed to investigate the pair of attacks published its findings.[42] "[T]he destruction of the aircraft structure in flight [is a] result of exposure to explosive charges in passenger salons," the final report stated. "Under these conditions, the crews did not have the ability to safely complete the flight."[43] Within one second, the document revealed, the blasts in the fuselages had caused the cabins to depressurize.

Although investigators recovered the flight data recorders and cockpit voice recorders from both planes, it was found that those from the Volga-AviaExpress jet had ceased functioning within two to three seconds of the explosion. Consequently, they were of little value to the forensics team except to confirm a catastrophic onboard event.[44] By comparison, the CVR on the Sibir airliner was connected to an emergency source, an auxiliary power supply housed in the center of the fuselage. For two minutes and thirteen seconds after the blast, it continued recording the flight crew's exchanges as they struggled to contend with the airliner's depressurization. While initial reports had also suggested that the Sibir plane transmitted a "hijacker alert" signal, an action that would have required the pilot or co-pilot to flip a switch in the cockpit, investigators ultimately determined that the notification was merely a quirk that had occurred in the erratic course of the aircraft's destruction.

Claims of Responsibility

Four days after the midair catastrophes, a website known for posting statements by Islamist militants startled Russia's FSB. It carried a claim of responsibility by an unheard-of outfit calling itself the Islambouli Brigades. Evidently, the name was a tribute to Khaled al-Islambouli, the army officer who had assassinated Egyptian president Anwar Sadat decades earlier. "Very little is known about the Islambouli Brigades," reported the *Moscow Times*, "or whether the organization even exists."[45]

Whatever the case, the alleged terror group heralded the success of the mission it claimed to have conducted. "Our mujahedin in the Islambouli Brigades were able to hijack two Russian planes and they were successful despite the obstacles that faced them at the beginning," read the Arab-language declaration.[46] The synchronized terrorist mission, which the statement painted as a show of solidarity with Chechen separatists, supposedly included five operatives on each airliner. No details were

FIVE. *Over the Skies of Russia* 175

forthcoming about the methods the mujahedin had used to bring down the aircraft, however.[47]

From the start, Russian officials were skeptical of the claim, noting there was no plausible reason for a militant organization to place five guerrillas on a pair of suicide flights. Further undermining the claim: Amanta Nagayeva and Satsita Dzhebirkhanova were the only ones whose remains were not acknowledged or collected by families. All of the other passengers had been accounted for, and they did not include eight operatives.

And more problems were evident. On its web post, the Islambouli Brigades declared that the two airliners had been hijacked, which was, of course, wrong. This suggests that the statement's author was acting on the early, erroneous press accounts concerning the Sibir plane's "hijacking alert" glitch. In addition, global news agencies, shortly after the incidents, reported that the Domodedovo Airport police had initially detained two suspected terrorists. The Islambouli Brigade's reference to the "obstacles that faced them in the beginning," then, may have been based on this information gleaned from the news media. Still, despite the flaws in the Islambouli Brigades' claim of responsibility, the group was widely reported to be the source of the attacks.

The Beslan Siege. Eight days after the Russian airline bombings, there came another act of barbarity and it proved to be related to the midair explosions. On the opening day of classes in Beslan, a town in the North Caucasus, thirty-three guerrillas wearing masks and bomb belts stormed into School No. 1, which served elementary and secondary students, and took hostage more than 1,200 children and adults.[48] After steering the captives into a bomb-rigged gymnasium, the hostage-takers demanded that Russia begin removing its troops from Chechnya. Among the terrorists in the gym: Rosa Nagayeva and Mariam Taburova.

For the next three days, the Chechen terrorists refused to furnish the captives with food or water, prompting some of the hostages to resort to drinking their own urine.[49] It was also on the third day that the Russian soldiers surrounding the school reported hearing an explosion and gunfire inside the building. This prompted a raid on the school that killed all of the terrorists but one. Among the casualties were Rosa Nagayeva, who was identified through DNA analysis, and Mariam Taburova. Scores of students, teachers, parents, and others were also killed or wounded. In time, it was determined that 339 hostages had perished, among them 186 school children.[50]

Predictably, the Beslan massacre would set off political shockwaves. "The scale of the violence at Beslan and, in particular, the fact that the attackers deliberately targeted young children traumatized the Russian public and horrified the outside world," reported one source.[51] The bloodbath also shook public confidence in Russian law enforcement and eventually led to criticism from the European Court of Human Rights in Strasbourg, which criticized Russian authorities "for being unable to prevent the militants from meeting and travelling on the day of the attack, and failing to increase security at the school or warn the public of the threat."[52] Not only had intelligence reports pointed to a probable attack on a school in that area, but the weapons that Russian forces used were condemned for being unsuitable for a hostage-rescue strategy involving children. Indeed, the arsenal deployed in the operation included tanks, flame throwers, thermobaric charges, anti-tank rockets, machine guns, and grenade launchers. Not surprisingly, a group of the victims' families—the "Mothers of Beslan"—would file a lawsuit focusing on the Russian forces' incompetency and recklessness, with the court action resulting in a $3.1 million settlement.[53] "The court found that the use of such lethal force 'contributed to the casualties among the hostages' and violated the 'right to life' by failing to restrict lethal force to what was 'absolutely necessary,'" reported the *New York Times*.[54] Of course, the vile affair also reflected badly on the image-conscious Vladimir Putin, who would soon use the tragedy to centralize control over Russia's outlying regions.

Two weeks after the Beslan horror, Shamil Basayev posted a message on a Russian website. The Chechen warlord claimed that his group, now referred to as Shahid Brigade Riadus-Salahina, was behind the suicide bombings of Siberia Airlines Flight 1407 and Volga-AviaExpress Flight 1303 as well as the Beslan school siege. Basayev also boasted about having personally trained the terrorists for the Beslan massacre, and he provided financial details about both operations. "Basayev said he spent $4,000 on the airliner bombings," writes Jill Dougherty, "and 8,000 euros on the Beslan siege."[55] Today, it is generally accepted that Basayev and his outfit were, in fact, the perpetrators of the attacks on the two Russian aircraft and the Beslan school.

In regard to the three men at Domodedovo Airport who, through their negligence or corruptibility, unwittingly contributed to the destruction of the Sibir and Volga-Avia Express airliners, they would be arrested and held accountable by Russian courts. In 2005, Mikhail Artamonov, the airport police captain who failed to conduct the required security checks on the two black widows, was convicted on two charges of negligence and sentenced to the maximum allowed by law, seven years in prison.[56] As for Armen Arutyunyan, the ticker scalper, and Nikolai Korenkov, the Siberia Airlines official, each was sentenced to eighteen months in prison on charges of bribery and aiding and abetting terrorism.[57]

The fate of Shamil Basayev would be even worse. On July 10, 2006, in the Russian republic of Ingushetia, the rebel leader died in an explosion.

"Ingush officials say Basayev was killed near a truck that blew up while separatist fighters were loading it with explosives in the Ingushetian village of Ekazhev," reported Radio Free Europe.[58] Contradicting this narrative, Russian special forces took credit for Basayev's death, depicting it as the result of a covert mission designed specifically to locate and eliminate the most wanted man in Russia. "[T]he operation was successful because the Russian special services had established operational positions abroad, above all in countries where arms were collected and then brought into Russia with the purpose of committing terrorist acts," stated a Kremlin press release.[59]

Following Basayev's death, a seasoned field commander by the name of Aslan Butukayev took the reins of the Riyad-us Saliheen Brigade of Martyrs. But while the organization would continue to carry out strikes against Russia for the next nine years, it would no longer conduct suicide bombings on commercial airliners. In 2015, the organization disbanded.[60]

Notes

1. "Siberia Airlines Official Statement," Siberia Airlines, August 25, 2004, https://web.archive.org/web/20040828084026/http://english.s7.ru/.
2. C.J. Chivers, "2 Planes Crash Near Moscow; 88 Feared Lost," *New York Times*, August 25, 2004, https://www.nytimes.com/2004/08/25/world/2-planes-crash-near-moscow-88-feared-lost.html.
3. Peter Baker and Susan G. Glasser, "Russian Probers Find No Sign of Terror in Wrecks," *Washington Post*, August 26, 2004, https://www.washingtonpost.com/archive/politics/2004/08/26/russian-probers-find-no-sign-of-terror-in-wrecks/3cae8894-8c9e-438b-acca-68bfc3f8ecbf/.
4. C.J. Chivers, "Investigators Seek Causes of Near-Simultaneous Jet Crashes in Russia That Killed 89," *New York Times*, August 26, 2004, https://www.nytimes.com/2004/08/26/world/investigators-seek-causes-near-simultaneous-jet-crashes-russia-that-killed-89.html.
5. David Holley, "No Terrorist Link Found in Twin Russian Plane Crashes," *Los Angeles Times*, August 26, 2004, https://www.latimes.com/archives/la-xpm-2004-aug-26-fg-crash26-story.html.
6. "David Holley, "No Terrorist Link Found in Twin Russian Plane Crashes."
7. Ryan Chilcote, "Search for Russia Crash Clues," CNN, August 25, 2004, https://web.archive.org/web/20050406230859/http://www.cnn.com/2004/WORLD/europe/08/25/russia.planecrash/index.html.
8. Ryan Chilcote, "Russia's 'Black Widows' Wreak Terror," CNN, September 3, 2004, https://www.cnn.com/2004/WORLD/europe/09/01/russia.widows/.
9. Tanya Narozhna and W. Andy Knight, *Female Suicide Bombings: A Critical Gender Approach* (Toronto: University of Toronto Press, 2016), 67.
10. "Claim (in 2004, 2015 and 2017): The U.S. Government Supported Chechen Separatism," Russia Matters Project—Belfer Center of Science and International Affairs, accessed April 2, 2023, https://www.russiamatters.org/node/20317.
11. Mia Bloom, *Bombshell: Women and Terrorism* (Philadelphia: University of Pennsylvania Press, 2011), 235.
12. Robert A. Pape, Lindsey O'Rourke, and Jenna McDermit, "What Makes Chechen Women So Dangerous?" *New York Times*, March 30, 2010, https://www.nytimes.com/2010/03/31/opinion/31pape.html.
13. Anne Speckhard and Khapta Akhmedova, "Memorandum No. 84: Black Widows: The Chechen Female Suicide Terrorists," Tel Aviv: Jaffee Center for Strategic Studies

at Tel Aviv University, August 2006, 75, https://www.inss.org.il/publication/black-widows-chechen-female-suicide-terrorists/.

14. Anne Speckhard and Khapta Akhmedova, "Memorandum No. 84: Black Widows: The Chechen Female Suicide Terrorists," 66.

15. Anne Speckhard and Khapta Akhmedova, "Memorandum No. 84: Black Widows."

16. Robert A. Pape, Lindsey O'Rourke, and Kenna McDermit, "What Makes Chechen Women So Dangerous?"

17. "Suicide Bomb Kills 2 Soldiers in Chechnya," *Washington Post*, June 8, 2000, https://www.washingtonpost.com/archive/politics/2000/06/08/suicide-bomb-kills-2-soldiers-in-chechnya/1225456f-6c51-45d3-abfa-9ce253a6eb06/.

18. "Riyadus-Salikhin Reconnaissance and Sabotage Battalion of Chechen Martyrs," Center for International Security and Cooperation (CIASC), accessed April 22, 2023, https://cisac.fsi.stanford.edu/mappingmilitants/profiles/riyadus-salikhin#_ednref1.

19. Jonathan Steele, "Shamil Basayev," *The Guardian*, July 10, 2006, https://www.theguardian.com/news/2006/jul/11/guardianobituaries.chechnya.

20. Alisa Stack-O'Connor, "Picked Last: Women and Terrorism," *Joint Force Quarterly* 44 (2007).

21. Alisa Stack-O'Connor, "Picked Last: Women and Terrorism," 99.

22. Robert A. Pape, Lindsey O'Rourke, and Kenna McDermit, "What Makes Chechen Women So Dangerous?"

23. Caitlin Toto, "Behind the Veil: A Study of Chechen Black Widows' Web," *Elements* 11, no. 1 (Spring 2015): 28, https://doi.org/10.6017/eurj.v11i1.8817.

24. Reed Wood and Jakana Thomas, "Women on the Frontline: Rebel Group Ideology and Women's Participation in Violent Rebellion," *Journal of Peace Research* 54, no. 1 (2017): 2.

25. Mia Bloom, "Female Suicide Bombers: A Global Trend," *Daedalus* 136, no.1 (Winter 2007): 95, https://www.jstor.org/stable/20028092?seq=1.

26. Nabi Abdullaev, "Women to the Forefront in Chechen Terrorism," Center for Security Studies at ETH Zunich, accessed April 22, 2023, https://css.ethz.ch/content/specialinterest/gess/cis/center-for-securities-studies/en/services/digital-library/articles/article.html/108029.

27. Mia Bloom, "Female Suicide Bombers: A Global Trend," 97.

28. Mia Bloom, *Bombshell: Women and Terrorism* (Philadelphia: University of Pennsylvania Press, 2011), 53.

29. Mia Bloom, "Female Suicide Bombers: A Global Trend," 97.

30. Mia Bloom, *Bombshell: Women and Terrorism*.

31. "This Day in History: 2002 Hostage Crisis in Moscow Theater," History Channel, accessed April 6, 2023, https://www.history.com/this-day-in-history/hostage-crisis-in-moscow-theater.

32. "Sisters in Arms," *The Guardian*, August 31, 2005, https://www.theguardian.com/world/2005/sep/01/chechnya.russia.

33. "Sisters in Arms," *The Guardian*.

34. "Sisters in Arms," *The Guardian*.

35. "Sisters in Arms," *The Guardian*.

36. "Terrorists Bribed Way on Doomed Flights," *Irish Examiner*, September 16, 2004, https://www.irishexaminer.com/world/arid-10039795.html.

37. Jill Dougherty, "'Bribe' Got Bomber on Russian Jet," CNN, September 15, 2004, https://edition.cnn.com/2004/WORLD/europe/09/15/russia.planecrash/index.html.

38. Philip Baum, *Violence in the Skies: A History of Aircraft Hijacking and Bombing* (West Sussex, England: Summersdale, 2016).

39. C.J. Chivers, "Russians Cite Porous Security in Terror Bombings of 2 Planes," *New York Times*, September 16, 2004, https://www.nytimes.com/2004/09/16/world/europe/russians-cite-porous-security-in-terror-bombings-of-2-planes.html.

40. B. Raman, "The Russian Ordeal," *Outlook India*, February 3, 2022, https://www.outlookindia.com/website/story/the-russian-ordeal/225018.

41. Anatoly Medetsky, "Crash Probe Turns to Bombs, 2 Women," *Moscow Times*, August 30, 2004, https://www.encyclopedia.com/politics/energy-government-and-defense-magazines/crash-probe-turns-bombs-2-women.

42. "State Commission for the Establishment of Causes of Aircraft Disasters TU-154 no 85556 and TU-134 No 650800, Which Occurred on August 24, 2004," Investigative Committee of the Russian Federation (SKR), Russian Defense Ministry, accessed April 14, 2023, https://web.archive.org/web/20110927230333/http://www.mintrans.ru:8080/pressa/Novosty_150904_2.htm.
43. "State Commission for the Establishment of Causes of Aircraft Disasters TU-154 no 85556 and TU-134 No 650800, Which Occurred on August 24, 2004."
44. "State Commission for the Establishment of Causes of Aircraft Disasters TU-154 no 85556 and TU-134 No 650800, Which Occurred on August 24, 2004."
45. Roman Kupchinsky, "Analysis: Islambouli Brigades Issues New Warning to Russia," Radio Free Europe/Radio Liberty, September 13, 2004, https://www.rferl.org/a/1054816.html.
46. "Islamic Group Claims Russian Plane Crashes," United Press International, August 27, 2004, https://www.upi.com/Top_News/2004/08/27/Islamic-group-claims-Russian-plane-crashes/95671093637295/.
47. Anatoly Medetsky, "Crash Probe Turns to Bombs, 2 Women."
48. Jill Dougherty, "Chechen 'Claims Beslan Attack,'" CNN, September 17, 2004, https://edition.cnn.com/2004/WORLD/europe/09/17/russia.beslan/.
49. The Editors of *Encyclopædia Britannica*, "Beslan School Siege," *Encyclopædia Britannica*, accessed April 20, 2023, https://www.britannica.com/event/Beslan-school-attack.
50. The Editors of *Encyclopædia Britannica*, "Beslan School Siege."
51. The Editors of *Encyclopædia Britannica*, "Beslan School Siege."
52. "Beslan School Siege: Russia 'Failed' in 2004 Massacre," BBC, April 13, 2007, https://www.bbc.com/news/world-europe-39586814.
53. "Beslan School Siege: Russia 'Failed' in 2004 Massacre."
54. Sewell Chan, "European Court Faults Russia's Handling of 2004 Beslan School Siege," *New York Times*, April 13, 2017, https://www.nytimes.com/2017/04/13/world/europe/beslan-school-siege-european-court-ruling.html.
55. Jill Dougherty, "Chechen 'Claims Beslan Attack.'"
56. "Police Officer Convicted in Plane Bombings," United Press International, July 1, 2005, https://www.upi.com/Top_News/2005/07/01/Police-officer-convicted-in-plane-bombings/60031120197510/.
57. "Police Officer Convicted in Plane Bombings," United Press International.
58. Robert Parsons, "Basayev's Death Confirmed," Radio Free Europe/Radio Liberty, July 10, 2006, https://www.rferl.org/a/1069732.html.
59. "The Elimination of Shamil Basayev and a Number of Other Terrorists Is Just Retribution for the Children of Beslan, for Budyonnovsk and for All the Acts of Terrorism They Have Committed in Moscow and Other Parts of Russia," President of Russia, July 10, 2006, http://www.en.kremlin.ru/events/president/news/35884.
60. "Riyadus-Salikhin Reconnaissance and Sabotage Battalion of Chechen Martyrs."

Bibliography

Abdullaev, Nabi. "Women to the Forefront in Chechen Terrorism." Center for Security Studies at ETH Zunich. Accessed April 22, 2023. https://css.ethz.ch/content/specialinterest/gess/cis/center-for-securities-studies/en/services/digital-library/articles/article.html/108029.
Baker, Peter, and Susan G. Glasser. "Russian Probers Find No Sign of Terror in Wrecks." *Washington Post*, August 26, 2004. https://www.washingtonpost.com/archive/politics/2004/08/26/russian-probers-find-no-sign-of-terror-in-wrecks/3cae8894-8c9e-438b-acca-68bfc3f8ecbf/.
Baum, Philip. *Violence in the Skies: A History of Aircraft Hijacking and Bombing*. West Sussex, England: Summersdale, 2016.
"Beslan School Siege: Russia 'Failed' in 2004 Massacre." BBC, April 13, 2007. https://www.bbc.com/news/world-europe-39586814.
Bloom, Mia. "Female Suicide Bombers: A Global Trend." *Daedalus* 136, no. 1 (Winter 2007): 94-102. https://www.jstor.org/stable/20028092?seq=1.

Bloom, Mia. *Bombshell: Women and Terrorism*. Philadelphia: University of Pennsylvania Press, 2011.

Chan, Sewell. "European Court Faults Russia's Handling of 2004 Beslan School Siege." *New York Times*, April 13, 2017. https://www.nytimes.com/2017/04/13/world/europe/beslan-school-siege-european-court-ruling.html.

Chilcote, Ryan. "Search for Russia Crash Clues." CNN, August 25, 2004. https://web.archive.org/web/20050406230859/http://www.cnn.com/2004/WORLD/europe/08/25/russia.planecrash/index.html.

Chilcote, Ryan. "Russia's 'Black Widows' Wreak Terror." CNN, September 3, 2004. https://www.cnn.com/2004/WORLD/europe/09/01/russia.widows/.

Chivers, C.J. "Investigators Seek Causes of Near-Simultaneous Jet Crashes in Russia That Killed 89." *New York Times*, August 26, 2004. https://www.nytimes.com/2004/08/26/world/investigators-seek-causes-near-simultaneous-jet-crashes-russia-that-killed-89.html.

Chivers, C.J. "Russians Cite Porous Security in Terror Bombings of 2 Planes." *New York Times*, September 16, 2004. https://www.nytimes.com/2004/09/16/world/europe/russians-cite-porous-security-in-terror-bombings-of-2-planes.html.

Chivers, C.J. "2 Planes Crash Near Moscow; 88 Feared Lost." *New York Times*, August 25, 2004. https://www.nytimes.com/2004/08/25/world/2-planes-crash-near-moscow-88-feared-lost.html.

"Claim (in 2004, 2015 and 2017): The U.S. Government Supported Chechen Separatism." Russia Matters Project—Belfer Center of Science and International Affairs. Accessed April 2, 2023. https://www.russiamatters.org/node/20317.

Dougherty, Jill. "'Bribe' Got Bomber on Russian Jet." CNN, September 15, 2004. https://edition.cnn.com/2004/WORLD/europe/09/15/russia.planecrash/index.htm.

Dougherty, Jill. "Chechen 'Claims Beslan Attack.'" CNN, September 17, 2004. https://edition.cnn.com/2004/WORLD/europe/09/17/russia.beslan/.

The Editors of *Encyclopædia Britannica*. "Beslan School Siege." *Encyclopædia Britannica*. Accessed April 20, 2023, https://www.britannica.com/event/Beslan-school-attack.

"The Elimination of Shamil Basayev and a Number of Other Terrorists Is Just Retribution for the Children of Beslan, for Budyonnovsk and for All the Acts of Terrorism They Have Committed in Moscow and Other Parts of Russia." President of Russia, July 10, 2006. http://www.en.kremlin.ru/events/president/news/35884.

Holley, David. "No Terrorist Link Found in Twin Russian Plane Crashes." *Los Angeles Times*, August 26, 2004. https://www.latimes.com/archives/la-xpm-2004-aug-26-fg-crash26-story.html.

"Islamic Group Claims Russian Plane Crashes." United Press International, August 27, 2004. https://www.upi.com/Top_News/2004/08/27/Islamic-group-claims-Russian-plane-crashes/95671093637295/.

Kupchinsky, Roman. "Analysis: Islambouli Brigades Issues New Warning to Russia." Radio Free Europe/Radio Liberty, September 13, 2004. https://www.rferl.org/a/1054816.html.

Medetsky, Anatoly. "Crash Probe Turns to Bombs, 2 Women." *Moscow Times*, August 30, 2004. https://www.encyclopedia.com/politics/energy-government-and-defense-magazines/crash-probe-turns-bombs-2-women.

Narozhna, Tanya, and W. Andy Knight, *Female Suicide Bombings: A Critical Gender Approach*. Toronto: University of Toronto Press, 2016.

Pape, Robert A., Lindsey O'Rourke, and Jenna McDermit. "What Makes Chechen Women So Dangerous?" *New York times*, March 30, 2010. https://www.nytimes.com/2010/03/31/opinion/31pape.html.

Parsons, Robert. "Basayev's Death Confirmed." Radio Free Europe/Radio Liberty, July 10, 2006. https://www.rferl.org/a/1069732.html.

"Police Officer Convicted in Plane Bombings." United Press International, July 1, 2005. https://www.upi.com/Top_News/2005/07/01/Police-officer-convicted-in-plane-bombings/60031120197510/.

Raman, B. "The Russian Ordeal." *Outlook India*, February 3, 2022. https://www.outlookindia.com/website/story/the-russian-ordeal/225018.

"Riyadus-Salikhin Reconnaissance and Sabotage Battalion of Chechen Martyrs." Center for

International Security and Cooperation (CIASC). Accessed April 22, 2023. https://cisac.fsi.stanford.edu/mappingmilitants/profiles/riyadus-salikhin#_ednref1.
"Siberia Airlines Official Statement." Siberia Airlines, August 25, 2004. https://web.archive.org/web/20040828084026/http://english.s7.ru/.
"Sisters in Arms." *The Guardian*, August 31, 2005. https://www.theguardian.com/world/2005/sep/01/chechnya.russia.
Speckhard, Anne, and Khapta Akhmedova. "Memorandum No. 84: Black Widows: The Chechen Female Suicide Terrorists." Tel Aviv: Jaffee Center for Strategic Studies at Tel Aviv University, August 2006. https://www.inss.org.il/publication/black-widows-chechen-female-suicide-terrorists/.
Stack-O'Connor, Alisa. "Picked Last: Women and Terrorism." *Joint Force Quarterly* 44 (2007): 95-100.
"State Commission for the Establishment of Causes of Aircraft Disasters TU-154 no 85556 and TU-134 No 650800, Which Occurred on August 24, 2004." Investigative Committee of the Russian Federation (SKR), Russian Defense Ministry. Accessed April 14, 2023. https://web.archive.org/web/20110927230333/http://www.mintrans.ru:8080/pressa/Novosty_150904_2.htm.
Steele, Jonathan. "Shamil Basayev." *The Guardian*, July 10, 2006. https://www.theguardian.com/news/2006/jul/11/guardianobituaries.chechnya.
"Suicide Bomb Kills 2 Soldiers in Chechnya." *Washington Post*, June 8, 2000. https://www.washingtonpost.com/archive/politics/2000/06/08/suicide-bomb-kills-2-soldiers-in-chechnya/1225456f-6c51-45d3-abfa-9ce253a6eb06/.
"Terrorists Bribed Way on Doomed Flights." *Irish Examiner*, September 16, 2004. https://www.irishexaminer.com/world/arid-10039795.html.
"This Day in History: 2002 Hostage Crisis in Moscow Theater." History Channel. Accessed April 6, 2023. https://www.history.com/this-day-in-history/hostage-crisis-in-moscow-theater.
Toto, Caitlin. "Behind the Veil: A Study of Chechen Black Widows' Web." *Elements* 11, no. 1 (Spring 2015): 23-32. https://doi.org/10.6017/eurj.v11i1.8817.
Wood, Reed, and Jakana Thomas. "Women on the Frontline: Rebel Group Ideology and Women's Participation in Violent Rebellion." *Journal of Peace Research* 54, no. 1 (2017): 31-46. 10.1177/0022343316675025.

Six

Libya and Terrorism I
The Downing of Pan Am Flight 103

In the late 1980s, two passenger jets were blown out of the sky, one over the Scottish Lowlands and the other over the Sahara Desert. Scrambling to identify the perpetrators, American, Scottish, and French investigators soon realized they were facing a staggering task, since a number of terrorist groups—and more than one Middle Eastern nation—had distinct motives for the carnage. It would be a challenge to pin down the responsible party. Yet the undertaking became even more daunting as the evidence increasingly suggested that a handful of extremist groups and sponsoring nations may have conspired in the midair atrocities, each for its own reasons. The two bombings, then, plausibly illustrated a multi-perpetrator terror operation, albeit an operation in which only a single nation, for political reasons, would be held accountable.

Noteworthy in both attacks was the presumed role of state-sponsored terrorism. Such support was, and remains today, essential for many extremist groups, including those suspected of involvement in the incidents to be discussed. "State sponsors provide funding, weapons, logistics, training, and bases," writes political scientist David B. Carter, citing the elements necessary for an effective terrorist enterprise.[1] Thus afforded safe haven and the requisite tools, the state-sponsored group may continue planning and executing, on its own, atrocious acts of political violence or, in other cases, the subsidizing nation may summon it to conduct or assist with a terrorist operation. Because the state does not perform the criminal act itself but rather hands it off to the extremist group, the former may hope to evade accountability. A number of countries, among them certain Middle Eastern nations, have long operated in this fashion.

Libya comes to mind. "Decades before al Qaeda would become a household name," writes Matthew Frakes of the Wilson Center, "the Libyan regime of Colonel Muammar Qadhafi [Gaddafi] stood as the locus of state-sponsored terrorism in the 1980s."[2] During Gaddafi's years as a Libyan strongman, the nation backed a wide range of extremist outfits. "Qaddafi [Gaddafi] has provided training, weapons, funding, safe haven, or other support to several Palestinian terrorist organizations and to the Irish Republican Army, the Basque separatist group ETA, and Sierra Leone's Revolutionary United Front," reports the Council on Foreign Relations.[3] As for targets of Gaddafi's attacks, they included U.S. interests, with the two nations sparring in a tit-for-tat pattern of hostilities over the course of the decade.

The Libyan secret service, for instance, acting through a diplomat at the Libyan embassy in East Berlin, orchestrated the bombing of a West Berlin discotheque in 1986 that was popular among American military personnel. Collaborating with the diplomat was a Palestinian man, a German woman (the bomber), and a Lebanese-born man. Two U.S. soldiers were killed in the blast, and another 229 patrons were wounded.[4]

The United States, in retaliation, launched airstrikes aimed at terrorist enclaves in and around the Libyan cities of Tripoli and Benghazi. During these sorties, Gaddafi's residence was hit, causing his eight children to be hospitalized for lacerations and shock. The family's pediatrician further claimed that Gaddafi's fifteen-month-old daughter died shortly after arriving at the hospital, although this has been disputed.[5] "I saw very much terror among the family," the doctor said.[6] It would be yet another reason for Gaddafi to abhor the United States.

Several months later, tensions between Libya and the United States ratcheted up even further during a North African border dispute. It was 1987, and Libya and its neighbor Chad were engaged in an armed conflict over Libyan encroachment into Chadian territory. At a critical juncture, the United States and France furnished the Chadian military with satellite intelligence, French troops, and millions of dollars' worth of weaponry. The upshot: Chad was victorious, while Muammar Gaddafi was incensed by the foreign military aid his enemy had received. He was convinced it had turned the balance against his country's armed forces.

According to the American government's version of events, Gaddafi subsequently set out to exact revenge on both the United States and France, and he did so by ordering terrorist strikes on their properties. Numerous Western political analysts contend that the destruction of Pan Am Flight 103 over Lockerbie, Scotland, during the Christmas holidays, a plane filled with Americans, was the first stage of Gaddafi's payback scheme. Buttressing this proposition was another act of sabotage nine months later, the presumed second stage of the revenge plan, which transpired over the Sahara Desert. The target, on this occasion, was a French commercial airliner.

And yet, while the motives for the two bombings seemed apparent, critics of the investigations raised doubts as to whether the African nation was solely responsible for the terrorist attacks or, for that matter, if it was involved at all. Submitted as likely actors in the multifaceted operations were Iran, Syria, and Lebanon as well as prominent Palestinian groups, all of which had discernible motives and were known to act in concert.

In this chapter, we revisit the first of this pair of aviation disasters, the targeting of an American jetliner, and assess the arguments offered by those who contend that Western nations, particularly the U.S. government, manipulated the inquiries so as to hold Libya, and only Libya, responsible for the crime. The next chapter will examine the second bombing, that of the French airliner.

Pan Am Flight 103

As the Christmas season approached in 1988, the United States Embassy in Helsinki received an unsettling message. "An anonymous caller told a US diplomatic facility in Europe on 5 December that a bombing attempt would be made against a Pan American aircraft flying from Frankfurt, West Germany to the United States," a classified CIA document stated.[7] The caller, a man with a Middle Eastern accent, said the Abu Nidal Organization (ANO) was behind the impending act of terror and that the operation would involve an unwitting accomplice. At the time, the ANO, a militant Palestinian group, had allied itself with Muammar Gaddafi's Libya, which was an avowed enemy of the United States. The ANO had previously aligned itself with Syria and Iraq.

Leaping into action, the U.S. government notified selected airports and airlines of the threat, and it called for tighter security measures, especially at the Frankfurt airport.[8] The State Department also informed U.S. embassies across Europe and Asia, with the notification prompting at least one of them, the mission in Moscow, to apprise its staff. On December 13, that particular embassy issued an internal memo disclosing the warning against Pan Am, stating that it "leaves to the discretion of individual travelers any decisions on altering personal travel plans or changing to another American carrier."[9]

It has been posited that officials of other governments were warned as well. The South African politician, Pik Botha, was scheduled to take Pan Am Flight 103 to New York City for the Namibian independence ratification ceremony. Accompanying him was a delegation of twenty-two South African officials. At the last minute, however, the group changed to another flight, prompting speculation that they had been advised to avoid the

Frankfurt-London route. According to Oswald LeWinter, who was a former CIA agent, and Walter Rowland, a British tycoon with business interests in South Africa, the warning came from the South African Bureau of State Security, which had close ties to the CIA and Israeli intelligence.[10] An intriguing claim, it has not been confirmed.

In contrast to such internal notifications, neither the American government nor Pan Am World Airways informed the one group that would be most affected by such an attack: traveling civilians. Instead, airline customers were kept in the dark about the danger. When spokespersons for the State Department and Pan Am were later grilled about why they had purposely withheld this information from prospective passengers, a handful of answers was offered, with one in particular catching the public's attention. It was the worry that customers would cancel their tickets if they were warned about a potential terrorist strike, and this would be disruptive to the airline industry if no attack was forthcoming.[11] Of course, far more disruptive than cancelled airfare was the abomination that was about to be unleashed over Lockerbie, Scotland, a tragedy supposedly set into motion in the Republic of Malta, two hundred miles east of Libya in the Mediterranean Sea.

It was here, on December 21, 1988, that many investigators contend that a thirty-six-year-old man believed to have been a member of the Jamahiriya Security Organization (JSO), the Libyan intelligence service, arrived at Luqa Airport. His name was Abdelbaset al-Megrahi, and he was the director of Libya's Center for Strategic Studies. More important, he was also the chief of security for Libya Arab Airlines. In the ensuing years, British and American investigators would suggest that Megrahi and an accomplice, Lamin Khalifah Fhimah, checked a brown Samsonite suitcase onto Air Malta Flight 180 to Frankfurt on this fateful morning, after which the bag was flown to the German airport. Neither Megrahi nor Fhimah boarded the plane.

On arrival at Flughafen Frankfurt Main, the Frankfurt facility, Pan Am personnel transferred the suitcase to the cargo hold of Pan Am Flight 103A, a feeder flight bound for London. The aircraft was a Boeing 727. The workers did not examine the bag, nor did they match it to a passenger on board the plane. In effect, it was a rogue piece of luggage, uninspected and unaccompanied, passing through a German airport that was classified as a high-risk site for terrorist activity.

Heathrow Airport in London was designated a high-risk facility as well, and it was here that baggage handlers transferred the suspicious suitcase to the front cargo hold of Pan Am Flight 103, a Boeing 747, bound for New York later that evening. Notably, a break-in at Heathrow had occurred the previous night, and it was in the area in which Pan Am 103's luggage was processed and loaded. Despite the questions prompted by the crime, however, Heathrow did not ground any flights that utilized this section of the facility for its baggage transfers. It was a lapse for which the airport would be deservedly criticized.

Concerning the brown Samsonite suitcase, once again Pan Am personnel, this time in London, neglected to pair it with a boarded passenger or examine its contents. Had they inspected it, they would have spotted a Babygro or "onesie," a cotton sleepsuit for an infant, inside of which was wrapped a Toshiba BomBeat radio-cassette player. A popular "boom box" of the era, it concealed a bomb. Consisting of a timing mechanism and Semtex, the odorless plastic explosive, the incendiary device was likely intended to detonate over the Atlantic.[12] A common practice among terrorists, the criminal evidence in such attacks is largely unrecoverable because it rests at the bottom of the ocean.

In London, all appeared normal to travelers and bystanders as Pan Am Flight 103 commenced its boarding process. An anti-terrorism squad stationed at Heathrow had no indication that a bomb was in its midst, just as they were unaware that the U.S. Embassy in Helsinki had received a warning earlier in the month. "We were never told, but we certainly should have been," said a member of the team.[13]

Captain James MacQuarrie was at the controls of the plane, which was the largest commercial aircraft in the world at the time. Fifty-five years old, Macquarrie had been with Pan Am for a quarter of a century and ranked as one of its most experienced pilots. Captain Raymond Wagner was his co-pilot, a father of three who had been slated to fly to South America but switched flights so he could return home to New Jersey to enjoy the Christmas holidays with his family.[14]

The flight would carry sixteen crew members and 243 passengers, most of whom were American. Among the latter were thirty-five students from Syracuse University's Study Abroad Program who were on their way home for Christmas. Also onboard were five U.S. intelligence officers, including Mark Gannon, the CIA's deputy station chief in Lebanon. Among the handful of people who changed their travel plans at the eleventh hour and did not board the doomed flight were actress Kim Cattrall; John Lydon, punk rocker with the Sex Pistols; and the Motown group The Four Tops, which was running late after a London recording session.

As it happened, the Pan Am airliner, dubbed the Clipper Maid of the Seas, was scheduled to fly out of Heathrow at 6:00 p.m. but was delayed twenty-five minutes. A fairly common holdup late in the day, it would have ramifications for the time bomb concealed in its cargo hold. The airliner's route would follow the "Daventry Departure," a pre-set flight path that, tracing the curvature of Earth, would guide the plane northward to

Scotland and then westward over the Atlantic Ocean. At 6:25 p.m., Pan Am Flight 103 lifted off from Heathrow.

Lockerbie, Scotland

Nestled in the Scottish Lowlands is the town of Lockerbie, home to 3,500 people at the time. Near the border with England, it is situated 280 miles northwest of London and seventy-five miles southeast of Edinburgh. Although it goes largely unnoticed by those on the ground, air traffic on the Daventry route routinely passes overhead. And this was the case four days before Christmas in 1988.

On this cold, windy Wednesday, residents of the provincial market town had spent the afternoon browsing its shops. Some were still milling about as the skies darkened, the stores remaining open into the evening hours to accommodate the holiday shoppers. The more generous merchants plied their customers with wine, in this way adding to the cheerful mood in the close-knit community and presumably to sales as well. Yet not all of the townspeople were purchasing gifts. Some were attending Christmas parties with friends and coworkers, while others were enjoying high tea in their homes.

Eighty miles to the northwest in Prestwick, the staff at the Scottish Air Control Centre was neither dining nor celebrating; the specialists were managing the traffic over northern England, Scotland, and Northern Ireland. Although they had been inundated with flights throughout the afternoon owing to the holidays, conditions had calmed by 7:00 p.m. In fact, Alan Topp, an air traffic controller, was tracking only two planes at the moment, and a third was just entering radar range. It was Pan Am Flight 103 from London, and it was crossing the border into Scottish airspace.

On the plane, the "no smoking" and seat belt signs had been switched off and passengers were settling in for the overnight trip to New York. It was at this juncture that Captain Macquarrie radioed Topp and reported that the jetliner would be maintaining an altitude of 31,000 feet. At nearly six miles over Lockerbie, the plane was cruising at 360 miles per hour. When Shanwick Oceanic Control contacted MacQuarrie moments later to grant Flight 103 clearance for the upcoming journey over the Atlantic, the pilot did not acknowledge the message. Likewise, air traffic controller Topp did not receive any further transmissions from MacQuarrie. Instead, shortly after 7:02 p.m., as the timer on the Semtex bomb reached zero, Topp watched as the blip on his radarscope, the one denoting Flight 103, suddenly became four blips. "I had never seen anything like this happen before," said Topp.[15] At the same moment, the residents of Lockerbie heard an unusual sound overhead.

It began as a low rumble in the distance and rapidly came closer and became more thunderous, causing objects in residents' houses to shake as if in an earthquake. "I wondered if my central heating boiler was about to explode," said Marjorie McQueen, who was watching *This Is Your Life* on television with her two children.[16] A nearby hotelier feared that the inn's roof might be collapsing, the vibration was so intense.

The crew members of Pan Am Flight 103 had no warning of the blast, meaning that the pilot had neither the time nor the opportunity to issue a mayday call or implement emergency procedures. So abrupt and complete was the detonation that the aircraft's oxygen masks did not have time to drop. Within three seconds of the explosion, the plane's nose section broke off, the cockpit and engines began plunging to the ground, and the fuselage gyrated and tumbled out of the sky. By the time the latter had fallen to 19,000 feet, it was in a full-on vertical dive and headed toward Lockerbie. At this altitude, it has been posited that up to 60 percent of the passengers might still have been alive but unconscious.[17] That said, a smaller number may have been semiconscious or perhaps fully conscious on impact. A disturbing prospect, it was suggested by the first responders' observations and noted in the subsequent inquest. "Rescuers found [such passengers] clutching crucifixes, or holding hands, still strapped into their seats," writes journalist and author Hugh Miles.[18]

To residents on the ground, the rumbling now took on more definition. "It began to sound like a fighter jet," recalled one eyewitness.[19] Another described it as a screaming sound as segments of the aircraft descended at a speed of up to 500 miles an hour.[20] And it was at this point that flaming wreckage began pummeling the town. "It was like liquid fire started to rain down, and bits of concrete and debris," said one man who was in his vehicle during the maelstrom. "[W]e even found a piece of the aluminium buried in the car."[21]

Michael Gordon, a police officer, was on the phone at his home when he heard the deafening noise, and he hurried to the window. "[Q]uite high on my right, I could see a long, thin, black object, which had a fire on the upper surface ... and it was making its way toward Lockerbie," he said. "When it hit, there was a horrendous explosion, and I could hear the tiles on the roof of my house lifting."[22] Elsewhere in Lockerbie, resident Bill Parr was taken aback by the luminosity of the impact. "[T]his noise, it's just best described as a gradually increasing roar," he said, "and then it all went quiet [and] there was a very, very, very white light."[23] Seconds later, the sky glowed orange, the scent of jet fuel permeated the air, and smoke billowed across Lockerbie as stunned townspeople emerged from their homes. "The only way I can describe it was like walking into hell," said retired chief inspector George Stobbs.[24]

Hundreds of tons of wreckage littered the region, giving rise to a debris field extending 845 square miles. Among other structures, the expanse of wreckage encompassed the Chapelcross Power Station, a facility that manufactured plutonium for nuclear weapons and a site that was only a fifteen-minute drive from Lockerbie. As it turned out, the most devastating property damage was in Lockerbie itself, the Chapelcross facility having not been affected, although more than a few locals initially feared that the blast may have originated at the nuclear reactor.

The fact is, much of the damage was the consequence of the jetliner's formidable engines—they were Pratt & Whitney JT9D-7As—which were in full throttle when they struck the ground, erupting into fireballs. The wings and their connecting structure, coupled with a section of the fuselage's midsection, crashed into a housing area known as Sherwood Crescent and the spectacle was ghastly. The wings, which still contained 180,000 pounds of fuel on impact, obliterated several houses and their occupants. Attesting to the intensity of the event, no traces would remain of the wreckage, the houses, or the victims on the ground except for the artificial knee of an eighty-one-year-old Lockerbie woman.[25] Eleven residents perished in the impact and conflagration.

Besides pulverizing the houses, the wings also gouged an enormous trench in Sherwood Crescent, one that was thirty feet wide and twenty feet deep. "There was a great roaring noise and flames coming out of a great big hole in the ground and dense, dense smoke," said Stobbs.[26] A number of townspeople dared to approach the fiery crater, anguished over the undeniable deaths of their friends and neighbors whose homes had stood in this neighborhood.

While the devastation in Sherwood Crescent was catastrophic, other parts of town sustained horrific damage as well. Most notably, Rosebank Crescent was struck by the rear section of the fuselage, with sixty-one bodies falling onto the one-block area. And the heat radiating through Sherwood and Rosebank Crescents was brutal. "I could remember seeing a wrought iron gate that had been at one of the houses," Stobbs recalled, "and this wrought iron gate was actually melting just as if it was butter being melted by heat."[27] Nearby, falling debris struck a gasoline station, causing its diesel tanks to trigger another fireball, while a local roadway, also afire, lit up the night sky. Worsening matters, the crash had severed the town's gas, electrical, phone, and water lines, meaning that residents were literally in the dark, unable to communicate by phone and powerless to extinguish fires in the usual fashion. In an inventive moment, the townspeople loaded water into a dairyman's milk truck and used it to dowse the flames.

For the people of Lockerbie, the experience was mystifying, since it was not immediately clear what had caused the inferno. Regardless, many residents found themselves face to face with the human price of the disaster. As lawns and streets blazed, the townsfolk discovered Christmas gifts that had dropped from the aircraft, some of them still in their wrappings, strewn about in the debris. Other items ranged from charred plastic cutlery, dolls, and clothing to cash, letters, and an undamaged PA103 ticket. Most upsetting, though, were the bodies, some intact and others unrecognizable, scattered across the town. "They lay alone or in groups of five or 10 or 20 in fields and parking lots, in gardens and on pavements, next to telephone booths and on top of roofs," reported *The Observer*.[28]

Within minutes of the crash, law enforcement moved into action. The Dumfries and Galloway Constabulary, the smallest police force in Scotland, was in charge of the region and had never encountered such an apocalyptic scene. "The previous year," writes Richard Marquise, "the most significant crime they had dealt with was bicycle theft."[29] It was Marquise, a noted counterterrorism expert, who would helm the American task force investigating the tragedy.

Fortunately, law enforcement officers from Edinburgh and Glasgow rushed to the scene as well, as did medics, firefighters, and military personnel from across northern England and southern Scotland. One Lockerbie resident recalled how the hazy orange sky became an electric blue as police cars swarmed the streets.[30] The media descended on the town as well, with reporters ditching their vehicles on the outskirts of Lockerbie and continuing on foot, as traffic was at a standstill for several miles around the town. Among the journalists was Alan Dron, who was taken aback by the nightmarish vision that confronted him. "What I saw recalled photos from the London Blitz of 1940," he said.[31]

Within twenty-five minutes of the crash, the Royal Air Force (RAF) ordered its teams to Lockerbie, their helicopters crowding the airspace over the town and surrounding areas. Then, at 7:33 p.m., newscasters in the United Kingdom and the United States set about airing their jarring announcements, reporting that Pan Am Flight 103 had gone down over the Scottish town. As could be expected, the families and friends of those assumed to have perished in the crash were stunned, with some becoming angry when Pan Am initially refused to release the passenger list to the public. Had the company done so, however, it would have violated protocol in this early phase of the disaster.

Into the night, the frantic search for survivors continued as hospitals, placed on alert, prepared to treat what were anticipated to be scores of life-threatening injuries. Yet as the hours passed, the emergency rooms remained vacant. "We waited, and we waited," said Emma Harper, a nurse.[32]

As it became obvious there would be no wounds to treat, the focus shifted from hospitals to morgues, with volunteers concocting makeshift mortuaries in the basement of the town hall and at a local ice rink. In the meantime, fires still raged in the streets as residents and first responders continued to come upon the deceased and their possessions. "What really brought it home," said David Nelson, a police officer, "was when you were picking up toys, dolls, kids' rucksacks."[33]

At first light, the extent of the catastrophe became apparent, and it was worse than anyone could have known. Teams from the U.S. government also touched down at dawn and set about establishing temporary headquarters for the FBI and the CIA. And as Wessex and Chinook helicopters from the British military dominated the skies, British prime minister Margaret Thatcher arrived to tour the gruesome scene and express her condolences. Prince Andrew put in an appearance as well, during which he made an unfortunate statement to reporters, a careless slip that riled people across the UK and especially in Lockerbie. "[It was] much worse for the Americans," said Prince Andrew, adding that such a disaster was bound to happen sooner or later.[34] Predictably, his comments were received as callous, and his older brother, Prince Charles, flew to Lockerbie shortly thereafter to clarify that the royal family grasped the magnitude of the tragedy and stood with those who were distraught.

As the day proceeded, more and more rescuers converged on the scene. One cadre was from the Mountain Rescue Service, a part of the Royal Air Force, and its task was to locate wreckage in the areas encircling Lockerbie. Another unit was from the Royal Highland Fusiliers, an infantry battalion, and its mission was to gather human remains. Other squads searched for passengers and crew members who might still be alive, including teams from the Fell Rescue Association, the Cave Rescue Organization, and the Search and Rescue Dog Association. The latter made use of thirty-seven canines, some of them becoming briefly ill or suffering burned paws due to the presence of spent jet fuel. "I felt sorry for the dogs," said Andy Colau, a rescuer and geography teacher. "[A]viation fuel is strong and can affect [those] working near it."[35]

All told, an estimated 5,000 responders combed the mammoth debris field in the days after the crash. A grueling process, it resulted in the retrieval of four million pieces of wreckage, or 319 tons, in what was deemed the largest crime scene in British history.[36] The methods ranged from satellite imaging and surveys by helicopter to arduous searches on foot, sometimes in heavily wooded areas with no roads. A ten-day undertaking, it was especially distressing for those who encountered human remains.

As copious accounts attest, the hunt for survivors left emotional scars on the first responders and the accident investigators who arrived early at the scene. One man whose memories of the macabre display remained distinct is Steve Moss, an investigator with the Air Accidents Investigation Branch (AAIB), an arm of Britain's Department for Transport. The work of Moss and his colleagues was the first to point to a bomb as the cause of the crash. In 2018, he recalled the startling vista, as seen from a helicopter, that stretched out before him over the meadows of southern Scotland. "Looking down from that helicopter," said Moss, "[I saw] people spreadeagled on the ground, almost as far as the eye could see."[37]

For seventeen-year-old David Stewart, who came upon three bodies on his family's sheep farm—a woman, a toddler, and a baby—the memory likewise endured. Upon discovering the deceased, he and his father gathered the remains within an hour's time, but the ordeal haunted David for years. "What we done stayed with me for the rest of my life," he said.[38]

Not surprisingly, civilians were not alone in their reactions; military personnel also suffered emotional pain when faced with the vast stretches of human devastation. For the seventeen members of the Derby Mountain Rescue Team who were dispatched to the crash site, their work, like that of so many others, came at an emotional cost. "[V]olunteers had to deal with sights that nobody should have to see," said a team spokesperson thirty years later, "the toll of which is probably being felt to this day."[39]

In the town of Lockerbie, meanwhile, townspeople exchanged their Christmas holidays for an impressive humanitarian operation to help the casualties' families. Longtime residents provided lodging in their homes for the victims' grieving loved ones who had traveled to Lockerbie from the United States. Others prepared Christmas dinners for the rescuers. And in a particularly stirring display of kindness, a handful of local women washed, ironed, folded, and mailed to victims' loved ones articles of clothing whose owners had perished. In all, the "Lockerbie Laundry Ladies," as they came to be known, cleaned an estimated 10,000 garments after the items had been examined for forensic evidence. By any measure, it was an immense task and a time-consuming one. "It took them the better part of a year to launder all the clothes, figure out who they belonged to and return them to the victims' families," said Deborah Brevoort, who wrote a play about the project, titled *The Women of Lockerbie*.[40]

While it would require considerable time for the emotional wounds to heal for those living in and around Lockerbie, the local population, as well as the victims' families, seemed to be buoyed by the criminal investigations that were set into motion soon after the crash. In both the United States and the United Kingdom, people were optimistic that the perpetrators would be identified, apprehended, and prosecuted.

The Investigations

The investigations, one of them American and other British, would be extensive and stretch over a decade. Both started in Lockerbie.

During the on-site salvage operation in the Scottish town and its surroundings, workers transported each piece of debris to the Central Ammunition Depot, which was situated twenty miles southeast of Lockerbie in Longtown. Here, experts identified and catalogued it. The plane's wreckage would be moved to a facility near London, one operated by the Department for Transport (Air Accidents Investigation Branch), where the aircraft would be partially reconstructed. The AAIB was the body charged with conducting the British investigation into the tragedy.

The notion that a bomb had brought down Flight 103 emerged within a day of the crash, when searchers discovered the airliner's nose section, which contained the cockpit. They spotted it three miles east of Lockerbie in a meadow near Tundergarth Church. This segment, which lay crumpled on its side, appeared to have snapped off cleanly from the rest of the aircraft and plummeted to earth "as a separate item," according to an AAIB representative.[41] Given its features and the precise location of the fracture, a proximate explosion was judged to be the probable cause.

The nose section also contained the first-class passengers and the crew of the cockpit, many of whom were still wearing their seat belts. "There was a mark on the thumb of the right hand of the pilot that suggests the pilot was holding the yoke of the plane on impact and was alive and holding on for dear life," said Dr. William G. Eckert of the Milton Helpern International Center of Forensic Sciences.[42] Nothing on the control panel indicated a problem with the jetliner itself, which had remained in cruise mode.

A few days later, investigators would announce that they had in their possession additional materials indicative of sabotage. "Just before Christmas a strut, which once served as the framing for an aluminum cargo container, was recovered from the fields near Lockerbie," said Richard Marquise. "A closer examination of the strut showed black marks as well as pitting and cratering which indicated to experts it had come into contact with a high velocity explosive."[43]

Most damning, though, was the finding that Michael "Mick" Charles, chief of the AAIB, revealed shortly before New Year's Day. Explaining that cargo holds are lined with Kevlar, a lightweight polymer, Charles reported that the Kevlar on the Pan Am's front cargo hold showed signs of concentrated heat damage. Also telling were the deposits extracted from the scorched polymer. "The explosive's residues recovered from the debris have been positively identified and are consistent with the use of a high-performance plastic explosive," an AAIB press release stated.[44] Side by side with this development, medical examiners discovered metal shards in the bodies of passengers and crew members. Little doubt remained that a bomb had brought down Flight 103.

Although investigators determined within days of the disaster that an IED had triggered the explosion, they could not yet pinpoint the type that had been used. If they could distinguish it, they would be better able to identify the terrorist organization behind the bombing, since bombmakers for extremist groups typically favor certain IED designs. In many cases, the technical features of an attack, from the makes and models of the firearms to the construction of the incendiary devices, inadvertently serve as an organization's signature.

Commencing shortly after the Pan Am tragedy, a multinational effort was launched to understand the intricacies of the bomb, a painstaking enterprise in which forensics experts at the Royal Armament Research and Development Establishment, or RARDE, took the lead. It was at the RARDE facility in Halstead, located an hour southeast of London, that specialists analyzed the baggage retrieved from Flight 103 and detected explosive damage on numerous pieces of luggage. And this was not all they found.

On February 2, 1989, the public learned that a RARDE team possessed a piece of debris—a strip of charred cloth from a garment—from which they were able to extract smaller pieces of potential evidence. "[T]here were found fragments of the lining and internal divider of the primary suitcase, five black plastic fragments which could have come from a Toshiba radio, four fragments of an RT-SF 16 owner's manual, and five clumps of blue/white fibres consistent with having come from a Babygro," reads a document released by the Scottish court.[45] Months later, investigators would claim to have also recovered a tiny green fragment, one that suggested electronic circuitry, in this clump of debris.

Forensic analyses confirmed that one of the items was, in fact, part of a twin-speaker Toshiba BomBeat RT-SF16 radio-cassette recorder. Testing also confirmed that another remnant had come from a Pan Am luggage container which had been placed on Flight 103 at the Frankfurt airport. That said, while investigators welcomed this new set of information, it did mark the beginning of a rather strained and at times contentious search for further answers.

"Some people were excited at the news," said Marquise, "but it did not sit well in Germany."[46] The reason was because the West German federal police, two months earlier, had taken pride in proclaiming that they had uncovered and halted a terrorist undertaking, one that could have resulted in a bombing. In their operation, dubbed "Autumn Leaves," police stormed numerous businesses and homes, seizing evidence and arresting seventeen suspects. (A judged promptly released fifteen of them.) As for the terrorist cell they thought they had broken up, it was a German unit of the Popular Front for the Liberation of Palestine–General Command or PFLP–GC. Funded by Iran, the PFLP–GC was based in Syria and enjoyed the protection of the Syrian government.

Among the incriminating evidence that German law enforcement officers seized in Operation Autumn Leaves was a flight timetable and four bombs.[47] Previous intelligence had indicated there were five IEDs, but police were unable to track down the fifth device. Tellingly, one of the bombs was concealed in a Toshiba BomBeat radio-cassette recorder along with five kilos of Semtex. The bomb was found in the car of Hafez Dalkamoni, a Syrian-born terrorist associated with the PFLP–GC and the head of its German cell, and its design suggested it was meant for use against a large aircraft. In addition, undercover surveillance had previously shown Dalkamoni bearing a brown Samsonite suitcase. To investigators, it seemed obvious that the PFLP–GC was behind the strike on Flight 103.

In terms of motives, political analysts believed the attack sprang from a dispute between Iran and the United States that had erupted a few months earlier, in the summer of 1988. At that time, the Iran-Iraq War was underway and American military ships were patrolling the Persian Gulf as part of a peace-keeping mission. On the day in question, July 3, Iranian gunboats in the Strait of Hormuz began firing on a U.S. Navy missile cruiser, the USS *Vincennes*, during which the ship's crew targeted an Iranian commercial airliner reportedly by accident. It seems that the crew, viewing the aircraft as a blip on a radar screen, mistook the passenger plane, Iran Air Flight 655, for an F-14 fighter jet. Firing two surface-to-air missiles, the *Vincennes* brought down the Airbus, killing all 290 people on board, many of them Iranian citizens on a pilgrimage to Mecca. The Navy warship left the area at once, offering no help to the downed Iranian airliner.[48] Both the Iranian leadership and the Iranian people were convinced that the destruction of the planeload of devotees had not been accidental.

Predictably, Tehran's response was swift and hot. "Death to America!" chanted thousands of Iranians at a mass funeral on the streets of Tehran four days later.[49] "We will not leave the crimes of America unanswered!" railed a commentator on Iran's official radio network.[50] Iran's spiritual leader, Ayatollah Khomeini, called for war against the United States, and the acting commander of Iran's military, Ali Akbar Hashemi Rafsanjani, promised a reprisal. "We cannot allow ourselves to refrain from taking revenge," Rafsanjani said, "and the choice of timing is up to us and not up to America."[51]

Astutely, the U.S. military placed its installations on alert, while notifying American interests in the civilian sphere, particularly those in Western Europe, of the potential for violent reprisals. Certainly, there was reason to worry. A report in the *New York Times* would subsequently confirm that Iran was actively seeking revenge against the United States. "American intelligence had solid evidence that ... a detachment of Iranian Revolutionary Guards stationed in Lebanon had ordered a series of attacks on Americans ... including the bombing of a civilian jetliner," writes journalist Stephen Engelberg.[52] It further appeared that the Iranian Revolutionary Guard was considering a terrorist group headquartered in Damascus to conduct the airliner bombing.

"Within days of the Airbus incident Iran's plan for retaliation seemed to be taking shape," write Matthew Cox and Tom Foster. "U.S. intelligence officials received information that Ahmad Jibril, leader of a Syrian-backed terrorist group known as the Popular Front for the Liberation of Palestine-General Command (PFLP-GC), had paid a visit to government officials in Teheran," they state. "It appeared that Jibril might be offering his services for a retaliatory strike."[53]

It was during this period that Israeli intelligence officers who were monitoring the PFLP-GC's internal communications discovered the terrorist organization was indeed making plans to attack an airliner. "There was a 'huge alert' in the Israeli security establishment because of indications that the PFLP-GC was about to strike," a source told the *Times of Israel*.[54] In Tel Aviv, officials believed the target would be an Israeli passenger plane, but they nevertheless notified their U.S. and British counterparts of the impending terrorist operation so as to keep them in the loop.

Scottish and American investigators, meanwhile, soldiered on through the remainder of 1989 and into 1990, but no new breakthroughs were forthcoming in the case. While it remained the belief that the PFLP-GC and the Iranian Revolutionary Guard were jointly responsible for the atrocity, investigators lacked the incontrovertible evidence that would provide a prosecutable case. In June 1990, the situation appeared to change.

It stemmed from the green fragment, the one that purportedly derived from electronic circuitry and which Scottish forensics experts had extracted from the clump of debris embedded in a charred garment. Unable to identify it, experts shared images of the item with fifty-five electronics businesses around the world, but none recognized it. The Scottish team sent a photograph to Tom Thurman, an FBI bomb expert, who ostensibly identified the fragment within forty-eight hours with the help of a CIA colleague. "I have you now!" Thurman recalled exclaiming.[55] But even as Thurman was delighting in his feat in the summer of 1990, he was also presenting a mystery to investigators. It seems the fragment was a piece of a timer attached to a green circuit board, and Thurman claimed it was different from those the PFLP-GC used in its explosive devices.

As it stood, the four bombs that West German police retrieved at the PFLP-GC's hideouts in the course of Operation Autumn Leaves were barometric bombs. Connected to altimeters, which measure altitude, a barometric bomb is designed to explode at a pre-set elevation. When used to blow up an aircraft, its atmospheric pressure-sensitive detonator is typically programmed to trigger an explosion at a high altitude. However, the green fragment that purportedly came from the Lockerbie wreckage was not part of a barometric bomb, according to Thurman, meaning that altitude had not been a factor in the Flight 103 explosion. If true, this would explain why the IED did not detonate while the aircraft was flying at a high altitude from Frankfurt to London. Instead, the sole factor was time itself.

"[T]he Pan Am 103 bomb had been activated by a sophisticated electronic timer, in contrast to the PFLP–GC bombs, which had altimeter switches and relatively crude timers," reads a U.S. State Department fact sheet.[56] With this, the investigation veered, practically overnight, in a radically different direction.

It was now determined that the mechanism was identical to those that had been used in terrorist campaigns in Togo and Senegal. By dismantling one of those that the FBI had in its possession, Thurman was able to trace the timing mechanism to MEBO, an electronics outfit in Zurich, Switzerland. "There can be no doubt," said Alan Feraday, a Scottish forensics explosive expert, "[that] the fragment of circuit board originated from a circuit board with a MEBO brand MST type 13 timer."[57]

The company's name, MEBO, was drawn from its founders' last names. Formally known as "Erwin Meister and Edwin Bollier, Ltd., Telecommunications," it was a lucrative business dealing in surveillance equipment, electronics, and telecommunications. MEBO's clientele reached far and wide, all the way to Libya. It was certainly no secret that the Libyan military was its main customer, a business relationship that was entirely legal.

In terms of the timer in question, MEBO, in the mid–1980s, received an order for, and manufactured, a version of its model MST-13 timing mechanism for Libya, delivering twenty of them to the North African nation. Although MEBO understood that the devices were to be used for training by the Libyan army, it was the Jamahiriya Security Organization (JSO), Libya's national intelligence agency, that ultimately took possession of them.[58] It was supposedly for this reason, then, that American investigators turned their attention away from the PFLP–GC and the Iranian Revolutionary Guard and placed it squarely on Libya and Muammar Ghaddafi.

Distrust and Denunciations

Here it is important to note that many people, including numerous family members of the Flight 103 victims, did *not* turn their attention away from the Syria-based PFLP–GC or the Iranian Revolutionary Guard. In fact, they were upset and quite outspoken about the fact that the United States had decided to focus exclusively on Libya at this point. They argued that there was sufficient reason to suspect that Iranian, Palestinian, and Syrian entities had contributed to the attack on Pan Am 103 and should not be let off the hook so easily. In the view of these critics, such entities may have collaborated in the terrorist bombing at the request of Muammar Gaddafi and the JSO, or, alternatively, they may have had their own motives for downing an American jumbo jet. It was well known that both the PFLP–GC and the Iranian Revolutionary Guard regarded the United States as an enemy, and, as noted earlier, Iran had recently and publicly vowed to exact revenge for the U.S. Navy's missile strike on Iran Air 655.

As questions mounted about the investigation's newly narrowed focus on Libya, the integrity of the undertaking itself came into question. Forensics experts, victims' families, and journalists openly speculated that the American government might be manipulating the Lockerbie case for political purposes.

One plausible reason that was, and continues to be, put forth in this regard involves the state of U.S.-Syrian relations during that period. It was August 1990. As investigators worked on the Pan Am Flight 103 case, the United States launched Operation Desert Storm in Iraq and Kuwait and it needed Syria's support in its military campaign. This development, many experts believe, dramatically altered the political equation.

"If Lockerbie had been on the mind of Western leaders ... suddenly it was completely forgotten and instead all effort went into ... winning over the government of Syria into the Western-led coalition that was going to attack Iraq," says Hazir Teimourian, historian, author, and Middle East expert. Teimourian adds that "some effort was [also] devoted to making sure that Iran was not going to ally itself with Saddam Hussein against the West."[59]

As the historical record reveals, the United States did succeed in persuading Syria's leader, Bashar al-Assad, to back Operation Desert Storm. Not only did Assad voice his support for the U.S. military campaign but he also dispatched Syrian troops to Kuwait and Iraq to fight in it. Of course, once Syria's participation was secured, the presidential administration of George H.W. Bush had no intention of jeopardizing it, and for this reason, the theory goes, the United States would not be returning its attention to the PFLP–GC's likely role in the Lockerbie case.[60] By extension, if the United States was now absolving PFLP–GC of the Flight 103 mass murder, there would be no justification for pursuing its Iranian sponsors. Even today, numerous political analysts remain convinced that Operation Desert Storm was at least part of the reason the United States spared Syria and Iran from accountability in the Flight 103 inquiry.

Another plausible explanation for the sharp turn in the American investigation, a premise that has been proposed as often as that of Operation Desert Storm, centers on the delicate, back-channel negotiations that were underway to obtain the release of prominent Westerners who were being held hostage by Shiite extremists in Lebanon. It was widely assumed that Iran and Syria were complicit in the kidnappings. As to the captives, they included Terry Waite, an Anglican Church emissary; Thomas Sutherland, a British professor and dean at the American University of Beirut; and Terry Anderson, an American journalist. Not wishing to risk the safety and possible release of these and other hostages, the theory contends, the powers-that-be in the U.S. government decided to refrain from antagonizing Syria and Iran by pursuing the PFLP–GC. It has further been suggested that an under-the-table deal was reached for the captives' release, one predicated on the United States paying no notice to Iran or Syria in the Pan Am investigation. "It seems to me," says Jim Swire, whose daughter perished on Flight 103, "that by far the most likely explanation for the blaming of Libya was to secure the release of Terry Waite and other hostages."[61] Tellingly, perhaps, four days after the Bush administration announced its intention to indict only Libyan nationals in the Pan Am Flight 103 bombing, Islamist extremists freed Terry Waite, Thomas Sutherland, and other hostages.

And so, in view of the questions raised by these and other political developments in the Middle East, coupled with the growing sense that American and British investigators may have been manipulating the inquiry for political purposes, the question arises: what critical information was accessible to investigators and, eventually, to government attorneys before the case went to trial, information that was unavailable or only partially available to the public? The answer, it turns out, is that the legal parties in the Lockerbie case were privy to at least four significant facts in advance of the proceedings, some of them potential game-changers, but they do not appear to have acted on them. The four pieces of information are summarized below.

Pre-Trial Information

The first concerns the authenticity of the MST-13 timer. Questions about its provenance first emerged in 1998, doubts that were expressed by MEBO co-owner Edwin Bollier. As it happened, Scottish investigators, in 1990, sent Bollier a photograph of the MST-13 fragment that was supposedly recovered in the Pan Am wreckage so he could verify that it was, in fact, a MEBO product. And he did confirm it. Bollier explained, however, that in 1998 he asked to see the fragment itself, not just a photograph of it, and upon inspecting the item under magnification, he noticed that an essential characteristic was missing.[62] It lacked traces of soldering, which would have been present if the timer had actually been used.[63] It was, he contended, "a fabricated fragment, never from a complete, functional timer."[64]

The next day, Bollier asked to re-examine the fragment. On this second occasion, however, the fragment *did* show traces of soldering, making it indistinguishable from a timer that had triggered a relay.[65] Bollier's conclusion: a person or persons were tampering with the evidence.

Second, there were questions about RARDE's examination of the MST-13 timer fragment as well as the piece of circuit board. It seems the agency did not analyze them for explosive residue. Of course, this was a stunning revelation, since the timer and circuit board were at the heart of the disaster and arguably the most vital pieces of evidence in the investigation.[66] As to the explanation, the RARDE expert who had been assigned to examine these items said they were too damaged for analysis.[67] It was also said that the remnants were too small to be tested for bomb residue, despite the fact that tinier pieces of debris had, in fact, been checked.

It would later emerge that a senior investigating officer in the Pan Am 103 disaster did, in 1990, address the issue of explosive residue. A Scottish detective, Stuart Henderson, dispatched a confidential memo to a French forensics team that was studying the case for its own edification. Referring to the Pan Am evidence, Henderson wrote, "the piece of PCB [printed circuit board] from the Toshiba [cassette player] bore no trace of explosive contamination."[68] Likewise, the timer fragment showed no signs of it. To explain how this might be the case, Henderson suggested that all of the explosive residue may have been consumed in the blast. Numerous pieces of the Pan Am debris did test positive for explosive residue, however.

Third, lawyers for one of the defendants in the Lockerbie case deposed a man by the name of Dr. Richard Fuisz who, besides being an international businessman, was a deep-cover CIA agent. Among his contacts were several high-level figures in the Syrian government. In early 2001, attorneys questioned Fuisz privately, under oath, at the United States District Court in Alexandria, Virginia.

A few years after the trial, Channel 4 News in London succeeded in gaining access to a transcript of Fuisz' deposition.[69] In it, the CIA agent testified that Ahmad Jibril's organization, the PFLP-GC, had in fact perpetrated the attack on Pan Am Flight 103. The operative added that the terrorist organization had done so on Iran's behalf as retaliation for the U.S. military's downing of Iran Air Flight 655.

Fuisz' sources were solid, his disclosures sobering. "Numerous high officials in the Syrian government were quite affirmative of Jibril's involvement in Pan Am 103," Fuisz testified. When asked how many Syrian officials, he answered, "ten to fifteen."[70] In a televised report, Channel 4 News correspondent Julian Rush was unsparing in his synopsis of Fuisz' testimony. "The CIA, we can reveal, was being told by one of its own spies with access to sources high in a key Middle Eastern government that it wasn't the Libyans," Rush stated.[71]

Unfortunately, the court decided that Fuisz' sworn statement had come too late. Its use in the legal proceedings would not be permitted.

Lastly, a former Iranian official, Abolghasem Mesbahi, provided a nugget of potentially pertinent information. A co-founder of the Iranian intelligence service, Mesbahi defected to Germany in the 1990s. In 1997, Germany's Federal Criminal Police Office questioned him about any knowledge he might have about the Flight 103 disaster, and *Der Spiegel* newsmagazine reported the substance of his response.[72]

Among other capacities, Mesbahi had served as head of Iranian intelligence operations in Europe, and he had remained in close contact with well-placed colleagues in Iran after his departure. To the German authorities, he asserted that Iran had commissioned the attack on Flight 103 as a reprisal for the U.S. military's destruction of Iran Air 655. "The decision was made by the whole system in Iran and confirmed by Ayatollah Khomeini," said Mesbahi.[73] Elaborating, he claimed that the Iranian leadership had originally sought the help of Abu Nidal, the leader of a renegade Palestinian terrorist organization, and also the Gaddafi regime in Libya.

Concerning the details of the bombing itself, Mesbahi explained the process by which the IED had ended up on the Pan Am jet at Heathrow. "According to the [*Der Spiegel*] report, Iran Air's representative in Frankfurt at the time smuggled parts for the bomb through airport security in Frankfurt; the bomb was assembled in London and placed aboard Pan Am Flight 103 from London to New York," reported the *Chicago Tribune*.[74] Mesbahi's account dovetailed with the break-in that occurred in Heathrow's luggage section the night before the Pan Am 103 disaster.

By any measure, the former operative's account of the Pan Am tragedy was a revelation, and it was consistent with the testimony of Dr. Richard Fuisz. "If Mesbahi's statements are correct," reports *Der Spiegel*, "the previous theory that Libya was the sole culprit is passé" ("Treffen Mesbahis Angaben zu, ist die bisherige Theorie von der libyschen Alleintäterschaft passé").[75] That said, it should be kept in mind that Mesbahi's reliability as a source has been questioned on occasion, with his detractors stating that his accounts of previous operations have vacillated between accurate and problematic.[76]

Thus, by the time the Lockerbie proceedings rolled around in 2000, it appeared that the MEBO timer which investigators had in their possession was not the one used in the Pan Am Flight 103 attack, and, moreover, there were multiple indicators that the PFLP, Iran, and Syria were quite possibly implicated in the mass murder. All the same, the notion that there may have been Palestinian, Syrian, or Iranian collaboration in the murder of 270 passengers, crew members, and residents of Lockerbie would remain off-limits as the case against Libya inched closer to the courtroom. Ultimately, prosecutors would pursue guilty verdicts against a pair of Libyan nationals, Abdelbaset al-Megrahi and Lamin Khalifah Fhimah.

The Lockerbie Trial

In 1991, the United States and the United Kingdom set out to extradite the defendants, but Libya did not have an extradition treaty with either country and did not comply. The reasons for its refusal, however, went beyond the absence of such an agreement. For one thing, the Libyan government noted that it had the right to conduct its own trial in the Lockerbie bombing, since the country was a signatory to the Convention for the Suppression of Unlawful Acts Against the Safety of Civil Aviation (Montreal, 1971).[77] Second, the Libyan leadership worried that the two defendants would be unsafe once they were no longer inside the nation's borders. And third, the United States and UK were denying Megrahi's and Fhimah's defense teams access to the totality of evidence to be used against them, meaning that their lawyers would be unable to construct the most comprehensive arguments for their innocence. So it was that an impasse existed for the next four years. "Al-Megrahi and Fhimah were placed under house arrest in Libya," reports the risk-intelligence company RANE, "a comfortable existence that, more than actually confining them, served to protect them from being kidnapped and spirited out of Libya to face trial."[78] Megrahi was allowed to continue teaching during this period.

To compel the North African nation to hand over the defendants, the United States, in 1995, classified Megrahi and Fhimah as "fugitives from justice" and stepped up measures to secure them. "[A]rmed and extremely dangerous" is the label the FBI now affixed to Megrahi specifically, on whose head it placed a multi-million-dollar bounty.[79] In 1992, the United Nations joined the pressure campaign and adopted Resolutions 731 and 748, which leveled hefty economic sanctions against Libya, restricted air travel to or from the country, and blocked arms sales to it.[80] In November 1993, Resolution 883 was added, which barred petroleum-related equipment from being sold to Libya, thereby undermining its oil industry as well as freezing Libyan assets.[81]

Hurt by the embargoes, boycotts, and related measures, the Gaddafi regime agreed in 1998 to a U.S./UK proposal whereby the defendants would stand trial in a neutral setting—Camp Zeist in the Netherlands—with the proceedings conducted under Scottish law by three judges representing the Scottish High Court of Justiciary. To help ensure the integrity of the trial, the UN Security Council appointed four individuals to observe it. These international monitors represented the League of Arab Nations, the European Commission, the Organization of African Unity and the Non-Aligned Movement, and the International Progress Organization.[82] The UN designated one of them, Hans Köchler, to compose a formal report at the end of the proceedings.

On May 3, 2000, the trial commenced, and it was controversial from the start. The defendants were charged with 270 counts of murder, conspiracy to commit murder, and violations of the Aviation Security Act of 1982, which seeks to guarantee the safety and protection of aircraft. The pair pleaded not guilty to all charges.

The rationale for accusing Megrahi centered on his membership in the Libyan intelligence service, his business relationship with the Swiss firm MEBO, his alleged purchase of an incriminating article of clothing in Malta, and his movements during the months prior to the Pan Am 103 disaster. Concerning the latter, it was established that he had entered a handful of nations without a valid passport. "Megrahi was accused of travelling to a string of countries in Africa, Europe and the Middle East to further the terrorist aims of the Libyan state," writes James Cook.[83] Megrahi would concede that he had passed through these regions using a doctored passport but would claim it was to purchase parts for Libyan aircraft.[84] Doing so was illegal at the time, since Libya was under sanctions.

The prosecuting attorneys would call 227 witnesses, which, on the surface, implied a formidable case. Defense attorneys, by comparison, would call only three, and they would not include the accused.

When it came to the central argument, the prosecution's case was straightforward: Megrahi and Fhimah entered Luqa Airport in Malta on December 21, 1988. Here, Megrahi, accompanied by Fhimah, planted a suitcase bomb on an Air Malta Flight 180.

For its chief witness, the lawyers produced a Maltese shopkeeper, Tony Gauci, who claimed to have sold a shirt to Megrahi prior to the Pan Am 103 crash. It was a charred fragment of this garment that investigators allegedly found in the Lockerbie wreckage.

The prosecutors also brought before the court a witness by the name of Abdel Majid Gialka. The deputy station manager of Libyan Airlines at Luqa Airport and a member of the Libyan intelligence community, Gialka claimed to have been aware that an incendiary device was on the Air Malta flight. He further stated that he had discovered plastic explosives in his office at the airport, explosives that Fhimah had hidden in his, Gialka's, desk. And Gialka said he had watched Megrahi and Fhimah load a brown Samsonite suitcase onto the Air Malta flight in question.

Lastly, the prosecution submitted as material evidence the fragment of the MEBO timer. It was the piece investigators claimed to have retrieved from the crime scene.

In terms of the defense team's strategy, it would entail dismantling, step by step, the prosecution's narrative, and it would begin with a cross-examination of Tony Gauci, the Maltese shopkeeper. It did not go well for him. On the stand, Gauci admitted that he did not remember when he sold the incriminating shirt to Megrahi or, for that matter, if it was Megrahi to whom he had actually sold it. He was also unable to identify Megrahi, who was seated in the courtroom, until an attorney pointed out the defendant. And there were other problems. "Gauci described the purchaser as being considerably older and larger than Megrahi," said a member of Parliament who was present for the proceedings.[85] For such reasons, reservations about Gauci's viability as the prosecution's chief witness mounted as the trial proceeded. "[A]n apple short of a picnic," is how Lord Fraser, the senior law officer who had overseen the Pan Am Flight 103 investigation, described him.[86]

The defense team also cross-examined Abdel Majid Gialka, and he too proved to be a mediocre witness. According to the *New York Times*, Gialka was not only a Libyan double agent but a CIA informant as well, and his account of events leading up to the Pan Am 103 was littered with fabrications and errors.[87] In his testimony, Gialka misrepresented both his role and his importance in the Libyan intelligence community, including the degree to which he enjoyed access to classified materials, and in other ways he undermined his own trustworthiness. His testimony, moreover, created problems for a U.S. intelligence agency. "Prodded by three Scottish law lords hearing the case," reported *Newsweek*, "the CIA was forced to declassify dozens of reports portraying Gialka as a money-grubbing hustler and a liar."[88] In the end, he was simply not believed. Even the judges said they were "unable to accept Abdul Majid [Gialka] as a credible and reliable witness on any matter," writes journalist Corey Charlton.[89] His integrity aside, Gialka contributed little of value to the case. "He never said he saw a bomb put in the suitcase or the suitcase put aboard a flight," said Donald G. McNeil, Jr.[90] In addition, Gialka's assertion that he had found plastic explosives stashed in his office desk was dismissed as a falsehood.

Regarding the foremost piece of evidence, the fragment of a MEBO MST-13 timer, Bollier testified that it was not the type his firm had sold to the Libyan military. The court rejected his statement, however, on the grounds that Bollier could not be believed. When he further explained that MEBO had supplied MST-13 timers to the Stasi, the East German secret police, which, in turn, was discovered to be supplying such devices to the Popular Front for the Liberation of Palestine–General Command, the court accepted the first part of Bollier's statement but rejected the second part. That is, the judges acknowledged that MEBO had sold timers to the Stasi but not that the Stasi then provided them to the PFLP-GC.[91] In the end, prosecutors succeeded in rendering the timer fragment that it presented in court as definitive proof—the "smoking gun"—of Libyan causation.

Lastly, the defense introduced a former suspect whom many still believed had been instrumental in the Pan Am 103 atrocity. Mohammed Abu Talb was his name, and he was an Egyptian-born, Palestinian militant who lived in Syria before illegally relocating to Sweden. In the 1970s, Talb joined the Palestinian Liberation Organization (PLO), and in the 1970s he became a principal member of the Palestinian Popular Struggle Front (PPSF). In the wake of the Flight 103 attack, investigators discovered that Talb had been in Malta a few weeks before the bombing. Although the authorities questioned him about the Pan Am explosion, they ultimately decided not to pursue an indictment.

The following year, Swedish authorities arrested Talb on other charges, with a court subsequently convicting him of a series of 1985 bombings carried out in Denmark and the Netherlands. A police search of Talb's apartment in Uppsala uncovered three items that alarmed officers, since the articles appeared to point to the earlier Lockerbie bombing. The potentially incriminating items: an electronic timing device, a 1988 calendar on which the date of the Pan Am 103 bombing was circled, and clothing purchased in Malta.[92] It soon came to light that the police had previously wiretapped Talb's phone and had intercepted a call between his Palestinian wife in Sweden and an unidentified figure in Palestine. "Get rid of the clothes immediately," she directed.[93]

Additional reasons to suspect Mohammed Abu Talb of having caused, or contributed to, the Pan Am disaster centered on his past actions in Malta. The defense revealed that Tony Gauci, the shopkeeper, originally identified Talb as the man who had purchased clothing at his shop in Malta, not Megrahi.[94] Gauci's description of the customer's physical attributes also matched those of Talb, not Megrahi. Despite the implications of this collection of information, however, the three judges ruled out Talb as a possible conspirator in the Flight 103 disaster. "We accept that there is a great deal of suspicion as to the [actions] of Abu Talb and his circle," the court stated, "but there is no evidence to indicate that they had either the means or the intention to destroy a civil aircraft in December 1988."[95]

After thirty-six weeks, the trial concluded. Unlike the legal system in the United States in which a verdict is either "guilty" or "not guilty," the Scottish system allows for one of three verdicts—"proven," "not proven," or "not guilty."

In the end, the court acquitted Fhimah, his attorneys having established that he was in Sweden, not Malta, on December 21, 1988. The case against Megrahi, on the other hand, was deemed proven and he was sentenced to life in prison, Scotland having abolished the death penalty.

According to Michael Scharf, a law professor and counsel to the U.S. State Department during the Pan Am 103 investigation, four factors were responsible for the court holding Megrahi to blame. They were the same four outlined in his indictment: he had conducted business with MEBO, he was a member of the Libyan intelligence community, he had traveled using an altered passport, and Gauci had been identified him as the man who bought the incriminating clothing in Malta.[96] After handing down the verdict, the judges conceded that the prosecution's case was flawed, not the least because it had presented witnesses who lied to the court. Nevertheless, the judges classified its case as "proven."

Legal appeals would follow, with the courts typically postponing them. In 2003, however, there came an important development when the Scottish Criminal Cases Review Commission (SCCRC) announced that it planned to conduct a judicial review of the Lockerbie proceedings to determine if there was reason to suspect that a miscarriage of justice had taken place. If so, Megrahi could appeal his conviction. It was Megrahi's attorneys who had petitioned the SCCRC to reconsider the trial.

Accusations of Injustice

As one might expect given the defects in the prosecution's case, the defense was not alone in crying foul over both the legal process and the consequent verdict. Dr. Hans Köchler, the lead United Nations observer at the proceedings, characterized the trial as a sham. A law professor at the University of Innsbruck, Köchler argued that a perversion of justice had occurred and that the true identities of the terrorists and their sponsors would possibly never be known.[97]

Robert Black, the distinguished professor of Scottish law at the University of Edinburgh Law School and the man who crafted the structure of the Camp Ziest proceedings, was equally outraged. "Every lawyer who has ... read the judgment says 'this is nonsense,'" said the architect of the Lockerbie trial.[98] Black ranked it as the most profound miscarriage of justice Scotland had endured in a century. "The evidence does not show [Megrahi] to have had anything to do with [the Lockerbie bombing]," Black later added.[99]

Former South African president Nelson Mandela spoke out as well, even though Tony Blair, the British prime minister, had asked him to remain silent on the matter. Mandela visited Megrahi in the prison near Glasgow and was distressed not only by the tainted trial and resultant conviction but also by the prisoner's treatment in the penitentiary. Megrahi was held in solitary confinement, and he was harassed by other inmates when he was permitted brief moments outside of his isolation cell.[100] "From the point of view of fundamental principles of natural law," said Mandela, "it would be fair if he is given a chance to appeal either to the privy council or the European Court of Human Rights."[101]

And then there was Sir Tam Dalywell, the designated "Father of the House of Commons" because he was the longest serving member of Parliament at the time. Dalywell now regarded Megrahi as a political prisoner.[102] The MP asserted that vital evidence had been withheld during the trial, including the fact that Iran paid eleven million dollars to a Palestinian extremist group forty-eight hours after Pan Am Flight 103 exploded.[103]

In the ensuing weeks, months, and years, even more disturbing facts would come to light. It was learned, for instance, that Tony Gauci, the prosecution's chief witness who identified Megrahi in a police lineup before the indictment, knew what the suspect looked like four days prior to fingering him in the lineup. "[H]e saw a photograph of [Megrahi] in a magazine article linking him to the bombing," reports Alan Cowell.[104]

The defense also obtained confidential documents that had been in the possession of prosecutors during the trial, and it posted them online for public scrutiny. The materials centered on witnesses being paid for their testimony. The documents showed that the U.S. Department of Justice had been requested to pay two million dollars to Tony Gauci and one million dollars to his brother Paul, who co-owned the shop in Malta, in exchange for the former's testimony.[105] Writes Severin Carrell of *The Guardian*: "The DoJ said their reward could be increased and that the brothers were also eligible for the US witness protection programme."[106]

Along the same lines, Edwin Bollier, co-owner of the Swiss firm MEBO, reported an unsettling interaction to Hans Köchler, the aforementioned UN observer. Bollier, of course, was the man who had initially confirmed, based on a photograph, that the MST-13 timing device allegedly recovered in the Lockerbie debris field was indeed a MEBO product. "During a visit to the headquarters of the American FBI in Washington DC at the beginning of 1991 [Bollier] was offered an amount of up to USD 4 million plus a new identity (name) in the United States if he would testify in court that the timer fragment that was allegedly found on the crash site around Lockerbie stemmed from a MST-13 timer that his company had delivered to Libya," reads an I.P.O. press release.[107] Bollier turned down the offer and subsequently reported it to the federal police in Switzerland. In addition, Bollier provided the UN observer with the name of the FBI agent who offered the deal as well as that of another official who was present during the exchange.

Maltese officials likewise came forth after the trial, puzzled that the information they had provided to investigators was upended in court. Contrary to the prosecution's argument, they insisted that no luggage had traveled unaccompanied on Air Malta Flight 180. George Grech, Malta's police commissioner, for one, asserted that fifty-five bags had been checked in and all of them had been claimed by passengers or otherwise accounted for.[108] Eddie Fenech Adami also made a striking pronouncement (he had served as president of the island nation and as its prime minister twice). "Malta's longest-serving prime minister has claimed it was 'impossible' for the Lockerbie bomb to have left the island and suggested that a miscarriage of justice had taken place," writes Marc Horne.[109] Of principal concern to Maltese officials and witnesses from the airport was the fact that the Scottish and American investigators who came to Malta to examine the matter had returned to their home countries fully aware that all of the luggage had been accompanied and thereafter accounted for.[110]

Finally, there was the fragment of charred Babygro fabric that prosecutors stated was wrapped around the bomb and that had been recovered from the Pan Am wreckage. In reality, the fragment exhibited in court had apparently not been retrieved from the debris field. Rather, it was sample of a new Babygro obtained months later and subjected to explosives tests by forensics experts. Thereafter, the prosecution presented it to the court, purportedly by accident, as having been found in the Lockerbie debris field.[111] "To say that the evidence recovered from the ground at Lockerbie and the material produced during the tests became mixed up would be something of an understatement," a person close to the case told *The Observer*.[112]

As could be predicted, the above revelations sparked considerable concern. To summarize, the authenticity of the timer that prosecutors exhibited during the proceedings was now widely doubted; the U.S. Department of Justice had offered money to witnesses for testimony favoring the prosecution; key testimony was largely or completely specious; and prosecutors withheld potentially exonerating materials from the defense team.

Wrongful Conviction

This last finding—the prosecution had suppressed seven significant pieces of evidence—would constitute part of the reason that the Scottish Criminal Cases Review Commission concluded, on June 28, 2007, that the trial may have produced a wrongful conviction. "[T]he Commission believes not only that there may have been a miscarriage of justice in the applicant's case, but also that it is in the interests of justice to refer the case to the High Court," declared the SCCRC.[113]

A meticulous undertaking, the SCCRC's four-year review had entailed, among other tasks, five trips to Malta to re-interview witnesses. All cooperated except for Tony and Paul Gauci, who steadfastly refused to speak to the review team—that is, until the Maltese and UK governments brought pressure to bear on them.[114]

Since the original trial, new material had also come to light, including the millions of dollars the U.S. Department of Justice had indeed proceeded to pay, covertly, to the two Gauci brothers for testimony. During the review, it also was discovered that the incriminating clothing which Megrahi had ostensibly bought at the Gaucis' shop had, in fact, been purchased *before* the date claimed at the trial and at a time when Megrahi was not in Malta.[115] Other problems in the proceedings were uncovered and the SCCRC identified six distinct issues that could justify deeming the trial a miscarriage of justice.

On one subject, however, the reviewers upheld the prosecution's case. The SCCRC said there was no indication that the MST-13 timer exhibited at the trial had been fabricated.[116] But even this assertion would soon be proven incorrect.

It was three weeks later—July 18, 2007—when a Swiss electronics engineer at MEBO by the name of Ulrich Lumpert showed up at a Zurich police station and asked to make an affidavit. Investigators had questioned him nearly twenty years earlier in the Lockerbie inquiry, and now he was confessing to having perjured himself at that time. In a sworn statement, Lumpert admitted that he stole a prototype of an MST-13 timer on June 22, 1989, at the request of a figure involved in the Flight 103 investigation.[117] The latter was an official with the Swiss secret service who procured the item on behalf of an unnamed American entity.[118]

"It did not escape me," Lumpert said in his confession, "that the MST-13 fragment shown on the police photograph No. PT/35(b) came from the nonoperational MST-13 prototype PC-board that I had stolen."[119] A startling admission, it vindicated those who, since the early days of the Lockerbie crash, had argued that the U.S. investigation, in particular, had been corrupted and that the MST-13 timer was "a probable fake," as one reporter put it.[120] Certainly it began to appear that the undisclosed American acquisition of the MST-13 prototype from Lumpert had been part of a strategy. "You have to wonder whether the investigation was subsequently already following a prepared script," said a law enforcement official close to the case.[121]

One year later, fundamental metallurgical differences would be reported between the timer fragment allegedly found near Lockerbie and the circuit boards manufactured by Thüring AG, the company that supplied them to MEBO for its timing devices. The staff at Thüring checked the firm's records from 1985 and confirmed that it had built twenty timer boards for MEBO, the same year that MEBO, in turn, constructed twenty MST-13 timers for the Libyan military. The salient point: all of the circuitry on Thüring's circuit boards was composed of 70 percent tin and 30 percent lead alloy; the company did not have the capability in 1985 to manufacture them in any other composition.[122] Yet the circuitry in the fragment allegedly recovered in the Pan Am wreckage was 100 percent tin.[123] "The inevitable conclusion was that the [Pan Am fragment] could not have come from a Thüring board," writes Jim Swire. "It therefore was not from one of the twenty boards [MEBO] provided to Libya in 1985."[124]

The Second Appeal

Like nearly all aspects of the Lockerbie case until 2009, Megrahi's second appeal turned out to be rather controversial. This is because the Scottish court decided that access to the entirety of the prosecution's materials would still not made be available to the defense and that the appeal proceedings themselves would not be held, as previously agreed, in a neutral nation like the Netherlands. Accordingly, the international observer for the United Nations, Hans Köchler, decried what he regarded as the lack of transparency and the totalitarian tone of the appeals process, the Scottish government having intervened and placed stark restrictions on the affair. "The entire procedure," Köchler wrote, "looks more like an intelligence operation than a genuine undertaking of criminal justice."[125]

During his second appeal, Megrahi was required to remain behind bars, even after he was diagnosed with terminal cancer. Still insisting on his innocence, he petitioned the court to permit him to return to his Libyan home so he could live out his final months with his loved ones. And then came an interesting turn of events. Whereas the court had initially refused Megrahi's request to leave the UK, observers in the legal community sensed that the Scottish court was becoming increasingly concerned about what additional evidence might come to light during the appeals process and, for this reason, was becoming more receptive to having Megrahi off its hands. Some speculated that Scottish prosecutors, along with the Scottish government and the FBI, were worried that the latter's manipulation and possible fabrication of evidence, namely the MST-13 timing device, might now be exposed during the proceedings.

And there was another concern as well. "Britain was aware that Libya would be upset if Mr. Megrahi died in a UK jail," reports the *Financial Times*, "and that British interests could then be affected."[126]

On August 14, 2009, Megrahi's lawyers withdrew his appeal, gambling that the court would release him on "compassionate grounds" because he had cancer. "Review Commission chief executive Gerard Sinclair said al-Megrahi abandoned his second appeal as he held a genuine and reasonable belief that such a course of action would result in him being able to return home to Libya, at a time when he was suffering from terminal cancer," reports *The Associated Press*.[127] He was correct.

So it was that Megrahi arrived in Libya on August 20, 2009, against the wishes of many Scottish and American officials. They considered it wise to keep him behind bars until he was dead. Regardless, Megrahi received a grand welcome when he stepped off the plane in Tripoli, the public viewing him as an ailing political prisoner. And although there was speculation that his release may have been partially related to a $900 million deal that was being negotiated at precisely that moment—BP (British Petroleum) was wooing Libya's new government for the drilling rights off its oil-rich coast—a quid pro quo has never been proven. It is known, however, that BP wanted him released. "Part of the transaction involved BP lobbying the British government to release Libyan prisoners back to their home country," reported *Energy* magazine.[128] Later that year, BP was awarded the drilling rights it was seeking. On May 20, 2012, Megrahi succumbed to cancer.

Five years later, Megrahi's family filed an appeal on his behalf, determined to clear his name, and in 2018 the Scottish Criminal Cases Review Commission was again requested to reassess the proceedings. "When we referred this case [to the High Court of Judiciary] in 2007," said Gerard Sinclair, the commission's chief executive, "I never expected that, over 10 years later, we would be asked not only to revisit our original decision, applying the law as currently stated, but also consider a whole new set of materials which had become available in the intervening years."[129] The result was that the SCCRC notified the High Court once again that a review of the case indicated that a miscarriage of justice may have taken place and that Megrahi may have been wrongly convicted. And the High Court countered as before.

On April 2, 2021, the Court of Criminal Appeal ruled that there had been no miscarriage of justice. In so doing, the Scottish court closed the door on the efforts of Megrahi's loved ones to absolve him of murdering 270 people. "I regard my father Abdelbaset al-Megrahi as the 271st victim of Lockerbie," said his son, Ali al-Megrahi.[130]

Interestingly, as the legal saga of Abdelbaset al-Megrahi was receding in the public mind, the U.S. government accused another Libyan man of involvement in the Lockerbie tragedy. On December 21, 2020—the thirty-second anniversary of the Pan Am 103 tragedy—the U.S. Department of Justice made known that it had indicted an alleged bomb maker in the attack, a Libyan intelligence officer by the name of Masud (Abu Agela Mas'ud Kheir Al-Marimi).[131] The announcement was made by William "Bill" Barr, the controversial U.S. attorney general under Donald Trump. Proposing, again, the hypothesis of a Maltese connection, Barr stated that Masud was at the Luqa Airport with Megrahi and Fhimah when the explosive device was allegedly placed on the Air Malta flight. The affidavit supporting the criminal complaint reads, "[T]he suitcase used by Masud was a medium-sized Samsonite suitcase that he used for traveling. Megrahi and Fhimah were both at the airport on the morning of Dec. 21, 1988, and Masud handed the suitcase to Fhimah after Fhimah gave him a signal to do so. Fhimah then placed the suitcase on the conveyor belt. Masud then left. He was given a boarding pass for a Libyan flight to Tripoli, which was to take off at 9:00 a.m."[132]

As noted earlier, it had already been proven in court that Fhimah was not in Malta on that date, and for this reason the charges against him were dropped. It further appeared that Megrahi had been elsewhere at the time as well.

In all likelihood, there will never be a satisfactory resolution of the Pan Am Flight 103 case. While some accept the verdict against Megrahi as the outcome of a fair and just trial, other legal observers dismiss the proceedings as clumsy political machinations that damaged the reputations of both the Scottish and U.S. legal systems, not to mention convicting an innocent man. But while differing views may exist in terms of the integrity of the legal proceedings, one fact is indisputable: the terrorist attack helped kill Pan American World Airways.

The downward spiral began when the victims' families filed a $300 million lawsuit against the carrier on the grounds that it had exhibited willful misconduct, the airline's security team at Heathrow having knowingly permitted a piece of unauthorized baggage to be placed on the aircraft.[133] Certainly it was true that Pan Am's failure to comply with mandatory security regulations had cost 270 lives. And so it was the beginning of the end for the company. Within two years of the disaster, Pan Am was bankrupt, its reputation for public safety was in tatters, and the financially crippled carrier was facing soaring fuel costs. On December 4, 1991, it shuttered operations.

Regarding Muammar Gaddafi's government, it agreed, in 2003, to issue a letter of "responsibility for the actions of its officials" in the Pan Am Flight 103 disaster as well as pay $2.7 billion to the victims' families as part of an arrangement designed to bring about the lifting of the economic

Six. Libya and Terrorism I

sanctions against the North African nation.[134] "Libyan officials," writes television journalist and author Lindsey Hilsum, "quite openly said that they were 'buying peace' rather than accepting blame."[135]

The payments would occur in stages, as components of the UN sanctions were rescinded. And while some observers viewed the arrangement as coercive—Libya had little choice but to comply if it wished to salvage its plunging economy—others would trumpet its letter of responsibility as proof of guilt. Those in the latter category frequently voiced the opinion, however, that Libya's culpability in the terrorist operation may have been partial rather than total.

Once again, the prospect of state-sponsored terrorism arises. Due partly to the deeply flawed legal proceedings in the Pan Am 103 case, the question remains as to whether the horrific bombing of the commercial airliner was a single-nation operation or a sophisticated endeavor that entailed state-sponsored terrorism, with Iran or Libya acting through the PFLP-GC and such figures as Ahmad Jibril or Mohammed Abu Talb to destroy an American aircraft as an act of vengeance. Both Iran and Libya had the motives and the means and Iran in particular had threatened to perpetrate such an abomination.

It is the same question that presents itself in the bombing of a French passenger plane eight months later, UTA Flight 772. As with Pan Am Flight 103, suspicion abruptly shifted to Libya a few months into the investigation, with the United States once again attributing the attack to Muammar Gaddafi's regime. The story of the doomed French airliner is the subject of the next chapter.

Notes

1. David B. Carter, "A Blessing or a Curse? State Support for Terrorist Groups," *International Organization* 66, no. 1 (2012): 129, https://www.jstor.org/stable/41428948.
2. Matthew Frakes, "Reagan, Rogue States, and the Problem of Terrorism," Wilson Center, September 17, 2020, https://www.hornecenter.org/blog-post/reagan-rogue-states-and-problem-terrorism.
3. "State Sponsors: Libya," Council on Foreign Relations, December 1, 2005, https://www.cfr.org/backgrounder/state-sponsors-libya.
4. Steven Erlanger, "4 Guilty in Fatal 1986 Berlin Disco Bombing Linked to Libya," *New York Times*, November 14, 2001, https://www.nytimes.com/2001/11/14/world/4-guilty-in-fatal-1986-berlin-disco-bombing-linked-to-libya.html.
5. "Doctor Describes Terror among Qaddafi Family," *New York Times*, April 16, 1986, https://www.nytimes.com/1986/04/16/world/doctor-describes-terror-among-qaddafi-family.html.
6. Doctor Describes Terror among Qaddafi Family."
7. "Pan Am 103: Analysis of Claims," Central Intelligence Agency, December 22, 1988, https://www.cia.gov/readingroom/docs/CIA-RDP89G01321R000500180003-6.pdf
8. John H. Cushman, Jr., "The Crash of Flight 103; Pan Am Was Told of Terror Threat," *New York Times*, December 23, 1988, https://www.nytimes.com/1988/12/23/world/the-crash-of-flight-103-pan-am-was-told-of-terror-threat.html#:~:text=Acting%20on%20

an%20unsubstantiated%20threat, Federal%20Aviation%20Administration%20said%20 today.&text=The%20bomb%20threat%2C%20received%20on%20Dec.

9. *Foreign Airport Security: Hearing Before the Committee on Foreign Affairs, House of Representatives, One Hundred First Congress, First Session, February 9, 1989*, United States Congress (Washington, D.C.: U.S. Government Printing Office, 1989), 54.

10. Chris Nicholson, "Pik Botha's Lockerbie Mystery," *The Independent—Online* (South Africa), October 24, 2018, https://www.iol.co.za/ios/behindthenews/pik-bothas-lockerbie-mystery-17617534.

11. John H. Cushman, Jr., "The Crash of Flight 103; Pan Am Was Told of Terror Threat."

12. "Exhibits—Terrorist Bombing of Pan Am Flight 103," CIA Legacy Museum, accessed July 28, 2022, https://www.cia.gov/legacy/museum/exhibit/terrorist-bombing-of-pan-am-flight-103/.

13. John Dickie and David Gardner, "Why Weren't They Told?" *Daily Mail*, December 23, 1988, https://panam103.syr.edu/pdf/timeline/103HUDSON0002.pdf.

14. Anna Fenton, "Veteran at the Front," *The Sun*, December 23, 1988, http://clippercrew.com/pan-am-crew-flight-103/captain-james-bruce-macquarrie/.

15. Ian Black and Gerard Seenan, "Court Told How Jet's Radar Blip Broke Up at 7:02 pm," *The Guardian*, May 3, 2000, https://www.theguardian.com/uk/2000/may/04/lockerbie.gerardseenan1#:~:text=The%20final%20dramatic%20moments%20of,accused%20of%20 murdering%20270%20people.

16. *Lockerbie: Terror at 31,000 Ft.*, written and produced by David Harvey, Circle Films, airdate May 17, 2014, on Channel 5 (Britain), https://www.youtube.com/watch?app=deskto p&v=zCpCJCuB3ZM.

17. "Two Passengers on Flight 103 Might Have Survived, Pathologist Says," Associated Press, October 17, 1990, https://apnews.com/article/6630a187dd9a67416a8cfac908eb33c2.

18. Hugh Miles, "Inconvenient Truths," *London Review of Books* 29, no. 12, June 21, 2007, https://www.lrb.co.uk/the-paper/v29/n12/hugh-miles/inconvenient-truths.

19. *Mayday: Air Disaster*, season 7, episode 2, "Lockerbie Disaster," Cineflix Productions, airdate November 4, 2009, on Discovery Channel Canada, https://www.youtube.com/watch?app=desktop&v=_PqPKjWabio.

20. BBC News Bulletin: Lockerbie Air Disaster, presented by Michael Beck, airdate December 21, 1988, on BBC-1 (British Broadcasting Corp.), https://www.youtube.com/watc h?app=desktop&v=jPZVoHt5nTc.

21. BBC News Bulletin: Lockerbie Air Disaster.

22. *Mayday: Air Disaster*, season 7, episode 2, "Lockerbie Disaster."

23. *Mayday: Air Disaster*, season 7, episode 2, "Lockerbie Disaster."

24. *It Happened in Lockerbie, Part 1*, Bill Cran (director), Al Jazeera—English, airdate August 7, 2007, https://www.youtube.com/watch?v=R_USFvnaSSU.

25. "What Really Happened on Flight 103?" *The Observer*, February 27, 2000, https:// www.theguardian.com/uk/2000/feb/27/lockerbie.life1.

26. George Stobbs (interviewee), "Remembering Pan Am 103: George Stobbs," Federal Bureau of Investigation, accessed Jun 8, 2022, https://www.fbi.gov/video-repository/george-stobbs-30-years-pan-am-103-lockerbie-2018.mp4/view.

27. *It Happened in Lockerbie, Part 1*.

28. "What Really Happened on Flight 103?"

29. Richard A. Marquise, *Scotbom: Evidence and the Lockerbie Investigation* (New York: Algora Publishing, 2006), 16.

30. *Minute by Minute*, "Pan Am Flight 103," directed by Lisa Shaughnessy, presented by Bill Kurtis, A&E Channel, airdate 2001.

31. Alan Dron, "A News Reporter at Lockerbie," *Air and Space Magazine*, November 2016, https://www.smithsonianmag.com/air-space-magazine/above-beyond-Lockerbie-180960971/.

32. Rachael Kennedy, "Lockerbie Disaster 30 Years On: People Share Their Memories of Pan Am Flight 103 Tragedy," *EuroNews*, December 21, 2018, https://www.euronews.com/2018/12/21/lockerbie-disaster-30-years-on-people-share-their-memories-of-pan-am-flight-103-tragedy.

33. Lindsey Johnstone, "Lockerbie Bombing: 'What Really Brought It Home Was When You

Were Picking Up Toys,'" *EuroNews*, December 21, 2018, https://www.euronews.com/2018/12/21/lockerbie-bombing-what-really-brought-it-home-was-when-you-were-picking-up-toys.

34. Abbie Llewelyn, "Prince Andrew's Astonishing Comment to Terrorism Victims as He Was Accused of 'No Empathy,'" *Daily Express*, July 31, 2020, https://www.express.co.uk/news/royal/1317194/prince-andrew-duke-york-royal-family-news-lockerbie-queen-elizabeth-ii-spt.

35. "Craven Rescuers Who Joined the Search at Lockerbie," *The Craven Herald & Pioneer*, January 4, 2014, https://www.cravenherald.co.uk/nostalgia/nostalgia_history/10911251.craven-rescuers-who-joined-the-search-at-lockerbie/.

36. "Pan Am 103 Bombing," Federal Bureau of Investigation, accessed June 7, 2022, https://www.fbi.gov/history/famous-cases/pan-am-103-bombing.

37. Andrew Nicoll, "Ex-Air Accident Investigator Reveals He Saw Lifeless Bodies of Lockerbie Disaster's Crew among Wreckage," *The Scottish Sun*, December 16, 2018, https://www.bbc.com/news/uk-scotland-highlands-islands-16307355.

38. David Cowan, "Farmer's Tribute to Young Lockerbie Victims," BBC Scotland, December 20, 2018, https://www.bbc.com/news/uk-scotland-south-scotland-46613309.

39. Bob Smith, "Derby Rescuers Recall Team's Search on 30th Anniversary of Lockerbie Bombing," *Grough Magazine*, December 21, 2018, https://www.grough.co.uk/magazine/2018/12/21/derby-rescuers-recall-teams-search-on-30th-anniversary-of-lockerbie-bombing.

40. Paul Hyde, "One Town's Response to Terrorism: Women of Lockerbie," *Greenville News*, November 3, 2016, https://www.greenvilleonline.com/story/entertainment/arts/paul-hyde/2016/11/03/one-towns-response-terrorism-women-lockerbie/93250420/.

41. Andrew Nicoll, "Ex-air Accident Investigator Reveals He Saw Lifeless Bodies."

42. Michael Bates, "Researcher: Many Lockerbie Victims May Have Lived until Impact," Associated Press, October 6, 1990, https://apnews.com/article/acdaad08cbee147122a54b5592f26ec2.

43. Richard A. Marquise, *Scotbom: Evidence and the Lockerbie Investigation*, 20.

44. Robert Barr, "Investigators Say Bomb Caused Pan Am Crash," Associated Press, December 28, 1988, https://apnews.com/article/d9b45b0424c1952d50b4103bef415051.

45. *Opinion of the Court Delivered by Lord Sutherland in Causa Her Majesty's Advocate v Abdelbaset Ali Mohmed Al Megrahi and Al Amin Khalifa Fhimah (Case No: 1475/99)*, High Court of Justiciary at Camp Zeist, January 1, 2001, https://www.scotcourts.gov.uk/docs/default-source/sc---lockerbie/lockerbiejudgement.pdf.

46. Richard A. Marquise, *Scotbom: Evidence and the Lockerbie Investigation*, 38.

47. Katie Worth, "Lockerbie: The Alternate Theories," PBS, October 6, 2015, https://www.pbs.org/wgbh/frontline/article/lockerbie-the-alternate-theories/.

48. "Iranian Spiritual Leader Ayatollah Ruhollah Khomeini Called for 'All-Out…,'" United Press International, July 5, 1988, https://www.upi.com/Archives/1988/07/05/Iranian-spiritual-leader-Ayatollah-Ruhollah-Khomeini-called-for-all-out/9763584078400/.

49. Yeganeh Rezaian, "Opinion: A Grim Anniversary Reminds Us of the Potential For Tragedy in the Persian Gulf," *Washington Post*, July 2, 2019, https://www.washingtonpost.com/opinions/2019/07/02/grim-anniversary-reminds-us-potential-tragedy-persian-gulf/.

50. Valerie Strauss, "Iran Says U.S. Action Deliberate, Threatens Unspecified Retaliation," *Washington Post*, July 4, 1988, https://www.washingtonpost.com/archive/politics/1988/07/04/iran-says-us-action-deliberate-threatens-unspecified-retaliation/90aa6983-3be6-40f2-ab02-d11178dd36e4/.

51. "Iranian Spiritual Leader Ayatollah Ruhollah Khomeini Called for 'All-Out….'"

52. Stephen Engelberg, "U.S. Suspects Iran Unit in the Pan Am Bombing," *New York Times*, February 25, 1989, https://www.nytimes.com/1989/02/25/world/us-suspects-iran-unit-in-the-pan-am-bombing.html.

53. Matthew Cox and Tom Foster, *Their Darkest Day: The Tragedy of Pan Am 103 and Its Legacy of Hope* (New York: Grove Weidenfeld, 1992), 20.

54. David Horovitz, "Who Made the Bomb? The Full Truth about Lockerbie Is Still Not Being Told," *Times of Israel*, November 26, 2020, https://www.timesofisrael.com/who-made-the-bomb-the-full-truth-about-the-lockerbie-bombing-has-yet-to-be-told/.

55. Richard A. Marquise, *Scotbom: Evidence and the Lockerbie Investigation*, 60.
56. *U.S. Department of State Dispatch: Fact Sheet: The Iranians and the PFLP-GC—Early Suspects in the Pan Am Flight 103 Bombing*, United States Department of State (Ann Arbor: University of Michigan Press, January 1, 1990), p. 858.
57. "Trial Shown Cassette 'Bomb,'" BBC, June 14, 2000, http://news.bbc.co.uk/2/hi/790805.stm.
58. Matthew Cox and Tom Foster, *Their Darkest Day: The Tragedy of Pan Am 103 and Its Legacy of Hope*.
59. Shelley Jofre (reporter) and Murdoch Rodgers (producer), "Silence over Lockerbie," *Frontline Scotland* (BBC), airdate December 22, 1993, http://plane-truth.com/Aoude/geocities/silence.html.
60. John Biewen and Ian Ferguson, "Shadow over Lockerbie: Mass Murder over Scotland," *American RadioWorks* (CPB), March 2000, https://americanradioworks.publicradio.org/features/lockerbie/story/printable_story.html.
61. Robert Mendick, "Was Terry Waite Freed as Part of Secret Lockerbie Deal with Iran?" *The Independent*, December 15, 2013, https://www.telegraph.co.uk/news/uknews/10518045/Was-Terry-Waite-freed-as-part-of-secret-Lockerbie-deal-with-Iran.html.
62. Alex Duval Smith, "Vital Lockerbie Evidence 'Was Tampered With,'" *The Guardian*, September 1, 2007, https://www.theguardian.com/business/2007/sep/02/theairlineindustry.libya.
63. John Biewen and Ian Ferguson, "Shadow over Lockerbie."
64. John Biewen and Ian Ferguson, "Shadow over Lockerbie."
65. John Biewen and Ian Ferguson, "Shadow over Lockerbie."
66. "New Doubts in Crucial Evidence in Lockerbie Trial," *The Herald* (Scotland), July 16, 2011, https://www.heraldscotland.com/news/13033151.new-doubts-crucial-evidence-lockerbie-trial/.
67. "New Doubts in Crucial Evidence in Lockerbie Trial."
68. "New Doubts in Crucial Evidence in Lockerbie Trial."
69. Julian Rush (correspondent), "Secret CIA Testimony Identified Real Lockerbie Mastermind," Channel 4 News (London), airdate December 20, 2013, https://www.youtube.com/watch?v=26GonRZrWw0.
70. Julian Rush (correspondent), "Secret CIA Testimony Identified Real Lockerbie Mastermind."
71. Julian Rush (correspondent), "Secret CIA Testimony Identified Real Lockerbie Mastermind."
72. "Die Mullah-Spur," *Der Spiegel*, July 6, 1997, https://www.spiegel.de/politik/die-mullah-spur-a-e737e9aa-0002-0001-0000-000008741161.
73. TOI Staff, "'Bomb-maker' Brags about El Al Blast, Posts Lockerbie Photos," *Times of Israel*, March 19, 2014, https://www.timesofisrael.com/bomb-maker-brags-about-el-al-blast-posts-lockerbie-photos/.
74. Tribune News Services, "Iran's Former Top Spy Reportedly Links Khomeini to Pan Am Blast," *Chicago Tribune*, July 6, 1997, https://www.chicagotribune.com/news/ct-xpm-1997-07-06-9707060208-story.html.
75. "Die Mullah-Spur," *Der Spiegel*.
76. John Ashton, "Review of Aljazeera Documentary 'Lockerbie: What Really Happened?'" *Megrahi: You Are My Jury*, March 12, 2014, https://www.megrahiyouaremyjury.net/?p=1031.
77. *Convention for the Suppression of Unlawful Acts Against the Safety of Civil Aviation*, United Nations Treaty Series, July 18, 1975, https://treaties.un.org/doc/Publication/UNTS/Volume%20974/volume-974-I-14118-english.pdf.
78. "Libya: A Hero's Welcome," *RANE Worldview*, August 26, 2009, https://worldview.stratfor.com/article/libya-heros-welcome.
79. "Lockerbie Bomber Abdel Basset Ali al-Megrahi Dies at 60, Report Says," *Washington Post*, May 20, 2012, https://www.washingtonpost.com/local/obituaries/lockerbie-bomber-abdel-basset-al-megrahi-dies-at-60-report-says/2012/05/20/gIQAxRo3cU_story.html.
80. Michael P. Scharf, "A Preview of the Lockerbie Case," *ASIL Insights* 5, issue 5 (May 4, 2000), https://www.asil.org/insights/volume/5/issue/5/preview-lockerbie-case.

81. Kenneth Katzman, "Terrorism: Near Eastern Groups and State Sponsors, 2002," Federation of American Scientists, February 13, 2002, https://irp.fas.org/crs/RL31119.pdf.
82. Kofi A. Annan, "Letter Dated 25 April 2000 from the Secretary-General Addressed to the President of the Security Council," UN Security Council, April 26, 2000, http://i-p-o.org/nomination-observers.pdf.
83. James Cook, "Megrahi Dies Protesting Lockerbie Bombing Innocence," BBC, May 20, 2012, https://www.bbc.com/news/uk-scotland-south-scotland-14707355.
84. James Cook, "Megrahi Dies Protesting Lockerbie Bombing Innocence."
85. John Ashton, "Tam Dalyell's Last Interview: Going to the Grave Convinced of Lockerbie Bomber's Innocence," *The Herald* (Scotland), January 29, 2017, https://www.heraldscotland.com/news/15055570.tam-dalyells-last-interview-going-grave-convinced-lockerbie-bombers-innocence/.
86. Brian Wilson, "Lord Fraser of Carmyllie Obituary," *The Guardian*, June 24, 2013, https://www.theguardian.com/politics/2013/jun/24/lord-fraser-of-carmyllie.
87. Donald G. McNeil, Jr., "Libyan Double Agent Testified in Lockerbie Bomb Trial," *New York Times*, September 27, 2000, https://www.nytimes.com/2000/09/27/world/libyan-double-agent-testifies-in-lockerbie-bomb-trial.html.
88. Mark Hosenball, "Why One Defendant Got Off," *Newsweek*, February 11, 2001, https://www.newsweek.com/why-one-defendant-got-155315.
89. Corey Charlton, "Spook Cables Hidden: Lockerbie Bombing CIA Documents Reveal Secret Evidence That Could Have Helped Prosecution Was Withheld from Trial," *The Sun*, February 8, 2017, https://www.thesun.co.uk/news/2812566/lockerbie-bombing-cia-evidence-withheld/.
90. Donald G. McNeil, Jr., "Libyan Double Agent Testified in Lockerbie Bomb Trial."
91. Michael P. Scharf, "The Lockerbie Trial Verdict," *ASIL Insights* 6, issue 2 (February 13, 2001), https://www.asil.org/insights/volume/6/issue/2/lockerbie-trial-verdict.
92. Michael P. Scharf, "The Lockerbie Trial Verdict."
93. Eva Janzon, "Flight 103 Suspect Convicted on Separate Terrorism Charge with AM-Flight 103," Associated Press, December 21, 1989, https://apnews.com/article/c598ea591dadb77ef634f18da82dcab9.
94. Michael P. Scharf, "The Lockerbie Trial Verdict."
95. Michael P. Scharf, "The Lockerbie Trial Verdict."
96. Michael P. Scharf, "The Lockerbie Trial Verdict."
97. "Statement of Dr. Hans Koechler, International Observer at the Lockerbie Trial, on Recent Reports in the Scottish and British Media," I.P.O. Information Service, October 14, 2005, http://i-p-o.org/nr-lockerbie-14Oct05.htm.
98. The Newsroom, "Architect of Lockerbie Trial Vows to Fight for an Appeal," *The Scotsman*, November 1, 2005, https://www.scotsman.com/news/architect-lockerbie-trial-vows-fight-appeal-2509587.
99. David Horovitz, "Editor's Notes: Lockerbie—A Miscarriage of Justice?" *Jerusalem Post*, October 11, 2007, https://www.jpost.com/opinion/columnists/editors-notes-lockerbie-a-miscarriage-of-justice.
100. Staff and Agencies, "Mandela Appeals on Behalf of Lockerbie Bomber," *The Guardian*, June 10, 2002, https://www.theguardian.com/uk/2002/jun/10/lockerbie.nelsonmandela.
101. Staff and Agencies, "Mandela Appeals on Behalf of Lockerbie Bomber."
102. Staff and Agencies, "Mandela Appeals on Behalf of Lockerbie Bomber."
103. Staff and Agencies, "Mandela Appeals on Behalf of Lockerbie Bomber."
104. Alan Cowell, "Scottish Panel Challenged Lockerbie Conviction," *New York Times*, June 29, 2007, https://www.nytimes.com/2007/06/29/world/europe/29lockerbie.html.
105. Severin Carrell, "U.S. Paid Reward to Lockerbie Witness, Abdelbasset al-Megrahi Papers Claim," *The Guardian*, October 2, 2009, https://www.theguardian.com/world/2009/oct/02/lockerbie-documents-witness-megrahi,
106. Severin Carrell, "U.S. Paid Reward to Lockerbie Witness."
107. "Statement of Dr. Hans Koechler."
108. John Biewen and Ian Ferguson, "Shadow Over Lockerbie."
109. Marc Horne, "Ex-Leader of Malta Casts Doubt on Conviction of Lockerbie Bomber Abdul Baset Ali al-Megrahi," *The Times* (London), December 19, 2018, https://www.

thetimes.co.uk/article/ex-leader-of-malta-casts-doubt-on-conviction-of-lockerbie-bomber-abdul-baset-ali-al-megrahi-8bfvpwtps.

110. John Biewen and Ian Ferguson, "Shadow Over Lockerbie."

111. "Statement of Dr. Hans Koechler."

112. Tony Thompson, "Forensic Mix-Up Casts Fresh Lockerbie Doubt," *The Observer*, October 8, 2005, https://www.theguardian.com/business/2005/oct/09/theairlineindustry.libya.

113. "Maltese Lockerbie Trial Witnesses Were Reluctant to Meet Scottish Review Commission," *Times of Malta*, March 26, 2012, https://timesofmalta.com/articles/view/maltese-lockerbie-trial-witnesses-were-reluctant-to-meet-scottish.412782.

114. "Maltese Lockerbie Trial Witnesses Were Reluctant to Meet Scottish Review Commission."

115. Pioneer Press, "Review Calls for New Trial in Lockerbie Case," *Pioneer Press/TwinCities.com*, November 14, 2015, https://www.twincities.com/2007/06/28/review-calls-for-new-trial-in-lockerbie-case-2/.

116. Mark Trevelyan, "Lockerbie Investigation Spurns Conspiracy Theories," Reuters, June 28, 2007, https://www.reuters.com/article/us-lockerbie-conspiracies/lockerbie-investigation-spurns-conspiracy-theories-idUSL2679117620070628.

117. Ludwig De Braeckeleer, "Key Lockerbie Witness Admits Perjury," *Scoop Independent News* (New Zealand), September 20, 2011, https://www.scoop.co.nz/stories/HL1109/S00189/key-lockerbie-witness-admits-perjury.htm.

118. Marcello Mega, "Doubts Over Lockerbie Bomb Timer Fragment," *The Sunday Times* (London), December 17, 2018, https://www.thetimes.co.uk/article/doubts-over-lockerbie-bomb-timer-fragment-2vqgm6wxn.

119. Ludwig De Braeckeleer, "Key Lockerbie Witness Admits Perjury."

120. Alex Duval Smith, "Vital Lockerbie Evidence 'Was Tampered With.'"

121. Marcello Mega, "Doubts over Lockerbie Bomb Timer Fragment."

122. Lucy Adams, "Megrahi: Eight Pieces of Evidence," *The Herald* (Scotland), February 27, 2012, https://www.heraldscotland.com/news/13048661.megrahi-eight-key-pieces-evidence/.

123. Lucy Adams, "Megrahi: Eight Pieces of Evidence."

124. Jim Swire and Peter Biddulph, *The Lockerbie Bombing: A Father's Search for Justice* (Edinburgh: Birlinn Ltd., 2021), 235.

125. Mark Macaskill, "Lockerbie Bombing Hearing 'Flawed,'" *The Times* (London), March 16, 2010, https://www.thetimes.co.uk/article/lockerbie-bomber-hearing-flawed-8b0r33rnkwl.

126. Andrew Bolger and Andrew England, "Lockerbie Bomber Abandons Appeal," *Financial Times*, August 14, 2009, https://www.ft.com/content/1876eece-87dd-11de-82e4-00144feabdc0.

127. Associated Press, "Scotland to Review Lockerbie Plane Bombing Investigation," Canadian Broadcasting Corp., May 3, 2018, https://www.cbc.ca/news/world/lockerbie-scotland-appeals-review-1.4646250https://www.cbc.ca/news/world/lockerbie-scotland-appeals-review-1.4646250.

128. "BP May See Competition in Post-Conflict Libya," *Energy Digital Magazine*, May 17, 2020, https://energydigital.com/utilities/bp-may-see-competition-post-conflict-libya.

129. "Lockerbie: Scottish Criminal Cases Review Commission Refers Al Megrahi's Case to High Court Again," *Scottish Legal News*, March 11, 2020, https://www.scottishlegal.com/articles/lockerbie-scottish-criminal-cases-review-commission-refers-al-megrahi-s-case-to-high-court-again.

130. Greg Russell, "Family to Appeal to Supreme Court as Megrahi Appeal Rejected," *The National* (Scotland), April 2, 2021, https://www.thenational.scot/news/19205864.supreme-court-move-megrahi-appeal-rejected/.

131. "Former Senior Libyan Intelligence Officer and Bomb-Maker for the Muamar Qaddafi Regime Charged for the December 21, 1988 Bombing of Pan Am Flight 103," Office of Public Affairs, U.S. Dept. of Justice, December 21, 2020, https://www.justice.gov/opa/pr/former-senior-libyan-intelligence-officer-and-bomb-maker-muamar-qaddafi-regime-charged.

132. "Former Senior Libyan Intelligence Officer and Bomb-Maker for the Muamar Qaddafi Regime Charged."
133. Melissas Ludtke, "Keeping Lockerbie Alive," *TIME Magazine*, November 27, 1989, https://web.archive.org/web/20080307061423/http://www.time.com/time/magazine/article/0,9171,959126,00.html.
134. Lindsey Hilsum, *Sandstorm: Libya in the Time of Revolution* (New York: Penguin, 2013), 128.
135. Lindsey Hilsum, *Sandstorm: Libya in the Time of Revolution*, 128.

Bibliography

Adams, Lucy. "Megrahi: Eight Pieces of Evidence." *The Herald* (Scotland), February 27, 2012. https://www.heraldscotland.com/news/13048661.megrahi-eight-key-pieces-evidence/.

Al Jazeera. *It Happened in Lockerbie, Part 1*. Airdate August 7, 2007, Al Jazeera—English. https://www.youtube.com/watch?v=R_USFvnaSSU.

Annan, Kofi A. "Letter Dated 25 April 2000 from the Secretary-General Addressed to the President of the Security Council." UN Security Council, April 26, 2000. http://i-p-o.org/nomination-observers.pdf.

Ashton, John. "Review of Aljazeera Documentary 'Lockerbie: What Really Happened?'" *Megrahi: You Are My Jury*, March 12, 2014. https://www.megrahiyouaremyjury.net/?p=1031.

Ashton, John. "Tam Dalyell's Last Interview: Going to the Grave Convinced of Lockerbie Bomber's Innocence." The Herald (Scotland), January 29, 2017. https://www.heraldscotland.com/news/15055570.tam-dalyells-last-interview-going-grave-convinced-lockerbie-bombers-innocence/.

Associated Press. "Scotland to Review Lockerbie Plane Bombing Investigation." Canadian Broadcasting Corp., May 3, 2018. https://www.cbc.ca/news/world/lockerbie-scotland-appeals-review-1.4646250https://www.cbc.ca/news/world/lockerbie-scotland-appeals-review-1.4646250.

Barr, Robert. "Investigators Say Bomb Caused Pan Am Crash." Associated Press, December 28, 1988. https://apnews.com/article/d9b45b0424c1952d50b4103bef415051.

Bates, Michael. "Researcher: Many Lockerbie Victims May Have Lived until Impact." Associated Press, October 6, 1990. https://apnews.com/article/acdaad08cbee147122a54b5592f26ec2.

Beck, Michael, presenter. BBC News Bulletin: Lockerbie Air Disaster. Airdate December 21, 1988, BBC. https://www.youtube.com/watch?app=desktop&v=jPZVoHt5nTc.

Biewen, John, and Ian Ferguson. "Shadow over Lockerbie: Mass Murder over Scotland." *American RadioWorks* (*CPB*), March 2000. https://americanradioworks.publicradio.org/features/lockerbie/story/printable_story.html.

Black, Ian, and Gerard Seenan. "Court Told How Jet's Radar Blip Broke Up at 7:02 pm." *The Guardian*, May 3, 2000. https://www.theguardian.com/uk/2000/may/04/lockerbie.gerardseenan1#:~:text=The%20final%20dramatic%20moments%20of,accused%20of%20murdering%20270%20people.

Bolger, Andrew, and Andrew England. "Lockerbie Bomber Abandons Appeal." *Financial Times*, August 14, 2009. https://www.ft.com/content/1876eece-87dd-11de-82e4-00144feabdc0.

"BP May See Competition in Post-Conflict Libya." *Energy Digital Magazine*, May 17, 2020. https://energydigital.com/utilities/bp-may-see-competition-post-conflict-libya.

Carrell, Severin. "U.S. Paid Reward to Lockerbie Witness, Abdelbasset al-Megrahi Papers Claim." *The Guardian*, October 2, 2009. https://www.theguardian.com/world/2009/oct/02/lockerbie-documents-witness-megrahi.

Carter, David B. "A Blessing or a Curse? State Support for Terrorist Groups." *International Organization* 66, no. 1 (2012): 129–51. https://www.jstor.org/stable/41428748.

Charlton, Corey. "Spook Cables Hidden: Lockerbie Bombing CIA Documents Reveal Secret Evidence That Could Have Helped Prosecution Was Withheld from Trial." *The Sun*, February 8, 2017. https://www.thesun.co.uk/news/2812566/lockerbie-bombing-cia-evidence-withheld/.

Convention for the Suppression of Unlawful Acts against the Safety of Civil Aviation. United Nations Treaty Series. July 18, 1975. https://treaties.un.org/doc/Publication/UNTS/Volume%20974/volume-974-I-14118-english.pdf.

Cook, James. "Megrahi Dies Protesting Lockerbie Bombing Innocence." BBC, May 20, 2012. https://www.bbc.com/news/uk-scotland-south-scotland-14707355.

Cowan, David. "Farmer's Tribute to Young Lockerbie Victims." BBC Scotland, December 20, 2018. https://www.bbc.com/news/uk-scotland-south-scotland-46613309.

Cowell, Alan. "Scottish Panel Challenged Lockerbie Conviction." *New York Times*, June 29, 2007. https://www.nytimes.com/2007/06/29/world/europe/29lockerbie.html.

Cox, Matthew, and Tom Foster. *Their Darkest Day: The Tragedy of Pan Am 103 and Its Legacy of Hope*. New York: Grove Weidenfeld, 1992.

"Craven Rescuers Who Joined the Search at Lockerbie." *The Craven Herald & Pioneer*, January 4, 2014. https://www.cravenherald.co.uk/nostalgia/nostalgia_history/10911251.craven-rescuers-who-joined-the-search-at-lockerbie/.

Cushman, John H., Jr. "The Crash of Flight 103; Pan Am Was Told of Threat." *New York Times*, December 23, 1988. https://www.nytimes.com/1988/12/23/world/the-crash-of-flight-103-pan-am-was-told-of-terror-threat.html#:~:text=Acting%20on%20an%20 unsubstantiated%20threat, Federal%20Aviation%20Administration%20said%20 today.&text=The%20bomb%20threat%2C%20received%20on%20Dec.

De Braeckeleer, Ludwig. "Key Lockerbie Witness Admits Perjury." *Scoop Independent News* (New Zealand), September 20, 2011. https://www.scoop.co.nz/stories/HL1109/S00189/key-lockerbie-witness-admits-perjury.htm.

Dickie, John, and David Gardner. "Why Weren't They Told?" *Daily Mail*, December 23, 1988. https://panam103.syr.edu/pdf/timeline/103HUDSON0002.pdf.

"Die Mullah-Spur." *Der Spiegel*, July 6, 1997. https://www.spiegel.de/politik/die-mullah-spur-a-e737e9aa-0002-0001-0000-000008741161.

"Doctor Describes Terror among Qaddafi Family." *New York Times*, April 16, 1986. https://www.nytimes.com/1986/04/16/world/doctor-describes-terror-among-qaddafi-family.html.

Dron, Alan. "A News Reporter at Lockerbie." *Air and Space Magazine* (Smithsonian), November 2016. https://www.smithsonianmag.com/air-space-magazine/above-beyond-Lockerbie-180960971/.

Engelberg, Stephen. "U.S. Suspects Iran Unit in the Pan Am Bombing." *New York Times*, February 25, 1989. https://www.nytimes.com/1989/02/25/world/us-suspects-iran-unit-in-the-pan-am-bombing.html.

Erlanger, Steven. "4 Guilty in Fatal 1986 Berlin Disco Bombing Linked to Libya." *New York Times*, November 14, 2001. https://www.nytimes.com/2001/11/14/world/4-guilty-in-fatal-1986-berlin-disco-bombing-linked-to-libya.html.

"Exhibits—Terrorist Bombing of Pan Am Flight 103." CIA Legacy Museum. Accessed July 28, 2022. https://www.cia.gov/legacy/museum/exhibit/terrorist-bombing-of-pan-am-flight-103/.

Fenton, Anna. "Veteran at the Front." *The Sun*, December 23, 1988. http://clippercrew.com/pan-am-crew-flight-103/captain-james-bruce-macquarrie/.

Foreign Airport Security: Hearing Before the Committee on Foreign Affairs, House of Representatives, One Hundred First Congress, First Session, February 9, 1989. United States Congress. Washington, D.C.: U.S. Government Printing Office, 1989.

"Former Senior Libyan Intelligence Officer and Bomb-Maker for the Muamar Qaddafi Regime Charged for the December 21, 1988 Bombing of Pan Am Flight 103." Office of Public Affairs, U.S. Dept. of Justice, December 21, 2020. https://www.justice.gov/opa/pr/former-senior-libyan-intelligence-officer-and-bomb-maker-muamar-qaddafi-regime-charged.

Frakes, Matthew. "Reagan, Rogue States, and the Problem of Terrorism." Wilson Center, September 17, 2020. https://www.wilsoncenter.org/blog-post/reagan-rogue-states-and-problem-terrorism.

Harvey, David, writer/producer. *Minute by Minute*, "Lockerbie: Terror at 31,000 Feet." Circle Films, airdate May 17, 2014, on Channel 5 (UK), https://www.youtube.com/watch?app=desktop&v=zCpCJCuB3ZM.

Six. Libya and Terrorism I

Hilsum, Lindsey. *Sandstorm: Libya in the Time of Revolution.* New York: Penguin, 2013.
Horne, Marc. "Ex-Leader of Malta Casts Doubt on Conviction of Lockerbie Bomber Abdul Baset Ali al-Megrahi." *The Times* (London), December 19, 2018. https://www.thetimes.co.uk/article/ex-leader-of-malta-casts-doubt-on-conviction-of-lockerbie-bomber-abdul-baset-ali-al-megrahi-8bfvpwtps.
Horovitz, David. "Editor's Notes: Lockerbie—A Miscarriage of Justice?" *Jerusalem Post*, October 11, 2007. https://www.jpost.com/opinion/columnists/editors-notes-lockerbie-a-miscarriage-of-justice.
Horovitz, David. "Who Made the Bomb? The Full Truth About Lockerbie Is Still Not Being Told." *Times of Israel*, November 26, 2020. https://www.timesofisrael.com/who-made-the-bomb-the-full-truth-about-the-lockerbie-bombing-has-yet-to-be-told/.
Hosenball, Mark. "Why One Defendant Got Off." *Newsweek*, February 11, 2001. https://www.newsweek.com/why-one-defendant-got-155315.
Hyde, Paul. "One Town's Response to Terrorism: Women of Lockerbie." *Greenville News*, November 3, 2016. https://www.greenvilleonline.com/story/entertainment/arts/paul-hyde/2016/11/03/one-towns-response-terrorism-women-lockerbie/93250420/.
"Iranian Spiritual Leader Ayatollah Ruhollah Khomeini Called for 'All-Out…" United Press International, July 5, 1988. https://www.upi.com/Archives/1988/07/05/Iranian-spiritual-leader-Ayatollah-Ruhollah-Khomeini-called-for-all-out/9763584078400/.
It Happened in Lockerbie, Part 1. Bill Cran (director). Al Jazeera—English, airdate August 7, 2007. https://www.youtube.com/watch?v=R_USFvnaSSU.
Janzon, Eva. "Flight 103 Suspect Convicted on Separate Terrorism Charge with AM-Flight 103." Associated Press, December 21, 1989. https://apnews.com/article/c598ea591dadb77ef634f18da82dcab9.
Jofre, Shelley, reporter. *Frontline Scotland*, "Silence Over Lockerbie." Airdate December 22, 1993, BBC Scotland. http://plane-truth.com/Aoude/geocities/silence.html.
Johnstone, Lindsey. "Lockerbie Bombing: 'What Really Brought It Home Was When You Were Picking Up Toys.'" *EuroNews*, December 21, 2018. https://www.euronews.com/2018/12/21/lockerbie-bombing-what-really-brought-it-home-was-when-you-were-picking-up-toys.
Katzman, Kenneth. "Terrorism: Near Eastern Groups and State Sponsors, 2002." Federation of American Scientists, February 13, 2002. https://irp.fas.org/crs/RL31119.pdf.
Kennedy, Rachael. "Lockerbie Disaster 30 Years On: People Share Their Memories of Pan Am Flight 103 Tragedy." *EuroNews*, December 21, 2018. https://www.euronews.com/2018/12/21/lockerbie-disaster-30-years-on-people-share-their-memories-of-pan-am-flight-103-tragedy.
"Libya: A Hero's Welcome." *RANE Worldview*, August 26, 2009. https://worldview.stratfor.com/article/libya-heros-welcome.
Llewelyn, Abbie. "Prince Andrew's Astonishing Comment to Terrorism Victims as He Was Accused of 'No Empathy.'" *Daily Express*, July 31, 2020. https://www.express.co.uk/news/royal/1317194/prince-andrew-duke-york-royal-family-news-lockerbie-queen-elizabeth-ii-spt.
"Lockerbie Bomber Abdel Basset Ali al-Megrahi Dies at 60, Report Says." Washington Post, May 20, 2012. https://www.washingtonpost.com/local/obituaries/lockerbie-bomber-abdel-basset-al-megrahi-dies-at-60-report-says/2012/05/20/gIQAxRo3cU_story.html.
"Lockerbie: Scottish Criminal Cases Review Commission Refers Al Megrahi's Case to High Court Again." Scottish Legal News, March 11, 2020. https://www.scottishlegal.com/articles/lockerbie-scottish-criminal-cases-review-commission-refers-al-megrahi-s-case-to-high-court-again.
Ludtke, Melissas. "Keeping Lockerbie Alive." *TIME Magazine*, November 27, 1989. https://web.archive.org/web/20080307061423/http://www.time.com/time/magazine/article/0,9171,959126,00.html.
Macaskill, Mark. "Lockerbie Bombing Hearing 'Flawed.'" *The Times* (London), March 16, 2010. https://www.thetimes.co.uk/article/lockerbie-bomber-hearing-flawed-8b0r33rnkwl.
"Maltese Lockerbie Trial Witnesses Were Reluctant to Meet Scottish Review Commission." Times of Malta, March 26, 2012. https://timesofmalta.com/articles/view/maltese-lockerbie-trial-witnesses-were-reluctant-to-meet-scottish.412782.

Marquise, Richard A. *Scotbom: Evidence and the Lockerbie Investigation*. New York: Algora Publishing, 2006.
Mayday: Air Disaster, season 7, episode 2, "Lockerbie Disaster." Cineflix Productions, airdate November 4, 2009, on Discovery Channel Canada. https://www.youtube.com/watch?app=desktop&v=_PqPKjWabio.
McNeil, Donald G., Jr. "Libyan Double Agent Testified in Lockerbie Bomb Trial." *New York Times*, September 27, 2000. https://www.nytimes.com/2000/09/27/world/libyan-double-agent-testifies-in-lockerbie-bomb-trial.html.
Mega, Marcello. "Doubts over Lockerbie Bomb Timer Fragment." *The Sunday Times* (London), December 17, 2018. https://www.thetimes.co.uk/article/doubts-over-lockerbie-bomb-timer-fragment-2vqgm6wxn.
Mendick, Robert. "Was Terry Waite Freed as Part of Secret Lockerbie Deal with Iran?" *The Independent*, December 15, 2013. https://www.telegraph.co.uk/news/uknews/10518045/Was-Terry-Waite-freed-as-part-of-secret-Lockerbie-deal-with-Iran.html.
Miles, Hugh. "Inconvenient Truths." *London Review of Books* 29, no. 12 (June 21, 2007). https://www.lrb.co.uk/the-paper/v29/n12/hugh-miles/inconvenient-truths.
"New Doubts in Crucial Evidence in Lockerbie Trial." *The Herald* (Scotland), July 16, 2011. https://www.heraldscotland.com/news/13033151.new-doubts-crucial-evidence-lockerbie-trial/.
The Newsroom. "Architect of Lockerbie Trial Vows to Fight for an Appeal." *The Scotsman*, November 1, 2005. https://www.scotsman.com/news/architect-lockerbie-trial-vows-fight-appeal-2509587.
Nicholson, Chris. "Pik Botha's Lockerbie Mystery." *The Independent—Online* (South Africa), October 24, 2018. https://www.iol.co.za/ios/behindthenews/pik-bothas-lockerbie-mystery-17617534.
Nicoll, Andrew. "Ex-Air Accident Investigator Reveals He Saw Lifeless Bodies of Lockerbie Disaster's Crew among Wreckage." *The Scottish Sun*, December 16, 2018. https://www.bbc.com/news/uk-scotland-highlands-islands-16307355.
Opinion of the Court Delivered by Lord Sutherland in Causa Her Majesty's Advocate v Abdelbaset Ali Mohmed Al Megrahi and Al Amin Khalifa Fhimah (Case No: 1475/99). High Court of Justiciary at Camp Zeist, January 1, 2001. https://www.scotcourts.gov.uk/docs/default-source/sc---lockerbie/lockerbiejudgement.pdf.
"Pan Am 103: Analysis of Claims." *Central Intelligence Agency*, December 22, 1988. https://www.cia.gov/readingroom/docs/CIA-RDP89G01321R000500180003-6.pdf.
"Pan Am 103 Bombing." Federal Bureau of Investigation. Accessed June 7, 2022. https://www.fbi.gov/history/famous-cases/pan-am-103-bombing.
Pioneer Press. "Review Calls for New Trial in Lockerbie Case." *Pioneer Press/TwinCities.com*, November 14, 2015. https://www.twincities.com/2007/06/28/review-calls-for-new-trial-in-lockerbie-case-2/.
Rezaian, Yeganeh. "Opinion: A Grim Anniversary Reminds Us of the Potential for Tragedy in the Persian Gulf." *Washington Post*, July 2, 2019. https://www.washingtonpost.com/opinions/2019/07/02/grim-anniversary-reminds-us-potential-tragedy-persian-gulf/.
Rush, Julian (correspondent). "Secret CIA Testimony Identified Real Lockerbie Mastermind." Channel 4 News (London), December 20, 2013. https://www.youtube.com/watch?v=26GonRZrWw0.
Russell, Greg. "Family to Appeal to Supreme Court as Megrahi Appeal Rejected." The National (Scotland), April 2, 2021. https://www.thenational.scot/news/19205864.supreme-court-move-megrahi-appeal-rejected/.
Scharf, Michael P. "The Lockerbie Trial Verdict." *ASIL Insights* 6, issue 2 (February 13, 2001). https://www.asil.org/insights/volume/6/issue/2/lockerbie-trial-verdict.
Scharf, Michael P. "A Preview of the Lockerbie Case." *ASIL Insights* 5, issue 5 (May 4, 2000). https://www.asil.org/insights/volume/5/issue/5/preview-lockerbie-case.
Shaughnessy, Lisa, dir. *Minute by Minute*. "Pan Am Flight 103." Airdate 2001, on A&E Channel.
Smith, Alex Duval. "Vital Lockerbie Evidence 'Was Tampered With.'" *The Guardian*, September 1, 2007. https://www.theguardian.com/business/2007/sep/02/theairlineindustry.libya.
Smith, Bob. "Derby Rescuers Recall Team's Search on 30th Anniversary of Lockerbie

Six. Libya and Terrorism I

Bombing." *Grough Magazine*, December 21, 2018. https://www.grough.co.uk/magazine/2018/12/21/derby-rescuers-recall-teams-search-on-30th-anniversary-of-lockerbie-bombing.
Staff and Agencies. "Mandela Appeals on Behalf of Lockerbie Bomber." *The Guardian*, June 10, 2002. https://www.theguardian.com/uk/2002/jun/10/lockerbie.nelsonmandela.
"State Sponsors: Libya." Council on Foreign Relations, December 1, 2005. https://www.cfr.org/backgrounder/state-sponsors-libya.
"Statement of Dr. Hans Koechler, International Observer at the Lockerbie Trial, on Recent Reports in the Scottish and British Media." I.P.O. Information Service, October 14, 2005. http://i-p-o.org/nr-lockerbie-14Oct05.htm.
Stobbs, George (interviewee). "Remembering Pan AM 103: George Stobbs." Federal Bureau of Investigation website (video transcript). Accessed June 8, 2022. https://www.fbi.gov/video-repository/george-stobbs-30-years-pan-am-103-lockerbie-2018.mp4/view.
Strauss, Valerie. "Iran Says U.S. Action Deliberate, Threatens Unspecified Retaliation." *Washington Post*, July 4, 1988. https://www.washingtonpost.com/archive/politics/1988/07/04/iran-says-us-action-deliberate-threatens-unspecified-retaliation/90aa6983-3be6-40f2-ab02-d11178dd36e4/.
Swire, Jim, and Peter Biddulph. *The Lockerbie Bombing: A Father's Search for Justice*. Edinburgh: Birlinn Ltd., 2021.
Thompson, Tony. "Forensic Mix-Up Casts Fresh Lockerbie Doubt." *The Observer*, October 8, 2005. https://www.theguardian.com/business/2005/oct/09/theairlineindustry.libya.
TOI Staff. "'Bomb-maker' Brags About El Al Blast, Posts Lockerbie Photos." *Times of Israel*, March 19, 2014. https://www.timesofisrael.com/bomb-maker-brags-about-el-al-blast-posts-lockerbie-photos/.
Trevelyan, Mark. "Lockerbie Investigation Spurns Conspiracy Theories." Reuters, June 28, 2007. https://www.reuters.com/article/us-lockerbie-conspiracies/lockerbie-investigation-spurns-conspiracy-theories-idUSL2679117620070628.
"Trial Shown Cassette 'Bomb.'" BBC, June 14, 2000. http://news.bbc.co.uk/2/hi/790805.stm.
Tribune News Services. "Iran's Former Top Spy Reportedly Links Khomeini to Pan Am Blast." *Chicago Tribune*, July 6, 1997. https://www.chicagotribune.com/news/ct-xpm-1997-07-06-9707060208-story.html.
"Two Passengers on Flight 103 Might Have Survived, Pathologist Says." Associated Press, October 17, 1990. https://apnews.com/article/6630a187dd9a67416a8cfac908eb33c2.
U.S. Department of State Dispatch: Fact Sheet: The Iranians and the PFLP–GC—Early Suspects in the Pan Am Flight 103 Bombing. United States Department of State. Ann Arbor: University of Michigan Press, January 1, 1990.
"What Really Happened on Flight 103?" *The Observer*, February 27, 2000. https://www.theguardian.com/uk/2000/feb/27/lockerbie.life1.
Wilson, Brian. "Lord Fraser of Carmyllie Obituary." *The Guardian*, June 24, 2013. https://www.theguardian.com/politics/2013/jun/24/lord-fraser-of-carmyllie.
Worth, Katie. "Lockerbie: The Alternate Theories." PBS, October 6, 2015. https://www.pbs.org/wgbh/frontline/article/lockerbie-the-alternate-theories/.

SEVEN

Libya and Terrorism II
The Downing of UTA Flight 772

The McDonnell Douglas DC-10 was six and a half miles over the Sahara Desert when it crashed, and Nigerian aviation officials at once suspected a terrorist operation. In part, this was because only nine months earlier Pan Am Flight 103 had blown apart in the skies over Scotland—a Semtex bomb obliterated the jumbo jet—with the attack sensitizing authorities in Niger to the possibility of such a tragedy within their own borders.

On this occasion, the aircraft was a French airliner, and the probe would follow the same course as that of the Pan Am investigation: it would begin as an inquiry into Middle Eastern extremist groups, then turn to the North African nation of Libya. In time, French and American investigators would depict the disaster as the second act of a two-act revenge scheme ordered by Muammar Gaddafi. (Chapter Six focuses on the purported first act of the plot.) Other experts would emphasize the plausibility of it having been a Hezbollah operation on behalf of Iran or Syria or, alternatively, a product of the Abu Nidal Organization (ANO), perhaps at the direction of, or in alliance with, Libya.

MURDER OVER THE SAHARA

The aircraft was owned and operated by Union de Transports Aériens (UTA), a French company. Departing from Brazzaville in the Republic of Congo shortly after noon on Tuesday, September 19, 1989, it carried 170 passengers and crew. Among the travelers were fifty French citizens as well as three employees of Esso, the oil conglomerate, and Bonnie Pugh, wife of the U.S. ambassador to Chad. The final destination was to be Charles de Gaulle Airport in Paris after a brief stopover in N'Djamena, Chad. As it happened, the four African nations that Flight 772 would traverse—Congo, Chad, Niger, and Algeria—were former colonies of France.

At take-off, the skies were partly cloudy, the temperature was rising, and the baggage-check procedure without incident. The first leg of the flight was uneventful, the aircraft flying from Brazzaville to N'Djamena and landing on time. After completing its stopover in the Chadian capital, the plane returned to the air at 1:13 p.m., with the pilot making his final contact with the N'Djamena control tower twenty minutes later. The aircraft would now climb to 35,100 feet and fly over the Sahara Desert, more precisely, an expanse of the Sahara the size of France, known as the Ténéré Desert. Owing to the remoteness of the region, the plane would be out of radar range until it approached Niger, when protocol dictated that the pilot inform Niamy Airport that the aircraft was entering Nigerian airspace. No notification was forthcoming, however.

When UTA 772 failed to appear at the expected time, air traffic controllers went into action. After several failed attempts to contact the pilot, the Flight Information Center in Niamy issued a DETRESFA alert in the late afternoon (DETRESFA is a code word meaning "distress [French: *détresse*] phase"). It is a signal that is rarely used, and author Stuart H. Newberger explains that air traffic controllers obviously "believed there was a very high probability that something catastrophic had happened to the aircraft, and the 170 human beings sealed inside the pressurized cabin."[1]

Within hours, the French navy dispatched a reconnaissance plane from Senegal to track down UTA 772, but night had fallen by this point and there was no sign of the missing aircraft. Then, shortly after 5:00 the next morning, the French army sent a transport plane, a Transall C-160, over the Sahara. The team that it carried was retracing the French airliner's designated flight path after its departure from Chad.

Two hours into their mission, the airborne soldiers spied something in the desert sands that was mirroring the morning sunlight. Their position was 400 miles northwest of N'Djamena in the nation of Niger. As they neared the glistening entity, an expanse of wreckage began to take shape. The team could now confirm that Flight 772 had not experienced mechanical problems and landed at another location, but that the worst-case scenario had transpired: it had crashed. The debris field stretched forty square miles.

By the next morning, the site was swarming with paratroopers and rescue workers, some of the latter having struggled to make it to the scene isolated in the desert. There were few roads or villages in the far-flung region. Yet even before the first responders arrived, authorities held out little hope that anyone had survived the crash, partly because of the terrain. Any survivor, presumably badly injured, would have had to contend with the extreme conditions of the desert itself, meaning searing days and frigid nights. And this was a near impossibility.

Although investigators had not officially determined the reason for the plane to plummet to the ground, it seemed obvious to the rescue teams that an improvised explosive device (IED) was the likely cause. "One team discovered pieces of metal laid out in a neat pattern fifty meters by twenty meters, perhaps a slice of the aircraft's aluminum outer skin, cleanly severed from the body of the DC-10 several miles above the desert," writes Newberger. "Another found one of the three huge engines, the aircraft having had one bolted to each wing and a third mounted high on the tail."[2] The remaining engines were recovered several miles away. And then there were the innumerable fragments of the DC-10 that littered the sand. The pattern of wreckage pointed to UTA 772 blowing apart in midair, then shattering, which was typical of a high-altitude blast triggered by an improvised explosive device.

Besides the debris pattern, three additional factors suggested a terrorist strike: the skies had been calm, the pilot had not reported any mechanical problems, and there had been no mayday call. "If there had been a very serious and violent problem on board, unless it was an explosion or the plane suddenly and completely disintegrated, there would have been several seconds or minutes, probably tens of minutes, for the crew to lose altitude or re-establish radio contact," said UTA spokesman Michel Friess.[3] Three days after the crash, the authorities announced that an analysis of the airliner's black box confirmed that a catastrophic blast had indeed been the cause.[4] Furthermore, the International Civil Aviation Organization (ICAO) team revealed that a suitcase bomb in the front cargo hold had caused the explosion.

As anticipated, news bureaus began receiving messages from groups claiming responsibility for the mass murder. One arrived at a Middle Eastern newsroom in the form of a typewritten statement ostensibly prepared by the "Secret Chadian Resistance," a group opposed to the administration of Hissen Habré, the president of Chad. Although Chad had been a sovereign nation since 1960, France nevertheless maintained 19,000 troops in its former colony to help Chad defend against Libyan incursions. Even so, a portion of the Chadian population was unsettled by the troops' presence, hence the resistance group. "The struggle will continue until the complete withdrawal of all military colonial forces from Africa," read its statement.[5]

Other claims, in the view of French officials, emerged from "strangers with questionable mental health."[6] What *were* taken seriously were three claims phoned in to Western news agencies and UTA offices from a single terrorist entity, one that counterterrorism experts deemed the most inclined to target French interests. A militant pro–Palestinian Shiite organization, it was known as Islamic Jihad, although it was more familiar to Westerners as Hezbollah. Based in Lebanon and reinforced by neighboring Syria, the organization, since 1987, had received military, monetary, and political support from Iran.

One of the calls from Islamic Jihad asserted that the Flight 772 bombing was retribution for the Israelis' kidnapping of Sheik Abdul Karim Obeid in Lebanon. "We would like to say the French are warned not to exchange information regarding Sheik Obeid with the Israelis no more," the caller said.[7] Officials discounted this explanation, since it was unclear what, if any, information the French had supposedly shared about the man.

Soon came another claim from Islamic Jihad, but this time experts accorded it more credibility. Since March 1989, a bloody conflict had been raging in Lebanon between Maronite Christians and a combination of Muslim and pro–Syrian forces. In August, the situation became even more precarious when François Mitterrand dispatched his nation's military to the region, the French president having long favored the Maronites. "[T]he French government sent a naval task force of five warships into Lebanese waters as part of what President Francois Mitterrand called a 'rescue mission' for several thousand French nationals living in the war-torn country," write journalists Rone Tempest and Jim Mann.[8] Not surprisingly, Muslim and pro–Syrian forces, which already mistrusted Mitterrand, considered the warships' unsolicited presence a threat. Convinced that the French had arrived to protect and perhaps augment the Maronite fighters, the Muslim and pro–Syrian forces ordered Mitterrand to remove the vessels or face fierce reprisals. The warnings were issued by, among others, Islamic Jihad and a pro–Syrian militant group, and they went unheeded by French authorities.

Two weeks later, in early September, the *New York Times* revealed that the dispute was intensifying. "The warships remain, and France may yet take economic, and perhaps military, action against Syria," reported Youssef M. Ibrahim.[9] Political analysts speculated that Mitterrand had calculated that the pro–Syrian forces were flagging and was seizing the opportunity to intimidate them.

It was during this volatile period that a French intelligence officer received word that terrorist elements were planning to retaliate; French airliners were the targets.[10] For this reason, when UTA 772 was bombed shortly thereafter, counterterrorism experts interpreted it as an admonishment of France over its perceived interference in Lebanon's domestic affairs. Even today, numerous experts contend that it was French naval aggression in Libya's territorial waters that set into motion the tragedy that would befall UTA 772.

The French Investigation

As to the subsequent probe, Jean-Louis Bruguière, a Paris judge whose job was to manage his nation's terrorism inquiries, would oversee it. Within hours of the explosion over the Sahara Desert, he and his staff opened an investigation that would become controversial.

Starting with the premise that a Middle Eastern militant organization was behind the attack, Bruguière and his team focused on Lebanese groups and those closely aligned with Lebanon. Number one on his list was Islamic Jihad. As previous noted, Islamic Jihad had a motive for the Flight 772 bombing—the incursion of French warships into Lebanese waters—and the group had warned that it would strike French interests in retaliation. Furthermore, it was among the first to take credit for the explosion and crash, and in three separate notifications. On top of that, it had a history of forceful actions against France, having kidnapped and murdered French military personnel and civilians earlier in the decade. But although the perpetrators seemed obvious, Bruguière kept open the possibility that sympathetic entities may have contributed to Islamic Jihad's deadly attack, that it may have been a multi-perpetrator operation incorporating state-sponsored terrorism, the type of operation examined in the previous chapter. Certainly, it is true that multifaceted terrorist strikes against superpowers, like the United States, may require such collaboration.

Regarding the evidence, Bruguière's team, early in the investigation, sought the help of the FBI crime lab with what appeared to be a charred fragment of luggage retrieved in the Sahara. The bureau's analysis confirmed that the fragment was from a Samsonite suitcase and that it was identical to those that French police had previously seized in their raids on the "15 May Organization." The latter was a breakaway faction of the Popular Front for the Liberation of Palestine–General Command (PFLP-GC), the Syria-based group that was originally implicated in the Pan Am 103 explosion.[11] Bombs constructed by the PFLP-GC and 15 May Organization were distinctive, unlike those of other terrorist outfits. Presumably, the PFLP-GC had built the explosive device at the request of Islamic Jihad.

"Until the beginning of the summer of 1990, Judge Bruguière was therefore working on the trail of the PFLP-GC and Shiite circles, a trail that was to lead his steps towards Damascus and Tehran" ("Jusqu'au début de l'été 1990, le juge Bruguière travaillait donc sur la piste du PFLP-GC et des milieux chiites, piste qui devait conduire ses pas vers Damas et Téhéran"), writes Pierre Péan, an investigative journalist and author.[12] But then, rather unexpectedly, came a development that, on the face of it, seemed to shift the blame to Muammar Gaddafi's Libyan regime. Bruguière therefore dropped Islamic Jihad from further consideration, as well as the PFLP-GC and their possible accomplices in Syria, Iran, and Lebanon, and set his sights exclusively on Libya. The timing of this new development was striking, coinciding, as it did, with a similar about-face in another investigation in which the FBI crime lab was intricately involved, namely, that of Pan Am 103. "The reversal occurred on the same date as in the Lockerbie affair" ("Le revirement se produisit à la même date que dans l'affaire de Lockerbie"), writes Péan, who was suspicious of the coincidence.[13]

This fresh development in the UTA inquiry came in the form of a discovery by Bruguière. "[H]e found a file compiled by Congolese security describing close contacts between Libyan intelligence agents and an anti-Congo group based in Zaire," reports Sharon Waxman of the *Chicago Tribune*.[14] It contained a statement by a Congolese man, Bernard Yanga, which directly implicated Libya in the Flight 772 crime.

The official narrative that arose from Yanga's version of events was intriguing: an impoverished man by the name of Apollinaire Mangatany, a citizen of the Republic of Congo, placed a suitcase bomb on UTA 772. Mangatany's family and friends did not know how he could afford the new suitcase or the airfare to Paris or why he would be traveling to a non-existent street address in the French capital. All the same, Mangatany purportedly boarded the passenger plane in Brazzaville and flew, with the bomb in the cargo hold, to N'Djamena, Chad. Here, he presumably deplaned. In Yanga's account, the IED was supposed to denotate while the plane was on the ground at the Chadian airport and was meant to send a message to France. Property damage and public fear were the intended result, but not a massive loss of life.[15]

Yanga further explained that he and Mangatany were lifelong friends as well as members of a resistance organization aimed at liberating a Congolese state from its corrupt administration. Mangatany managed the group. Yanga said that he and Mangatany underwent paramilitary training in Libya, which was sympathetic to their cause, and that their resistance group had received funding through the Libyan Embassy in Brazzaville.[16] So it was that one of Mangatany's contacts in Libya asked him to plant a bomb on Flight 772, the reason being to punish France for having helped Chad militarily. It was a quid pro quo.

Before long, journalists and independent investigators began voicing doubts about the veracity of Yanga's claim, not only because he was the lone source for his belated account but also because he was connected to Congo's intelligence apparatus. "[T]he investigators," reported the French newspaper *Le Monde diplomatique*, "had to rely on extremely fragile testimony by a Congolese national, Bernard Yanga, in Brazzaville who [had] links with his country's security services" ("Les enquêteurs se replient alors, pour incriminer la Libye, sur le témoignage extrêmement fragile, recueilli à Brazzaville, d'un Congolais, Bernard Yanga, lié aux services de son pays").[17] Also problematic, Yanga's account did not match the evidence. It was at odds with the Samsonite suitcase, the one that the FBI confirmed was identical to those used by the PFLP–GC and the 15 May Organization in their terrorist operations. Thus, Yanga's version of events, by itself, was unpersuasive. Auspiciously, the FBI uncovered a "smoking gun" at this moment, and once again it pointed to Muammar Gaddafi.

It seems that the FBI's Tom Thurman, without informing Jean-Louis Bruguière or the French forensics teams, scrutinized photos of the UTA 772 wreckage and detected a green circuit board fragment on which the initials "TY" were engraved.[18] "It had been miraculously recovered from the tons of debris scattered over miles of barren desert," writes Newberger.[19] Thurman asserted that the fragment was the product of a Taiwanese firm, Tai Youn Electronics, and that the company manufactured circuit boards. After Thurman notified the French investigators, they proceeded to link the TY fragment to a second company that made timing devices for use in home appliances and industrial equipment. Next, they tracked these devices to a firm in Germany, which had supplied more than a hundred of them to Libya in 1989 for use in runway beacons for desert landings. So now, Bruguière and Thurman posited that Libyan intelligence had used one of the timers in the bomb that demolished UTA 772 in mid-flight. This stage of the investigative process paralleled the discovery and analysis of the green circuit board fragment that was ostensibly recovered from the Pan Am 103 wreckage as well as its connection to Libya. The breakthroughs were timely and impressive, but some observers were skeptical.

"It is striking how similar the findings, by the FBI, to the 'scientific' evidence of the two cases of Lockerbie and Ténéré [UTA 772]" ("Il est frappant de constater la similitude des découvertes, par le FBI, de la preuve 'scientifique' des deux affaires de Lockerbie et du Ténéré [UTA772]"), writes Péan. "In the thousands, if not tens of thousands, of [pieces of] debris collected from the scene of the disaster, a single piece of circuit board was found, and in both cases—miraculously—this single small piece of circuit board bore an indication that allowed identification: MEBO for Lockerbie, TY for UTA's DC10" ("Dans les milliers, voire les dizaines de milliers, de [morceaux de] débris ramassés sur les lieux de la catastrophe, un seul fragment de circuit imprimé a été trouvé et, dans les deux cas—miracle— cet unique petit bout de circuit imprimé portait une indication qui en permettait l'identification: Mebo pour Lockerbie, TY pour le DC10 d'UTA").[20] Both fragments, of course, implicated Libya.

And there was another coincidence: in the Pan Am 103 inquiry, forensics analyses revealed that the piece of MST-13 timer contained no traces of explosive residue, a remarkable finding since the fragment had supposedly been situated at the nucleus of the blast. Even more stunning, the timer that was purportedly extracted from the Flight 772 debris also did not test positive for explosive residue.

While Thurman and his FBI unit stood firmly behind the notion that it was a TY timer that had triggered the UTA 772 bomb, French scientists, a year later, arrived at a different conclusion. The latter experts worked for three separate investigative bodies, each of which operated its own crime lab: the Direction de la Surveillance du Territoire (DST), the Direction Centrale de la Police Judiciaire (DCPJ), and the Préfecture de Police (PP). While all of the specialists were well respected in professional circles, one in particular stood out. His name was Claude Calisti, he worked for the PP forensics lab, and he was among the world's leading explosives experts. Upon analyzing the timer fragment, Calisti, as well as the members of the other three teams, determined that the TY timer had not been concealed in a Samsonite suitcase on Flight 772 and thus could not have been part of the bomb that brought down the French airliner. Besides the fact that the device did not contain traces of explosive residue, they also noted that it was too large to have been incorporated into the Samsonite casing. Such troubling incongruities notwithstanding, Bruguière deferred to Thurman's opinion, and the official French investigation formally shifted to Libya as the perpetrator.

Owing to his critical role in both the French (UTA) and Scottish (Pan Am) inquiries, it may be informative to take note of Thurman's career subsequent to these cases. In the mid–1990s, a high-level whistleblower disclosed scientific misconduct at the FBI crime laboratory, which prompted the Office of the Inspector General (OIG), an independent entity within the U.S. Department of Justice, to launch an intensive investigation into the lab and its Chemistry and Toxicology Unit (CTU), Materials Analysis Unit (MAU), and Explosives Unit (EU). Thurman was chief of the latter component.

Over the course of eighteen months, investigators interviewed more than one hundred witnesses and examined roughly 60,000 pages of "case files, work notes, test results, policies, internal memoranda, and other materials."[21] In April 1997, the OIG released its conclusions in a document titled *The FBI Laboratory: An Investigation into Laboratory Practices and Alleged Misconduct in Explosives-Related and Other Cases*.[22] "The conclusions were damning and dangerous," write journalists John F. Kelly and Phillip K. Wearne.[23]

As the findings pertained to Thurman, he turned out to be one of the most criticized FBI figures in the inquiry, with investigators finding "ambiguities and other errors" in his lab reports.[24] Even more concerning, they discovered that he had altered or rewritten such reports.[25] Regarding the question of "prosecutorial bias," meaning whether he had adjusted them to favor prosecutors and win guilty verdicts, the inquiry confirmed that "the effect of his overstating ... conclusions in certain reports was favorable to the prosecution."[26] While the Office of the Inspector General did not cite him for willful misconduct, it did single out Thurman for special censure, and the FBI removed him from his position in the Explosives Unit on the grounds that he lacked the necessary scientific background.[27]

Unfortunately, the OIG did not review Thurman's role in the UTA 772 and Pan Am 103 inquiries, in which he was acclaimed for having more or less cracked the cases. And this raises questions about the findings of the two terrorism investigations, including the provenance of the incriminating circuit board fragments. In his study of the Flight 772 disaster, Péan voiced grave concerns about Thurman's involvement in the French investigation, describing the former FBI officer as a "specialist in fabricating evidence" ("spécialiste de la fabrication de preuves").[28] Be that as it may, the general consensus, which was fostered by both the American and French governments and news media, was that Muammar Gaddafi was behind the attack on the French aircraft and that he must pay for his crime.

Legal Proceedings

In late October 1991, magistrate Jean-Louis Bruguière issued four arrest warrants, all of which named Libyan nationals. Most imposing among them was Abdallah al-Sanussi (alternatively Abdullah al-Senussi), the brother-in-law of Muammar Gaddafi. Sanussi, who had been drawn into Gaddafi's political circle through marriage, rose to the position of deputy chief of the country's intelligence apparatus, and it proved to be a role he savored. "He was nicknamed 'the butcher' because of his reputation for brutal behaviour," reads a BBC profile.[29] Allegedly, it was Sanussi who conceived the attack on Flight 772. Given his status, French officials were well aware that imprisoning him would deal a formidable blow both to Libya's intelligence community and the Gaddafi family itself.

Bruguière's arrest warrants also targeted Abdullah Elazragh (Abd al-Azragh), a diplomat at the Libyan embassy in Brazzaville. If Bernard Yanga's testimony was accurate, it was Elazragh who claimed that the reason for the UTA bombing was to punish France for its assistance to Chad. Elazragh, according to Yanga, was also the diplomat who supplied Apollinaire Mangatany with a plane ticket to Paris, a Samsonite suitcase, and new garments. "The clothing—including a bright-red tie—were intended to allow another Libyan agent in N'Djamena to recognize Mangatany at the stopover, so that [Mangatany] could slip off the plane and out of the airport during the panic that would follow the explosion," writes Newberger.[30]

The remaining set of warrants was issued to Ibrahim Naeli (Nayil Ibrahim) and Abbas Musbah (Musbah Arbas). Naeli, a captain in the Libyan intelligence service, was responsible for security at Libyan Arab Airlines, while Musbah, who purportedly functioned as Naeli's right-hand man in the bombing, was an intelligence officer and explosives expert. As per the court documents, the men "ensured the inspection and set-up of the explosive device in Brazzaville," thus tying them directly to the atrocity.[31]

In the course of Bruguière's eight-year investigation, further material came to light and, in 1997, resulted in two additional warrants. Like the four men before them, this final pair of suspects was connected to the Libyan intelligence service. One was Abdelsalam Issa Shibani, a colonel who ostensibly acquired the timing device used in the UTA 772 bombing, and Bedelsalam Hammouda El Ageli, a lieutenant who was believed to have coordinated the terror attack.[32]

On March 27, 1998, French prosecutors brought formal charges against the six men, with the allegations consisting of murder, complicity to commit murder, and complicity to destroy property through the use of explosives. As anticipated, Gaddafi refused to extradite the defendants, so they were put on trial in absentia on March 8, 1999, in Paris.

The prosecution's narrative was straightforward: the Flight 772 attack was formulated in Tripoli, overseen by Elazragh at the Libyan embassy in Brazzaville, managed on the ground by Hammouda, and implemented by a Congolese resistance agent, Mangatany, who was supposedly unaware of the full ramifications of his role.[33] In effect, the latter had been an unwitting pawn. Unfortunately, investigators would never succeed in locating Mangatany, assuming he actually existed.

The overarching question in the trial centered on the reason for the mass homicide. "The prosecutor," writes Jon Henley in *The Guardian*, "cited two possible motives: the desire to kill a Libyan opponent on the plane or retaliation for French troops' blocking Libyan designs on Chad in the 1970s and 1980s."[34]

The trial itself was swift. Seventy-two hours after the proceedings commenced, the court determined that the prosecution's arguments were persuasive and brought the case to a close. Guilty verdicts followed, with the court handing down life sentences to all of the defendants.

In spite of the ruling, a number of experts continued to speculate that Libya had not been the perpetrator of the attack or, alternatively, that the North African nation had not acted alone in planning and executing it. Conjecture persisted that the United States and France had either framed Libya or sequestered it from its co-conspirators in order to preserve their relationships with Syria and Iran, which were of immediate value to Operation Desert Storm.[35]

Settlements

On the subject of penalties, the Libyan government, while not acknowledging culpability, acquiesced to court orders and paid $33 million in judgments against the six men. Five years later, in response to additional legal rulings, the Gaddafi Foundation agreed to further compensate the UTA 772 victims' loved ones, paying one million dollars to each family of a casualty. But this was not the end of it.

In 2004, Libya reached yet another agreement whereby it would pay millions more to the African and European families of the Flight 772 casualties.[36] Then, in 2007, the U.S. government conducted its own proceedings. Since Gaddafi still scoffed at handing over the defendants, it was in the form of a bench trial, with the judge ruling, as had the French court, that Libya was liable for the downing of the French airliner. The defendants were again sentenced to life in prison for the midair bombing in which seven Americans perished.[37]

Owing to the protracted litigation against the North African country for its alleged roles in terror operations in the 1980s, the United States decided in 2008 to resolve the matter with a single, comprehensive settlement. To this end, it established, but did not pay into, a $1.8 billion fund that would encompass a handful of incidents that killed or injured American or Libyan citizens. Of this sum, $1.5 billion would be earmarked for American victims and $300 million would be set aside for Libyan victims.

The acts of violence covered by the fund consisted of the UTA 772 and Pan Am 103 bombings as well as the 1986 La Belle discotheque attack in Berlin. The human cost of the U.S. air strikes in Tripoli and Benghazi, which came in response to the Berlin bombing, were included as well.[38] Libya could thus draw on the fund to compensate its own citizens who were victims of the U.S. sorties. "State Department spokesman Robert Wood," reported Reuters, "said the deal was pursued on a 'purely humanitarian basis' and did not constitute an admission of fault by either party."[39] The State Department also insisted that no U.S. taxpayer money would be transferred into the fund, although it was rumored that American companies, with their own financial interests in mind, may have contributed to it in an effort to speed up the normalization of relations.[40] Lastly, the settlement would protect Libya from future litigation stemming from its past terrorist activities. It was a status that would help the nation attract Western businesses, since the latter would be more likely to invest in Libyan enterprises if it was known that massive compensation claims would not be filed against the country in the future.

In terms of Libya's compliance with, and contribution to, the fund, it was total and substantial, with the Gaddafi administration providing three payments that amounted to $1.5 billion. Subsequent to this, the former pariah nation rejoined the international community.

Libya and the Abu Nidal Organization

As it happened, the question of Libya's culpability in the Flight 772 disaster would not disappear after the legal settlements were honored. It would reemerge in February 2011, as the Arab Spring was spreading across much of the Arab world, and would focus on a Palestinian militant organization.

"A former official from the radical Palestinian group Abu Nidal said that the attacks against the Pan Am and UTA planes were conducted 'in conjunction' with Libya," reported the Agence France-Presse news bureau.[41] In light of the close relationship between Abu Nidal, the organization's founder and namesake, and Muammar Gaddafi when the Pan Am and UTA attacks transpired, the former official's assertion would seem to warrant consideration.

Chapter Six recounted how the first of the two midair bombings began with a man who claimed to represent the Abu Nidal Organization phoning into the U.S. embassy in Helsinki on December 5, 1988. The caller warned of a plot to destroy a Pan Am airliner on a flight that passed through Frankfurt. It is also important to understand that Libya harbored the ANO from 1987 to 1999, after Syria, under pressure from the United States, ejected the terrorist outfit. But Libya did more than merely shelter the ANO; it capitalized on it. "Gaddafi," writes journalist Lindsey Hilsum, "needed someone he could task with getting rid of enemies overseas."[42]

In 1985, the two men allegedly collaborated on their first mission when the ANO devised a diabolical operation to be carried out in Europe. The objective was to slaughter customers, presumably Israelis, waiting in line at El Al ticket counters at two international airports.[43] Those waiting at the TWA counter, presumably Americans, would be targeted too, albeit secondarily. A reprisal for a recent attack by the Israeli military on the headquarters of the Palestinian Liberation Organization in Tunis, the ANO mission was set for the Christmas holidays when the airports would be teeming with travelers.

In the horrific operation, the Abu Nidal Organization dispatched two teams of young Palestinian commandos to Leonardo da Vinci Airport in Rome and Vienna International Airport. Initially, the Frankfurt airport was to have been a target as well, but this element of the plan was scrapped. Also ditched was a particularly nefarious scheme, which the gunmen abandoned when they were confronted by heavy security at the Italian airport. "[T]he commandos planned to take American and Jewish hostages in the terminal, hijack an El Al jet to Tel Aviv and blow it up over the Israeli city, ending their suicide mission," reported the Associated Press.[44]

The seven terrorists came of age in Palestinian refugee camps in Lebanon, with the ANO subsequently exploiting their loyalties to their families and country. Idealistic and angry, the young commandos launched their simultaneous assaults on the Austrian and Italian airports in the morning, a time when such facilities are most crowded and chaotic. Armed with Soviet-made assault rifles and hand grenades, the terrorists were hungry for bloodshed. "Doped on amphetamines," writes Middle East expert Patrick Seale, "the young killers had been told to throw grenades and fire blindly at checkout counters."[45] By all accounts, hell ensued. "It was an inferno," said Dora Silvestri, who was injured in the assault. "[T]hey started throwing hand grenades and firing with submachines guns."[46] In all, 121 civilians were wounded and another eighteen people, including a child and an American diplomat, died in the onslaught, according to the U.S. Office of the Director of National Intelligence.[47]

Pertinent to our discussion of Libya, defectors from the ANO later revealed that the Gaddafi regime had played a vital role in the attacks. "Libyan intelligence took part in the planning and supplied the weapons," writes Seale.[48] In addition, Libyan intelligence furnished the Palestinian commandos with stolen Tunisian passports for entry into Austria and Italy.[49] And lastly, the Libyan media, under Gaddafi's thumb, heralded the Christmastime carnage as heroic.

It was also in 1985 that Nidal began relocating his organization to Libya, where he promptly selected an official from the Libyan Intelligence Directorate to serve as his personal liaison to the nation's intelligence network. Gaddafi, for his part, was thrilled that Nidal and his organization were now based in Libya, and he wasted no time bestowing on the guerrilla leader considerable real estate. To Nidal, he gave apartments in the capital city, a villa, and two farms, together with access to Libyan embassies, classified intelligence communications, diplomatic pouches, and even aircraft. And so the two men, throughout the remainder of the 1980s and into the 1990s, were joined at the hip. "[Gaddafi] and Abu Nidal had now become partners," writes Seale. "[T]hey spent their time together abusing their enemies—before plotting how best to destroy them."[50]

Because the planning and execution of the Flight 772 attack occurred while the ANO was ensconced in Libya and collaborating with Libyan intelligence services, it is not a stretch to posit that Nidal and his group may have teamed up with Libya in the bombing of the French airliner. That said, it should be borne in mind that evidence is lacking; only the 2011 declaration of the former ANO official exists. It is worth noting, too, that Abu Nidal, who died in 2002 in Baghdad, was known to take credit for terrorist incidents in which he and his organization had played no part.[51] We are left, then, with a claim that is plausible but unsubstantiated.

Shortly after the former ANO official made his assertion about his organization's involvement in the Flight 772 attack, a second figure, perhaps seeking to refute the claim, spoke out about Libyan culpability in the operation. His name was Abdel Rahman Shalgam, and he was Libya's former foreign minister and representative to the United Nations. In March 2011, Shalgam defected from the Gaddafi administration and set about re-establishing himself as the regime collapsed. It was at this juncture that Shalgam told the media that Libya had indeed been responsible for the Flight 722 attack, that its intelligence services were attempting to assassinate Mohammed Magariaf, the leader of the National Front for the Salvation of Libya (NFSL). Allegedly, Libyan operatives believed this political rival of Gaddafi would be on the flight.[52] Magariaf was not on board, of course, and would proceed to become the president of Libya the following year.

Shalgam also offered his perspective on the Pan Am 103 disaster. "The Lockerbie operation was more complex," he noted. "The role of states and organizations has been discussed, and while the Libyan services were implicated, I do not think it was a purely Libyan operation."[53]

In the end, the entity or entities that destroyed UTA Flight 772 and Pan Am Flight 103, as well as their motives for doing so, is still uncertain, despite the Libyan government having been prosecuted and legal closure achieved. It is possible, of course, that Libya was wholly responsible for both of the attacks. It is a fact, however, that the investigations and resultant trials in the UTA and Pan Am cases were characterized by such irregularities and incongruities that the question of political machinations on the part of the American government, in cooperation with the French and Scottish governments, persists.

Sahara Silhouette

Just as Pan Am World Airways folded shortly after the Flight 103 disaster, so too did UTA begin to fade in the months following the Flight

772 bombing. In the latter case, however, it was for a much different reason.

In 1990, leaders of the commercial airline industry in France, anticipating the economic boost that would emerge from the impending formation of the European Union, set about crafting a national airline to compete with those of other countries. As a part of this process, Groupe Air France purchased two successful French airlines, one of which was Union de Transports Aériens. Over the next two years, Air France integrated UTA's operations, after which it retired the UTA appellation. The acquisition was widely regarded as a smart, forward-thinking strategy.

The means by which the victims of the Pan Am 103 and UTA 772 bombings were honored also share certain features. Memorials to those who perished in the Lockerbie disaster were constructed at the Arlington National Cemetery near Washington, D.C., as well as Syracuse University in New York, the Sherwood Crescent neighborhood in Lockerbie, and nearby Tundergarth Church, where first responders discovered the airliner's cockpit. Most prominent, though, was the Lockerbie Air Disaster Memorial and Garden of Remembrance, which includes a stone cenotaph onto which are inscribed the victims' names. Situated a mile west of the Scottish town, the expansive floral garden was fashioned for contemplation, and each year thousands of people visit it, keeping alive the memory of the deceased.

As to the victims of Flight 772, memorials were erected in Brazzaville, Niger, and N'Djamena, Chad, as well as at the site of the crash in the Sahara Desert, where a group of Esso (Exxon) employees fashioned a tribute to their three colleagues who perished in the bombing. In the UTA debris, they attached a plaque bearing the names of their deceased coworkers to the airliner's starboard wing, which was standing upright and embedded in the sand. It was also in this patch of desert, but four miles from the site of impact, that the UTA 772 DC-10 Memorial was built.

The brainchild of Guillaume Denoix de Saint Marc, a Paris businessman whose father was killed in the UTA 772 attack, the desert memorial is a tribute to all of the casualties. Denoix de Saint Marc, with the support of an organization comprised of the UTA victims' loved ones—Les Familles de l'attendtat du DC10 d'UTA (The Families of the UTA DC10 Attack)—created the extraordinary memorial, which was designed to be observable by those flying over the Sahara Desert.[54] Denoix de Saint Marc and the Les Familles organization used funds that the Libyan government had paid as part of its settlement with the U.S. government.

Here, in the desert, teams of workers from three indigenous tribes—the Hausa, Toubou, and Tuareg—constructed an immense stone circle, more than 200 feet in diameter, to represent a compass. A wing salvaged from the airliner was positioned as a compass point, and around the circumference of the circle tribesmen placed 170 broken mirrors signifying the 170 lives that were cut short by the terrorist attack.

Using dark stones, the workers next formed a life-sized silhouette of the DC-10 inside the compass. Visible from satellites and aircraft, as well as viewable on Google Earth, the enormous memorial resembles a black tattoo on the sand, that of the UTA 772 pointing toward Paris, its destination. A work of art that is timeless and ethereal, the UTA 772 DC-10 Memorial is a uniquely serene tribute. "We want to show there is not a spirit of vengeance," said Denoix de Saint Marc, "just justice and peace."[55]

Notes

1. Stuart H. Newberger, *The Forgotten Flight: Terrorism, Diplomacy and the Pursuit of Justice* (London: Oneworld Publications, 2017), 5.
2. Stuart H. Newberger, *The Forgotten Flight*, 7.
3. Youssef M. Ibrahim, "Bomb Suspected in Midair Wreck of French DC-10," *New York Times*, September 21, 1989, https://www.nytimes.com/1989/09/21/world/bomb-suspected-in-midair-wreck-of-french-dc-10.html.
4. "Jet's Black Box Confirms That Blast Caused Crash," *Deseret News*, September 22, 1989, https://www.deseret.com/1989/9/24/18824991/jet-s-black-box-confirms-that-blast-caused-crash.
5. "Jet's Black Box Confirms That Blast Caused Crash."
6. Stuart H. Newberger, *The Forgotten Flight*, 29.
7. Edward Cody, "Air Crash Attributed to Bomb," *Washington Post*, September 21, 1989, https://www.washingtonpost.com/archive/politics/1989/09/21/air-crash-attributed-to-bomb/b175b3c2-5208-48f7-9385-4a282005900b/.
8. Rone Tempest and Jim Mann, "Bomb Suspected in Crash of French Plane in Africa," *Los Angeles Times*, September 21, 1989, https://www.latimes.com/archives/la-xpm-1989-09-21-mn-888-story.html.
9. Youssef M. Ibrahim, "The World; A French Presence in Lebanon, A Lebanese Presence in France," *New York Times*, September 3, 1989, https://www.nytimes.com/1989/09/03/weekinreview/the-world-a-french-presence-in-lebanon-a-lebanese-presence-in-france.html.
10. Rone Tempest and Jim Mann, "Bomb Suspected in Crash of French Plane in Africa."
11. Stuart H. Newberger, *The Forgotten Flight*.
12. Pierre Péan, *Manipulations Africaines: Qui Sont les Vrais Coupables de l'Attentat du Vol UTA 772?* (Paris: Plon, 2001), 95.
13. Pierre Péan, *Manipulations Africaines*, 95.
14. Sharon Waxman, "Judge's Pursuit of Terrorist Annoys the French Government," *Chicago Tribune*, August 10, 2021, https://www.chicagotribune.com/news/ct-xpm-1991-11-15-9104120524-story.html.
15. Stuart H. Newberger, *The Forgotten Flight*.
16. Stuart H. Newberger, *The Forgotten Flight*.
17. "Les Preuves Trafiquées du Terrorisme Libyen," *Le Monde—Diplomatique*, March 2001, https://www.monde-diplomatique.fr/2001/03/PEAN/6174.
18. Pierre Péan, *Manipulations Africaines*.
19. Stuart H. Newberger, *The Forgotten Flight*, 55.
20. Pierre Péan, *Manipulations Africaines*, 98.
21. "The FBI Laboratory: An Investigation into Laboratory Practices and Alleged Misconduct in Explosives-Related and Other Cases," Office of the Inspector General, United States Department of Justice, April 1997, https://irp.fas.org/agency/doj/oig/fbilab1/fbil1toc.htm.

22. "The FBI Laboratory: An Investigation into Laboratory Practices and Alleged Misconduct in Explosives-Related and Other Cases."

23. John F. Kelly and Phillip K. Wearne, *Tainting Evidence: Inside the Scandals at the FBI Crime Lab* (New York: The Free Press, 1998), 126.

24. "The FBI Laboratory: An Investigation into Laboratory Practices and Alleged Misconduct in Explosives-Related and Other Cases—Section H10: Thurman's Alleged Alteration of Dictation," Office of the Inspector General, U.S. Department of Justice, April 1997, https://irp.fas.org/agency/doj/oig/fbilab1/18thurma.htm.

25. John Biewen and Ian Ferguson, "Shadow over Lockerbie: Mass Murder over Scotland," *American RadioWorks* (CPB), March 2000, https://americanradioworks.publicradio.org/features/lockerbie/story/printable_story.html.

26. "The FBI Laboratory: An Investigation into Laboratory Practices and Alleged Misconduct in Explosives-Related and Other Cases—Section H10: Thurman's Alleged Alteration of Dictation."

27. David Johnson, "Report Criticizes Scientific Testing at F.B.I. Crime Lab," *New York Times*, April 16, 1997, https://www.nytimes.com/1997/04/16/us/report-criticizes-scientific-testing-at-fbi-crime-lab.html.

28. Pierre Péan, *Manipulations Africaines*, 98.

29. BBC News, "Profile: Abdullah al-Senussi," BBC, October 15, 2016, https://www.bbc.com/news/world-middle-east-17414121.

30. Stuart H. Newberger, *The Forgotten Flight*, 38.

31. *Robert L. Pugh, et al. [Plaintiffs] v. The Socialist People's Libyan Arab Jamahiriya, et al. [Defendants]*, United States District Court for the District of Columbia, September 19, 2005, https://www.crowell.com/PDF/UTA-Flight-772/Statement_of_Facts.pdf, 19.

32. *Robert L. Pugh, et al. [Plaintiffs] v. The Socialist People's Libyan Arab Jamahiriya, et al. [Defendants]*.

33. Sharon Waxman, "Judge's Pursuit of Terrorist Annoys the French Government."

34. Jon Henley, "France Finds Six Libyans Guilty of 1989 Airliner Bombing," *The Guardian*, March 10, 1999, https://www.theguardian.com/world/1999/mar/11/jonhenley.

35. Pierre Péan, *Manipulations Africaines*.

36. Reuters Staff, "U.S. Court Orders Libya to Pay $6 Billion for Bombing," Reuters, January 16, 2008, https://www.reuters.com/article/us-libya-bombing-lawsuit/u-s-court-orders-libya-to-pay-6-billion-for-bombing-idUSN1657189520080116.

37. Reuters Staff, "U.S. Court Orders Libya To Pay $6 Billion for Bombing."

38. "Libya Pays $1.5 Billion to Settle Terrorism Claims," CNN, October 31, 2008, https://edition.cnn.com/2008/WORLD/africa/10/31/libya.payment/index.html.

39. Salah Sarrar, "Libya Signs Bombing Compensation Deal with U.S.," Reuters, August 14, 2008, https://www.reuters.com/article/us-libya-usa/libya-signs-bombing-compensation-deal-with-u-s-idUSLE22721120080814.

40. "Libya Compensates Terror Victims," BBC, October 31, 2008, http://news.bbc.co.uk/2/hi/americas/7703110.stm.

41. Agence France-Presse—Dubai, "Ex-Foreign Minister Says Libya Behind 1989 Airline Attack," *Al Arabiya News*, July 18, 2011, https://english.alarabiya.net/articles/2011%2F07%2F18%2F158145.

42. Lindsey Hilsum, *Sandstorm: Libya in the Time of Revolution* (New York: Penguin, 2013), 120.

43. John Tagliabue, "Airport Terrorists Kill 13 and Wound 113 at Israeli Counters in Rome and Vienna," *New York Times*, December 28, 1985, https://www.nytimes.com/1985/12/28/world/airport-terrorists-kill-13-and-wound-113-at-israeli-counters-in-rome-and-vienna.html.

44. Frances D'Emilio, "Survivors of Airport Attack Describe Horror of Massacre," Associated Press, January 15, 1988, https://apnews.com/article/7a32e5d41f0812bdf9a049250f2f53d3.

45. Patrick Seale, *Abu Nidal: A Gun for Hire* (New York: Random House, 1992), 244.

46. John Tagliabue, "Airport Terrorists Kill 13 and Wound 113 at Israeli Counters in Rome and Vienna."

47. "Counterterrorism Guide: The Methods and Tactics of Global Terrorism—Timeline,"

Office of the Director of National Intelligence, accessed November 16, 2022, https://www.dni.gov/nctc/timeline.html.
 48. Patrick Seale, *Abu Nidal: A Gun for Hire*, 245.
 49. Lindsey Hilsum, *Sandstorm: Libya in the Time of Revolution*.
 50. Patrick Seale, *Abu Nidal: A Gun for Hire*, 150.
 51. Lindsey Hilsum, *Sandstorm: Libya in the Time of Revolution*.
 52. Agence France-Presse—Dubai, "Ex-Foreign Minister Says Libya Behind 1989 Airline Attack."
 53. Lindsey Hilsum, *Sandstorm: Libya in the Time of Revolution*, 187–188.
 54. Alex Davies, "There's a Beautiful Plane Crash Memorial in The Middle of the Niger Desert," *Business Insider*, May 17, 2013, https://www.businessinsider.com/uta-flight-772-memorial-pictures-2013-5.
 55. Alex Davies, "There's a Beautiful Plane Crash Memorial in the Middle of the Niger Desert."

Bibliography

Agence France-Presse—Dubai. "Ex-Foreign Minister Says Libya Behind 1989 Airline Attack." Al Arabiya News, July 18, 2011. https://english.alarabiya.net/articles/2011%2F07%2F18%2F158145.
BBC News. "Profile: Abdullah al-Senussi." BBC, October 15, 2016. https://www.bbc.com/news/world-middle-east-17414121.
Biewen, John, and Ian Ferguson. "Shadow over Lockerbie: Mass Murder over Scotland." *American RadioWorks* (CPB), March 2000. https://americanradioworks.publicradio.org/features/lockerbie/story/printable_story.html.
Cody, Edward. "Air Crash Attributed to Bomb." *Washington Post*, September 21, 1989. https://www.washingtonpost.com/archive/politics/1989/09/21/air-crash-attributed-to-bomb/b175b3c2-5208-48f7-9385-4a282005900b/.
"Counterterrorism Guide: The Methods and Tactics of Global Terrorism—Timeline." Office of the Director of National Intelligence. Accessed November 16, 2022. https://www.dni.gov/nctc/timeline.html.
D'Emilio, Frances. "Survivors of Airport Attack Describe Horror of Massacre." Associated Press, January 15, 1988. https://apnews.com/article/7a32e5d41f0812bdf9a049250f2f53d3.
Davies, Alex. "There's a Beautiful Plane Crash Memorial in the Middle of the Niger Desert." Business Insider, May 17, 2013. https://www.businessinsider.com/uta-flight-772-memorial-pictures-2013-5.
"The FBI Laboratory: An Investigation into Laboratory Practices and Alleged Misconduct in Explosives-Related and Other Cases." Office of the Inspector General, U,S, Department of Justice, April 1997. https://irp.fas.org/agency/doj/oig/fbilab1/fbil1toc.htm.
"The FBI Laboratory: An Investigation into Laboratory Practices and Alleged Misconduct in Explosives-Related and Other Cases—Section H10: Thurman's Alleged Alteration of Dictation." Office of the Inspector General, U.S. Department of Justice, April 1997. https://irp.fas.org/agency/doj/oig/fbilab1/18thurma.htm.
Henley, Jon. "France Finds Six Libyans Guilty of 1989 Airliner Bombing." *The Guardian*, March 10, 1999. https://www.theguardian.com/world/1999/mar/11/jonhenley.
Hilsum, Lindsey. *Sandstorm: Libya in the Time of Revolution*. New York: Penguin, 2013.
Ibrahim, Youssef M. "Bomb Suspected in Midair Wreck of French DC-10." New York Times, September 21, 1989. https://www.nytimes.com/1989/09/21/world/bomb-suspected-in-midair-wreck-of-french-dc-10.html.
Ibrahim, Youssef M. "The World; A French Presence in Lebanon, A Lebanese Presence in France." *New York Times,* September 3, 1989. https://www.nytimes.com/1989/09/03/weekinreview/the-world-a-french-presence-in-lebanon-a-lebanese-presence-in-france.html.
"Jet's Black Box Confirms That Blast Caused Crash." *Deseret News*, September 22, 1989. https://www.deseret.com/1989/9/24/18824991/jet-s-black-box-confirms-that-blast-caused-crash.

Johnson, David. "Report Criticizes Scientific Testing at F.B.I. Crime Lab." *New York Times,* April 16, 1997. https://www.nytimes.com/1997/04/16/us/report-criticizes-scientific-testing-at-fbi-crime-lab.html.
Kelly, John F., and Phillip K. Wearne. *Tainting Evidence: Inside the Scandals at the FBI Crime Lab.* New York: The Free Press, 1998.
"Les Preuves Trafiquées du Terrorisme Libyen." Le Monde—Diplomatique, March 2001. https://www.monde-diplomatique.fr/2001/03/PEAN/6174.
"Libya Compensates Terror Victims." BBC, October 31, 2008. http://news.bbc.co.uk/2/hi/americas/7703110.stm.
"Libya Pays $1.5 Billion to Settle Terrorism Claims." CNN, October 31, 2008. https://edition.cnn.com/2008/WORLD/africa/10/31/libya.payment/index.html.
Newberger, Stuart H. *The Forgotten Flight: Terrorism, Diplomacy and the Pursuit of Justice.* London: Oneworld Publications, 2017.
Péan, Pierre. *Manipulations Africaines: Qui Sont les Vrais Coupables de l'Attentat du Vol UTA 772?* Paris: Plon, 2001.
Reuters Staff. "U.S. Court Orders Libya to Pay $6 Billion for Bombing." Reuters, January 16, 2008. https://www.reuters.com/article/us-libya-bombing-lawsuit/u-s-court-orders-libya-to-pay-6-billion-for-bombing-idUSN1657189520080116.
Robert L. Pugh, et al. [Plaintiffs] v. The Socialist People's Libyan Arab Jamahiriya, et al. [Defendants]. United States District Court for the District of Columbia, September 19, 2005: 1–82. https://www.crowell.com/PDF/UTA-Flight-772/Statement_of_Facts.pdf.
Sarrar, Salah. "Libya Signs Bombing Compensation Deal with U.S." Reuters, August 14, 2008. https://www.reuters.com/article/us-libya-usa/libya-signs-bombing-compensation-deal-with-u-s-idUSLE22721120080814.
Seale, Patrick. *Abu Nidal: A Gun for Hire.* New York: Random House, 1992.
Tagliabue, John. "Airport Terrorists Kill 13 and Wound 113 at Israeli Counters in Rome and Vienna." New York Times, December 28, 1985. https://www.nytimes.com/1985/12/28/world/airport-terrorists-kill-13-and-wound-113-at-israeli-counters-in-rome-and-vienna.html.
Tempest, Rone, and Jim Mann. "Bomb Suspected in Crash of French Plane in Africa." *Los Angeles Times,* September 21, 1989. https://www.latimes.com/archives/la-xpm-1989-09-21-mn-888-story.html.
Waxman, Sharon. "Judge's Pursuit of Terrorist Annoys the French Government." Chicago Tribune, August 10, 2021. https://www.chicagotribune.com/news/ct-xpm-1991-11-15-9104120524-story.html.

Eight

Aircraft as Guided Missiles
Kamikazes, al-Qaeda, and the 9/11 Attacks

The terrorist strikes on the Twin Towers and the Pentagon stunned and appalled the world in equal measure, not least because of the unorthodox method of attack: the perpetrators commandeered four airliners bound for Los Angeles, then repurposed them as missiles. A diabolical strategy, it proved to be an exceptionally effective means of committing murder on a monumental scale. But while the media portrayed the aircraft-as-weapon approach as unprecedented, the rationale behind it does, in fact, have a noteworthy history.

It was the novelists Jules Verne and H.G. Wells who, in the late 1800s, acquainted the reading public with the concept of "heavier-than-air" flying machines, including airborne apparatuses that could be used aggressively. The only competitors of the era, "airships" like the German Zeppelin and hot air balloons, were lighter than air and, in the pages of science fiction, defenseless against such fantastical contrivances.

Several years later, the thought experiments of aviation enthusiasts Carl Diesnstbach and T.R. MacMechen further explored the notion of airborne aggression, but these men focused their attention on existing technology. "It will soon be realized that the entire design of the Zeppelin lends itself to the conversion of the craft into an aerial man-of-war," they wrote in the September 1909 issue of *American Aeronaut*.[1] The duo proceeded to describe in detail how a weighty object, one that was suspended on a rope from a Zeppelin, could demolish a target beneath it. "The blow that the implement at the end of the guide-rope is capable of giving will be some twenty tons delivered at 60 miles an hour, plus the pressure of propulsion, plus the power of the wind," they estimated.[2] "[It] might be tried against all sorts of structures on the ground, even against living objects."[3]

Such flights of fancy were joined in World War I by real-life events when a Russian aircraft designer and military pilot, Pyotr Nesterov, purposely slammed his glider into an Austrian aircraft in flight. Praised in Russia as an intrepid feat, the incident, one in which both pilots perished, was the first recorded aerial ramming.[4] But it would be during the final months of World War II that airplanes would be methodically deployed as weapons, and it would be the Japanese military that would inaugurate the practice.

Kamikaze Attacks in the Pacific War

It was the spring of 1944 and the East Asian nation was suffering a substantial loss of troops, weapons, aircraft, and airfields in its battle against the Allies in the Pacific. In this dispiriting milieu, numerous Japanese pilots, when confronted with their inevitable deaths during surveillance or bombing missions, took it upon themselves to hallow their final moments through an act they considered at once personal and patriotic. "Individual Japanese pilots, deciding they were doomed anyway, chose to 'take one with them,' deliberately ramming [Allied] aircraft or crashing into ships," writes Mark Lardas.[5] Some pilots thought that doing so would fulfill the traditional Japanese code of the Bushidō, thus ensuring an honorable death and immortality.[6]

As the number of pilots who spontaneously pursued this course of action mounted—and as the tactic was observed to diminish the enemy's resources and morale—the Japanese High Command decided to form a special unit composed exclusively of aviators willing to dive-bomb their planes into the Allies' high-value assets. Judged to be essential under the circumstances, it was a last-ditch military campaign to save the nation. As for its implementation, the program would rest with the Imperial Japanese Navy, soon to be joined by the Imperial Japanese Army.

On October 25, 1944, the first such sortie was carried out by volunteers in the Tokubetsu Kōgeki tai, or the Special Attack Unit. In the West, "kamikaze," meaning "divine wind," became the commonly-used term for these self-sacrificial missions. In the initial attack, five airplanes were fitted with explosives. The aircraft, Mitsubishi A6M2 Zero planes, were selected for use because they were lightweight, fast, and highly maneuverable.[7] Accompanying them in the formation were three fighter planes whose role was to shield the kamikazes from enemy fire.

Absent the suicidal element, the concept was a rather conventional one. "The best way to consider a kamikaze is as a cruise missile or precision-guided munition with a human being substituting for a digital computer as the guidance system," explains Lardas.[8] Evidently, the pilots held a similar perspective. The typical aviator who flew to his death, or attempted unsuccessfully to do so, did not view his actions as suicidal in the usual sense but rather as a transformation of the self into a component of the emperor's war machine.[9] "He looked upon himself as a human bomb which would destroy a certain part of the enemy fleet for his country," recalled a Japanese general.[10]

As could be expected given the cultural divide between East and West, kamikaze missions were perceived quite differently by those from the other side of the globe. "The Japanese consider it noble sacrifice; the Americans consider it inhuman warfare," reported documentary filmmaker Dan J. Wolf.[11] Certainly, the macabre spectacle succeeded in attracting the attention of the Allied forces at sea. "There was a hypnotic fascination to a sight so alien to our Western philosophy," recalled Vice Admiral C.R. Brown.[12]

As the Allies' march to victory continued, the Imperial Japanese Navy and Army suffered a staggering attrition of pilots. Needing to retain those who were well equipped for combat missions, military leaders turned in 1945 to men with little or no aviation experience and trained them for kamikaze strikes. Their preparation was brief and focused. What the pilots learned, in essence, was how to take off and reach a target.

In the end, the kamikaze strategy failed to win the war for Japan. It did, however, constitute the most formidable line of attack the Allies would confront in the Pacific theater.

In retrospect, it appears that the Japanese pilots, especially those zealous volunteers at the outset of the "divine wind" campaign, shared certain characteristics with the 9/11 terrorists who would fly jetliners into the World Trade Center and the Pentagon. Both the kamikazes and the al-Qaeda operatives viewed their nations or cultures as being under threat from the United States and therefore considered their deeds to be justified. They also looked upon their human marks as malevolent beings deserving of death, whether the targets were military or civilian. Many additionally believed that a rich afterlife awaited them as a reward for their acts of self-sacrifice. And lastly, their flight preparation came to be geared explicitly toward reaching, then breaching, large structures to commit mass murder.

THE SEPTEMBER 11 OPERATION

In the case of the al-Qaeda team, the pilots' training in the United States began in mid-2000, when three men from a terrorist cell in

Hamburg, Germany, relocated to South Florida. Although they would keep their American flight instructors in the dark, the trio was, in fact, planning to act as hijacker-pilots on September 11, with a fourth hijacker-pilot joining the lineup at a later date and in another U.S. state.

The Hijacker-Pilots

While the 9/11 attacks are thought to have been broadly planned in Afghanistan and fine-tuned in Germany, their commander, once the mission was afoot in the United States, would be a thirty-three-year-old Egyptian national, Mohamed Atta. By all accounts, the man was an enigma. His father would later tell the media that Atta, as a child and young man, was "a gentle person, very shy, unassuming, and highly sensitive," an indulged son who did not stop sitting on his mother's lap until he entered Cairo University to study architecture.[13] "I used to tell her that she is raising him as a girl," the senior Atta said, "but she never stopped pampering him."[14] After years of involvement in an al-Qaeda cell, Atta came to be viewed quite differently. "We didn't like him," says Rudi Dekkers, the owner of the flight academy in Venice, Florida, where Atta underwent training in June 2000. "For us, he was a dead man walking; his face was expressionless."[15] Although Atta was a graduate of Cairo University, his grades had been poor and he was not accepted into graduate school. At the Florida flight school—it was the now-defunct Huffman Aviation—he also was viewed as a second-rate student.[16] In terms of his assignment on September 11, it would be to fly a jetliner into the North Tower of the World Trade Center.

Alongside Atta at the flight academy was Marwan al-Shehhi, a citizen of the United Arab Emirates (UAE). Twenty-three-year-old Shehhi was a married man and an alumnus of the University of Bonn. Well liked, he was known for his cheery, sociable demeanor. "[H]e was funny, he had jokes," says Dekkers, "sometimes dirty jokes, but he was normal."[17] Shehhi's role would be to penetrate the South Tower.

It is worth noting that Atta and Shehhi, growing tense after several weeks at Huffman Aviation, withdrew and enrolled in September 2000 in a different flight school, Jones Aviation in nearby Sarasota. "According to the instructor at Jones, the two were aggressive, rude, and sometimes even fought with him to take over the controls during their training flights," revealed *The 9/11 Commission Report*. "In early October, they took the Stage I exam for instruments ratings at Jones Aviation and failed."[18] For this reason, the pair returned, grudgingly, to Huffman Aviation to finish their training.

Also worth noting, Atta and Shehhi refined their skills in "executing

EIGHT. Aircraft as Guided Missiles

turns and approaches" at still another facility in Florida, one situated in the city of Opa-Locka. The two sought out the flight center because it offered aviation enthusiasts access to flight simulators.[19] Tellingly, neither man demonstrated an interest in, or practiced, takeoffs or landings.

The third hijacker-pilot to arrive in Florida during the summer months was an associate of Atta and al-Shehhi from Hamburg. A twenty-six-year-old Lebanese man, Ziad Jarrah was amiable and seemingly well-adjusted. "[He] was the kind of boy that was raised well and was treated in a very good manner," said his uncle, Jamal Jarrah. "He was a happy boy."[20]

Ziad Jarrah attended the University of Greifswald but left after two semesters. When he moved to Florida, he also left behind a girlfriend in Germany. For personal reasons or perhaps strategic ones, Jarrah kept a distance from Atta and Shehhi as he prepared for the attacks. In Venice, for instance, he sought instruction at a different flight school, the Florida Flight Training Center, and he shared an apartment with some of its teachers. His target on September 11 would be the Capitol Building, based on information acquired after the attacks, but Jarrah would fail to fulfill that part of the mission. The same sources reported that the operation's mastermind in Afghanistan, Osama bin Laden, had wanted the White House, rather than the Capitol, to be struck, but Atta convinced him that the residence and offices of the president would be too well-defended.[21]

By the end of 2000, the three operatives who trained in Florida had received their commercial licenses. Subsequent to this, they once again trained on flight simulators that were designed to familiarize the users with large commercial jets.

The fourth and final hijacker-pilot was Hani Hanjour, a twenty-nine-year-old from Saudi Arabia. Years earlier, Hanjour had attended ESL (English as a Second Language) classes in Arizona and California but did not become proficient. Along the way, he also obtained a commercial pilot's license, one that was issued to him by an Arab-American instructor in Arizona. Then, in December 2000, Hanjour enrolled in a refresher course at JetTech flight school in Phoenix, where the facility's manager, on three occasions, contacted the FAA to voice her concerns about the Saudi's inadequate command of English. "I couldn't believe that he had a commercial license of any kind with the skills that he had," said Peggy Chevrette.[22] Despite the manager's alerts, the FAA reviewed the matter and allowed Hanjour to retain his license without any further action.

Hanjour next set about practicing on a Boeing 737 flight simulator in Mesa, Arizona, and he persevered over a three-month stretch despite his mentors informing him that his flight skills were "well below standard."[23]

Undaunted, he thereafter attended flight academies in Virginia, New Jersey, and Maryland, and he would remain in the latter state until the day of the attack. In terms of his target, it would be the Pentagon, an assignment the novice pilot would tackle with conviction. "Hanjour took many flights in the Washington DC metropolitan area, familiarizing himself with the airspace—the only pilot in the group to do so," writes William M. Arkin.[24]

As previously noted, the hijacker-pilots represented four Middle Eastern nations—Egypt, Lebanon, Saudi Arabia, and the United Arab Emirates. As it happened, two more al-Qaeda operatives, Khalid al-Mihdhar and Nawaf al-Hazmi, would also pursue flight training. It was in San Diego in late 2000 that the two Mecca-born Saudi nationals, neither of whom was fluent in English or possessed prior aviation experience, expressed a desire to undertake flight training from a local instructor who spoke Arabic. They did not, however, wish to learn the basics of flying a small airplane, which customarily is the first step. "Hazmi and Mihdhar emphasized their interest in learning to fly jets, Boeing aircraft in particular, and asked where they might enroll to train on jets right away," reads the 9/11 Commission document.[25] Due to their inability to communicate effectively coupled with their unrealistic expectations, their hopes of becoming hijacker-pilots were quickly dashed. That said, the fact that they attempted to become hijacker-pilots in San Diego raises the possibility that the original 9/11 plot may have included additional U.S. targets and that they were spared due to a lack of al-Qaeda aviators.

Although Hazmi and Mihdhar would not be at the controls of Boeing jetliners on September 11 as they had hoped, they would nevertheless participate in the mission, albeit in a lesser capacity. Their roles would be those of "muscle hijackers," the term used for the contingent of terrorists who would carry out the more savage aspects of the operation. Despite the term, these men were not physically imposing—their average height was five feet, six inches—but they were hardened, committed, and dutiful and thus deemed suitable for their assignments.[26]

The "Muscle Hijackers"

The architect of the September 11 attacks, Osama bin Laden, handpicked fifteen men from the network's ranks to serve as muscle hijackers. It was fundamentally a Saudi Arabian team, since fourteen of the men were citizens of that country. The remaining pick was an Emirati national. Nearly all of the muscle hijackers, regardless of their homelands, were single and poorly educated and with few aspirations or prospects.[27] They did have clean records, however, and thus were unlikely to invite scrutiny. In the mission, their function would be to secure the cockpits and control, through brute force, the passengers and crew.

In mid-2000, bin Laden sent these operatives to Afghanistan to undergo advanced training that was constructed expressly for the forthcoming mass murders. According to the 9/11 plan, each airliner would carry three or four muscle hijackers who would monitor the doors of the flight decks once the planes were aloft. As soon as the crews opened the doors, the muscle hijackers would storm the cockpits, incapacitate the flight crews, and install the hijacker-pilots. Subsequent to this, their focus would shift to subduing—that is, overwhelming—the passengers and the remainder of the aircrew. As part of their preparation in Afghanistan, the muscle hijackers practiced butchering animals, such as camels and sheep. Although the operatives knew they were being trained to kill, they were unaware that the victims were to be airline passengers and flight crews.[28]

The extent to which the muscle hijackers knew that death awaited them on September 11 has never been established. Unlike the hijacker-pilots who were informed about most aspects of the intricate plot more than a year in advance, the muscle hijackers may have been kept in the dark so as to ensure their cooperation. What is known is that, based on the items the men left behind on 9/11, they apparently were unaware that they would be part of a suicide mission on this day. "It looks as if they expected they might be going to prison, not paradise," a source told *The Guardian*.[29] Still, a videotape featuring bin Laden that was confiscated after the 9/11 attacks may shed some light on the matter, assuming that the radical Islamist's statements were true. In it, he tells a gathering of adherents that the muscle hijackers were apprised, while training in Afghanistan, that they would be contributing to a sacrificial mission. They were not told any details, however, and they were not permitted to have any contact with the men who would serve as hijacker-pilots. "[A]ll they knew was that they have a martyrdom operation and we asked each of them to go to America but they didn't know anything about the operation, not even one letter," said bin Laden. "[W]e did not reveal the operation to them until they are there and just before they boarded the planes."[30]

Between April and June 2001, the muscle hijackers arrived in the United States, primarily South Florida. Then, starting in August, numerous operatives, both hijacker-pilots and muscle hijackers, traveled periodically to the northeastern United States to establish bank accounts and purchase global-positioning devices, aeronautical charts, and Stanley knives (box cutters), among other weapons. As well, they researched car rental services, surveilled the layouts and security procedures at the relevant airports, and joined gyms to build their strength and stamina.

During this same period, al-Qaeda's archenemy, the U.S. government, was likewise submerged in the forthcoming terror operation. Analysts were receiving and analyzing a torrent of intelligence reports pointing to a cataclysmic al-Qaeda strategy, one that would soon be deployed against the United States.

"Bin Laden Determined to Strike in US"

The White House would present to the American people its version of events that led up to the September 11 disaster. Its narrative would contend that the U.S. intelligence community had provided the Bush-Cheney administration with insufficient information about the prospects of an al-Qaeda attack, that it had furnished strategic information that could be used for long-term planning but nothing usable, tactically, in the near future. For this reason, America had purportedly been caught off-guard.

It was an assertion that the U.S. intelligence community rejected. Top figures in the CIA and associated agencies maintained that they had, in fact, delivered actionable intelligence but that the White House had chosen not to respond. Certainly, it is true that the Bush-Cheney administration not only failed to prevent the 9/11 catastrophe but also made the decision not to warn the citizenry about the imminent threat that faced them. Among those left in the dark were the people who lived and worked in heavily-populated urban centers along the East Coast, the probable target of a major terrorist operation.

As it stands, the record confirms that President George W. Bush, Vice President Dick Cheney, National Security Advisor Condoleezza Rice, Deputy National Security Advisor Stephen Hadley, and others in the administration were apprised on numerous occasions that the terrorist network overseen by Osama bin Laden (AKA bin Ladin) was about to unleash an unparalleled assault on the United States. The awareness of these government leaders was evident in the tens of thousands of documents reviewed by, and interviews conducted by, the National Commission on Terrorist Attacks Upon the United States—"the 9/11 Commission"—during its 2002-2004 investigation. Additional material would come in the form of memoirs and other written works by U.S. and foreign figures who, during the lead-up to the al-Qaeda atrocities, were well placed to witness the inner workings of the government.

Internal communiqués and interviews reveal that the intelligence community was gripped with apprehension from April to September 2001, apprehension over what had already become "street knowledge" in parts of the Middle East. In short: al-Qaeda was preparing a strike, or a series of strikes, that would be far more extravagant than anything a terrorist

EIGHT. Aircraft as Guided Missiles

organization had ever attempted. To celebrate the mass murder of Americans once the mission had transpired, al-Qaeda was planning to host eight celebrations in assorted Middle Eastern locales.[31] Informants for the West further reported that al-Qaeda operatives had begun dropping out of sight—presumably, they were hiding from anticipated retaliation—and training camps in Afghanistan were being shuttered. The moment, it appeared, was fast approaching.

"Bin Ladin Planning Multiple Operations" was the title of an intelligence briefing that was convened on April 20, 2001, by Richard A. Clarke, the MIT-educated "terrorism czar."[32] Clarke was chairman of the Counterterrorism Security Group (CTSG), which was composed of top figures from the CIA, FBI, Joint Chiefs of Staff, State Department, Defense Department, and Justice Department. The members in attendance were notified that a multifaceted terrorist mission was being readied against the United States and the available materials were provided to them.

The following month, intelligence officials in the United States found themselves fielding even more phone tips from sources warning about the impending al-Qaeda operation. "By May of 2001," said Cofer Black, "it was very evident that we were going to be struck, we were gonna be struck hard and lots of Americans were going to die."[33] Black was the director of the CIA's Counterterrorism Center, and he went to considerable lengths to keep the Bush-Cheney administration abreast of developments as they occurred. He would later reveal his astonishment that the administration had ignored the increasing amount of credible intelligence that had been presented to it, a situation so bizarre that he likened it to a *Twilight Zone* episode.[34]

During this period, Richard Clarke also warned National Security Advisor Condoleezza Rice about the forthcoming terrorist assaults. He was dismayed that the Bush administration was not taking bold action to block them. "When these attacks occur, as they likely will, we will wonder what more we could have done to stop them," Clarke told Rice.[35]

Not surprisingly, the months of June and July would witness still more intelligence alerts from domestic sources and foreign agencies, even as a television station in an Arabic nation broadcast a news report on the subject. By all accounts, it was a nerve-wracking summer in intel circles. "One al Qaeda intelligence report warned that something 'very, very, very, very' big was about to happen, and most of Bin Ladin's network was reportedly anticipating the attack," reported *The 9/11 Commission Report*.[36] Distraught at the prospect of the fast-approaching catastrophe, the CIA's George Tenet, Director of National Intelligence, considered tendering his resignation so that he could alert the public.[37]

In his 2007 memoir, *At the Center of the Storm: My Years at the CIA*, Tenet recounts a July 10, 2001, meeting that included Richard Clarke,

Condoleezza Rice, and Rich Blee, who was the chief of the CIA's al-Qaeda unit. "The attack will be 'spectacular,' Rich told Condi [Rice] and the others, and it will be designed to inflict mass casualties against U.S. facilities and interests. 'Attack preparations have been made.... Multiple and simultaneous attacks are possible, and they will occur with little or no warning.'"[38] It was Blee's recommendation that the United States take preemptive action against bin Laden on the militant's home turf so as to avert the impending bloodbath on American soil. Confirming the uniformity of such dire predictions were the findings of the 9/11 Commission's investigation. "The intelligence reporting consistently described the upcoming attacks as occurring on a calamitous level, indicating that they would cause the world to be in turmoil and that they would consist of possibly multiple—but not necessarily simultaneous—attacks."[39]

It was also in July 2001 that the FBI office in Phoenix relayed to Washington, D.C., its concerns about the Middle Eastern men who had been seeking flight training in the city, a communiqué that alluded to Osama bin Laden. "[T]he agents recommended an urgent nationwide review of flight schools 'for any information that supports Phoenix's suspicions' of a terrorist connection," reported ABC News.[40] In certain respects, the FBI warning dovetailed with the contents of a classified document that would be hand-delivered to President Bush on August 6, 2001, for a special intelligence briefing at his ranch in Crawford, Texas.

"Bin Ladin Determined to Strike in US" was the title of the Presidential Daily Brief on this date.[41] The CIA-prepared document warned that the United States had received intelligence indicating that a group of al-Qaeda members was operating in, and planning to attack, the United States. The report also referred to Osama bin Laden's statements in which he made known his desire to stage terrorist operations inside the United States, singling out Washington, D.C., in the process. But there was one item, based on fresh intelligence gathered by the FBI, that eclipsed the others. "FBI information," the brief stated, "indicates patterns of suspicious activity in this country consistent with preparations for hijackings or other types of attacks, including recent surveillance of federal buildings in New York."[42]

When grilled by the 9/11 Commission in August 2004, Condoleezza Rice dismissed the CIA warning to the president. She described the document, which was still classified at the time of the hearing, as "historical information based on old reporting—there was no new threat information."[43] President Bush also appeared before the Commission, albeit on the condition that he not be questioned under oath, and he too characterized the brief as "historical."[44] Subsequent to this, the 9/11 Commission called for the document to be declassified and made available to the public, whereupon its portrayal as "old news" was roundly challenged. "In a single 17-sentence document," reported the *New York Times*, "the intelligence briefing delivered to President Bush in August 2001 spells out the *who*, hints at the *what* and points towards the *where* of the terrorist attacks on New York and Washington that followed 36 days later" (italics added).[45]

While the question remains as to why the Bush-Cheney administration did not act more decisively to protect the nation in the run-up to September 11, one thing is certain: it cannot be ascribed to a dearth of intelligence. Although the federal agencies that were in possession of crucial information during the spring and summer of 2001 did not always share it with other government organizations that likewise dealt with security matters, the sheer amount of credible and consistent intelligence was sufficient for any reasonable person to conclude that an extraordinary assault on the American people was just around the corner. As the director of National Intelligence stated, "The system was blinking red."[46]

THE ATTACKS

It was during those thirty-six days after the Daily Presidential Brief was entrusted to President Bush—and while the system was blinking red—that the four hijacker-pilots and fifteen muscle hijackers wrapped up their preparations. For the former, this included traveling round-trip to Las Vegas in mid-August, with each man flying on an airliner similar to the one he would be piloting on the day of the attacks. Two weeks later—it was now the first week of September—all nineteen terrorists began moving into position in the northeastern United States, booking hotel rooms near the airports from which the targeted airliners would be departing. The night of September 10 would find the men in Massachusetts, Virginia, and New Jersey, with the exception of Mohamed Atta and a fellow hijacker. This pair stayed overnight in Portland, Maine, where they ate pizza and shopped at a Walmart.[47] It has been speculated that Atta may have met with unknown supporters in that city, suggesting the existence of an underground al-Qaeda network operating in the United States.[48] At dawn, Atta and his accomplice would drive to the Portland International Jetport for a commuter flight to Boston.

Regarding the plan of attack, the strategy called for the terrorists to commandeer four aircraft shortly after takeoff, three of which would be bound for Los Angeles and the remaining one headed for San Francisco. West Coast destinations were presumably selected because the airliners would be heavily fueled for the coast-to-coast flights and thus more lethal upon impact. It was akin to the Japanese military's practice of loading extra fuel, and often explosives, onto kamikaze aircraft so as to cause maximal damage to the targets.

The airliners that the al-Qaeda group planned to seize consisted of the following:

- American Airlines (AA) Flight 11. A Boeing 767, it would carry 92 passengers and crew and was scheduled to depart from Logan International Airport in Boston at 7:59 a.m.
- United Airlines (UA) Flight 175. A Boeing 767, it would carry 65 passengers and crew and was scheduled to depart from Logan International Airport at 8:14 a.m.
- American Airlines (AA) Flight 77. A Boeing 757, it would carry 64 passengers and crew and was scheduled to depart from Dulles International Airport near Washington, D.C., at 8:20 a.m.
- United Airlines (UA) Flight 93. A Boeing 757, it would carry 44 passengers and crew and was scheduled to depart from Newark International Airport in Newark, New Jersey, at 8:00 a.m. Due to a delay, it would depart at 8:42 a.m.

The iconic buildings that al-Qaeda set out to obliterate would include both the North Tower and South Tower of the World Trade Center, which Mohamed Atta and his corps of hijackers referred to as the "Faculty of Architecture" in their communications.[49] Also in the crosshairs would be the Pentagon, which they code-named the "Faculty of Fine Arts," and the Capitol Building, designated the "Faculty of Law." The former two structures were situated in Manhattan, and the latter pair was located in or near Washington, D.C.

Airport Screening Issues

On the morning of 9/11, the four teams of hijackers began arriving at their assigned airports. Because Atta and his fellow hijacker had spent the night in Maine, it would be necessary for them to fly to Massachusetts to join the other members of their unit. It was at this early point that Atta encountered an obstacle, one that materialized at a U.S. Airways ticket counter at Portland International Jetport.

Here, the ticket agent explained to the hijacker that although he, Atta, would be passing through a security checkpoint in Portland, he would nevertheless be required to do it again in Boston. This angered Atta, his face flushed with emotion. "I said to myself, 'If this guy doesn't look like an Arab terrorist, then nothing does,'" recalled the ticket agent.[50]

It was also at the Portland facility that Atta was flagged by a program known as CAPPS (Computer-Assisted Passenger Prescreening System), the purpose of which was to detect suspicious travelers who might pose a bomb threat. In keeping with protocol, security officers were to examine such a passenger's checked baggage for explosives, following which, if cleared, it would be loaded onto the aircraft. But it would be loaded only after the passenger was already onboard. The reason was to ensure that the bag in question did not travel unaccompanied. In Atta's case, he was soon permitted to continue his trip to Boston.

In that city, an identical system was operational at Logan International Airport, where CAPPS flagged three hijackers. At the Newark airport, one more was singled out, while the Dulles program also identified three hijackers as dubious. In that none of the men's checked luggage was found to contain explosive materials, all were allowed to proceed with their flights unimpeded.

A note on metal detectors: two hijackers set off the magnetometers at the Dulles airport; one was subjected to a scan using a hand wand. Both men were subsequently allowed to board the plane, even though it had not been determined what triggered the magnetometers.

A review of Dulles surveillance videos ordered by the 9/11 Commission was critical of the procedure's implementation. "We asked a screening expert to review the videotape of the hand-wanding, and he found the quality of the screener's work to have been 'marginal at best,'" the commission reported. "The screener should have 'resolved' what set off the alarm."[51]

Shortly thereafter, the four airliners began departing for what were expected to be routine daily flights to Los Angeles and San Francisco.

American Airlines Flight 11

The first to take off was American Airlines Flight 11, departing from Boston at 7:59 a.m. On this sunny Tuesday morning, no one could have predicted that the airliner would soon be weaponized, that it would be transformed into a 200-ton guided missile—no one, that is, except Mohamed Atta and his four Saudi accomplices who were on the flight with him.

After a smooth departure, the Boeing 767 reached its initial cruising altitude of 29,000 feet, while the cabin crews turned off the "Fasten Seatbelt" signs and set about preparing for cabin service. Moments later, an air traffic controller at Boston Center directed the captain, John Ogonowski, to climb to 35,000 feet. The time was 8:14 a.m.

It was around this time, investigators believe, that an American-Israeli passenger seated in the business-class section began to suspect that a hijacking was in the works, and he confronted the al-Qaeda operatives.[52] Thirty-one years old, Danny Lewin was an MIT-educated mathematician and entrepreneur who had served as a captain in the Israeli Defense Forces. Seated in front of him were Mohamed Atta and an accomplice, and seated behind him was another terrorist. Presumably, Lewin, who was fluent in the Arabic language, overheard and understood what the men were saying to one another. "According to flight attendants' [phone] calls relayed to authorities on the ground," writes Todd Leopold, "the first passenger to be killed was seated in 9B."[53] It was Lewin's seat number. His throat had been slashed.[54]

A pair of muscle hijackers now forced their way into the locked cockpit, stabbing two flight attendants in the process. Razors and box cutters are believed to have been the hijackers' weapons, along with small knives hidden in cigarette lighters.[55] Once the cockpit door was open, Atta arrived and seized control of the airliner.

With the captain incapacitated—he most likely was murdered—the cockpit ceased responding to ground requests and the Mode-C transponder stopped transmitting. As intended, the latter made it difficult for Boston Center to monitor the plane's flight level, or altitude.

Shouting that they had a bomb, the muscle hijackers next released a chemical agent, presumably Mace or pepper spray, into the first-class cabin, forcing the passengers and crew to make their way to the rear of the aircraft. In so doing, the terrorists were confining them to a single, manageable area far away from the flight deck. Furthermore, the chemical agent would keep them in place, serving as barrier separating the cockpit and the coach seats. All of these actions were carried out within five minutes of the takeover.

At Boston Center, in the meantime, the controller who was tracking Flight 11 was trying, futilely, to restore contact with Captain Ogonowski. It was at this juncture that Betty Ong, a flight attendant on the hijacked plane, phoned an American Airlines reservations office in North Carolina to declare a midair emergency. A forty-five-year-old Chinese-American from the Chinatown neighborhood of San Francisco, Ong was drawing on her vigor and ingenuity, two qualities she had demonstrated often during her fourteen years at American Airlines. "This was the first of several occasions on 9/11 when flight attendants took action outside the scope of their training, which emphasized that in a hijacking, they were to communicate with the cockpit crew," reads *The 9/11 Commission Report*.[56] Because of Ong's emergency call, which lasted twenty-five minutes, she became the person who would alert the world to the maelstrom in the skies. In turn, her running commentary would help those on the ground better manage the national crisis that was unfolding.

"The cockpit is not answering, somebody's stabbed in business class," Ong told the airline's operations specialist, "and I think there's Mace ... we can't breathe.... I think we're getting hijacked."[57] Ong proceeded to report

EIGHT. *Aircraft as Guided Missiles* 257

on the other victims, among them the purser, who was unconscious and receiving oxygen. Throughout the lengthy conversation, the first-class cabin remained contaminated by the chemical agent.

At Boston Center, the controller persisted in his efforts to reach the captain of Flight 11 but to no avail. Then, a voice from the flight deck broke through the static at 8:24 a.m. "We have some planes," Atta said. "Just stay quiet and we'll be okay. We are returning to the airport."[58] Atta, it seems, had broadcast his ominous message not only to those on board the airliner but inadvertently to Boston Center as well. When the air traffic controller responded to it, Atta did not reply but instead issued another warning. "If you try to make any moves," he said, "you will injure yourself and the airplane."[59] The Boeing 767, which was flying over Albany, New York, began turning southward toward Manhattan. The time was 8:26 a.m.[60]

As it happened, Boston Center did not yet know about Betty Ong's emergency call to the American Airlines operations specialist, but the air traffic controller had already concluded that Flight 11 had been commandeered. The signs were obvious: the transponder had been shut off, the cockpit had remained silent, and the aircraft's path, as monitored by primary radar, had begun to veer from the flight plan. Although Boston Center knew the commercial airliner had been seized, it did not inform the U.S. Department of Defense, specifically NORAD's Northeast Air Defense Sector (NEADS), until the voice of Mohamed Atta confirmed the takeover. And this brings us to an important point.

Prior to September 11, the hijacking protocols that had been created by the FAA and NORAD (North American Aerospace Defense Command) were based on two unwavering beliefs. The first was that "aircraft pilots would remain at the controls and would be able to communicate their predicament to air traffic controllers," writes Priscilla D. Jones. The second centered on the assumption of self-preservation, namely that "hijackers did not know how to fly planes and did not want to die."[61] Both assumptions would be negated on this day.

Also relevant, NORAD, established in 1958, was designed to patrol the skies externally, not internally. Its purpose was to detect threats originating outside of U.S. and Canadian borders, such as missiles headed toward the North American continent. "NORAD did not anticipate attacks in which civil airliners would be hijacked from domestic airports and turned into weapons against US targets," writes Adam J. Hebert.[62] And so, just as the kamikazes changed the face of the Pacific war through their willingness to kill themselves in order to kill the enemy, so too would Osama bin Laden, Mohamed Atta, and their teams of operatives redefine the tactics of aviation terrorism.

It was against this confounding backdrop that the FAA alerted NEADS to the Flight 11 hijacking at approximately 8:38 a.m. Eight minutes later, the military issued a scramble order, which entailed two F-15 fighter jets from Otis Air National Guard Base in Falmouth, Massachusetts. Since the airliner's transponder had been turned off, however, and therefore the fighter pilots had no target, they were ordered to "hold as needed" in military airspace off the coast of Long Island.[63] Regarding American Airlines Flight 11, it was closing in on the North Tower of the World Trade Center. Because the building was wider than an airport runway, Atta would have sufficient room to breach the structure.

"I see water and buildings," shouted Madeleine "Amy" Sweeney, another flight attendant on Flight 11, who was relaying information to a ground manager in Boston.[64] The Boeing 767 was now soaring low over the Hudson River toward the World Trade Center. "Something is wrong. We are in a rapid descent," Sweeney cried out. "[W]e are all over the place."[65]

Betty Ong was also on the phone. "Oh my God, the flight, it's going down, it's going down," she shouted. And then Ong made a last request. "She did ask for us to pray for her," said the operations specialist.[66]

American Airlines Flight 11 flew into the North Tower at 8:46 a.m., slicing through floors 93–99 of the 101-story structure. The plane was loaded with 20,000 pounds of fuel and was traveling at 494 miles an hour, based on government estimates, a speed that is much faster than the federal limits imposed on aircraft traveling at such low altitudes.[67]

On impact, the airliner exploded and a massive fireball erupted, one composed of burning jet fuel, and it shot downward through the elevator shafts to the lobby. Black smoke billowed, fiery debris showered the streets below, and the stairwells above the 92nd floor became inaccessible.

United Airlines Flight 175

As Tower One blazed, the FAA notified NEADS of a second hijacking. United Airlines Flight 175 had departed from Boston Logan fifteen minutes after the American Airlines flight, altered its course without permission, and stopped communicating with air traffic controllers. It was between 8:42 a.m. and 8:46 a.m. that the takeover commenced.

Based on credit card receipts, it appears that the five hijackers were armed with short blade knives, box cutters, a Cliphanger Viper (knife), and an Imperial Tradesman Dual Edge knife.[68] They began by killing both the pilot and copilot, stabbing some of the flight attendants, spraying Mace, and claiming to possess a bomb. Paralleling the American Airlines hijacking minutes earlier, the terrorists next forced the passengers and crew to the rear of the aircraft.

As it happened, a few of the passengers were able to phone their loved ones during this time. Among these passengers was a man who called his mother and told her that the passengers were considering storming the flight deck. Another passenger, Peter Burton Hanson, called his father and instructed him to report the hijacking to United Airlines. Then, at 9:00 a.m., as Flight 175 headed toward Lower Manhattan, Hanson made another call, his last one. "It's getting bad, Dad," he said. "Passengers are throwing up and getting sick—the plane is making jerky movements.... I think we are going down.... Don't worry, Dad—if it happens, it'll be very fast—my God, my God."[69] Hanson's father heard a woman scream, then the call ended abruptly.[70] It was 9:03 a.m., and United Airlines Flight 175 now slammed into the South Tower at 586 miles an hour, an unheard-of speed for a Boeing 767 at such a low altitude. "It's off the chart," says Liz Verdier of the Boeing Company.[71] Numerous engineers have since voiced their surprise that the airliner actually made it to the South Tower rather than disintegrating in flight. As in the case of the North Tower, the crash triggered a monstrous explosion.

American Airlines Flight 77

Watching on television as United Airlines Flight 175 crashed into the South Tower were military leaders at the Pentagon. Little did they know that a third airliner would soon be arriving on their own doorstep.

In the interim, Indianapolis Center, which was tracking American Airlines Flight 77 on its westward journey to Los Angeles, noticed the aircraft's signal vanish from radar and its transponder cease transmitting. The time was 8:56 a.m. Without success, flight control tried to contact the pilot; the assumption was that the commercial jet was experiencing an electrical malfunction. As it turned out, twenty-four minutes would pass before Indianapolis Center would learn that two commercial airliners had crashed into the World Trade Center, that suicide hijackings were underway in the United States. Of course, this news placed Flight 77's unusual actions in a whole new light. The FAA also grounded all air traffic across the nation at this juncture.[72]

During the radio silence, the hijacker-pilot of the westward Flight 77 made a U-turn, meaning the aircraft was heading back toward the East Coast. Seven minutes later, a controller at Dulles spotted it on radar, a new "blip" that was moving at an unusually high rate of speed toward Washington, D.C. Langley Air Force Base would now dispatch jet fighters but from 150 miles away.

Without delay, flight control at nearby Reagan National Airport instructed the pilot of a C-130H cargo plane, already airborne in the region, to identify the phantom aircraft and follow it. It proved too late to make a difference, however. "[L]ooks like that aircraft crashed into the Pentagon, sir," the pilot reported.[73]

At 9:37 a.m., American Airlines Flight 77 slammed into the west side of the Pentagon and exploded. The plane was traveling at 530 miles an hour. The hijacker-pilot, Hani Hanjour, the Saudi terrorist who had trained so poorly in San Diego and Arizona, had completed his mission successfully. Hanjour was also the man that a JetTech manager in Phoenix, on three occasions, had reported to the FAA.

As could be predicted, the Boeing 757's collision with the Pentagon was ruinous and it traumatized scores of those who survived it. "For people in the immediate vicinity of impact and along the path of destruction the first minutes brought surprise, disorientation, fear, panic, danger, and death," write Alfred Goldbert and his colleagues at the U.S. Department of Defense. "They faced a host of instant hazards: utter darkness, toxic smoke, fire, immense heat, piles of hot debris, collapsed ceilings and walls, live electric wires, blocked exits and stairways, and the beginning of a structural collapse within the critical zone."[74]

Army major Craig Collier was among the officers who were on the job at the Pentagon, the headquarters of the Defense Department. "[T]he building jolted and we heard a muffled boom. Some loose plaster and dust fell from the ceiling," Collier recalled. "All of my peers in the area are experienced combat arms officers, and we quickly agreed that it sounded and felt like a bomb."[75]

Dr. Betty Maxfield was also in the Pentagon, and she recalled watching as a fireball rolled through the room in which she was talking to a coworker. "Everything went black," Maxfield said. "The smoke was very, very dense. And the burning ceiling tiles began to drop on us like hot cinder balls." Fortunately, Maxfield would escape without serious injury. "The only damage to me personally was that the hair on my arms ... [was] burned."[76]

First responders descended on the scene to extinguish the inferno and rescue those trapped inside the building. Five stories of the Pentagon's western flank would collapse.

United Airlines Flight 93

The one commercial jet that terrorists would fail to convert into a guided missile was scheduled to depart from Newark at 8:00 a.m., but due to congestion at the airport, it would not take off until 8:43 a.m. This unanticipated change in departure time may have played a role in the ensuing

EIGHT. Aircraft as Guided Missiles

events, since it delayed the hijacking and thus allowed the captain and first officer of United Airlines Flight 93, the fourth targeted aircraft, to learn about the previous hijackings and to be on their guard.

With a light passenger load—the cabins were only 20 percent filled—Flight 93 was still on the tarmac when the al-Qaeda plot commenced. By the time the United airliner was airborne, hijackers had already commandeered the two commercial carriers flying out of Boston Logan, one of which had just sliced into the North Tower in Manhattan. Even so, neither the passengers nor crew of Flight 93 knew about these startling developments; forty minutes would elapse before they would first hear about them. Until then, the Boeing 757 would travel westward, uneventfully, over Pennsylvania and Ohio at a cruising altitude of 35,000 feet.

In the first-class cabin, the three muscle hijackers and the hijacker-pilot, Ziad Jarrah, had taken seats but not together. In their pockets were red bandanas, which they would wear as headbands once the attack was underway. Unlike the three earlier hijackings, the United 93 takeover would not begin when the seatbelt sign was turned off. While the reason may never be known, it is plausible that Jarrah, the leader of the terrorist team, may have contemplated aborting the mission. He may have believed that Flight 93's prolonged delay at the Newark airport had eliminated the element of surprise and jeopardized the team's plan.

At 9:22 a.m., the wife of Flight 93's first officer, concerned about her husband's safety, contacted United Airlines and asked that they send him a text message. It was the first notification the flight deck would receive about the aerial terrorist operation that was in progress on the East Coast. Two minutes later, Jason Dahl, the captain, received an official warning from a United Airlines dispatcher. "BEWARE OF ANY COCKPIT INTRUSION," it stated. "TWO AIRCRAFT IN NY, HIT TRADE CNTER BLDS."[77] The captain responded by asking that the dispatcher confirm the message.

Although the precise order of events is unclear, we do know that the four hijackers now launched their assault by stabbing a passenger, forcing the remaining passengers to the rear of the aircraft, and breaking into the cockpit. At 9:28 a.m., Cleveland Center, which was tracking the airliner and was unaware of the cockpit breach, watched as Flight 93's altitude dropped nearly 700 feet in thirty seconds. "Mayday!" shouted the captain or first officer during the unauthorized, precipitous descent.[78] And the yelling persisted. "[G]et out of here—get out of here—get out of here!"[79] And then, for the next thirty-five minutes, radio transmissions became patchy.

As in the previous takeovers, the hijacker-pilot accessed the public-address system, declared that a bomb was on board, and ordered everyone to remain seated. Horrified, the passengers on Flight 93 began placing phone calls, nearly forty of them, and mostly by Airfone. The conversations furnished details about the aircraft, the terrorists and their apparent strategy, and eventually the passengers' own plan of action.

During this time, a flight attendant, Sandy Bradshaw, conversed with a United Airlines maintenance facility in San Francisco; the manager later described Bradshaw's voice as "shockingly calm."[80] Bradshaw revealed that the terrorists had just murdered a flight attendant.

Because the World Trade Center attacks were, at this juncture, being reported by the news media, those trapped on Flight 93 learned from friends and relatives about the three airliners crashing into the Manhattan skyscrapers and the Pentagon. Those on board evidently deduced that the Boeing 767 on which they were traveling would likely be used as a missile as well. Although it was undoubtedly a harrowing realization, it did prompt several passengers and flight attendants to become proactive in taking control of their collective fate. Based on the information gleaned during their phone conversations, they hatched a plan that would entail raiding the cockpit, disabling the terrorists, then either landing the plane with guidance from Cleveland Center or downing the aircraft to prevent it from striking a building.

In the galley, passengers set about preparing containers of hot water (their intention was to scald the hijackers) and creating other makeshift weapons. One man, Jeremy Glick, who was speaking to his wife on the phone, jokingly told her that four male passengers were "going to get the butter knives."[81] He was trying to ease her distress, it was surmised.[82]

Among those who would rush the flight deck was thirty-one-year-old Mark Bingham. A gay rugby champion and public relations executive, Bingham had founded a technology PR firm, the Bingham Group, with offices in San Francisco and New York City. "Calm, controlled, matter-of-fact, and focused" are the words his mother used to describe his voice during their brief conversation.[83]

Another passenger, Todd Beamer, was a thirty-two-year-old account manager at a software firm. Contacting an Airfone operator, he reported the hijacking and relayed the condition of the flight crew. "The captain and first officer were lying on the floor of the first-class cabin and were injured or possibly dead," recalled the operator whom Beamer updated.[84] Then, after asking the operator to join him in reciting the Lord's Prayer, Beamer addressed his fellow passengers. "Let's roll," he said.[85] He made it a point to leave open the phone connection throughout the remainder of Flight 93's ordeal so it would be audible to those on the ground.

A half an hour after the al-Qaeda terrorists captured the cockpit, the team of passengers moved into action. "Everyone's running up to first class," Sandy Bradshaw told her husband. "I've got to go."[86] The group descended on the cockpit at 9:58 a.m., and for the next five minutes, the brawl on the

EIGHT. *Aircraft as Guided Missiles* 263

flight deck was transmitted to controllers on the ground. The sounds of yelling, fighting, and shrieking in pain were ongoing, accompanied by loud thumps and the crash of breaking glass, presumably plates and drinking glasses.

Over and again, Ziad Jarrah rolled the airliner, trying to unbalance those who were overpowering him and his accomplices. At one point, he even pitched the aircraft's nose into a dive. Then, through the din of the cockpit combat came the voice of an English-speaking man shouting, "Let's get them," along with that of Jarrah proclaiming "Allah is the greatest!"[87] The last word received by Cleveland Center was from one of the native English speakers. "NO!" yelled the man.[88]

United Airlines Flight 93 crashed into a field near a small town in Pennsylvania at 10:03 a.m. Since it had been loaded with nearly 49,000 pounds of fuel for the nonstop flight to California, the explosion was formidable. Three miles away from the crash site, the residents of Shanksville heard and felt the Boeing 757's impact. As a precaution, teachers at a local school—the building was shaking and the window panes rattling—instructed their students to take shelter under their desks.

In the end, the intrepid men and women on Flight 93 had prevented the airliner from being used as a weapon of war. No buildings were struck and no one on the ground was injured or killed. Unfortunately, the airliner's passengers and crew did not survive.

AFTERMATH OF SEPTEMBER 11

The harm to the United States was unprecedented, both emotionally and economically. In addition to the deaths on Flight 93, nearly 3,000 people perished when the two aircraft slammed into the Twin Towers, which collapsed soon thereafter. Among this number were an estimated 200 people who leapt to their deaths as well as 403 first responders who died while attempting to extinguish the flames and rescue those trapped inside the burning buildings.[89]

In economic terms, the cost to replace the World Trade Center was estimated to be around four billion dollars, according to the Institute for the Analysis of Global Security.[90] And that was just the start. The City of New York suffered a nearly $100 billion loss owing to the cost of the clean-up, secondary infrastructure damage, and lost jobs and lost taxes.[91]

Regarding the Pentagon, 189 people were killed in the attack, most of them instantly or within minutes of the airliner's impact. In the edifice itself, 125 individuals died, while sixty-four passengers and crew on Flight

77 expired.⁹² Damage to the Pentagon was estimated to reach one billion dollars.⁹³

"Letter to the American People"

Months after the September 11 operation, Osama bin Laden, still in hiding, released a statement. It was already known, of course, that al-Qaeda's decision to launch the offensive was grounded in Islamic extremism, a radicalism that emerged from a confluence of events over the decades. "Islamic extremism was stirred by the Iranian Revolution, the Soviet invasion of Afghanistan and the assassination of the Egyptian president," writes Cara Reed.⁹⁴ The mounting influence of Western secularism and capitalism in the Middle East further alienated Islamic militants, as did the long-standing U.S. support for the State of Israel. Then, too, the American military operations carried out in the Middle East, such as the Gulf War and the U.S. intervention in Somalia, compounded the contempt.⁹⁵

For Osama bin Laden, a citizen of Saudi Arabia until he was banished in 1991, it was a rage that was fueled by the U.S. military presence in his homeland. The Saudis, it seems, had initially invited American troops to be a part of an international force, one intended to help shield Saudi oil fields from Iraqi aggressors. "Bin Laden—like many Muslims—consider[ed] the presence of these armed infidels in Saudi Arabia the greatest possible desecration of the holy land," writes David Plotz.⁹⁶

So it was that the fugitive terrorist posted a "Letter to the American People" on Arabic-language websites, some of which also published bomb-making instructions and materials on biological and chemical weapons.⁹⁷ In the document, bin Laden demanded that the United States leave the Middle East, stop interfering in the region's political affairs, and halt its support for Israel.⁹⁸ He also insisted that the United States, if it hoped to avoid future terror attacks, admit that, as a nation, it was immoral. "We call you to be a people of manners, principles, honour, and purity; to reject the immoral acts of fornication, homosexuality, intoxicants, gambling's [sic], and trading with interest."⁹⁹ And he stipulated that the American people adopt Islam.¹⁰⁰

Of course, the United States' response to the 9/11 attacks would not be to indulge bin Laden but rather to eliminate him. To this end, the Bush-Cheney administration launched a military operation in Afghanistan designed to decimate the Taliban, which was providing safe haven to both the fugitive and al-Qaeda. Although the U.S.-led coalition did succeed in toppling the regime, bin Laden eluded capture.

EIGHT. Aircraft as Guided Missiles

Unfortunately, the United States next invaded and occupied Iraq, which had played no role in the 9/11 attacks. The Bush-Cheney administration's pretext: Iraq was manufacturing weapons of mass destruction to be used against the American homeland. In reality, there was no evidence to support such a far-reaching claim, according to the UN weapons inspectors who were on the ground in Iraq.[101] Ultimately, the attack on the Middle Eastern nation, which was illegal under international law, "led to a near-decade of civil war and occupation, no discovery of weapons of mass destruction, the deaths of more than 4,400 American troops and an estimated 300,000 Iraqis," write Amna Nawaz and Dan Sagalyn.[102] Iraq was reduced to ruins, and the United States became an even greater object of disdain in the Middle East.

As for bin Laden, he would meet his fate on May 2, 2011, a decade after the World Trade Center and Pentagon attacks, when SEAL Team Six located and liquidated him at his compound in Abbottabad, Pakistan. "[J]ustice has been done," said President Barack Obama when announcing the death.[103]

Closer to home, the September 11 aftermath would include a string of new legislation. Among other controversial features, these laws would permit "eavesdropping on U.S. citizens without a court order, and [setting] up the detention camp at Guantanamo Bay, Cuba," states the Council on Foreign Relations.[104] The legislation would also establish the Department of Homeland Security, a Cabinet-level department that would combine all or portions of twenty-two federal agencies into a single, integrated entity that would be responsible for coordinating national, state, local, and private efforts to ensure security preparedness and enhance information-sharing. And within two months of the attacks, the Transportation Security Administration would come into existence and adopt a layered approach to ensure that transportation in the United States was safer and more efficient.

As a part of the TSA's mission, federal agents would now take control of security screening at all U.S. airports, X-ray machines and metal detectors would be employed more frequently and adeptly, cockpit doors would be fortified to the point of impenetrability, air marshals would vastly increase in number, and pilots would be authorized to carry weapons on commercial airliners through the Federal Flight Deck Officers program. Additionally, the national no-fly list would be updated and significantly expanded and programs would be created to accommodate "trusted travelers," expediting their passage through airport security procedures. Part I of this book provides more information about the establishment, development, and responsibilities of both the DHS and the TSA.

Further Improvements

As it stands, the numerous methods of enhancing passenger safety and security that were devised after the September 11 attacks have evolved over time, and today they are contributing to the protection of the public in unforeseen ways. "[A]fter 9/11, because of all the government money that funneled through the TSA and its centers of innovation, you saw people pitching different types of technology that changed aviation security," writes Mike Hofman, "and we now see that innovation being used in all different kinds of industries."[105]

Relevant to air travel, some of the above-mentioned advances are now being applied to passenger identification and verification. In particular, emergent facial, iris, and retinal scanning technologies are in use that do not require a traveler to be in close proximity to, or have direct physical contact with, airline staff or security officers. As a result, the risk of interpersonal transmission of viruses and bacteria during the validation process is diminished or eliminated. Without a doubt, such biometric technologies serve a valuable public health function in our post–Covid era, one in which Covid mutations or novel and potentially lethal pathogens may continue to materialize from time to time.

In that the 9/11 strikes marked the first time that commercial airliners had been weaponized against the continental United States, the federal government, as well as private-sector stakeholders, also set out to evaluate and improve existing methods of protecting those buildings considered to be high-value terrorist targets. As a part of this initiative, the Federal Emergency Management Agency (FEMA) published a manual after the al-Qaeda attacks, a guidebook intended to help mitigate the damage that could result from future terrorist strikes on critical structures.[106] The recommendations included intelligence-sharing to prevent an attack, dissuasion methods to render a potential target less accessible to extremists, and measures intended to reduce damage from a successful attack through materials "designed to withstand blast and chemical, biological, or radiological effects."[107]

To this end, structural engineers and their collaborators, acting on the third recommendation, expended considerable effort to determine why the Twin Towers had crumpled and the means by which such an occurrence could be averted. It was, in effect, a study in "progressive collapse," a process that has been aptly described by structural engineer Shih-Ho Chao.

"When the [Twin Towers'] steel columns were exposed to the high temperatures created by burning airplane fuel," writes Shih-Ho Chao, "they became weak, causing much of the structures' weight to be shifted onto other supports."[108] These secondary supports, in turn, were unable to shoulder the extra burden. The collapse was "like a row of dominoes falling down," write Thomas W. Eagar and Christopher Musso.[109]

Today, designated buildings are being constructed with sturdier, more flexible, and, of course, redundant support beams. The concrete in use is densely packed with metal so as to produce a material more capable of withstanding explosions. Yet such innovations do not mean that a high-rise structure can necessarily weather the impact of a Boeing jetliner. And this points to the need for additional approaches.

"It would be impractical to design buildings to withstand the fuel load induced by a burning commercial airliner," write Eagar and Musso. "Instead of saving the building, engineers and officials should focus on saving the lives of those inside by designing better safety and evacuation systems."[110] It is a viewpoint shared by FEMA and other organizations, which collectively emphasize the necessity of viable systems for the prompt alert and safe removal of those who may find themselves in buildings under attack.

Since the September 11 operation, the United States has not endured another aerial assault by a terrorist group with a political agenda. Furthermore, it is highly unlikely that such a well-organized series of strikes will recur any time soon in view of the numerous protections that have since been installed. Yet the possibility of a more modest attack does remain. Case in point: on February 18, 2010, Andrew Stack III, a stressed-out computer engineer who was angry at the Internal Revenue Service, flew his single-engine Piper Dakota into a seven-story building that housed IRS offices.[111] In the suicide attack, 190 employees were evacuated from the blazing structure, two were severely burned, and another worker was killed.[112] The incident occurred only seven miles from the Capitol Building in Austin, Texas.

In the end, the lesson is clear: from the Pacific Theatre in World War II to the urban landscapes of the twenty-first century, as long as there are aircraft in the skies, there will be a risk to those on the ground. It is merely a matter of degree.

Notes

1. T.R. *MacMechen and Carl Dienstbach*, "Fighting in the Air," *American Aeronaut* 1, no. 2 (September 1909): 60.
2. T.R. *MacMechen and Carl Dienstbach*, "Fighting in the Air," 60.
3. T.R. *MacMechen and Carl Dienstbach*, "Fighting in the Air," 61.
4. "Prominent Russians: Pyotr Nesterov," RT Russiapedia, accessed May 4, 2023, https://russiapedia.rt.com/prominent-russians/military/pyotr-nesterov/index.html.
5. Mark Lardas, *The Kamikaze Campaign 1944–45: Imperial Japan's Last Throw of the Dice* (Oxford: Osprey Publishing, Ltd., 2022), 29.
6. Bill Coombes, "Divine Wind: The Japanese Secret Weapon—*Kamikaze* Suicide

Attacks," *The Dispatch* 20, No. 1 (Spring 1995), http://rwebs.net/dispatch/output.asp?ArticleID=49.

7. "Mitsubishi A6M2 Zero," National Museum of the United States Air Force, accessed May 11, 2023, https://www.nationalmuseum.af.mil/Visit/Museum-Exhibits/Fact-Sheets/Display/Article/196313/mitsubishi-a6m2-zero/#:~:text=Beginning%20around%20October%201944%20during,aircraft%20for%20these%20suicide%20missions.

8. Mark Lardas, *The Kamikaze Campaign 1944-45*, 16.

9. Dan J. Wolf (writer, producer) and Jeff Wilburn (narrator), *The Battle of Okinawa in Color*, Smithsonian Channel, aired December 15, 2017, https://www.youtube.com/watch?v=PsI79eO23K0&t=131s.

10. Chalmer M. Roberts, "Did America Have to Drop the Bomb? With Japan Girding and American Lives at Stake, Truman Had No Choice," *Washington Post*, August 4, 1985, https://www.washingtonpost.com/archive/opinions/1985/08/04/did-america-have-to-drop-the-bombwith-japan-girding-and-american-lives-at-stake-truman-had-no-choice/f2e852d9-4e19-495a-b963-e32c2d9781fb/.

11. Dan J. Wolf (writer, producer) and Jeff Wilburn (narrator), *The Battle of Okinawa in Color*.

12. Bill Coombes, "Divine Wind," 1.

13. "Frontline: Inside the Terror Network—Who Were They?" PBS, accessed May 16, 2023, https://www.pbs.org/wgbh/pages/frontline/shows/network/personal/whowere.html.

14. Neil MacFarquhar, Jim Yardley, and Paul Zielbauer, "A NATION CHALLENGED: THE MASTERMIND; A Portrait of the Terrorist: From Shy Child to Single-Minded Killer," *New York Times*, October 10, 2001, https://www.nytimes.com/2001/10/10/world/nation-challenged-mastermind-portrait-terrorist-shy-child-single-minded-killer.html.

15. "SNNG: 9/11 Venice Flight School," *Sarasota Herald-Tribune*, May 12, 2015, https://www.youtube.com/watch?v=aibZJs89ABo.

16. "SNNG: 9/11 Venice Flight School."

17. Andy Johnson, "Flight School Owner Recalls Training 9/11 Hijackers," *CTV News*, September 11, 2012, https://www.ctvnews.ca/world/flight-school-owner-recalls-training-9-11-hijackers-1.951384?cache=yes%3FclipId%3D1723871.

18. National Commission on Terrorist Attacks upon the United States, *The 9/11 Commission Report, Executive Summary* (Washington, D.C., 2004), 224, https://www.9-11commission.gov/report/911Report.pdf.

19. Calvin Hughes (anchor), "Remembering 9/11: South Florida Was Home to Hijackers before the Attacks," Local10 (ABC), September 11, 2021, https://www.local10.com/news/local/2021/09/10/remembering-911-south-florida-was-home-to-hijackers-before-the-attacks/.

20. "Frontline: Inside the Terror Network—Who Were They?"

21. National Commission on Terrorist Attacks upon the United States, *The 9/11 Commission Report, Executive Summary*.

22. "FAA Received Alert about 9/11 Hijacker," ABC News, May 10, 2003, https://abcnews.go.com/U.S./story?id=91659&page=1#:~:text=W%20A%20S%20H%20I%20N%20G%20T%20O%20N%2C%20May%2010%20%E2%80%94%20Federal%20aviation,school%20and%20government%20officials%20say.

23. Joe Enea, "Old Time Crime: Arizona Was a Training Ground for the September 11th Attackers," KNXV-TV ABC-15 Arizona, September 10, 2021, https://www.abc15.com/news/crime/old-time-crime-arizona-was-a-training-ground-for-the-september-11th-attackers.

24. William M. Arkin, "9/11 Pilot Hani Hanjour Took Extra Flights to Check Out D.C. Airspace," *Newsweek*, August 10, 2021, https://www.newsweek.com/9-11-pilot-hani-hanjour-took-extra-flights-check-out-dc-airspace-1616398.

25. National Commission on Terrorist Attacks upon the United States, *The 9/11 Commission Report, Executive Summary*, 221–222.

26. "11 September: The Plot and the Plotters (CTC 2003-40044HC)," Central Intelligence Agency—Directorate of Intelligence, June 1, 2003, https://nsarchive.gwu.edu/document/24294-11-september-plot-and-plotters-ctc-2003-40044hc-central-intelligence-agency.

27. National Commission on Terrorist Attacks upon the United States, *The 9/11 Commission Report, Executive Summary*.

EIGHT. Aircraft as Guided Missiles   269

28. National Commission on Terrorist Attacks Upon the United States, *The 9/11 Commission Report, Executive Summary*.
29. David Rose, "Attackers Did Not Know They Were to Die," *The Guardian*, October 14, 2001, https://www.theguardian.com/world/2001/oct/14/terrorism.september111.
30. "Transcript of Usama bin Laden Video Tape," U.S. Department of Defense, November 2001, https://web.archive.org/web/20011214230828/http://www.defenselink.mil/news/Dec2001/d20011213ubl.pdf.
31. Gedeon Naudet and Jules Naudet (filmmakers), "The Spymasters—CIA in the Crosshairs," *Showtime Documentaries*, airdate May 2, 2016, https://www.cbsnews.com/video/48-hours-presents-the-spymasters-cia-in-the-crosshairs/#x.
32. National Commission on Terrorist Attacks Upon the United States, *The 9/11 Commission Report, Executive Summary*, 255.
33. Chris Whipple, "The Attacks Will Be Spectacular," *Politico Magazine*, November 12, 2015, https://www.politico.com/magazine/story/2015/11/cia-directors-documentary-911-bush-213353/#ixzz3rNFeL9Wb.
34. Chris Whipple, "The Attacks Will Be Spectacular."
35. National Commission on Terrorist Attacks Upon the United States, *The 9/11 Commission Report, Executive Summary*, 256.
36. National Commission on Terrorist Attacks Upon the United States, *The 9/11 Commission Report, Executive Summary*, 257.
37. National Commission on Terrorist Attacks Upon the United States, *The 9/11 Commission Report, Executive Summary*.
38. George Tenet, *At the Center of the Storm: My Years at the CIA* (New York: HarperCollins, 2007), 152.
39. National Commission on Terrorist Attacks Upon the United States, *The 9/11 Commission Report, Executive Summary*, 257.
40. ABC News, "Bush Warned of Hijackings Before 9-11," ABC News, May 15, 2002, https://abcnews.go.com/U.S./story?id=91651&page=1.
41. "Presidential Daily Brief: Bin Ladin Determined to Strike in U.S.," Office of the Director of National Intelligence, August 6, 2001, file:///C:/Users/MarcV/Downloads/Bin%20Laden%20Determine%20to%20Strike%20in%20US.pdf.
42. "Presidential Daily Brief: Bin Ladin Determined to Strike in U.S."
43. Philip Shenon, "THREATS AND RESPONSES: THE INQUIRY; 9/11 Panel Presses Rice on Early Warnings," *New York Times*, April 9, 2004, https://www.nytimes.com/2004/04/09/world/threats-and-responses-the-inquiry-9-11-panel-presses-rice-on-early-warnings.html.
44. National Commission on Terrorist Attacks Upon the United States, *The 9/11 Commission Report, Executive Summary*, 260.
45. Douglas Jehl, "A Warning, but Clear? White House Tries to Make the Point That New Details Add Up to Old News," *New York Times*, April 11, 2004, https://www.nytimes.com/2004/04/11/politics/a-warning-but-clear.html.
46. National Commission on Terrorist Attacks Upon the United States, *The 9/11 Commission Report, Executive Summary*, 259.
47. National Commission on Terrorist Attacks Upon the United States, *The 9/11 Commission Report, Executive Summary*.
48. "9/11 Mystery: What Was Atta Doing on 9/10?" NBC News, September 5, 2006, https://www.nbcnews.com/id/wbna14686192.
49. "11 September: The Plot and the Plotters."
50. "Ticket Agent Recalls Anger in Atta's Eyes," Associated Press, March 7, 2005, https://www.nbcnews.com/news/amp/wbna7117783.
51. National Commission on Terrorist Attacks Upon the United States, *The 9/11 Commission Report, Executive Summary*, 3.
52. National Commission on Terrorist Attacks Upon the United States, *The 9/11 Commission Report, Executive Summary*.
53. Todd Leopold, "The Legacy of Danny Lewin, the First Man to Die on 9/11," CNN, September 11, 2013, https://www.cnn.com/2013/09/09/tech/innovation/danny-lewin-9-11-akamai/index.html.

54. Eric Lichtblau, "Aboard Flight 11, a Chilling Voice," *Los Angeles Times*, September 20, 2001, https://www.latimes.com/archives/la-xpm-2001-sep-20-mn-47829-story.html.
55. Eric Lichtblau, "Aboard Flight 11, a Chilling Voice."
56. National Commission on Terrorist Attacks Upon the United States, *The 9/11 Commission Report, Executive Summary*, 5.
57. National Commission on Terrorist Attacks Upon the United States, *The 9/11 Commission Report, Executive Summary*, 5.
58. "The 9/11 Tapes: The Story in the Air," *New York Times*, September 7, 2011, https://archive.nytimes.com/www.nytimes.com/interactive/2011/09/08/nyregion/911-tapes.html?smid=nytcore-android-share.
59. "The 9/11 Tapes: The Story in the Air."
60. Priscilla D. Jones, "The First 109 Minutes: 9/11 and the U.S. Air Force," Air Force History and Museums Program, 2011 (updated 2018), https://media.defense.gov/2012/Sep/05/2001329941/-1/-1/1/First_109_Minutes(2018).pdf.
61. Priscilla D. Jones, "The First 109 Minutes: 9/11 and the U.S. Air Force."
62. Adam J. Hebert, "The Return of NORAD," *Air & Space Forces Magazine*, February 1, 2002, https://www.airandspaceforces.com/article/0202norad/.
63. National Commission on Terrorist Attacks Upon the United States, *The 9/11 Commission Report, Executive Summary*, 20.
64. Eric Lichtblau, "Aboard Flight 11, a Chilling Voice."
65. National Commission on Terrorist Attacks Upon the United States, *The 9/11 Commission Report, Executive Summary*, 6-7.
66. "9/11 Interviews: Transcription, Case #265D-NY-280350 (Betty Ong, Mark Bingham)," Federal Bureau of Investigation—The Vault, September 12, 2001, https://vault.fbi.gov/9-11%20Commission%20Report/9-11-interviews-2001-09-sep-04-of-08.
67. Brian Dakks, "Speed Likely Factor in WTC Collapse," CBS News, February 25, 2002, https://www.cbsnews.com/news/speed-likely-factor-in-wtc-collapse-25-02-2002/.
68. "Staff Report, August 26, 2004," National Archives—9/11 Commission Records, accessed June 8, 2023, https://www.archives.gov/files/research/9-11/staff-report-sept2005.pdf.
69. National Commission on Terrorist Attacks Upon the United States, *The 9/11 Commission Report, Executive Summary*, 8.
70. National Commission on Terrorist Attacks Upon the United States, *The 9/11 Commission Report, Executive Summary*.
71. Brian Dakks, "Speed Likely Factor in WTC Collapse."
72. National Commission on Terrorist Attacks Upon the United States, *The 9/11 Commission Report, Executive Summary*.
73. National Commission on Terrorist Attacks Upon the United States, *The 9/11 Commission Report, Executive Summary*, 26.
74. Alfred Goldberg, Sarandis Papadopoulos, Diane Putney, Nancy Berlage, and Rebecca Welch, *Defense Studies Series: Pentagon 9/11* (Washington, D.C.: Office of the Secretary of Defense, 2007), 25, https://history.defense.gov/Portals/70/Documents/pentagon/Pentagon9-11.pdf.
75. Alfred Goldberg, et al., "Defense Studies Series: Pentagon 9/11," 26.
76. Alfred Goldberg, et al., "Defense Studies Series: Pentagon 9/11," 40.
77. National Commission on Terrorist Attacks Upon the United States, *The 9/11 Commission Report, Executive Summary*, 616.
78. National Commission on Terrorist Attacks Upon the United States, *The 9/11 Commission Report, Executive Summary*, 616.
79. National Commission on Terrorist Attacks Upon the United States, *The 9/11 Commission Report, Executive Summary*, 616.
80. National Commission on Terrorist Attacks Upon the United States, *The 9/11 Commission Report, Executive Summary*, 619.
81. "Phone Calls from Flight 93," U.S. National Park Service, accessed June 17, 2023, https://www.nps.gov/flni/learn/historyculture/phone-calls-from-flight-93.htm.
82. "Phone Calls from Flight 93."
83. "Phone Calls from Flight 93."

EIGHT. Aircraft as Guided Missiles 271

84. "Phone Calls from Flight 93."
85. Ashlee Edwards, "List of the Crew and Passengers Aboard United Airlines Flight 93 on Sept. 11, 2001," ABC-27 News (WHTM), September 2, 2021, https://www.abc27.com/news/remembering-september-11/list-of-the-crew-and-passengers-aboard-united-airlines-flight-93-on-sept-11-2001/.
86. "Phone Calls from Flight 93."
87. "Phone Calls from Flight 93."
88. "Phone Calls from Flight 93."
89. History.com Editors, "September 11 Attacks," History Channel, March 23, 2023, https://www.history.com/topics/21st-century/9-11-attacks.
90. "How Much Did the September 11 Terrorist Attack Cost America?" Institute for the Analysis of Global Security, accessed on June 10, 2023, http://www.iags.org/costof911.html#:~:text=The%20destruction%20of%20major%20buildings,%2410%20billion%20 to%20%2413%20billion.
91. "How Much Did the September 11 Terrorist Attack Cost America?"
92. Alfred Goldberg, et al., "Defense Studies Series: Pentagon 9/11."
93. "How Much Did the September 11 Terrorist Attack Cost America?"
94. Cara Reed, "9/11: Causes and Lingering Consequences," Ohio State Impact, August 14, 2020, https://www.osu.edu/impact/research-and-innovation/hahn-september-11.
95. David Plotz, "What Does Osama Bin Laden Want?" *Slate*, September 14, 2001, https://slate.com/news-and-politics/2001/09/what-does-osama-bin-laden-want.html.
96. David Plotz, "What Does Osama Bin Laden Want?"
97. "Full Text: Bin Laden's 'Letter to America,'" *The Guardian*, November 24, 2002, https://www.theguardian.com/world/2002/nov/24/theobserver.
98. "November, 2002 Osama Bin Laden's Letter to America," Center for Online Judaic Studies, accessed June 18, 2023, https://cojs.org/november-2002-osama-bin-ladens-letter-america/.
99. "Full Text: Bin Laden's 'Letter to America.'"
100. "Full Text: Bin Laden's 'Letter to America.'"
101. World News, "Iraq War 10 Years Later: Where Are They Now? Hans Blix (U.N. Weapons Inspector)," NBC News, March 19, 2013, https://www.nbcnews.com/news/world/iraq-war-10-years-later-where-are-they-now-hans-flna1c8956460.
102. Amna Nawaz and Dan Sagalyn, "The Long-Lasting Impact of the U.S. Invasion of Iraq," PBS, March 29, 2023, https://www.pbs.org/newshour/show/the-long-lasting-impact-of-the-u-s-invasion-of-iraq.
103. Peter Baker, Helene Cooper, and Mark Mazzetti, "Bin Laden Is Dead, Obama Says," *New York Times*, May 1, 2011, https://www.nytimes.com/2011/05/02/world/asia/osama-bin-laden-is-killed.html.
104. "1999-2021: The U.S. War in Afghanistan," Council on Foreign Relations, accessed June 25, 2023, https://www.cfr.org/timeline/us-war-afghanistan.
105. Mike Hofman, "The Impact of 9/11 on Air Travel Prepared Us for a Post-COVID World," *Fortune Magazine*, September 11, 2012, https://fortune.com/2021/09/11/9-11-air-travel-impact-post-covid-20-years-later/.
106. "Reference Manual to Mitigate Potential Terrorist Attacks against Buildings (Risk Management Series #426)," FEMA/Emergency Preparedness & Response, December 2003, https://www.fema.gov/sites/default/files/2020-08/fema426_0.pdf.
107. "Reference Manual to Mitigate Potential Terrorist Attacks against Buildings," 9.
108. Shih-Ho Chao, "How Building Design Changed After 9/11," Associated Press, September 9, 2016, https://theconversation.com/how-building-design-changed-after-9-11-64580.
109. Thomas W. Eagar and Christopher Musso, "Why Did the World Trade Center Collapse? Science, Engineering, and Speculation," *Journal of the Minerals, Metals & Materials Society* 53, no. 12 (2001): 9.
110. Thomas W. Eagar and Christopher Musso, "Why Did the World Trade Center Collapse? Science, Engineering, and Speculation," 11.
111. Michael Brick, "Man Crashes Plane into Texas I.R.S. Office," *New York Times*, February 18, 2010, https://www.nytimes.com/2010/02/19/us/19crash.html.
112. CBS Austin Staff, "10 Years Ago, a Man Purposely Crashed His Plane into an

Austin IRS Office Building," CBS Austin, February 19, 2020, https://cbsaustin.com/news/local/10-years-ago-a-man-purposely-crashed-his-plane-into-an-austin-irs-office-building.

Bibliography

ABC News. "Bush Warned of Hijackings Before 9–11." ABC News, May 15, 2002. https://abcnews.go.com/U.S./story?id=91651&page=1.

Arkin, William M. "9/11 Pilot Hani Hanjour Took Extra Flights to Check Out D.C. Airspace." *Newsweek*, August 10, 2021. https://www.newsweek.com/9-11-pilot-hani-hanjour-took-extra-flights-check-out-dc-airspace-1616398.

Baker, Peter, Helene Cooper, and Mark Mazzetti. "Bin Laden Is Dead, Obama Says." *New York Times*, May 1, 2011. https://www.nytimes.com/2011/05/02/world/asia/osama-bin-laden-is-killed.html.

The Battle of Okinawa in Color. Wolf, Dan J. (writer, producer) and Jeff Wilburn (narrator). Smithsonian Channel, airdate December 15, 2017. https://www.youtube.com/watch?v=PsI79eO23K0&t=131s.

Brick, Michael. "Man Crashes Plane into Texas I.R.S. Office." *New York Times*, February 18, 2010. https://www.nytimes.com/2010/02/19/us/19crash.html.

CBS Austin Staff. "10 Years Ago, a Man Purposely Crashed His Plane into an Austin IRS Office Building." CBS Austin, February 19, 2020. https://cbsaustin.com/news/local/10-years-ago-a-man-purposely-crashed-his-plane-into-an-austin-irs-office-building.

Chao, Shih-Ho. "How Building Design Changed After 9/11." Associated Press, September 9, 2016. https://theconversation.com/how-building-design-changed-after-9-11-64580.

Coombes, Bill. "Divine Wind: The Japanese Secret Weapon—*Kamikaze* Suicide Attacks." *The Dispatch* 20, No. 1 (Spring 1995). http://rwebs.net/dispatch/output.asp?ArticleID=49.

Dakks, Brian. "Speed Likely Factor in WTC Collapse." CBS News, February 25, 2002. https://www.cbsnews.com/news/speed-likely-factor-in-wtc-collapse-25-02-2002/.

Eagar, Thomas W., and Christopher Musso. "Why Did the World Trade Center Collapse? Science, Engineering, and Speculation." *Journal of the Minerals, Metals & Materials Society* 53, no. 12 (2001): 8–11.

Edwards, Ashlee. "List of the Crew and Passengers Aboard United Airlines Flight 93 on Sept. 11, 2001." ABC-27 News (WHTM), September 2, 2021. https://www.abc27.com/news/remembering-september-11/list-of-the-crew-and-passengers-aboard-united-airlines-flight-93-on-sept-11-2001/.

"11 September: The Plot and the Plotters (CTC 2003-40044HC)." Central Intelligence Agency—Directorate of Intelligence, June 1, 2003. https://nsarchive.gwu.edu/document/24294-11-september-plot-and-plotters-ctc-2003-40044hc-central-intelligence-agency.

Enea, Joe. "Old Time Crime: Arizona Was a Training Ground for the September 11th Attackers." KNXV-TV ABC-15 Arizona, September 10, 2021. https://www.abc15.com/news/crime/old-time-crime-arizona-was-a-training-ground-for-the-september-11-attackers.

"FAA Received Alert about 9/11 Hijacker." ABC News, May 10, 2003. https://abcnews.go.com/U.S./story?id=91659&page=1#:~:text=W%20A%20S%20H%20I%20N%20G%20T%20O%20N%2C%20May%2010%20%E2%80%94%20Federal%20aviation,school%20and%20government%20officials%20say.

"Frontline: Inside the Terror Network—Who Were They?" PBS. Accessed May 16, 2023. https://www.pbs.org/wgbh/pages/frontline/shows/network/personal/whowere.html.

"Full Text: Bin Laden's 'Letter to America.'" *The Guardian*, November 24, 2002. https://www.theguardian.com/world/2002/nov/24/theobserver.

Goldberg, Alfred, Sarandis Papadopoulos, Diane Putney, Nancy Berlage, and Rebecca Welch. *Defense Studies Series: Pentagon 9/11*. Washington, D.C.: Office of the Secretary of Defense, 2007. https://history.defense.gov/Portals/70/Documents/pentagon/Pentagon9-11.pdf.

Hebert, Adam J. "The Return of NORAD." *Air & Space Forces Magazine*, February 1, 2002. https://www.airandspaceforces.com/article/0202norad/.

History.com Editors. "September 11 Attacks." History Channel, March 23, 2023. https://www.history.com/topics/21st-century/9-11-attacks.

Hofman, Mike. "The Impact of 9/11 on Air Travel Prepared Us for a Post-COVID

Eight. Aircraft as Guided Missiles

World." *Fortune Magazine*, September 11, 2012. https://fortune.com/2021/09/11/9-11-air-travel-impact-post-covid-20-years-later/.
"How Much Did the September 11 Terrorist Attack Cost America?" Institute for the Analysis of Global Security. Accessed on June 10, 2023. http://www.iags.org/costof911.html#:~:text=The%20destruction%20of%20major%20buildings,%2410%20billion%20to%20%2413%20billion.
Hughes, Calvin (anchor). "Remembering 9/11: South Florida Was Home to Hijackers before the Attacks." Local10 (ABC), September 11, 2021. https://www.local10.com/news/local/2021/09/10/remembering-911-south-florida-was-home-to-hijackers-before-the-attacks/.
Jehl, Douglas. "A Warning, but Clear? White House Tries to Make the Point That New Details Add Up to Old News." *The New York Times*, April 11, 2004. https://www.nytimes.com/2004/04/11/politics/a-warning-but-clear.html.
Johnson, Andy. "Flight School Owner Recalls Training 9/11 Hijackers." CTV News, September 11, 2012. https://www.ctvnews.ca/world/flight-school-owner-recalls-training-9-11-hijackers-1.951384?cache=yes%3FclipId%3D1723871.
Jones, Priscilla D. "The First 109 Minutes: 9/11 and the U.S. Air Force." Air Force History and Museums Program, 2011 (updated 2018). https://media.defense.gov/2012/Sep/05/2001329941/-1/-1/1/First_109_Minutes(2018).pdf.
Lardas, Mark. *The Kamikaze Campaign 1944–45: Imperial Japan's Last Throw of the Dice*. Oxford: Osprey Publishing, Ltd., 2022.
Leopold, Todd. "The Legacy of Danny Lewin, the First Man to Die on 9/11." CNN, September 11, 2013. https://www.cnn.com/2013/09/09/tech/innovation/danny-lewin-9-11-akamai/index.html.
Lichtblau, Eric. "Aboard Flight 11, a Chilling Voice." *Los Angeles Times*, September 20, 2001. https://www.latimes.com/archives/la-xpm-2001-sep-20-mn-47829-story.html.
MacFarquhar, Neil, Jim Yardley, and Paul Zielbauer. "A NATION CHALLENGED: THE MASTERMIND; A Portrait of the Terrorist: From Shy Child to Single-Minded Killer." *New York Times*, October 10, 2001. https://www.nytimes.com/2001/10/10/world/nation-challenged-mastermind-portrait-terrorist-shy-child-single-minded-killer.html.
MacMechen, T.R., and Carl Dienstbach. "Fighting in the Air." *American Aeronaut* 1, no. 2 (September 1909): 51–62. [Reproduced: MacMechen, T.R., and Carl Dienstbach, *American Aeronaut, Volume 1, Issues 1–3*. Charleston, South Carolina: Nabu Press, 2012.]
"Mitsubishi A6M2 Zero." National Museum of the United States Air Force. Accessed May 11, 2023. https://www.nationalmuseum.af.mil/Visit/Museum-Exhibits/Fact-Sheets/Display/Article/196313/mitsubishi-a6m2-zero/#:~:text=Beginning%20around%20October%201944%20during,aircraft%20for%20these%20suicide%20missions.
National Commission on Terrorist Attacks upon the United States. *The 9/11 Commission Report, Executive Summary* (Washington, D.C., 2004). https://www.9-11commission.gov/report/911Report.pdf.
Naudet, Gedeon, and Jules Naudet (filmmakers). "The Spymasters—CIA in the Crosshairs." *Showtime Documentaries*, airdate May 2, 2016. https://www.cbsnews.com/video/48-hours-presents-the-spymasters-cia-in-the-crosshairs/#x.
Nawaz, Amna, and Dan Sagalyn. "The Long-Lasting Impact of the U.S. Invasion of Iraq." PBS, March 29, 2023. https://www.pbs.org/newshour/show/the-long-lasting-impact-of-the-u-s-invasion-of-iraq.
"9/11 Interviews: Transcription, Case #265D-NY-280350 (Betty Ong, Mark Bingham)." Federal Bureau of Investigation—The Vault, September 12, 2001. https://vault.fbi.gov/9-11%20Commission%20Report/9-11-interviews-2001-09-sep-04-of-08.
"9/11 Mystery: What Was Atta Doing on 9/10?" NBC News, September 5, 2006. https://www.nbcnews.com/id/wbna14686192.
"The 9/11 Tapes: The Story in the Air." *New York Times*, September 7, 2011. https://archive.nytimes.com/www.nytimes.com/interactive/2011/09/08/nyregion/911-tapes.html?smid=nytcore-android-share.
"1999–2021: The U.S. War in Afghanistan." Council on Foreign Relations. Accessed June 25, 2023. https://www.cfr.org/timeline/us-war-afghanistan.
"November, 2002 Osama Bin Laden's Letter to America." Center for Online Judaic

Studies. Accessed June 18, 2023. https://cojs.org/november-2002-osama-bin-ladens-letter-america/.

"Phone Calls from Flight 93." U.S. National Park Service. Accessed June 17, 2023. https://www.nps.gov/flni/learn/historyculture/phone-calls-from-flight-93.htm.

Plotz, David. "What Does Osama Bin Laden Want?" *Slate*, September 14, 2001. https://slate.com/news-and-politics/2001/09/what-does-osama-bin-laden-want.html.

"Presidential Daily Brief: Bin Ladin Determined to Strike in U.S." Office of the Director of National Intelligence, August 6, 2001. file:///C:/Users/MarcV/Downloads/Bin%20Laden%20Determine%20to%20Strike%20in%20US.pdf.

"Prominent Russians: Pyotr Nesterov." RT Russiapedia, accessed May 4, 2023. https://russiapedia.rt.com/prominent-russians/military/pyotr-nesterov/index.html.

Reed, Cara. "9/11: Causes and Lingering Consequences." Ohio State Impact, August 14, 2020. https://www.osu.edu/impact/research-and-innovation/hahn-september-11.

"Reference Manual to Mitigate Potential Terrorist Attacks against Buildings (Risk Management Series #426)." FEMA/Emergency Preparedness & Response, December 2003. https://www.fema.gov/sites/default/files/2020-08/fema426_0.pdf.

Roberts, Chalmer M. "Did America Have to Drop the Bomb? With Japan Girding and American Lives at Stake, Truman Had No Choice." *Washington Post*, August 4, 1985. https://www.washingtonpost.com/archive/opinions/1985/08/04/did-america-have-to-drop-the-bombwith-japan-girding-and-american-lives-at-stake-truman-had-no-choice/f2e852d9-4e19-495a-b963-e32c2d9781fb/.

Rose, David. "Attackers Did Not Know They Were to Die." *The Guardian*, October 14, 2001. https://www.theguardian.com/world/2001/oct/14/terrorism.september111.

Shenon, Philip. "THREATS AND RESPONSES: THE INQUIRY; 9/11 Panel Presses Rice on Early Warnings." *New York Times*, April 9, 2004. https://www.nytimes.com/2004/04/09/world/threats-and-responses-the-inquiry-9-11-panel-presses-rice-on-early-warnings.html.

"SNNG: 9/11 Venice Flight School." *Sarasota Herald-Tribune*, May 12, 2015. https://www.youtube.com/watch?v=aibZJs89ABo.

"Staff Report, August 26, 2004." National Archives—9/11 Commission Records. Accessed June 8, 2023. https://www.archives.gov/files/research/9-11/staff-report-sept2005.pdf.

Tenet, George. *At the Center of the Storm: My Years at the CIA*. New York: HarperCollins, 2007.

"Ticket Agent Recalls Anger in Atta's Eyes." Associated Press, March 7, 2005. https://www.nbcnews.com/news/amp/wbna7117783.

"Transcript of Usama bin Laden Video Tape." U.S. Department of Defense, November, 2001. https://web.archive.org/web/20011214230828/http://www.defenselink.mil/news/Dec2001/d20011213ubl.pdf.

Whipple, Chris. "The Attacks Will Be Spectacular." *Politico Magazine*, November 12, 2015. https://www.politico.com/magazine/story/2015/11/cia-directors-documentary-911-bush-213353/#ixzz3rNFeL9Wb.

World News. "Iraq War 10 Years Later: Where Are They Now? Hans Blix (U.N. Weapons Inspector)." NBC News, March 19, 2013. https://www.nbcnews.com/news/world/iraq-war-10-years-later-where-are-they-now-hans-flna1c8956460.

Index

AAIB *see* Air Accidents Investigation Branch
Abarbanell, Oded, Capt. 1, 2
Abdulmutallab, Umar Farouk 58, 59
Abu Agela Mas'ud Kheir Al-Marimi *see* Masud
Abu Nidal 201
Abu Nidal Organization (ANO) 32, 33, 83, 184, 224, 235, 236, 237
Accuracy in Media (AIM) 143
Action Organization for the Liberation of Palestine *see* PLO
Adami, Eddie Fenech 208
ADS-B (technology) 97–100
ADS-B In 98
ADS-B Out 98–100
Advanced Imaging Technology (AIT) *see* screening, passenger
Agence France-Presse 235
Air Accidents Investigation Branch (AAIB) 192, 193
Air Line Pilots Association (ALPA) 16, 125, 140, 141, 149
Air Malta Flight 180 185, 203–204, 208, 212
air marshals 14, 22, 37, 265
air traffic control (ATC) 1, 52, 71, 89, 92, 97, 98, 99, 100, 115, 127, 151, 187, 225, 255, 256, 257, 258, 259, 263
Air Transportation Security Act of 1974 26
Airbus, targeted by terrorists
  Airbus A300 28, 58, 72
  Airbus A310 35
  Airbus A320 95
  Airbus A321-200 61, 72
  Airbus A350 97
  Airbus A380 97
Airfone 261, 262
Airplane Interior Documentation Group 111
airports, ensnared in terrorist attacks
  Aden Adde International Airport 62

Atlantic City International Airport 96
Ben Gurion Airport 166
Brussels Airport 85–86
Charles de Gaulle Airport 115, 121, 224
Cincinnati Airport 20
Damascus International Airport 19
Dar El-Beida Airport 2
Detroit Metropolitan Airport 58
Domodedovo International Airport 164, 171, 172, 173, 175, 176
Dulles International Airport 36, 121, 254, 255, 259
Frankfort International Airport (Flughafen Frankfurt Main) 3, 35, 184, 185, 194, 236
Hartsfield-Jackson Atlanta International Airport 113, 121
Heathrow Airport 57, 90, 185–187, 201, 212
JFK International Airport (JFK) 35, 69, 115, 121, 150
Jinnah International Airport 33
John F. Kennedy International Airport *see* airports, ensnared in terrorist attacks: JFK International Airport
José Marti Airport 13, 17
Kimpo Airport 83
LAX *see* airports, ensnared in terrorist attacks: Los Angeles International Airport
Leonardo da Vinci International Airport 1, 68, 82, 83, 236
Logan International Airport 36, 56, 254, 255, 258, 261
Los Angeles International Airport (LAX) 63–64
Luqa Airport 32, 185, 203–204, 212
Midway Airport (Chicago) 48
Munich-Reim Airport 3, 81
Newark International Airport (New Jersey) 36, 254, 255, 261

275

Niamy Airport 225
Portland International Jetport 253, 254
Reagan National Airport 259
"Revolution Airport" 21
Santander Airport 84
Sheikh Ul Alam International Airport 84
Tarragona International Airport 84
Vienna (Schwechat) International Airport 83, 236
"airships" 243
AK-47 assault rifle *see* weapons
Akache, Zohair Youssif (AKA Captain Mahmoud) 30
Akhmedova, Khapta 167
Al Shabaab 63
al-Arja, Jayel 28
al-Asiri, Ibrahim Hassan 61
Alaspa, Bryan 48
al-Assad, Bashar 198
al-Awlaki, Anwar 59
USS *Albuquerque* 127
al-Hazmi, Nawaf 248
al-Islambouli, Khaled 174
Alitalia (airline) 87
al-Maliki, Fadhel 63–64
al-Megrahi, Abdelbaset 185, 202, 211
al-Megrahi, Ali 211
al-Mihdhar, Khalid 248
Al-Nusra Front *see* al-Qaeda in Syria
ALPA *see* Air Line Pilots Association
Al-Qaeda 35–36, 54, 55, 57–59, 62, 70, 84, 113, 114, 168, 173; Nine-Eleven (9/11 attacks) 243, 245, 246, 248, 249–256, 261, 262, 263, 264, 266
Al-Qaeda in Syria 63
Al-Qaeda in the Arabian Peninsula *see* AQAP
al-Sanussi, Abdallah (Abdullah al-Senussi) 232
altimeter 197
al-Walid, Agu 167
Amati, Giacomo 54
American Aeronaut Magazine 243
American Occupied Zone (Germany) 9, 11
American Red Cross 121
American University of Beirut 199
amphetamines 236
amputation 82, 121
Amtrack 37
Anderson, Larry 88
Anderson, Terry 199
Andrew, Prince 191
ANO *see* Abu Nidal Organization
antimissile defense system 71–73
Antonov An-24 turboprop 69

APATA *see* Arming Pilots Against Terrorism Act
Apollo Project 146
AQAP (Al-Qaeda in the Arabian Peninsula) 60–61, 63
Arab Spring 235
Arafat, Yassar 24
ARAP *see* Associated Retired Aviation Professionals
Arlington National Cemetery 238
Arming Pilots Against Terrorism Act (APATA) 38
Artamonov, Mikhail 171–172, 176
Arutyunov, Armen 172, 176
ascending-fuselage hypothesis *see* "zoom-climb" scenario
Ashkenazi, Michael 66–67
ASPI *see* Australian Strategic Policy Institute
Associated Press 121, 211, 236
Associated Retired Aviation Professionals (ARAP) 112, 142, 143, 144
ATC *see* air traffic control
At the Center of the Storm: My Years at the CIA 252–253
ATF (Bureau of Alcohol, Tobacco, and Firearms) 130–132, 133, 142, 151
ATSA *see* Aviation and Transportation Security Act
ATSB *see* Australian Transport Safety Board
Atta, Mohamed 246–247, 253, 254, 255, 256, 257, 258
Australian Strategic Policy Institute (ASPI) 55
Australian Transport Safety Board (ATSB) 92
Automatic Control System (aircraft remote control) 94
Automatic Dependent Surveillance-Broadcast *see* ADS-B (technology)
"Autumn Leaves" (counterterrorism operation) 194, 195, 196
Aviation and Transportation Security Act (ATSA) 37, 38, 57
Aviation Safety Network (ASN) 53
Aviation Security Act of 1982 203

Baader-Meinhof Gang 28
Babbar Khalsa 52
Babygro (product) 186, 194, 208
backscatter X ray machine *see* screening, passenger
Bacos, Michel, Capt. 28, 29, 30
baggage reconciliation 39, 54, 185
Barayeva, Khava 168
Bar-Lev, Uri, Capt. 22

Index

Barr, William "Bill" 212
Basayev, Shamil 168, 169, 170, 172, 176–177
Bashar al-Assad *see* al-Assad, Bashar
Basque separatists 28, 84, 183
Batista, Fulgencio, President 11, 12, 13
Baum, Philip 11, 13, 33, 53
Baur, Christian "Chris," Capt. 116, 117, 120
BBC (British Broadcasting Corp.) 30, 52, 53, 232
Beach Lane Bridge 116
Beamer, Todd 262
Because He Could 151
Bednarek, Janet 26
behavioral profiling *see* screening, passenger
La Belle discotheque 234
Bergen, Peter 72
Beslan Seige 175–176
Bhanot, Neerja 34
Biello, David 57
Biles, Clay 14, 19
bin Laden, Osama 150, 247, 248, 249, 250, 252, 257, 264, 265
Bin Ladin Planning Multiple Operations 251
Bin Mohamad, Mahathir, Prime Minister 94
Bingham, Mark 262
Bingham Group 262
Biomedical and Behavioral Sciences Division (FAA) 20
biometric measures *see* identity verification methods
bipolar disorder 7
Black, Cofer 251
Black, Robert 206
"black box" *see* flight data recorder
Black Hawk (H-60) helicopter 116
black hole 92
Black Nationalists 15
Black Panther Party 15
"Black September" (event) 24
Black September (organization) 24, 68
"black widow" (definition) 166
black widow terrorist operation 167–177
Blair, Anthony "Tony," Prime Minister 207
Blee, Rich 252
Blitz (London) 190
Bloom, Mia 167, 169, 170
Bodansky, Yossef 150
body cavity bomb *see* bomb (types)
"body packing" 64
Boeing aircraft targeted by terrorists
  Boeing 247 48
  Boeing 707 1, 2, 18, 21, 68, 82
  Boeing 727 26, 30, 185
  Boeing 737 30, 32, 72, 95, 247

Boeing 747 21, 33, 34, 52, 53, 69, 112, 115, 143, 144, 146, 185
Boeing 757 70, 95, 96, 148, 254, 260, 261, 263
Boeing 767 55, 254, 255, 257, 258, 259, 262
Boeing 777 91, 92, 94
Boeing 787 81, 96, 97
Boeing Company 95, 259
Bollier, Edwin 197, 199, 200, 204–205, 207
bomb, types
  barometric 197
  body cavity 63–64
  IED (improvised explosive device) 39, 49, 50, 51, 52, 53, 54, 57, 58, 59, 60, 61, 62, 63, 64, 66, 86, 169, 173, 194, 195, 197, 201, 226, 229; innovative techniques 55–66
  laptop computer 57, 62–63, 95
  liquid 55, 57–58, 62, 66
  nail 86
  soda can 61–62
  surgically-implanted 63–64
  "thin bomb" 63
bombings, targeted airliners
  Air India Flight 181 52
  Air India Flight 182 52
  Canadian Pacific Airlines (CP Air) Flight 108 49–50
  Daallo Airlines Flight 159 62
  Flight 901 (Alas Chiricanas) 54
  Metrojet Flight 9268 61, 62
  Northwest Airlines Flight 253 (attempted) 58, 59
  Pan Am Flight 103 34, 53, 150, 182, 183–185, 186–213, 224, 237
  Philippine Airlines Flight 434 54, 113
  Siberia Airlines (Sibir) Flight 1407 170, 172, 176
  United Airlines (UA) Flight 23 48
  United Airlines Flight 629 50
  UTA (Union de Transports Aériens) Flight 772 213, 224, 225, 227–229, 230–238
  Volga-AviaExpress Flight 1303 164, 170, 176
Bonn International Center for Conversion (BICC) 66
boombox *see* Toshiba BomBeat radio-cassette player
Borjesson, Kristina 149
Bortnikov, Alexander 61
Böse, Wilfried 28
Boston Center 255, 256, 257
Botha, Pik, Foreign Minister 184
box cutter *see* weapons
BP (British Petroleum) 211

Index

Bradshaw, Sandy 262
breast *see* bomb types, surgically-implanted
British Petroleum *see* BP
Brown, C.R., Vice Admiral 245
Brown, James G. Capt. 16–17
Bruguière, Jean-Louis 228–229, 230, 231, 232, 233
Brumley, Dwight 118–119, 147
Bunker, Robert J. 57, 64
Bunn, Tom, Capt. 37
Bureau of Alcohol, Tobacco, and Firearms *see* ATF
Burkeman, Oliver 8
Burns, Nicolas 122
Burquest, Bret 114
Bush, George Herbert Walker, President 198, 199
Bush, George Walker, Jr., President 37, 38, 250, 251, 252, 253, 264–265
Bushidō 244
Butukayev, Aslan 177

C4 *see* plastic explosives
Cairo University 246
Calverton Hangar 130, 141
Camp Zeist 203
Canadian Pacific Air Lines (CP Air) 49, 52, 53
canine drug detection units 58, 85
canine search team (Lockerbie) 191
Capitol Building (Austin, Texas) 267
Capitol Building (Washington, D.C.) 247, 254
CAPPS (Computer-Assisted Passenger Prescreening System) 255
Captain Mahmoud *see* Akache, Zohair Youssif
card verification code (CVC) 90
Carlos the Jackal 28
Carter, David B. 182
Cashill, Jack 136
Castro, Fidel, President 11, 12, 13, 14, 15, 17
Castro, Raúl 11, 12
CAT scanner *see* screening, passenger
Cattrall, Kim 186
Catusi, Massimo 11
Cave Rescue Organization 191
Center for Strategic Studies (Libya) 185
center wing fuel tank (CWT) 125, 130, 134, 139, 141, 142, 145, 146
Central Ammunition Depot (Scotland) 193
Central Intelligence Agency *see* CIA
Centralsequence see FBI/CIA animated video
Channel 4 News (London) 200–201

Chao, Shih-Ho 266
Chapelcross Power Station 189
Charles, King 191
Charles, Michael "Mick" 193
Charlton, Corey 204
Ché Guevara Commando Unit 18, 28
Chechen rebels 166
Chechnya-Russia conflict 166, 168
checkpoint (airport) 13, 36, 65, 66, 85, 86, 87, 254; explosive chemical scan ("black box") 66
Cheney, Richard "Dick," Vice President 250, 251, 253, 264, 265
Chevrette, Peggy 247
Chicago Tribune 201, 229
Chilcote, Ryan 166
Chinatown 256
Chivers, C.J. 172
Choi, Jin-Tai 112
Christmas 35, 53, 58, 59, 145, 183, 184, 186, 187, 190, 192, 193, 235, 236
"Christmas Bomber" *see* Abdulmutallab, Umar Farouk
CIA 13, 24, 111, 112, 114, 124, 145, 184, 185, 186, 191, 196, 200, 201, 204, 250, 251, 252: role in TWA Flight 800 investigations. 133, 134, 135, 136, 137; "zoom-climb" scenario 136–137, 146–147
Clark, Nicola 24
Clarke, John H. 147
Clarke, Richard A. 151
Cleveland Center 261, 262
Clinton, William "Bill," President 112, 113, 114, 120, 122, 123, 124, 130, 131, 132, 144, 151
Clinton-Gore reelection campaign 131, 132, 151
Cliphanger Viper knife 258
Clipper Maid of the Seas 186
C-MUSIC (Commercial-Multi Spectral Infrared Countermeasure) 72
CNN (Cable News Network) 37, 62, 63, 94, 120, 151
cockpit voice recorder (CVR) 115, 116, 123, 144, 145, 146, 165, 174
Coconut Curtain hijackings 11–17
Cohen, Uri 81–82
Colau, Andy 191
Cold War 9, 10
Coletti, Adam 118
Collier, Craig, Major 260
Commercial-Multi Spectral Infrared Countermeasure *see* C-MUSIC
computed-tomography scanner *see* screening, passenger
Computer-Assisted Passenger Prescreening System *see* CAPPS

Index

Congressional Task Force on Terrorism and Unconventional Warfare 150
continuous-rod missile 128
Convention for the Suppression of Unlawful Acts Against the Safety of Civil Aviation 202
Convention for the Suppression of Unlawful Seizure of Aircraft 27
Convention on Offences and Certain Other Acts Committed on Board Aircraft 27
Cooper, Dan (D.B. Cooper) 25–26
coronavirus disease 2019 *see* Covid-19
Council on Foreign Relations 183, 265
Counterterrorism Security Group (CTSG) 124, 251
Court of Criminal Appeal (Scotland) 211
Covid-19 (coronavirus disease 2019) 65, 87–88, 266
Cowell, Alan 207
Cox, Matthew 196
Coyne, John 55
CP Air *see* Canadian Pacific Air Lines
Crimea 92
Crippin, James B. 64
CT scanner *see* screening, passenger
CTSG *see* Counterterrorism Security Group
Cuban Revolution 11, 18
CVC *see* card verification code
CVR *see* cockpit voice recorder
CWT *see* center wing fuel tank
cyberattack, airliner *see* United Airlines Flight 3642
cyberattack, methods 98–99
cybercrime (non-terrorism) 89–91
cyclotrimethylenetrinitramine (RDX) *see* plastic explosives

Dabiq (magazine) 62
Dahl, Jason 261
Dailey, John T. 20
Dalkamoni, Hafez 195
Dalywell, Tam 207
Danziger, Andrew 148
dark web 89, 90, 91
Daventry Departure 186, 187
Davey, Robert 143
Dawson Field 21, 23, 24, 82
DCPJ *see* Direction Centrale de la Police Judiciaire
decompression, cabin 32, 53
decompression chamber 23
DDoS attack *see* Distributed Denial of Service (DDoS) attack
Dekkers, Rudi 246
Democratic Popular Front for the Liberation of Palestine *see* DPFLP

Denial of Service (DoS) attack 89
Denning, Dorothy E. 91
Denoix de Saint Marc, Guillaume 238, 239
Department for Transport (UK) 192, 193
Department of Defense (DoD), United States 25, 150, 257, 260
Department of Energy (DOE), United States 96
Department of Homeland Security (DHS), United States 37, 39, 57, 70, 71, 96, 265
Department of Justice (DOJ), United States 207, 208, 209, 212, 231
Department of State (DOS), United States 114, 122, 150, 184, 185, 197, 206, 234
Department of Transportation (DOT), United States 24, 37
Department of the Treasury (USDT), United States 24
Der Spiegel 201
Derby Mountain Rescue Team 192
DETRESFA alert 225
Detsch, Jack 70
DHS *see* Department of Homeland Security, United States
Diego Garcia (military facility) 93, 94
Diehl, Jörg 61
Direction Centrale de la Police Judiciaire (DCPJ) 231
Direction de la Surveillance du Territoire (DST) 231
Distributed Denial of Service (DDoS) attack 89
DNA analysis 175
Docker's Restaurant 114
DoD *see* Department of Defense, United States
Doda, Bajazid 7
DOE *see* Department of Energy, United States
DOJ *see* Department of Justice, United States
Donaldson, William S., Cmdr. 135, 142
Doppler radar system 71
DoS attack *see* Denial of Service attack
DOS *see* Department of State, United States
DOT *see* Department of Transportation, United States
Dougherty, Jill 171, 176
DPFLP (Democratic Popular Front for the Liberation of Palestine) 81
Dreamliner *see* Boeing 787
Dron, Alan 190
drug smuggling 51, 63, 64, 172
DST *see* Direction de la Surveillance du Territoire
Dubrovka Theatre 169–170

Dugain, Marc 93
Dumfries and Galloway Constabulary 190
Dzhebirkhanova, Satsita 171, 175

Eagar, Thomas W. 267
Eastern Airlines (company) 20
Eckert, William G. 193
Eddy, Max 97
Edinburgh Law School 206
Edward R. Murrow Award 149
"Egypt Revolution" (terror cell) 32
ejection seat 17
El Ageli, Bedelsalam Hammouda, Lt. 233
Elazragh, Abdullah (Abd al-Azragh) 232, 233
Elliott, Christopher 87
Embry-Riddle Aeronautical University 98
Emmy Award 149
encryption 91, 99, 100
Energy Magazine 211
Engelberg, Stephen 196
English as a Second Language (ESL) 247
Erwin Meister and Edwin Bollier, Ltd., Telecommunications *see* MEBO
ESL *see* English as a Second Language
Essawi, Salim 18–19
Esso 224, 238
ETA (Basque separatist group) 84, 183
Ethiopian Airlines 1
EU *see* European Union
European Commission 203
European Court of Human Rights 176, 207
European Union (EU) 85, 238
Euskadi Ta Askatasuna *see* ETA
explosives-detection system 57
extraterrestrials 92
Exxon *see* Esso

F-14 fighter jet 195
F-15 fighter jet 258
FAA 14, 16, 17, 20, 21, 24, 26, 27, 31, 36, 37, 71, 88, 121, 127, 149, 247, 257, 258, 259, 260; "NextGen" system 97, 98, 99, 100
FAA Command Center 37
FAA Peace Officers *see* air marshals
facial-recognition technology *see* identity verification methods
"Faculty of Architecture" (World Trade Centers) 254
"Faculty of Fine Arts" (Pentagon) 254
"Faculty of Law" (Capitol Building) 254
Fadhel al-Maliki *see* al-Maliki, Fadhel
Les Familles de l'attentat du DC10 d'UTA 238
FBI 14, 24, 38, 50, 51, 56, 64, 95, 111, 112, 114, 120, 130, 131, 138, 139, 140, 141, 142, 145, 147, 148, 149, 151, 191, 196, 197, 202, 207, 208, 210, 228, 229, 230, 231, 232, 251, 252; "friendly fire" imbroglio 125–129; TWA 800 investigation 132–137
FBI/CIA animated video ("Speculated TWA Flight 800 Accident Sequence") 136, 146
FBI crime lab 228, 229, 231
FBI Laboratory: An Investigation into Laboratory Practices and Alleged Misconduct in Explosives-Related and Other Cases 231
FDR *see* flight data recorder
Federal Air Marshal Service *see* air marshals
Federal Aviation Act of 1958 14, 26
Federal Aviation Administration *see* FAA
Federal Bureau of Investigation *see* FBI
Federal Emergency Management Agency *see* FEMA
Federal Flight Deck Officer Program (FFDO) 38
Federal Security Service (FSB) 165, 170, 174
FedEx (Federal Express) 61 72
Fell Rescue Association 191
FEMA 266, 267
FFDO *see* Federal Flight Deck Officer Program
Fhimah, Lamin Khalifah 185, 202, 203, 204, 206, 212
Fifteen May ("15 May") Organization 228, 230
Financial Times 211
fingerprints *see* identity verification methods
"Fire Magic" *see* Operation Feuerzauber
firewall (network security) 91, 96
FIRO (Flight 800 Independent Researchers Association) 143, 144
First District Command Center, U.S. Coast Guard (Boston) 123
flak 116–117
flight attendants 1, 10, 11, 15, 16, 17, 18, 23, 27, 31, 32, 33, 34, 35, 56, 58, 62, 115, 256, 258, 262; pursers 22, 34, 257
flight data recorder (FDR, "black box") 115, 143, 144, 145, 146, 165, 174
Flight Deck Secondary Barrier 38
Flight 800 Independent Researchers Association *see* FIRO
Flight Guard 71, 72
Flight Information Center (Niamy, Niger) 225
Florida Flight Training Center 247
Florida State University 143
fluoroscope 50
FOIA *see* Freedom of Information Act

Fokker Friendship aircraft 69
Ford Trimotor transport aircraft 8
Foreign Policy (magazine) 70, 124
Foster, Tom 196
"four Rs" 167
Four Tops (band) 186
Frakes, Matthew 182
Fraser, Lord 204
Freedom of Information Act (FOIA) 144, 145, 146, 147
Freeh, Louis 135
friendly fire 125, 126, 127, 128, 129, 130, 132, 133, 137, 144
Friess, Michel 226
FSB *see* Federal Security Service
Fuisz, Richard 200–201
full-body scans (Advanced Imaging Technology) 39, 59, 60, 64

Gaddafi, Muammar, Col. 182, 183, 184, 198, 201, 203, 212, 213, 224, 228, 230; legal proceedings 232, 233, 234, 235, 236, 237
Gaddafi Foundation 234
Galal, Hani, Capt. 32
Gandhi, Indira, Prime Minister 52
Gannon, Mark 186
GAO *see* Government Accounting Office
Garden of Remembrance 238
gas chamber 50
Gauci, Paul 209
Gauci, Tony 203, 204, 205, 206, 207, 209
gay (same-sex orientation) 7, 262, 264
Gaza Unit—Popular Front for the Liberation of Palestine 28
Gebauer, Matthias 61
gender 60, 169
gender-nonconforming passengers 60
General Electric 140
Genzlinger, Neil 149
Gerace, Diane 60
German Federal Police (GSG 9) 31
Gestapo 11
Gialka, Abdel Majid 203, 204
Glick, Jeremy 262
Global Position System *see* GPS
Glusac, Elaine 65
Goldbert, Alfred 260
Goodman, Al 84
Goodman, Walter 122
Google Earth 239
Gordon, Michael 188
Gore, Albert "Al," Vice President 131, 132
Gorman, Siobhan 64
Gorokhov, Nikolai 164
Government Accounting Office (GAO) 95, 96, 97, 99
GPS (global positioning) 98, 99

Graeme Sephton v. F.B.I., 2005 145
Graham, Jack Gilbert 50
Grassley, Chuck 132, 133, 134, 135
"Great Balls of Fire" incident 59
Grech, George 208
Grenzschutzgruppe 9 *see* GSG-9
Greyhound Lines 37
groundstop 37
Groupe Air France 238
GSG-9 31
Guantanamo Bay 265
Guardian (UK) 59, 170, 207, 233, 249
Guay, Joseph Albert 49–50
Guevara, Ché 11
Guttmann, Avila 24

Haass, Jon C. 98–99
Habash, George 2
Haberman, Clyde 83
Habré, Hissen, President 226
Hadley, Stephen 250
The Hague 27
Halinski, John 63
Hall, Jim 126, 138, 140
Hammarskjöld, Dag 68
hand grenade *see* weapons
handgun *see* weapons
Hanjour, Hani 247, 248, 260
Hanson, Peter Burton 259
Harper, Emma 190
Harrison, Gregory 143
Hartuv, Ilan 29
Hasak, Amit 22
Hausa (tribe) 238
hazardous materials (HAZMAT) 64
HAZMAT *see* hazardous materials
Hebert, Adam J. 257
Henderson, Stuart 200
Henley, John 233
Hercules C-130 transport/cargo aircraft 30, 260
Herridge, Catherine 59
Hewlett-Packard laser printer 61
hexogen 166
Hezbollah 113, 150, 224, 227
Hezbollah International 150
Hickey, Robert 96
Higgins, Kelly Jackson 91
"hijacker alert" 174
hijacker-pilot 246–248, 249, 253, 259, 260, 261
hijackings, targeted airliners
 Air France Flight 139 28
 American Airlines (AA) Flight 11 254, 255–258, 260
 American Airlines Flight 77 254, 259–260

Index

BOAC (British Overseas Airways Corp.) Flight 775 23
Continental Airlines 14
Cubana de Aviación Flight 495 12
Czechoslovak National Airlines 9–10
Delta Airlines Flight 670 (attempted hijacking) 20
Eastern Air Lines 14, 16
EgyptAir Flight 648 32
El Al Flight 219 21–22
El Al Flight 426 1, 2, 3, 18, 22
Lufthansa Flight 181 30
Lufthansa Flight 592 35
National Airlines Flight 186 15–16
National Airlines Flight 337 13–14
Pan Am Flight 73 (attempted hijacking) 33–34
Pan Am (Pan American World Airways) Flight 93 21
Southern Airways Flight 49 26
Swissair Flight 100 21
TAME (Transportes Aéreo Militares Ecuatorianos) 19
TWA (Trans World Airlines) Flight 741 21
TWA Flight 840 18, 19
United Airlines (UA) Flight 93 254, 260–263
United Airlines Flight 175 254, 258–259
Hill, Mark, Rear Admiral 143
Hoffman, Bruce 2
Hofman, Mike 266
Hofmann, Paul 82
Holden, Robert T. 18
Holland, Tom 7
Homeland Security: Protecting Airliners from Terrorist Missiles 71
"homesick hijackings" 15
Horne, Marc 208
Huffman Aviation 246
Hughes, Henry F. 111, 112, 141, 149
Human Rights Watch 86
Humphreys, Todd 99
Hungarian Soviet Republic 7
Hussein, Saddam 198
hydrogen peroxide 57–58
"hypodermic injection apparatus" 17

identity verification methods 65, 266
   biometric measures
      facial recognition technology 65, 87
      fingerprints 65
      iris scans 65, 87
      retina scans 266
   identification photos 87
   security questions 53
IDF *see* Israeli Defense Forces

IED *see* bomb, types
IFALPA *see* International Federation of Air Line Pilots Associations
IFE *see* in-flight entertainment system
Ignatchenko, Sergei 165
Imperial Japanese Army 244, 245
Imperial Japanese Navy 244, 245
Imperial Tradesman Dual Edge knife 258
improvised explosive device (IED) *see* bomb, types
Indianapolis Center 259
in-flight entertainment (IFE) system 95
infrared (IR) countermeasure *see* C-MUSIC
Inside Terrorism 2
Institute for the Analysis of Global Security 263
Internal Revenue Service *see* IRS
International Air Transport Association 32
International Airline Pilots Association 2
International Association of Machinists and Aerospace Workers (IAMAW) 141–142
International Civil Aviation Organization 226
International Federation of Air Line Pilots Associations (IFALPA) 31
International Olympic Committee 121
International Progress Organization 203
IOActive 91
IRA (group) *see* Provisional Irish Republican Army
Iranian Revolution 264
Iranian Revolutionary Guard 196, 197, 198
Iran-Iraq War 195
iris scans *see* identity verification methods
Irish Examiner 171
Iron Curtain hijackings 9–11
IRS 267
ISIS 61, 62, 63, 85, 86
Islambouli Brigades 174, 175
Islamic Jihad 227, 228
Islamic Movement for Change *see* Movement of Islamic Change
Islamic State of Iraq and Syria *see* ISIS
Israeli Air Force 72
Israeli Defense Forces (IDF) 29, 256
Israeli-Palestinian conflict 51–52

Jaber, Fayez Abdul-Rahim al 28
Jafry, Syed 58
Jamahiriya Security Organization *see* JSO
Japanese High Command 244
Japanese Red Army 28
Jarrah, Ziad 247, 261, 263
Jenkins, Brian Michael 54

Index

"Jetosaurus Rex" 130
JetTech flight school 247, 260
Jewish Telegraphic Agency (JTA) 82
Jibril, Ahmad 196, 200, 213
John Paul II, Pope 54
Johnson, Howard 49
Johnson, Keith 64
Johnson, Lyndon B., President 125
Johnson, Raymond 15–16
Joint Chiefs of Staff 143, 251
Joint Force Quarterly 168
Joint Terrorism Task Force (FBI) 120
Jones, Priscilla D. 257
Jones Aviation 246
JSO 185, 197, 198

Kallstrom, James 125, 126, 129, 130, 131, 132, 133, 134, 135, 137, 139, 145
kamikaze 244, 245, 254, 257
Kelly, John F. 231
Kennedy, John F., President 12, 14, 125
Kerry, Bob 151
Kevlar 38, 193
Kevorkian, Ralph, Capt. 115
KGB *see* Federal Security Service
Khaled al-Islambouli *see* al-Islambouli, Khaled
Khaled, Leila 18, 19, 22, 23, 24
Khobar Towers 113, 124, 150
Khomeini, Ayatollah Ruhollah 195, 201
Kieler, Ashlee 31
"Killnet" 89
King Hussein (Jordan) 21, 23, 24
knife *see* weapons
Knight, W. Andy 166
Köchler, Hans 203, 206, 207, 210
Koerner, Brendan J. 15, 17
Kommando Siegfried Hausner 30
Korean War 125
Korenkov, Nikolai 172, 176
Kramek, Robert E. 123
Kuhlmann, Brigitte 28
Kumar, Rajesh 34

Lahr, Ray, Capt. 146–147
Laird, Melvin 25
Lake, Anthony 120
Langewiesche, William 92
Langley Air Force Base 259
laptop computer, as weapon *see* bomb, types
Lardas, Mark 244, 145
Larson, George C. 25
Lashkar-e-Toiba (terror group) 84
Latner, Teishan A. 15
lead azide 61
League of Arab Nations 203

Lee, Jong K. 72
Legally Blonde 56
Leopold, Todd 256
Letter to the American People 264
Lewin, Danny 256
LeWinter, Oswald 185
Liberation of Palestine (aircraft) 1
Liberation Tigers of Tamil Eelam *see* LTTE
Libya Arab Airlines 185
Libyan army 197
Libyan Embassy in Brazzaville, Congo 229
Libyan Intelligence Directorate *see* JSO
Libyan Intelligence Service *see* JSO
life insurance payouts 49, 50
"liquid bomb" plot 62
lithium ion batteries 63
Lockerbie, Scotland (town) 187
Lockerbie Air Disaster Memorial 238
Lockerbie Laundry Ladies 192
Loeb, Bernard 139
London Blitz *see* Blitz
London Times 122
London Underground (transport) 57
Lord's Prayer 262
Louis Armstrong International Airport 25
LTTE 69–70
luggage inspections 39, 50, 57, 65, 171, 172
Lumpert, Ulrich 209
Lydon, John 186

Mace *see* weapons
MacQuarrie, James, Capt. 186, 187
Maelbeek Metro Station 86
Magariaf, Mohammed, President 237
Magdomadova, Luiza 168
Magecart (hacker network) 90
magnetic tape 143, 145
magnetometers *see* metal detectors
Malay Peninsula 92
Malaysia Airlines Flight 370 91–94
Mandela, Nelson, President 207
Mangatany, Apollinaire 229, 323–233
Mann, Howard, Capt. 143
Mann, Jim 227
MANPAD (man-portable air-defense system) 66–70
  "beam rider" 67
  "command line of sight" (CLOS) 67
  infrared (IR) 67, 71
man-portable air-defense system *see* MANPAD
Marinello, Del 18
Maron, Hanna 82
Maronite Christians 227
Marquise, Richard 190, 193, 194
Marsh, Rene 63

284 Index

Massachusetts Institute of Technology (MIT) 96, 251, 256
Masud (Abu Agela Mas'ud Kheir Al-Marimi) 212
Maxfield, Betty 260
mayday notification 52, 123, 188, 226
Mazzoleni, Nicoletta 11
McCurry, Mike 123–124
McDonnell Douglas aircraft, targeted by terrorists
  DC-2 67–68
  DC-3 9, 12, 49
  DC-4 68
  DC-6 68
  DC-8 21
  DC-9 20
  DC-10 224, 226, 238, 239
  Douglas C-47B 49
McKinney, David D. 25
McLaughlin Group 132
McNeil, Donald G., Jr. 204
McQueen, Marjorie 188
MEBO 197, 199, 201, 203–210, 230
Meir, Golda, Prime Minister 29, 68
Meister, Erwin 197
Memorandum of Understanding on Hijacking of Aircraft and Vessels and Other Offenses 17
Mesbahi, Abolghasem 201
metal detectors 16, 20, 25, 26, 31, 36, 50, 60, 64, 82, 255, 265
Meyer, Frederick "Fritz," Major 116, 117, 147
microscopic analysis 49
Middle Eastern hijackings 17–24
Miles, Hugh 188
Miller, Joy 50
Miller, Judith 151
Milton Helpern International Center of Forensic Sciences 193
Ministry of Foreign Affairs (Israel) 29
missile hypothesis (TWA Flight 800) 123–125
missile non-proliferation efforts 71
missile strikes, targeted airliners
  Air Rhodesia Flight 825 68
  Air Rhodesia Flight 827 69
  Air Vietnam 68
  Arkia Israeli Airlines Flight 582 (attempted) 70
  DHL Express 72
  Lion Air Flight 602 69
  Polar (research aircraft) 68
  Sudan Airways Flight 109 69
  TWA Flight 800 (possible strike) 124–125
MIT *see* Massachusetts Institute of Technology

Mitsubishi A6M2 Zero aircraft 244
Mitterrand, François, President 227
Mode-C transponder 256
Moisant Field 25
Molenbeek district 85
Le Monde diplomatique 229
Morris, Dick 151
Moss, Steve 192
Mossad 120
Mothers of Beslan 176
Motown 186
Mountain Rescue Service 191
Moutardier, Hermis 56
Movement of Islamic Change 114, 122, 123
mujahedeen 167
"mule" *see* drug smuggling
Mundo, Al, Capt. 143
Murdock, Jason 96
Musbah, Abbas (Musbah Arbas) 233
"muscle hijackers" 248–249
Musso, Christopher 267
"mystery vessel" (TWA 800 case) 119

Naeli, Ibrahim (Nayil Ibrahim) 233
Nagayeva, Amanta 170, 171, 173, 175
Nagayeva, Rosa 171, 175
nail bomb *see* bomb, types
Narozhna, Tanya 166
NASA (National Aeronautics and Space Administration) 146
Nasser, Gamal Abdel, President 24
National Airlines 13–14, 15, 16
National Airspace System (NAS) 97
National Commission on Terrorist Attacks Upon the United States *see* 9/11 Commission
National Explosives Detection Canine Team Program (NEDCTP) 58
National Front for the Salvation of Libya *see* NFSL
National Guard (United States) 37, 116, 119, 121, 149, 258
National Institute of Standards and Technology (NIST) 65
National Security Council (NSC) 124
National Transportation and Safety Board (NTSB) 111, 112, 120, 126, 129, 130, 131, 133, 136, 137; and the TWA Flight 800 Investigation 138–150; 151, 152
NATO (North Atlantic Treaty Organization) 135
Navy Air Corps 146
Nawaz, Amna 265
NBC News 150
NEADS (Northeast Air Defense Sector) 257, 258

Index 285

NEDCTP *see* National Explosives Detection Canine Team Program
negative-G mode 22
Nelson, David 191
Nesterov, Pyotr 244
Netanyahu, Benjamin, Prime Minister 30, 70
Netanyahu, Yonathan "Yoni" 30
Neubiberg Air Base 9
New York Air National Guard (NYANG) 116
New York Police Department 120
New York Times 3, 31, 48, 53, 113, 121, 129, 140, 149, 151, 176, 195, 204, 227, 253
New Yorker 50, 124
Newberger, Stuart H. 225, 226, 230, 233
Newsweek 204
"Next Generation Air Transportation System" *see* "NextGen" system
"NextGen" system 97–98
NFSL (National Front for the Salvation of Libya) 237
Nine-Eleven (9/11) attacks (September 11 attacks) 4, 24, 35, 36, 37, 38, 39, 55, 56, 70, 84, 88, 151, 172, 243–263, 264, 265, 266, 267
Nine-Eleven (9/11) Commission 36, 250, 251, 252, 255
Nine-Eleven (9/11) Commission Report 246, 248, 251, 256
NIST *see* National Institute of Standards and Technology
nitroglycerin 49, 55, 65, 139, 166
Nixon, Richard, President 24, 25, 26, 128
no-fly list 38, 265
"no pax, no bags" 54
nonbinary passengers 60
non-government organization (NGO) 68
nonstate armed group (NSAG) 68
Nopsca, Baron Franz von Felsö-Szilvás 7–8
NORAD (North American Aerospace Defense Command) 257
USS *Normandy* 114–115, 127
North American Aerospace Defense Command *see* NORAD
North Atlantic Treaty Organization *see* NATO
North Tower *see* World Trade Center
Northeast Air Defense Sector *see* NEADS
NSC *see* National Security Council
NTSB *see* National Transportation and Safety Board
Nugent, James 119
NYANG *see* New York Air National Guard

Oak Ridge National Laboratory 26
OAS *see* Organization of American States
Oasis sports drink 57
Obama, Barack H., President 59, 148, 265
Obeid, Sheik Abdul Karim 227
Observer (UK) 119, 190, 208
Occupied Palestinian Territories 2, 51
O'Donnell, J.J., Capt. 16
Office of Aviation Safety (NTSB) 139
Office of Science and Technology Policy (OSTP) 24
Office of Special Counsel (OSC) 111, 141
Office of the Director of National Intelligence 236
Office of the Inspector General (OIG) 131, 132
Ogonowski, John 255, 256
OIG *see* Office of the Inspector General
Olympic Games, 1996 (Summer), Atlanta 113–114, 121, 138
O'Neill, John 134, 135
"onesie" *see* Babygro (product) 186
Ong, Betty 256, 257, 258
Operation Blue Star 52
Operation Desert Storm 198, 199, 234
Operation Entebbe 29
Operation Feuerzauber ("Fire Magic") 31
Oplan Bojinka (Operational Plan Bojinka) 54
Organization of African Unity and the Non-Aligned Movement 203
Organization of American States (OAS) 12–13
Osama bin Laden *see* bin Laden, Osama
OSTP *see* Office of Science and Technology Policy
Otis Air National Guard Base 258

P-3 Orion surveillance aircraft 118, 119, 127
Pacific Northwest National Laboratory 96
Pacific War (World War II) 244–245, 257, 267
"packs" 115
paleobiology 7
Palestine 24, 51, 205
Palestine Liberation Organization *see* PLO
Palestinian Popular Struggle Front (PPSF) 205
Pan American-Grace Airways 8
Panasonic Corp. 95
Paris Match 128
Parr, Bill 188
Partin, Ben, Brig. Gen. 143
pat-downs *see* screening, passenger
Paul VI, Pope 68
Péan, Pierre 228, 229, 230, 232

286 Index

Pearson, Erica 34
pentaerythritol tetranitrate (PETN) *see* plastic explosives
Pentagon 3, 36, 37, 38, 84, 125, 126, 127, 129, 243, 245, 248, 254, 259, 260, 262, 263, 264, 265
pepper spray *see* weapons
PETN *see* plastic explosives
PFLP 1, 2, 3, 18, 19, 21, 22, 23, 24, 28, 30, 81
PFLP-EO (Popular Front for the Liberation of Palestine—External Operations) 28
PFLP-GC (Popular Front for the Liberation of Palestine—General Command) 195, 196, 197, 198, 199, 200, 205, 213, 228, 230
photo ID *see* identity verification methods
Piette, Lauren 93
Piper Dakota 267
plastic explosives 60, 62, 64, 193, 204; C4 166; PETN (pentaerythritol tetranitrate) 56, 58, 59, 61, 139; RDX (cyclotrimethylenetrinitramine) 139–140; Semtex 140, 186, 187, 195, 224; *see also* hexogen; nitroglycerin
PLO (Palestine Liberation Organization) 1, 2, 21, 23–24, 28, 205
plutonium 189
Polisario Front 68
Popular Front for the Liberation of Palestine *see* PFLP
PP *see* Préfecture de Police
PPSF *see* Palestinian Popular Struggle Front
Pratt & Whitney JT9D-7A 189
PreCheck *see* TSA PreCheck
Préfecture de Police (PP) 231
Presidential Daily Brief 252
Preston Sugar Mill 12
Prevost, Stéphane 90
printer cartridge bomb plot 60–61
"progressive collapse" (structural design) 266
projectile *see* surface-to-air missile
Proteus Airlines 93
Provisional Irish Republican Army (IRA) 28, 183
proximity missile 149
Psiaki, Mark 99
Public Law 87–197 14
pursers *see* flight attendants
Putin, Vladimir, President 165, 172, 174, 176

Qadhafi, Muammar *see* Gaddafi, Muammar, Colonel
QED Secure Solutions 96
queer *see* gay (same-sex orientation)

Rabin, Yitzhak, President 18
Radio France Internationale 85
Radio Free Europe 177
RAF *see* Royal Air Force; Red Army Faction
Rafsanjani, Ali Akbar Hashemi 195
Ramsdell, Kellyn Wagner 98
RAND Corp. 51, 68
RANE (business) 202
RARDE *see* Royal Armament Research and Development Establishment
Rauf, Rashid 58
razor *see* weapons
RDX *see* plastic explosives
Reconsideration and Modification of the National Transportation Safety Board's Findings and Determination of the Probable Cause for the Crash of TWA Flight 800 149
rectum 64
Red Army Faction (RAF) 28, 30
Red Brigades 28
Red Cross *see* American Red Cross
Reed, Cara 264
Reid, Richard 55–57
remote control *see* Automatic Control System
Reno, Janet 122
residue (explosive deposit) 59, 65, 139, 140, 149, 193, 200, 230, 231
retina scans *see* identity verification
Reuters 234
Revolutionary Cells 28
Revolutionary United Front 183
Reyat, Inderjit Singh 53
Rice, Condoleezza 250, 251, 252
Ripp, Irving 16
Riyad-us Saliheen Brigade of Martyrs 168, 177
Roberts, John B., II 132, 134
Rogg, Margaret 69
Ron, Rafi 166
Rosebank Crescent 189
Rostov Oblast 165
Rowland, Walter 185
Royal Air Force (RAF) 9, 10, 11, 21, 190, 191
Royal Armament Research and Development Establishment (RARDE) 194
Royal Highland Fusiliers 191
Rush, Julian 201
Russell, Richard 125, 126, 127, 128

Sadat, Anwar, President 174
Sagalyn, Dan 265
saline solution 55
Salinger, Pierre 125–129

Index

SALT I *see* Strategic Arms Limitation Treaty I
SAM *see* surface-to-air missile
Samsonite luggage 52, 185, 186, 195, 204, 212, 228, 230, 231, 232
Sánchez, Ilich Ramirez *see* Carlos the Jackal
Sanders, James 136, 147
Sanger, David E. 63
Santamarta, Ruben 96–97
SARS-CoV-2 *see* Covid-19
SAS *see* Special Air Service
SATCOM 96
Satellite Communication *see* SATCOM
Saudi Hezbollah al-Hejaz 113; *see also* Hezbollah International
SCCRC *see* Scottish Criminal Cases Review Commission
Scharf, Michael 206
Schiavo, Mary 36
Schiliro, Lewis 133
Schmitt, Eric 63
School No. 1 *see* Beslan Seige
Schroeder, Matthew 124
Schulze, Glen 145–146, 147
Schuringa, Jasper 58
Scientific American 57
Scott, Erik R. 9
Scottish Air Control Centre 187
Scottish Criminal Cases Review Commission 206, 208, 211
Scottish High Court of Justiciary 203
screening, passenger
  Advanced Imaging Technology (AIT) 39, 59, 60, 64
  backscatter X-ray machine 60
  behavioral profiling 20, 23, 24, 25, 26, 85
  computed-tomography scanner (CAT or CT scanner) 66
  explosive trace detection (swabbing) 59, 65
  pat-downs 59, 64, 65
  three-dimensional (3D) imaging technology 39
  X-ray technology 26, 31, 37, 54, 60, 62, 63, 265
SEAL Team Six 265
Seale, Patrick 236
Search and Rescue Dog Association 191
Second Sino-Japanese War 67
Secret Chadian Resistance 226
Secret Service, United States 126
Semtex *see* plastic explosives
Senate Intelligence Committee 151
Sephton, Graeme 144, 145, 147
September 11th attacks *see* Nine-Eleven (9/11) attacks

Sex Pistols 186
Shahid Brigade Riadus-Salahina 176; *see also* Riyad-us Saliheen Brigade of Martyrs
Shalgam, Abdel Rahman 237
Shani, Joshua, Lt. Col. 29
Shanwick Oceanic Control 187
Sharkey, Joe 39
Sharon, Ariel, Prime Minister 2, 70, 229
Shazar, Zalman 2
Shelton, Chris 61
Sherwood Crescent 189, 238
Shibani, Abdelsalam Issa, Col. 233
shoe bomb plot 55–57, 59
shootdowns, targeted airliners
  China National Aviation Corporation (CNAC) 67–68
  El Al Flight 435 81
  Iran Air Flight 655 195, 200
Shorter, Wayne 115
shoulder-fired missile *see* surface-to-air missile
Sikh extremists 52, 53
Silvestri, Dora 236
Sinclair, Gerard 211
Six-Day War 1
The Skies Belong to Us 15
Skyjack Sunday 21–24
Skylab Project 146
Smith, Paul J. 54
smoke bomb 32–33
smoke inhalation 33
"smoking gun" 205, 230
Snyder, Steven 115
soda can bomb *see* bomb, types
South African Bureau of State Security 185
South Tower *see* World Trade Center
Southern University (New Orleans) 15
Special Air Service (SAS) 31
Special Attack Unit (Japan) 244
Speckhard, Anne 167
Speers, Richard 140–141, 147
spike-tooth fracture 148, 149
SPLA (Sudan People's Liberation Army) 69
Stack, Andrew III 267
Stack-O'Connor, Alisa 168
Stalcup, Tom 137, 143, 147, 149, 152
Stanley knife 249
Starr, Barbara 63
Stasi 205
state-sponsored terrorism 182–183, 213
Steele, Jonathan 168
stewardesses *see* flight attendants
Stewart, David 192
Stinger missile 70, 124
Stobbs, George 189

Index

Strait of Hormuz 195
Strategic Arms Limitation Treaty 1 (SALT 1) 128
Strela-2 (SA-7) *see* surface-to-air missile
submachine gun *see* weapons
Sudan People's Liberation Army *see* SPLA
suicide bombing 49, 59, 62, 83, 149, 166, 236, 259; Chechen suicide bombers 167–177
surface-to-air missile (SAM) 3, 66, 67, 69, 70, 72, 112, 124, 195
surgically-implanted bomb *see* bomb (types)
Sutherland, Thomas 199
swab *see* screening, passenger
Sweeney, Madeleine "Amy" 258
Swire, Jim 199, 210
Syracuse University 186, 238
syringe 17, 57, 58, 61, 64

Tai Youn Electronics (TY) 230, 231
Talb, Mohammed Abu 205, 213
Taliban 124, 264
TATP 56
Tavurova, Mariyam 171
Teimourian, Hazir 198
Teledyne Ryan Aeronautical 128–129
Tempest, Rone 227
Tenet, George 251–252
terrorism czar *see* Clarke, Richard A.
Terzi, Zehdi Lahib 2
Thales (company) 95
Thatcher, Margaret, Prime Minister 191
This Is Your Life 188
Thomas, Jakana 169
three-dimensional (3D) imaging technology *see* screening, passenger
Thüring AG (firm) 210
Thurman, Tom 196, 197, 230, 231, 232
Thurner, Leopold 10
TIME Magazine 2
time warp 92
timers (timing devices) 173, 187, 196, 205, 210, 230, 233; MST-13 timing device 197, 199, 200, 204, 205, 207, 209, 210, 230
Times of Israel 196
TNT (trinitrotoluene) 61
Tokubetsu Kōgeki tai *see* Special Attack Unit (Japan)
Tokyo Convention" *see* Convention on Offences and Certain Other Acts Committed on Board Aircraft
toner 60
Topp, Alan 187–188
Toshiba "Bombeat" radio-cassette player 186, 194, 195, 200
Toto, Caitlin 169

Toubou (tribe) 238
Trajectory-Based Operations (TBO) 97
tranquilizer darts 17
Transall C-160 transport aircraft 225
transgender passengers 60
transponder 92, 127, 256, 257, 258, 259
Transportation Security Administration (TSA) 37, 38, 39, 55, 57, 58, 59, 60, 62, 63, 64, 65, 66, 87, 88, 265, 266
USS *Trepang* 127
triacetone triperoxide *see* TATP
trinitrotoluene *see* TNT
Tristam, Pierre 24
Trump, Donald 212
"trusted traveler" programs 39, 265
TSA *see* Transportation Security Administration
TSA PreCheck 39
Tuareg (tribe) 238
Tula Oblast 164
Tundergarth Church 193, 238
Tupamaros 28
Tupolev 134 165
Tupolev 154 165
TWA Flight 800 (documentary) 149
Twilight Zone 251
Twin Towers *see* World Trade Center

underwear bomb plot 58–59, 61
Union of Soviet Socialist Republics *see* USSR
United Airlines Cyber Security Division 95
United Airlines Flight 3642 (cyber attack) 95
United Arab Emirates (UAE) 246, 248
United Nations 2, 27, 68, 202, 206, 210, 237
United Nations Resolution 731 202
United Nations Resolution 748 202
United Nations Resolution 883 202
United Nations Security Council 203
United Parcel Service *see* UPS
United Press International (UPI) 128
United States Air Force 9, 11, 113, 116, 259
U.S. Coast Guard 114, 123
United States District Court, Alexandria, Virgina 200
United States Embassy in Helsinki, Finland 184, 186
U.S. Naval Research Labs 145–146
United States Navy 114, 125, 126, 127, 128, 129, 195, 198, 244, 245
U.S. Office of Special Counsel 111, 141
U.S. Patent and Trademark Office 93
U.S. Senate 16, 132, 133, 135, 151
University of Greifswald 247
UPS (United Parcel Service) 61, 72

USAir Flight 217 118
USDT *see* Department of the Treasury
USSR 8, 9, 11, 12, 13, 67, 72
UTA 772 DC-10 Memorial 238–239

Valley, Bruce, Cmdr. 143
Vanguardia, Mike 91
Vatican 68
Verdier, Liz 259
Verne, Jules 243
vertical launch system (VLS) 127
Vesuwala, Sunshine 33
vetting, airport employees 85, 86
Vickers VC10 airliner 23
Vickers Viscount airliner 68
Vietnam 92
Vietnam War 15, 51, 68, 117, 135
USS *Vincennes* 195
Violence in the Skies 11
VLS *see* vertical launch system
Vrzáňová, Alena 10

Wagner, Raymond, Capt. 186
Waite, Terry 199
Wall Street Journal 142
Wallis, Rodney 32
Walmart 253
war games 127, 128
Waxman, Sharon 229
weapons, used on board
  AK-47 assault rifle 33, 88
  box cutter 36, 37, 249, 256, 258
  hand grenade 1, 13, 21, 28, 32, 33, 34, 81, 82, 176, 236
  handgun 13, 16, 21, 22, 28, 32, 33, 34, 35
  knife 13, 14, 20, 36, 37, 249, 256, 258, 262; *see also* Cliphanger Viper knife, Imperial Tradesman Dual Edge knife, Stanley knife
  Mace 256, 258
  pepper spray 256
  razor 256
  submachine gun 19, 81, 82, 236

Wearne, Phillip K. 231
Weiss, Philip 119
Weizman, Ezer, President 82
Wells, H. G. 243
Wetli, Charles 121, 125, 149
White House Commission on Aviation Safety and Security 131, 132
Wi-Fi 96–97
Willoughby, Gloria 15
Wilson Center 182
Wire, Mike 116
Withington, Thomas 70
Wolf, Dan J. 245
Women of Lockerbie 192
Wong, Stephen Kai-yi 90
Wood, Reed 169
Wood, Robert 234
World Trade Center 3, 36, 38, 84, 113, 138, 243, 245, 246, 254, 258, 259, 261, 262, 263, 265, 266
World War I 243
World War II 8, 244, 267
Wright, Lawrence 124
Wright, Stephen J. 94
Wright Brothers 7
USS *Wyoming* 127

X-ray technology *see* screening, passenger

Yanga, Bernard 229, 230, 232
Yastrzhembsky, Sergei 168
YNET (*Yedi'ot Aharonot*) 82
Yousef, Ramzi Ahmed 113, 123

Zalchenko, Aleksander 165
Zarqa (Jordan) 21
Zeppelin 243
Zetter, Kim 95, 97
Zimbabwe People's Revolutionary Army *see* ZIPRA
ZIPRA 68–69
"zoom-climb" scenario (TWA 800) 136–137, 145, 146, 147

www.ingramcontent.com/pod-product-compliance
Lightning Source LLC
Chambersburg PA
CBHW032032300426
44117CB00009B/1036